DATE DUE			

PENDLETON HERRING, President of the Social Science Research Council since 1948, has been a college professor, a foundation executive, a United Nations official, and a consultant to various governmental agencies. He received his doctorate in political science from Johns Hopkins and taught at Harvard from 1928 to 1946; for the first ten years of the Harvard Graduate School of Public Administration he held the post of Secretary. He was for two years on the staff of the Carnegie Corporation.

During the attempt in 1946 to negotiate an international control agreement he was head of the Secretariat of the United Nations Atomic Energy Commission. He has served the United States government in the Bureau of the Budget and has been a consultant to the War Department, the Navy Department, the Air Force, and more recently, the National Science Foundation. He holds the Navy Department's Civilian Distinguished Service Award, an M.A. (hon.) from Harvard and an LL.D. from Princeton.

He was president of the American Political Science Association in 1953, and is currently president of the Woodrow Wilson Foundation and vice-president of the International Social Science Council.

He has been associated in an editorial capacity with the *Public Administration Review*, the *American Political Science Review*, and the *Public Opinion Quarterly*, and has served on the Board of Franklin Publications and the Inter-University Case Program, Inc.

He is the author of *Group Representation Before Congress* (1929); *Federal Commissioners, Study of their Careers and Qualifications* (1936); *Public Administration and the Public Interest* (1936); *The Politics of Democracy* (1940); *Presidential Leadership* (1940); and *The Impact of War* (1941).

THE POLITICS OF DEMOCRACY

The Politics of Democracy

American Parties in Action

PENDLETON HERRING

New York

W · W · Norton & Company · Inc ·

Publishers

Preface to the New Edition

MUCH writing on American politics has been concerned with how best to insure a more responsible party system and to this end the supposed merits of party government in Great Britain have been advanced as a model. I began this study not with the thought of arguing the case for establishing a new or improved party system but rather with the intention of explaining what the functions of parties seemed to be and perhaps deriving from this evidence a model consistent with prevailing democratic values. As an active participant in the committee that prepared the report on *The Power of the Democratic Idea*,[1] I had the stimulating experience in 1960 of helping to formulate in many sessions of free discussion the meaning of democracy as understood by a broad cross-section of fellow citizens. The report provides a philosophic view of democracy, it seems to me, that is in harmony with the analyses offered in *The Politics of Democracy*. And as Austin Ranney[2] has so well demonstrated, most of the disagreement concerning what kind of party system the United States should have has been the direct result of differing views upon the nature and institutional requirements of democracy itself. The debate con-

[1] VI Report of the Rockefeller Brothers Fund Special Studies Project (Garden City, N. Y.: Doubleday & Company, 1960).
[2] *The Doctrine of Responsible Party Government* (Urbana, Ill.: University of Illinois Press, 1962), pp. 158-159.

tinues,[3] but in my opinion the events of the last twenty-five years fortify confidence in the adaptability and strength of our political institutions·and their compatibility with underlying political attitudes and values.

When *The Politics of Democracy* was published in 1940, the view presented was not in accord with interpretations of party politics in much current writing. A new alignment was urged of distinctive parties with programs that offered clear alternatives; all this, it was argued, was long overdue.

Since then vast changes have taken place through the very processes of party government which were described as outmoded and ineffective. Yet despite such a demonstration the dialogue continues between those who would substitute parties with sharply divergent programs for the present practice of seeking a broad middle ground of agreement for effectuating policy. The most striking recent change has been the desire of the conservatives to control a right-wing party. In the 1930's it was the liberals who were seeking a partisan vehicle for their objectives.

During that decade a major transition was made in the United States. Although feelings were bitter, the readjustment was carried forward under the orderly procedures of government. There were protest demonstrations and occasional riots. Those who were young voters in the 1930's can vividly recall the resentment of the older generation of well-to-do citizens at the changes underway and the fear that haunted those threatened by unemployment. The New Deal reforms and innovations we now see as merely preliminary and hesitant steps toward the present scope and possible future sweep of the Welfare State. Over the years since this book was written, nuclear armament, the balance of terror and the whole configuration of world politics, military intervention, foreign aid

[3] See, for example, the eloquent and challenging statement by James MacGregor Burns in *The Deadlock of Democracy* (Englewood Cliffs, N. J.: Prentice-Hall, 1963). For a fresh and rigorous analysis from a different standpoint, see Charles E. Lindblom's *The Intelligence of Democracy: Decision Making through Mutual Adjustment* (New York: The Free Press, 1965). For a clarifying review of the issues, see Part Six, especially pp. 514 ff., in *Democarcy and the American Patry System*, by Austin Ranney and Willmoore Kendall (New York: Harcourt, Brace & Co., Inc., 1956).

and relations with allies and with new nations have imposed on the United States a burden of responsibility in world affairs inconceivable in the 1930's.

A new consensus for supporting foreign policy and domestic changes gives a range to public authority that brings government more intimately into daily life than ever before. And this intimacy is given expression through public-relations practices and the media of mass communication that is direct and inescapable. Television opens a window to the world in the family living room. Homes are more and more urban and suburban dwellings. Class mobility, educational demands, automation, urban congestion and renewal: each of these familiar words evokes problems that must be dealt with through public policies — politically, with the involvement of political parties. And yet, it seems to me, the explanation of the party system set forth in *The Politics of Democracy* is basically as valid today as ever. A thoughtful reading discloses the essential continuity in our party system. In so many ways we are living in a new world and facing an ever more challenging future. Yet our traditional party system continues to fulfill the vital need for compromise, for consensus seeking, for finding the terms upon which governance by consent can go forward.

The fact that the United States in the 1930's underwent a great change through methods short of violence, then engaged in total mobilization for a global war, and today functions as a free and powerful nation bespeaks its political resilience.

Much of the portentous political writing of the 1930's seems dated. Some of the warnings were directed to dangers that never materialized and in the interim unimagined horrors indeed have transpired, some that were far beyond the endurance of those affected. There is today a more pervasive air of realism and qualified assertion than in the days when the coming of fascism or of communism or of revolutions by managers or bureaucrats or technocrats or what you will was foretold. Too often descriptive textbooks presented governance "as it was supposed to be," in terms of statutory authority and formal organization, rather than attempting to depict the complexities of actual political behavior. Many political studies, in offering "conclusions," contrasted observed practices unfavorably with conventional views of what "ought to be" if so-called democratic theory were to be followed.

A retrospective view of this literature suggests the need for further inquiry into the innovative arrangements in our policy. In the identification of interests, their articulation and realization in public policies, what are the dynamic forces and the accommodative institutions? In response to this question recent research provides a much better understanding of the political process and of the function of the party within this process. There is a growing body of empirical evidence pertinent to many isolated aspects of political behavior; we still lack a well-articulated body of propositions and a methodology adequate for systematic, analytical purposes.

The effort in this book is to see what sense, what rationale, can be discovered when we try to understand our own political behavior as revealed largely by the historical record and by diverse research inquiries. Admittedly, insight and "hunch," intuition and estimates are part of this diagnostic process. There is a limit to the uses of "detachment," as the experienced diagnostician will readily admit. The game, if you will, is to maximize the number of variables that can be visualized in a significant and interdependent relationship. The most embracing theory is obviously the most useful in explaining the phenomena under investigation. A conceptual scheme is sought that delineates and clarifies relationships without making data conform to subjective preferences. Only when a very substantial measure of understanding is achieved can prescription be prudently essayed.

Much of the writing on American politics continues to be prescriptive. The author chooses his materials to highlight current problems that need attention and then advances recommendations for improvement. This stimulates debate, promotes a keener awareness of situations that call for rectification, and contributes to step-by-step change based on rational considerations. The publicist, the reforming editor, the specialist trained in some aspect of administration or social science discipline contributes his bit, but the specialist by definition cannot be expected to grasp the whole scheme of things. In this discourse where appeals are directed to winning public acceptance for particular public policies or specific governmental reforms, politicians and party leaders come into the specialists' direct line of vision. When their response is dilatory or indifferent or unfavorable, they are criticized heartily for being what they are — politicians and, as such, "generalists."

There is, and I think must be, a recurrent tension between the role of the politician as "generalist" and the role of the specialist. The latter, whether as technical expert, special-interest spokesman, or crusader, has in any of these roles a directness and intensity of purpose that is different from the broader imperative driving the politician to seek support from the varied forces in his constituency in order to establish a basis for "living together."

This study tries to identify what in fact the operational utility of our parties appears to be in the light of their actual functioning and to suggest the value this has as a part of the larger political process. What then are the criteria that seem appropriate for judging the role of the parties in this system?

Merely to ask this question provokes thought concerning the interplay of interest groups, the press, the bureaucracies of industry, labor, the military, and the many competing areas and levels of governmental activity. In this array of forces the need is seen more clearly for parties to assist in the accommodative role of seeking some agreement on men or measures that will make governmental action possible. If today there is less fear and less hope, there is, I think, a steadiness of nerve and a readiness to face whatever facts seem to make sense. Political apathy and civic indifference can be regarded with less moralistic disapproval.

Views of politics based on normative aspirations did no particular harm so long as Americans treated "theory" as something divorced from the work-a-day world. Inconsistencies between standards of ideal performance and the realities of American politics were of no great consequence so long as these contradictions were not taken seriously enough to interfere with the operating necessities of governance. Now that we are advising countries undergoing political and economic development, it is very important that we understand the nature of our own political system. With the crucial role taken by intellectuals in nation building, the views of American publicists and political scientists assume a practical meaning. If many foreigners find it difficult to understand actual political practices and abstract formulations of democratic theory in the United States, one reason may be that we find it difficult to explain such matters to ourselves. When intellectuals in non-Western countries see how far everyday political behavior falls short of democratic ideals, they may despair of the effectiveness of representative institutions. Theories of class conflict and Marxist doctrine they may regard as more nearly fitting the conditions with which they are familiar.

For the political questions facing other democracies, the United States cannot provide ready-made answers. But if this book serves to emphasize that politics at best is an ever-developing process and that the search for answers is a continuing one, we will have established a mutual understanding among all men who aspire to freedom.

There is always a future for the truly developing nations; the mature, by definition, can only look forward to decline. The United States surely remains a new nation and a developing society. Perhaps by keeping in mind some of the questions that outsiders may be curious about and by trying to keep separate "what is" from "what should be," we may succeed in some measure in analyzing our politics.

The guiding curiosity in this analysis of democracy is to seek out the factors or forces that appear to hold the system together, that serve to integrate rather than to disintegrate. Many writers dealing with the democratic process operate under the guidance of a different interest: namely, to discover how special viewpoints may be expressed and distinctive programs enacted into law. My basic question is: how has the political process operated in the United States so that democracy has survived? This experience may be found relevant for democratic practices under conditions where unity and stability are under great strain. For my premise is that the United States started with a high degree of individualism and had to struggle toward unity and even fight for union. We still have a long way to go. As a country of colonists and pioneers, entrepreneurs, traders, and independent farmers, there has been from the outset a strong spirit of enterprise; the political task has been to harness this dynamic force and turn it to broader social purposes. To a remarkable degree change has been achieved and stability preserved. This is a somewhat paradoxical feat that other nations presently facing the necessity for rapid adjustment may well ponder. Indeed, a political question of very general interest is how to bring about the drastic adjustments demanded by modernization through the instrumentalities of self-government. In the developing countries the problem is to generate enough power in the organs of free government to satisfy ambitious politicians and to control self-seeking leaders. When the political realities in the new nations of Africa and Asia and in many of the Latin-American countries are candidly faced, it is clear that their basic problem is to achieve national unity. As Rupert Emerson writes, "The prime requirement is not for more freedoms but for discipline and hard work, not for opposition but for a national consolidation of all forces and talents."[4]

Yet the prevailing assumption is that the essential requisite, if new nations are to qualify as democracies, is the existence of one or more political parties in opposition. Too much is overlooked in making this conventional prescription for free government. Parties are presumed to be necessary organs for a healthy aligning of interests into two or more camps. The factors making for integration and for strengthening national loyalties perhaps have a prior claim to attention in nation building: an effective educational system, an enlightened press, a unified elite, a well-developed "infrastructure" of active and varied associational relationships. Even the nations of the West, where such institutions are embedded in the very culture, can safely endure only parties that represent a *loyal* opposition.

By our conventional assumption that the primary function of political parties in a democracy is to be distinctive and competitive, and that nations without such a system cannot be regarded as democratic, a dismal future is very logically predicted for most of the new nations and for many others in the early stages of moderni-

[4] From *Empire to Nation* (Cambridge, Mass.: Harvard University Press, 1960), p. 290.

zation. Before accepting this widely current syllogism let us not overlook our history of one-party domination in the states and regions of the United States. The political process is deeper and more encompassing than partisan politics.

Stresses may differ in origin, in force, in incidence; but democracy must meet the test through its own internal strength — and to this end self-comprehension is the essential means. This quest for understanding presents common problems for all men who value freedom and who undertake to govern themselves, however different their history and culture may be. My hope is that this volume may stimulate further analysis and also strengthen confidence in the ways of democracy.

Pendleton Herring

New York
May, 1965

Foreword

THE purpose of this book is to analyze the politics of democracy in order to show the nature of our party system and its relations to other social processes. We shall examine the factors which are commonly treated as grave dangers to democracy: machine control, pressure politics, propaganda, monied interests, patronage, and bureaucracy. This is the rogues' gallery of American politics. Undoubtedly much evil finds expression here. Yet these factors are but the reverse side of elements integral to the democratic process. Organization is essential to political party activity. Groups and associations of citizens must not be denied the right to advance their political ends. Wide avenues of advertising, persuasion, and promotion must be open to all. Money cannot be an economic instrument without serving also as a political tool. Wealth and political preferment are two strong inducements for loyalty and support. Government cannot function without a strong administrative service.

The good and the bad are inextricably mixed under democracy as under any other human institution. Both passion and reason motivate political behavior. As Ralph Waldo Emerson has pointed out, passion is as integral to politics as to personality. Only the spinster-minded would wish it otherwise. Special pleading and partisan zeal have been as much a part of government as has loyalty to broad principles of public welfare.

"Better, certainly," Emerson wrote, "if we could secure the strength and fire which rude, passionate men bring into society, quite clear of their vices. But who dares draw out the linchpin from the wagon-wheel?"

In this study I stress the premise that man is both rational and nonrational and capable of both love and hate. The politics of democracy allows for both the strength and the weakness of mankind. Dictatorships tend to be more selective: more heroism, more sacrifice, more discipline and obedience are demanded than men can freely give without fatal strain. Democracy asks for reason, tolerance, and sympathy, but paradoxically enough it takes full account of the fallibility of human nature.

The ultimate evaluation of democracy is to be found in the procedures through which it works, but it is not enough to understand merely the mechanics of our political system. Equally important, though more difficult to examine, are the workings of our own mental machinery when we think and talk about government. The study of popular government requires asking how man behaves as well as how political institutions operate.

A process cannot be described without a selection of facts, and this selection necessitates subjective judgment of two sorts. The more subtle and difficult is the personal motivation that leads the investigator to note certain aspects of reality and to disregard others. The student may be aware of this psychological bias, but he may not hope to escape it since he must remain himself. The second problem of evaluation is simpler. The adequacy or even the nature of a process cannot be judged without some conception of its ultimate purpose. In this book I attempt to evaluate our political process as a method for reconciling change with stability. Of course, many persons are ready to repudiate stability and to tempt violence and bloodshed if necessary to forward their own purposes. I have no concern with these purposes other than to suggest that those advocating a line of policy which appears either radical or reactionary for the climate of opinion wherein it is advanced must be either content to wait or prepared to fight. Since on most occasions human inertia serves as a deterrent, efforts to arouse society in battle array are usually limited to a small and innocuous area. When this is not so we all pay a heavy price in suffering and disruption for whatever benefits accrue from violent social change. Individuals may at times much prefer to pay the price, but that a promissory note must always be met is often overlooked by those seeking the promised land.

In this book I wish to stress the extralegal implementation that helps make democracy work; this emphasis does not imply any lack of appreciation for the profound significance of our constitutional settlement and legal tradition as a part of the democratic process. The importance of considering the adequacy of the governmental structure is acknowledged though questions of reforms in the formal system will not concern us here. Neither do I propose to argue what should be done in terms of a substantive program. The liberal weeklies are full of suggestions; the conservative press is full of forebodings. The specialists who have delved deepest into the intricacies of particular fields of policy are least ready to adhere to any over-all plan. My purpose is to show that through its toleration of attitudes and proposals our political process provides the milieu within which a science of society may be developed and intelligence may be applied to our common problems. It cannot guarantee the "good life" or an "economy of abundance," but it does not eliminate such hopes through a regimented loyalty to dictated myths. Sanguine men are free to plan and skeptics to scoff.

This does not imply a brake on reforming zeal. On the contrary, I would cheer the zealots on; they are an essential part of the democratic process.

My concern is with the domestic rather than with the international scene. This implies no unawareness of external factors, but one book should not attempt too much. Moreover, if democratic government is to win a lasting victory, this must be an internal conquest. One can but express the belief that the nation will preserve its democratic institutions and direction only through intelligent control of our own political processes. The stresses at home and from abroad may differ in origin, in force, in incidence; but democracy can withstand the test only through its own internal strength—a strength to which self-comprehension is a primary requisite.

A highly critical attitude toward our institutions and their operation is an almost conventional attitude for the student of politics. Accepting as a truism that such vigilance for error is the price of freedom, I believe that the application of critical standards too high for human attainment does tend toward an unhealthy sense of frustration which may lead to disillusionment and even cynicism. This is simply to suggest that a sympathetic understanding of the weaknesses of our system may at times be as effective a starting point for improvement as a sharp sense of our political shortcomings. Satire has its place, but as an antidote to smugness rather than as a daily tonic. And who of us can be complacent about the future of free institutions!

Thanks are due to the publishers who have kindly granted permission for quoting from the books bearing their imprint. In several instances portions of chapters have already appeared as articles. I wish to express my appreciation for the privilege of using this material to the editors of the following journals: *Journal of Social Philosophy*, *North American Review*, *Yale Law Review*, *The Harvard Guardian*, and the *Virginia Quarterly Review*.

Since the thoughts in this book have grown over a period of years, the debts accrued are many: to my colleagues and students for stimulation and sympathetic criticism; to the Committee on Research in the Social Sciences for assistance at the outset of this research, and to the Harvard Graduate School of Public Administration for help during its final stages of preparation. Under the consultantship program of the School it was possible to invite to seminar meetings political leaders whose comments on the political process led to a fresh appreciation of the vital realities of our party system and the tolerant empirical spirit that animates so many who succeed in public life. For deepening this sense of appreciation thanks are due to Mr. James A. Farley, Mr. John Hamilton, Mr. Emil Hurja, Mr. Franklyn Waltman, and to all the others who brought to our seminar the keenness of insight and intuitive awareness of the nature of the politics of democracy that comes from daily participation. However diverse the personal convictions of these men, their pragmatic temper helps explain the adaptability of democracy to a society of conflicting desires.

The one constant in the varied fortunes of writing has been the sympathetic understanding that my wife brought to my task. At various stages in the preparation of this book friends have generously assisted with comments and suggestions: C. B. Marshall, Roland Young, Charles A. H. Thomson, and Oliver Garceau have been particularly helpful. To all of these kind critics I wish to express my gratitude. To my colleague Carl Joachim Friedrich I want to acknowledge a deep sense of appreciation for the stimulus and encouragement he has given me in the writing of this volume. W. W. Norton and Addison C. Burnham have contributed not only valuable criticism but have contrived to make the task of publication the pleasantest stage in a lengthy journey.

As to the ultimate product of all this kind assistance, I can only say with Chaucer's Squire,

> "Hold me excused, if I say ought amiss,
> My aim is good, and lo, my tale is this."

Contents

Preface to the New Edition   ix

Foreword   xvii

Illustrations   xxv

PART I

CHAPTER

1. *The Faith of Democracy*   23
2. *The State Spiritual and the State Temporal*   36
3. *Conditions Favorable to Popular Rule*   47
4. *Leadership Under Party Government*   64
5. *Innovation and Conservatism*   74
6. *Banners of Belief*   87
7. *Standards for Judging the American Party System*   100

PART II

8. *Our Parties Take Their Stand*   119
9. *The Traditional Politician and the Service State*   134
10. *Community Standards and Political Ethics*   146
11. *Looking Forward*   159

12. *Class Cleavage and Party Loyalties* 169
13. *The Significance of Third Party Activities* 179
14. *Left! Right! Left! Right!* 191

PART III

15. *The Structure of Our Party System* 203
16. *The Uses for National Conventions* 225
17. *Channeling Intelligence into Party Activities* 240
18. *The Talk in Campaigns* 251
19. *Propaganda in Politics* 261.
20. *Doctrinaires and Demagogues* 272
21. *The Limitations of Debate* 288

PART IV

22. *Why Believe in Public Opinion?* 305
23. *Consummating Reform: Two Illustrations* 314
24. *Roots of Consent* 326
25. *Money as Political Currency* 336
26. *The Struggle with Spoils* 349
27. *A Democratic Bureaucracy* 368
28. *Can Officials Be Neutral?* 378
29. *The Impact of Economic Inequality on Politics* 391
30. *The Animating Spirit of American Progress* 419

Footnotes 437

Index 455

Illustrations

BETWEEN PAGES 120-121

THE illustrations in this book are offered not as a mere embellishment but rather as a reminder that the spirit of our democratic system finds artistic as well as political expression. In a nation where free government is taken for granted one would not expect to find any extensive treatment of political subjects. Prints and paintings dealing with democratic government are not abundant. Nevertheless throughout our history American artists have depicted various phases of political behavior. In varying modes and in succeeding periods they have recognized that argument and debate—talk, talk, talk—are an essential of democratic rule. Dictators appeal to the masses and secure vast plebiscites of acquiescence, but in a democracy we insist that this is not enough. It is true that the appeal to the voter is important and the verdict of the electorate is essential, but the keystone in the democratic structure is the discussion that comes between appeal and verdict. The pictures selected for this volume span a large part of our history, the costumes of the subjects suggest their generation, and each artist speaks in his own tones, but the common underlying ideal is the same. Free talk marks a free people. Someone has told the story of three Germans seated at a restaurant table reading their newspapers. The first reader cleared his throat and wrinkled his brow; the second emitted a low whistle and shifted his position uneasily. The third looked up from his paper and whispered harshly: "If you two insist upon discussing politics, I'm leaving." This caricature is not without point. Only so long as men are free to talk politics can we feel confident that the bill of rights is in working order. The intimate give-and-take of man-to-man argument is the surest defense against the demagogue and the humbug.

In the spirit of personal and continual argumentation and in the mere fact of its existence rather than in its intellectual level lies an essential of the democratic way of life. This is vividly brought to our attention through the intuition of artistic perceptions. The illustrations state in various ways that the politics of democracy finds fulfillment in appeals for political support, in discussion, and in final accountability to the electorate. That such fundamentals are habitually interpreted with humor and simple directness is in itself significant. Human frailties appear side by side with human strength and purpose. The holiday spirit in which election results are habitually depicted is a commentary in itself. The illustrations in this volume serve to suggest that the politics of democracy are in essence American parties in action.

Concerning the pictures reproduced in this volume a few comments are pertinent. Not until the eighteen thirties and forties do we find American artists turning their attention to the homely realities of American politics. The great work of the earlier period was in portraiture or dealt with historical scenes in the heroic manner. During the nineteenth century genre artists appeared, but relatively little of their work dealt with the political scene.

The best examples, however, are reproduced in this volume. The greatest of our politically-minded painters, without question, was George Caleb Bingham. He grew up in the West and drew his inspiration from his surroundings. His portrayal of political subjects was one expression of his active interest in politics.

Today Thomas Hart Benton is in a sense carrying on the Bingham tradition. A comparison of Benton's "Political Meeting" with Bingham's "Stump Speaking" reveals point for point a modern reinterpretation. The only new note is the mother and child introduced by Benton, though this can hardly be taken as a reflection of woman's attitude toward politics!

In all this genre painting the artists are ready to accept the fact that man as a participant in politics is a creature of emotions as well as an interested citizen. Men are accepted for what they are. The artist is content to tell a story; he seldom tries to preach a sermon. The voter casts his vote in his capacity as a citizen— he stops to argue and discuss politics—he may also take a drink before he is through. Human appetites are put side by side with human aspirations and logical processes. Another recurrent item is the inclusion of the newspaper. In picture after picture a newspaper is found in what amounts to an almost symbolic use. While artists have depicted the citizen and voter with humor and understanding, their ire is aroused when dealing with efforts to interfere with the free operation of democratic procedures. Don Freeman's "Trickery at the Polls" is an excellent example of this attitude. Other illustrations of the same point could have been given had space permitted.

Understanding of the common man and sympathy for his approach to government are the dominant note in the interpretation that American artists have given us—philosophers and publicists cannot find any better vantage point from which to view the politics of democracy.

Grateful acknowledgment is made to the artists, collectors, dealers, and curators who have advised me in gathering these illustrations and who have given permission for the reproduction of the works in their possession.

Part I

Part I

☆ 1 ☆

The Faith of Democracy

> "In the darkness with a great bundle of grief
> the people march.
> In the night, and overhead a shovel of stars
> for keeps, the people march:
> 'Where to? what next?' "
>
> CARL SANDBURG

THE future of democracy is uncertain. Today two basically divergent ideals of human progress—totalitarianism and individualism—stand mutually defiant. The people march, but no confident answer can be offered to their query—where to? what next? The world of this age is divided in its objectives. We lack that sense of direction which made so many men of an earlier generation feel a certain kinship even in the face of national differences and the friction of economic rivalry. Henry Adams reminds us of the time when "the Paris of Louis Philippe . . . and the London of Robert Peel . . . and John Stuart Mill were but varieties of the same *bourgeoisie* that felt instinctive cousinship with the Boston of Ticknor, Prescott and Motley. . . . The system had proved so successful that even Germany wanted to try it, and Italy yearned for it. England's middle-class government was the ideal of human progress." [1]

When the same human values pass current, the trends they encourage may be hopefully projected into the future. We are denied this hope today. Even within the democracies liberalism is under attack as a kind of intellectual laissez faire unsuited to present needs. Within the United States our political parties are criticized as meaningless and negative. No one can feel complacent about our political future.

23

The world-wide challenge confronting democratic government prompts a reconsideration of our political system. Both
political ideals and parties become encrusted with extraneous
associations; a continuing readaptation to current needs is the
price of their vitality. Can we distinguish essential values from
traditional attitudes which may have lost their usefulness? No
theory can confidently plot the future. No inevitable road lies
ahead. From the confusion of tendencies about us, however, a
selection to suggest a pattern for development may be made.
Much depends upon our wisdom of choice, not of any such over-
all alternative as fascism or communism, but rather in the more
limited alternatives that arise from day to day, from Congress
to Congress, from administration to administration. The specific
quandaries of local government and everyday politics are the
parts that relate to our more distant quest. Through our wisdom
in making these smaller decisions the path ahead is laid step by
step. A general agreement on direction is obviously desirable
though unlikely; yet some awareness of our drift seems essential
if intelligence is to contribute to public affairs.

The task of democratic politics is to evolve and execute a
policy reflecting the desires of the community and capable of
meeting current demands for security and prosperity. This must
be accomplished through a system of free partisan struggle
wherein office seeking is often put before considerations of public
policy. Moreover, hard experience has diminished the hope with
which institutional safeguards were once regarded.

Henry Adams, archpessimist though he was, could look back
upon a time when the perplexities of politics were not so overwhelming. "Viewed from Mount Vernon Street," he wrote of
the Boston of his boyhood, "the problem of life was as simple
as it was classic. Politics offered no difficulties, for there the moral
law was a sure guide. Social perfection was also sure, because
human nature worked for Good, and three instruments were all
she asked—Suffrage, Common Schools, and Press. On these
points doubt was forbidden." [2]

We have learned since that suffrage, our public schools, and
the press are not neutral tools working toward an abstraction

called good government. We now recognize them as channels for expressing the social content of the community. As that community changes, its teaching changes, its press changes, and the kind of men chosen by popular suffrage changes. No ultimate harmony can be taken for granted as the product of these democratic institutions. The sharpness with which rival interests clash seems at times to threaten our governmental machinery for reaching agreement through discussion, education, and the ballot box.

Today we feel the political repercussions of profound economic disturbances. Even though in this regard we are not in such severe straits as any other major power, the politics of our democracy faces a sterner test than ever before. Mr. Dooley once remarked that "Politics isn't Beanbag." It has long been a rough-and-tumble game, but as played under popular government it has been a sporting proposition. The participants have been agreed that victory was worth while only if attained under the rules of the game. What was once a debating match or a tug-of-war reserved for election days threatens at times to become a free-for-all struggle to determine who shall eat and how much; and who shall work and for what compensation.

Democratic government has been based on assumptions requiring as much faith as do authoritarian dogmas. On the plane of theory we argue that men are equal, that they will put the community welfare before private greed, that they will carry their proper burden in the task of self-government. Notwithstanding his pragmatism, William James wrote that "democracy is a kind of religion and we are bound not to admit its failure." [3]

The strength of democracy lies not in the complete accuracy of its assumptions about the nature of man nor in discovering a perfect system for adjusting rival interests or ideas. The crux lies here—that with all the wishful thinking in the words of democracy and with all the faults of operation in its institutions, both its words and its forms permit a higher degree of flexibility and experimentation in the adjustment of human affairs than man has yet achieved through any other means. The politics of democracy, with all its weaknesses, hesitations, and irrationalities, is realistically based upon human nature; hence it has a resiliency that competing forms of governance lack. Whether we have the intelligence and will to realize its potentialities is the unanswerable question. Its avowed objectives have held persistent meaning in our culture: for democracy means, as Maury Maverick has said, "being able to talk, pray and think as you please, and eat regular." [4]

The unvarying truth or falsity of the democratic dogma is not of determinant importance. Daily we see instances that deny this creed: many men are lazy, stupid, and selfish; at times their right to talk, pray, and think freely is threatened, and often their diet is scanty and irregular. The significant thing is that the ideology of democracy permits the peaceful resolution of interest conflicts through accepted institutions. The hungry have a recognized right to protest, and the stupid to debate. The unemployed have marched on state capitals, and gone as "petitions in boots" to Washington. They have been met with soup kitchens and sheltered in army tents. Their want and their methods could not affect their essential right to be heard. Their plight indicated grave flaws in our economic order, but our political system provided the milieu under which protest could be peacefully made and belated readjustment set in motion for meeting relief needs.

Government, whether good or bad, is a problem of relationships. For our purposes I suggest that we consider as factors in the political equation: (a) individuals and the groups into which their common interests cluster them; (b) ideas, aspirations, and philosophies which men accept for belief and guidance; (c) institutions and organizations which channel human behavior.

Good government I would define as that condition which results in the most harmonious interrelationship of all these factors. To answer the question of how such an accord may be achieved requires assumptions about the nature of men, the validity of certain principles, and the value of particular institutions. If you assume that men prefer to identify themselves solely with the state, to embrace the principles of hierarchy and discipline as maximizing human welfare, and the institution of the *Fuehrerprinzip* as essential to security, then totalitarianism is good government. On the other hand, if you assume that regardless of status or ability individuals have a right to share in the responsibilities of political control, that the principles of "rule by law" and "supremacy of the popular will" are patterns of thought capable of safeguarding individual freedom, and that men can find satisfying loyalties with many groups besides the state, then democracy is good government.

Domination by no one class, administration by no one set of institutions, and adherence to no one fixed set of principles may be set forth as the proper course for all communities. The question is one of the interrelationships of all these factors. Under the assumptions of democracy, good government might be defined as that form of control most representative of the freely accepted and freely urged values that win out in the competition of political debate.

Good government, if it means anything, must mean government that is good for someone in terms of recognized satisfactions enjoyed through workable institutions. Government, however, remains a process of adjusting the interrelations of individuals, institutions, ideals, and interests. Obviously, then, we cannot argue that to adopt the city-manager plan, proportional representation, civil service reform, or any other institutional change is an absolute good in itself. The significance of such an institution is inseparable from the configuration of interests that it is to serve and the values prevalent in a given context. Nor can we take the welfare of any one class or group as a final basis for public policy.

The specific content of events classified as good government under democratic control remains relative according to the narrowness or breadth of current views concerning the proper sphere of governmental activity. In so far as these views are broadly or narrowly based they will affect the efficiency of the functions carried on by government. If the community reaches wide agreement on the duties to be performed by government, the groundwork necessary for the efficient administration of those functions is thereby laid.

We stand at a mid-point in an historical trend. As we look

backward, we see the theories and practice of limited governmental activity; as we look forward, we discern an increased range of governmental activity and theories that validate it by stressing the new liberties and services resulting from the further extension of government in the economic realm.

At this mid-point, some of our traditional and historic ideals lack significance for many people. It will not do to attempt to recall the wayward to the eternal verities by urging them to be good citizens. This is preachment, not therapy. It will not close the gap between the established concepts of what should be and the demands made by everyday life.

This maladjustment appeared first in local government, since here the state touched the citizen most directly. Symptoms of a sick society were treated as immoral aberrations from an abstraction called good government. Fred Howe, after his experience as a reformer in New York City, came to the conclusion that Tammany survived despite periodic scandals because people liked it.[5] They voted for it because they deemed it a good thing, because it answered their conception of government. Confronted with a limited choice, they found that Tammany accorded more nearly with their view of life than did the program of the opposite party. Good government was government that supplied services to the community and gave personal attention to the unfortunate. The beefsteak parties and the picnics down the bay appealed to people who were emotional, gregarious, and responsive to simple pleasures. If indirectly they paid too high a price for such services, the cost was ignored.

Political power has been built on the satisfaction of such simple wants. Boss Pendergast gave as his formula for ruling Kansas City: "I take care of the poor. I give out all the jobs I can find. I never ask a man his politics, but I do him a good turn if I can. When I have treated the people right, they will vote my way on election day—that is 75% of them will. The other 25% aren't worth bothering about." [6] Here is a caricature of the service state and a travesty on good government. There is no recognition of the need for proper administrative tools or for a careful appraisal of social cost and social need. It is the politics of the handout to be paid for on election day. The stuffed ballot box does not explain the boss's power. His crude view of public policy has won on election day because with all its inefficiency it has come closer to satisfying human wants than the more coldly calculated policy followed in legitimate governmental institutions to conform with laissez-faire notions. For citizens of this latter faith it is enough if the law is impartially executed and if taxes are kept low, economically collected, and spent for clean streets and schools on the right side of the railroad tracks. Good government should lock up burglars, extinguish fires, remove garbage, supply water, and prevent epidemics. Beyond this, government may from time to time place limits on the enjoyment of the minor vices. If this policing develops into a major political issue, as it often does, the pinochle players rally to the defense of their game and churchgoers sooner or later give in.

That the citizenry today is awakening to the services available for the political asking is strikingly demonstrated in the record of Robert Moses [7] as park commissioner of New York. Moses is a boss in that he could not perform his job without ample power, but he works through official institutions, is identified with respected values, and is supported by intelligent and educated interest groups in the community. He makes the petty favors of a Tammany politician seem as tawdry as they are expensive.

The development of accepted standards of proper administration plus agreement on social goals has shifted the realization of many public policies from the realm of partisan conflict. This means, for example, that a sufficiently powerful combination of interests is in agreement on the desirability of parks and public recreation facilities and on the means best suited to this goal. Today politicians may sponsor social services within broad limits without damaging their respectability in the eyes of middle-class voters. Relief and social services even emerge as basic objectives in framing public policy. What once the local party boss alone was ready to recognize is now the concern of the President of the United States and his Cabinet.

The balance between the services the citizen wants and the

taxes he is willing to pay cannot be determined by any absolute concept of good and bad economics. The citizen's interest as a taxpayer must be balanced against his other interests as a member of a political community.

To seek a balance of interests is part of our quest. We cannot foretell the optimum proportions, but this is a remote consideration. Disproportions soon bring evidence of maladjustment. Here is problem enough. No subtleties of argument need reinforce the urgency of redressing conditions that create the distress of tenant farmers in the South or of migratory laborers in California. We have seen their faces! The politics of democracy cannot turn aside from their woe. Dawning awareness of abuses is followed by attempts at amelioration. Freedom of speech is more than a chance to speak one's own mind. It is a means for detecting the sore spots in our system; it gives direction to the process of adjustment.

Good government—traditionally deemed the area of activity of the expert as contrasted to the politician—has no tangible nonpolitical course separable from a definite declaration of policy. All policy is based on a pattern of interests. The major contribution that the expert can make depends upon the gradual establishment of an area within which he may work unmolested by the jungle law of political strife. Good government in regard to sewage disposal, fire and police protection, cost accounting, and public instruction may be measured by relatively objective criteria. The determination of public policy by experts alone, however, cannot be accepted as a definition of good government unless we accept also the Platonic assumptions of rule by philosopher-kings—who were a different sort of expert from the accountant or the physician.

Public policy as a concept implies a plan of governmental action for promoting the welfare of the whole community. Party politics connotes the efforts of one group to manipulate the rest of the community into supporting one interpretation of public policy. Yet we assume that party government is the essential form for democratic control and that through the hot conflict of partisan wills liberty and tolerance can best be preserved and efficient administration provided. Are these assumptions dependent for their validity upon the presence of a large body of public-spirited citizens ready to put the common welfare before self-interest? I believe that the continuance of democracy is not dependent upon an ideal that sets so high a standard. So much disillusionment with the democratic process arises from the alleged disregard of civic duties that the implications of citizenship under democracy may well be reduced to their essential minima.

The good-citizen ideal places an unnecessarily heavy burden on mere man. In contrast to the role assigned the "economic man" by classical theorists, the political man is expected to eschew self-interest. The economic man may be a grasping, hard-headed, rational-minded entrepreneur—a Scrooge before the ghost appeared. The political man is envisaged as being more like Mr. Pickwick—unselfish, well meaning, and with a tremendous interest in the affairs of his fellows. He is intelligent enough to voice opinion on all public affairs; he is vitally interested in all contenders for public office; he knows the candidates for coroner as well as those for governor; and he chooses among them without hesitation. He is ready to initiate legislation if the state assembly fails to voice his views. He would consider recalling judges whose decisions are unwise. He supports the Constitution without doubt as to its meaning. He is as ready to serve for a month on the jury, grand or otherwise, as he is responsive to the demands of his fellows that he become city alderman, sheriff of the county, or President of the United States. Above all the political man is motivated by reason in all things and by the desire to place the general welfare before all else. He is confident in his judgments because he realizes that the voice of the people is the voice of God. Such a fictional character is no more pertinent to a realistic understanding of political behavior than the economic man is to an analysis of economic relationships. Insistence upon good citizenship as a rigid moral concept can lead to an unrealistic and hence unsympathetic attitude toward popular government. The uncritical acceptance of such traditional symbols tends to obstruct the flexibility needed in political affairs today.

Faith in high standards of political behavior is helpful in maintaining respect for government, but respect is most firmly based where government is responsive to the needs of mankind. Underlying most pleas for participation by good citizens is the thought that men detach themselves from their self-interests and act for the commonweal. Consequently at critical junctures men are urged to intervene in political contests to which they are not immediate parties. Municipal reforms have been achieved by an aroused public which bursts with indignation and then subsides.

This generally deplored recession is, I think, a movement of great importance. Reaction from tension is inevitable in human affairs. A reform accomplished means a realignment of interests, held together long enough to throw the rascals out and substitute another crowd presumably of superior virtue. Only a continued crisis could sustain wide popular participation. Intensive organization to this end would be inescapable. Disciplined control of the mass would necessarily arise. The interest cleavages among politicians would have to be projected into great areas of the general public. The neutral body of opinion to which the newly emerging leaders could turn in a crisis would be lacking. If all are partisans, who is to umpire?

The concept of the popular will can be given substance so long as a large mass of uncommitted minds can be aroused for a brief crisis of decision making. Policy is worked out by bargaining among individuals in terms of their conflicting ideals and interests. If a great mass is aligned behind each interest group leader, the bargaining process becomes all the more difficult. Thus the citizen who is not identified with a party, who does not habitually participate in politics, and whose support cannot be counted upon by any one group is the agent that keeps politicians uncertain of power and therefore responsive to the current of opinion. If all men were good citizens in the sense of being participants in all contests they would have to act in practice like declared partisans. This would bring too many political contests to a danger point of intensity.[8]

So many books on politics have concluded with a sermon on citizenship that it seems desirable at the outset to note the limitations of this hope for a better world. No theme recurs more often than the plea for interest and participation on the part of the citizens if a democracy is to work. Citizenship is interpreted as a matter of voting in all elections and participating in partisan activities. Participation becomes of major importance. Yet what is gained if participation is treated as an end in itself? It seems to me that this confuses a means with an end. Citizenship is reduced to mere activism. Such values as justice, wisdom, and the like are left in mid-air.

An example of this viewpoint is the plea for college men to take a greater interest in local party politics. If this means a class dominance of the political process by a group assumed to have a common outlook because of a mutual educational experience, it is certainly open to challenge as an infringement of democratic theory. If it means that college graduates in proportion to their number are underrepresented in local party organizations, it is open to examination as a question of fact. If it means that more intelligence is needed in politics and that a college education is clear evidence of a highly enlightened attitude toward public questions, then the question is open for debate. It would seem that intelligent men by definition have the advantage in politics as well as in any other field of activity should they care to apply their talents. If they fail to do so when their best interests call for such effort, then they can scarcely be regarded as intelligent men. As we have suggested, political activity has in fact been of less importance to the individual than economic affairs. A change seems under way, and as one accompaniment more and more men of training and talents are finding their way into public life.

The problem of popular participation in government can be met only when men find personally significant values in public affairs. Democracy cannot be maintained solely by rallying the voter to vote and the individual to reform. Preachment cannot meet the problems of government. Only as government is charged with greater responsibilities affecting their well-being do citizens follow governmental activities with more attention.

Unless participation without regard to aims is deemed desirable in itself, the good citizen cannot act without allying himself with various interests. The question then is: What interests? The question of ends and hence of values is here inescapable. Interest and participation by the good citizen mean little in themselves. Rather ask: What pattern of interests emerges in a given instance from citizen activity?

Political action—the behavior of the citizen—does not occur as a pure element of the social world. Men find their interest in the political process, and their civic behavior is determined by their connections with churches, labor unions, business associations, fraternal organizations, and so on. As political issues involve industry, labor, social status, or religion, they bring about the intervention of men whose welfare is involved through common concern with these problems.

William Bennett Munro has said: "Government is not, fundamentally, either an affair of laws or of men, but of imponderables behind both of them. To these imponderables, which constitute the invisible government, we have given very little of our attention. Yet we must do it if political science is to maintain any contact with the realities." [9] The citizen cannot be considered alone, Munro believes: get away from the atomic view of citizenship, break down the atom, examine the electrons; note the various impulses affecting the action of the citizen. These influences are those which "compose the individual's immediate environment—his race, his religion, his political party, his labor union, his club, his newspaper, and all the rest. These influences are so penetrating, indeed, that for most of our citizenship the dogma of individual freedom is hardly more than a myth." [10]

Our subjective conceptions of good citizenship are drawn in large part from the social context in which we live. Martin Lomasny, the boss of Boston's old Ward Eight, saw social needs that could not be satisfied merely by emphasizing the moral values current among the substantial citizens living comfortably in the Back Bay. "I think that there's got to be in every ward somebody that any bloke can come to—no matter what he's done—and get help. Help, you understand, none of your law and your justice, but help," Lomasny said to Lincoln Steffens.[11]

It is futile to appeal to the unselfishness of hypothetical good citizens or to the sanctity of abstract principles as a warrant for denying human needs. The time for traditional politics is past. Power conflicts call for interest adjustments through the careful formulation of public policy. Democracy now makes a greater demand than ever before on men of intelligence and good will; but through the rule of law and the common acceptance of our procedural devices we have machinery and traditions for adjusting human passions and aspirations. Belief in the will of the people and the rationality of the common man, while primarily based on faith, still fosters the attitudes which facilitate compromise and adjustment. The people march. Change is inevitable. The future is unknowable, but men at some time are masters of their fates. The faith of democracy may not prove workable, but it holds the clearest hope for civilization today. To a world threatened by Caesarism it has the courage to declare: "The fault, dear Brutus, lies not in our stars but in ourselves that we are underlings."

☆ 2 ☆

The State Spiritual
and the State Temporal

"We must think things not words, or at
least we must constantly translate our words
into the facts for which they stand if we are
to keep to the real and the true."

JUSTICE OLIVER WENDELL HOLMES

THE state spiritual voices the words of what should be; the
state temporal confronts the things that are. But the man on the
street no less than the judge on the bench finds difficulty in
translating abstract ideals into the facts for which they stand.
As a consequence there is usually a hiatus between aspiration
and performance. This, however, is no necessary occasion for
satiric merriment. Man has been called a word-bearing animal.
Words not only protect him from the blasts of cold reality: they
also clothe him with dignity and influence his responses to his
surroundings.

In a democracy the "conditioning" effects of prevalent creeds
are of vast importance. The symbols of democracy may bring
an indulgent smile if seriously offered as a description of what
men do, but their value rests in their acceptance as beliefs.

This distinction is essential: political analysis is one thing;
political philosophy is another. The talk of the Nazis about discipline and leadership is not significant as a description of what
actually exists. No human relations could be as solid, unified, and
monolithic as their ideal would envisage. But the existence of a
symbolism stressing obedience and solidarity is enormously im-

portant in its effect on human behavior. So too the acceptance of democratic beliefs conditions rather than describes political behavior within a democracy.

In this country bloodshed and violence have occurred in strikes; strong-arm methods, espionage, and vigilantism are not infrequent, but the symbols of democracy prompt an indignant reaction to such infringements of the beliefs we hold. Men may suffer when the abstraction is accepted as sufficient in itself, even in the face of new factual situations that contradict the theory. Principles and symbols are needed to give meaning to social relationships, but since these relationships can never be static the ideology also must be open to change.

One task of politics is to assist in the search for the ideals that suit the interests and the institutions, for the institutions that implement the ideals and the interests, and for the interests that will support the ideals and the institutions. The problem might well be stated as a mathematical equation involving the inter-relations of these three factors, each variable to the nth degree. Some interests may find existing institutions well suited to their purposes; other interests may not. Thus the consumer is at a disadvantage with reference to the producer under our industrial setup; so is employee to employer. Consumers turn to co-opera-tives for a remedy. Industrial unions and the National Labor Relations Board are contrived as means to a better balance. Ideals and beliefs established as rationalizations of the status quo, however, overshadow the search for new instruments.

Leaders in all regimes invoke symbols, slogans, and prin-ciples to elicit loyalty. A strong tendency to cherish an established symbol develops even though in time it may cease to be the best means of dissolving social conflicts. Symbols may serve to obscure reality and may indeed become much more influential than the demands of actual practice. They are familiar, while facts may be confusing and strange. Political action is stimulated more readily by pointing to accepted symbols than by enunciating a program developed from cold analysis of specific needs. As Crane Brinton suggests,[1] permanence in accepted ideals and the repeti-tion of manifestoes may add stability to popular institutions. On the other hand, the tenacity with which beliefs are held gives rise to serious difficulty when the symbol no longer suits the fact. An inevitable battle ensues between men holding to the commonly accepted symbols and those urging new values.

There is an area of belief and of talk that is fully as real to the individual as the material evidence of his senses. Men demand that principles be maintained—that is, that ideals be enunciated by the right people at the right times. One result of this is to place in positions of influence in public life men adept in manipulating abstractions. What statesmen say is thus often more important than what they do. The man in public life must protect the totems of the tribe. Whether graven images or noble ideals, these are useful in the maintenance of communal stability, faith, and integrity. The very fervor with which they are held makes change difficult. It is pointless to argue that these sentiments lack a clear "referent." So long as they exist in the area of belief and discussion, they can fulfill their role without unduly interfering with social activity.

When government is called upon to act, the traditional attitude toward state action interferes. Both conservative and radical thinkers in the nineteenth century discredited state action. To Marx the government was the tool of the exploiting class; to the classical economists governmental intervention meant disrupting the natural interplay of economic forces. As Charles E. Merriam has stated, "Both ignored the social function of political direction, ignored or understated. They helped to set up the nineteenth-century plan of two worlds—one of which, politics, is vile; and the other of which, economics, is from on high." [2]

The nineteenth century doctrines which stressed the importance of economic considerations and understated the significance of political factors fitted conditions prevailing in the United States. The Revolution, the extension of popular control over government, and Jacksonian democracy provided a receptive environment. The development of the West, the growth of industry, the increase in national wealth, added apparent factual evidence to economic theories.

The United States has felt severely the consequences of the

deliberate discrediting of state action. Negative attitudes on political activity handicap even efficient governmental agencies. Thinkers of a previous generation and their present echoes condemn governmental intervention as an interference with the liberty of the individual. Governmental activity is inherently inefficient, they argue, and bureaucracy must be abolished. Much has been written about the need for more business in government, and the moral usually asserts the greater efficiency in the management of private affairs. Evidence might prove this assertion true or false. The controls imposed upon the individual by the social and economic order are often ignored while state regulation is condemned merely because it bears the imprint of government. The economic sphere is sustained by symbols and attitudes encouraging freedom, enterprise, and experimentation for the economic order; activity in the political realm is to be confined largely to upholding the principles of free government.

We often overlook the difference between our assumptions concerning government and those concerning business. The businessman engages in no great bother in adjusting his aims to concrete requirements. He must get on. This he tries to do with reasonable honesty and courage. Government, on the other hand, is supposed to be conducted in accordance with impartial standards which restrict the official.

The concept of what the state should do had little significance so long as officials did little. As the British scholar K. Smellie has said:

"For the United States we must grasp the continued insignificance of politics as compared with industry. This contrast between the richness of American economic life and the poverty of its political cannot too often be stressed. The United States has been described as 'not so much a democracy as a huge commercial company for the discovery, cultivation, and capitalisation of its enormous territory.' " [3]

Economic factors have been of foremost significance; but it does not follow logically that the government is therefore incapable of taking a positive and socially desirable role in the expanding industrial life of the nation. Such assumptions have had a more profound effect in the United States than in either Great Britain, France, or Germany. In those countries, the economic doctrines of the nineteenth century were valuable chiefly as a protest. They met a concept of statehood and government well armed with existing beliefs, symbols, doctrines, and resistant traditions. Hegelianism, the Napoleonic system of law and administration, and the Mother of Parliaments, as a symbol of liberation and popular authority, flowered abroad; and more important still, there was either an established bureaucracy or a ruling class with a strong sense of its own competence and authority. It seems likely that, since a bureaucratic tradition was not firmly established in the United States, laissez-faire doctrines reduced confidence in the state and thereby vitally affected the character of our civil service.

While government assumes more responsibility for the direct management of economic affairs, in deference to demands from large segments of the body politic, official action continues to be hedged about with verbalisms of the past. Under laissez faire business administrators had the freedom they desired, including the right to government services for their own purposes. Some abused their power; others achieved admirable results. The traditions of commerce did not restrain experimentation. As their activities brought far-reaching social consequences, however, the state intervened. Yet it came trailing clouds of concepts that impeded management.

The broad problem today is to work out the ways best suited to the attainment of various social needs. Democratic government is not a set of principles which must be consistently followed but rather a method for compromising differences and for freely expressing disagreement according to generally accepted rules of procedure. The forming of policy can await neither the crystallization of a popular will nor agreement among economists upon what is sound. Policy is the product of political compromise, dressed in the language of justification by the philosophers of the winning side.

We turn to government when we find that we cannot administer our affairs through other channels. The government is thought of as the repository of the ultimate power of the community; it is expected to realize ends that other institutions have failed to attain. When social need calls for action the government must respond. The traditional view of state action interferes with the service view, however. Much of our confusion today arises from lip service to principles which no longer accord with the institutions actually used in the service of social needs. Those institutions lacking a theoretical justification in accepted ethical or rational norms are not recognized as respectable or legitimate. This is unfortunate because the most talented individuals are not attracted to these institutions, and disgust and disillusionment with the political process result. The citizens' picture of what should be is besmirched by what is.

The Lynds note how the citizens of Middletown believe that the status quo is the inevitable consequence of progress. The economic system, education, and religion are accepted as the products of an evolutionary process toward better things. Free competition and individualism are credited with maintaining progress, even when their alleged tendency to "make the city a better place to live in" is not supported by evidence. When faced with deciding whether or not to support a zoning law or a slum clearance project, the citizen is as likely to act in accordance with his concept of the proper sphere of government and the necessity for competition as he is to be swayed by the particular need before him. Whether he is wise or foolish is another question. That he is concerned more with broad abstractions than with a specific problem is clear. The Lynds find Middletown torn between faith in democratic symbols and the urgencies of reality. Apathy toward public affairs alternates with feelings of "indignant frustration." "There is no area of Middletown life save religion," the Lynds write, "where symbol is more admittedly and patently divorced from reality than in government, or no area where the functioning of an institution is more enmeshed in undercover intrigue and personalities." [4] This condition is, of course, not confined to Middletown. It reflects a common attitude.

Our traditional view of politics invites comparison with religious behavior. Men are drawn together as they profess a common creed. Underlying that attraction is a common acceptance of the Christian ethic. Abstract doctrine and the interpretation of the scripture become of tremendous importance. People split into sects because of their disagreement about the details of baptism or the selection of the proper Sabbath. Is there not a parallel with the state? Citizens profess the creed of popular government. Strong doctrinal differences arise over what this means. Men believe in the Holy Trinity and with a similar piety in the trinity of powers—legislative, executive, and judicial. They believe in free will and popular will, in the voice of God and the voice of the people. I do not mean to belittle the importance of faith either in government or in religion. I wish to emphasize that community without it is unthinkable. Both citizen and churchman must have their Rock of Ages. Belief in principles and doctrines seems to satisfy basic desires.

Unfortunately dogma both in religion and in government has, however, sometimes become more important than the underlying ethic. Men have denied Christ in fighting over forms of worship. Men have disrupted the peace of the community in the name of common living. Thinking in abstractions, giving loyalty to symbols, is well enough in a period when a loyalty and a faith must be established through the exaltation of an ideal. When the church, once established, turns to social service, theological subleties are of less interest as questions to debate. When the state does likewise it enters a similar phase.

The consequence of a literal acceptance of political theology is seen when abstract doctrines, as for example states rights, are invoked to bar the government from a field where other less orthodox conceptions of social welfare dictate action. Today the doctrinal foes are not the Mohammedan and the heathen, but the fascist and the communist. We profess under democracy a common political ethic, but we split into sects over the details of practical application. Government must take some part in business, but shall it be total immersion or simply a gentle sprinkling? Cromwell knew the Levelers. Wall Street fears their counterparts. Our parallel indicates the difficulties arising from our supernatural view of the state. Religion demands an attitude of mind suited to a structure built on faith alone. The state, too, is built on faith, but it is a man-made affair. To operate successfully it must be dealt with for what it is.

We could afford our traditional approach to the state when the government was less concerned with community affairs. The real job of administering social business was done by private initiative. If we analyze power as it touches men, we cannot confine our attention to the institutions of the state. In any analysis of the actual exercise of power over men, one finds a great variety of power-units attempting to rule the behavior of those individuals falling under their jurisdictions. These groups compete for the wealth or the loyalty of the community. They reflect different traditions, different aims, different standards of right and wrong. Some demand special privileges; others ask simply to be let alone. Superimposed upon these complex forces are democratic ideals for which general recognition is expected. These concepts are supposed to condition the activities of men.

The great repositories of power are those institutions that determine the routine behavior of men, which, for want of a better term, we call power-units. The church and the merchant guilds of the Middle Ages were such. Today great industrial organizations, labor unions, professional associations, and the like perform a similar function within their respective fields.[5] Such groups actually govern the lives of their members much more intimately than do many official regulatory agencies of control. They affect profoundly the daily activities of all who deal with them.

Thus if the problem of government is approached by simply inquiring, "Who tells whom what to do and when?" we find that the routine actions of men are determined largely by non-state agencies and that the official agencies doing most of the actual governing are cities rather than states. The distinctions among federal, state, and city governments and between public and private affairs are but partial formulations of the distribution of authority; the exercise of power escapes the bounds of both.

Many power-units appear as national associations rather than as industrial hierarchies. Though less powerful financially and though employing fewer people, they may yet exercise greater influence by governing the actions of men through bonds of belief, professional standards of ethics, or class loyalties rather than economic sanctions. The size and the strength of power-units of this nature are indications of a significant development.

Control over the actions of individuals is for the most part conducted through nonstate agencies. Government in the legal sense is the institutionalization of the desires of politically effective power-units. We are witnessing not only more governmental control by the state but also more control over the individual by other bureaucracies as well. Government in the legal sense enters the picture (a) where parties in conflict are strong and rich enough to go to court, (b) where one party is influential enough to secure favorable action by the legislature or the executive, and (c) where a violation of mores or existing laws brings officialdom into action. As the statutes and precedents enforced in (c) are crystallizations resulting from (a) and (b), however, the last contingency is but an end product.

Government in the broad sense is the direction of the life of men. Social controls are growing through the expanding jurisdictions of legal, social, and economic power-units. On many fronts the dominance of society over the individual increases.

Because of the disappearance of the frontier, the increase in our population, and the effects and interrelations of technological economic change upon our social life, we in America are passing into a new era. We are entering a time when the exigencies of life impose a greater socialization upon us, such as has already occurred in Europe, with concomitant political and sociological results. The scope of national advertising, newspapers, motion pictures, urbanization, and the greater size of human aggregates in many fields stress the contemporary social controls on the individual. He can hope to find fulfillment only as he pools his interests with like-minded fellows and seeks expression of his beliefs and desires through organized efforts.

Today we witness an impounding of social power in large organizations. Power becomes centralized through the use of the political process as a way of fighting economic or moral battles. Business is characterized by large corporative structures. Social and economic aggregates seem directed toward increasing size.

Fifty-six per cent of the population now dwells in urban areas. One-quarter of the people live in the ten largest cities. The growth of our cities means the concentration of innumerable power-units in urban areas; it means also greater demands on government and perhaps greater political rivalries. Arthur N. Holcombe concludes that the

"demands of modern urban society upon government ensure that the urbane politics of the future will be something radically different from both the rustic and the municipal politics of the past. Urbane politics means not only that government must play a larger part in life, but also that the structure of government must be strengthened and the processes of government improved to the end that public enterprise may respond acceptably to the greater expectations of the people." [6]

By a legal fiction the state may be said to possess final authority, but actually the extent to which it serves as a power-unit depends on the relative strength of the many competing power-units. Law is not a power in itself but rather a channel through which social forces choose to seek their objectives. The authority of the state, like water from a spring, cannot rise above its own source. While we entertain the concept of state power, we accept the fact that it must be exercised through political institutions. These are the channels through which alliances of sections or factions seek to promote their own welfare in the name of the public interest. If we seek the forces which actually govern society, we must look beyond those few sources enumerated in the law.

We are today shifting to governmental institutions an ever greater share of the responsibility for adjusting human relationships. This entails, of course, a greater dependence on the institutions and ideology of the state. The struggle of politics becomes more intense as the stakes grow higher. It results, moreover, in greater reliance upon a peculiar process of adjustment. The political process has never before in this country been put to such a task of formulating and executing policy as at present. The extension of governmental activity means that the many administrative functions are removed from private power-units and centralized under public officials. These officials may themselves develop a power-unit—a bureaucracy. To prevent this, we limit their discretion at the cost of administrative efficiency, to the end, it is urged, that we may thus live under a government of laws and not of men.

The state can offset the power of nonofficial bureaucracies as we shift to the political process adjustments heretofore left to fortuitous or arbitrary settlement. Behind this development, however, lies the assumption made explicit by the Supreme Court in these words: "The theory of our government state and national is opposed to the deposit of unlimited power anywhere." [7] To this dictum we may add another: Power must be finally identified with no one class or group; it must be handled like a loving cup and passed about lest one of the company grow drunk.

As a consequence of greater governmental participation in the economic life of the nation, interests which once battled outside the government now fight inside and use the instruments of popular control as additional weapons. More government by the state does not necessarily result in less freedom. The control exercised over an individual by a private agency may be far more tyrannical than anything the state imposes. Under democracy many hierarchies of power exist side by side. Their interrelationship we are trying to adjust by rule, by discussion, by negotiation. The higher the stakes in economic terms, the more intense the struggle may be.

☆ 3 ☆

Conditions Favorable to Popular Rule

> "To hold men together by paper and seal or
> by compulsion is no account.
> That only holds men together which aggre-
> gates all in a living principle, as the hold
> of the limbs of the body or the fibres
> of plants."
>
> WALT WHITMAN

FOR its successful functioning democracy assumes a society naturally integrated. There must be a pattern of community life with
meaning to its people. There must be a core of spiritual values
generally conceded to be sound. Within such a social frame of
reference freedom of thought can operate. Disagreement can
be tolerated since most men feel confident that violent change
will not result from new and unorthodox ideas. In most democratic countries unity has gone further. Not only has there been
developed a common code of values, but also these values have
been the spiritual heritage of a relatively homogeneous class.
Our economic order has produced the conditions for a large,
stable, adequately fed middle class.[1] This has been the very back-
bone of democracy. In France, Great Britain, and the United
States such a class has evolved. In countries where such a class
has been weak, self-government has also been weak. A broad
middle class may offer an effective basis for a stable society but
within this society there must be competition among groups of
citizens for political control. This is not the whole answer. Middle-
class solidarity is not likely to continue in the form in which we

have known it, since the conditions that gave rise to this attitude are undergoing rapid change. Mindful of such social changes, and of the underlying economic factors, we must examine our governmental structure and reconsider the place of the political party. In totalitarian countries the first function of party is to establish a unified basis of support for the government. Integration is essential for a democratic society, too, but to maintain it will probably require a broader synthesis of interests than can be included within the traditional concept of middle-class loyalties. This promises to be a more urgent problem in the future than it has been in the past.

Like any other political pattern, democracy will persist so long as it responds to social needs. Our party system will continue to be justified in the extent to which it contributes as an instrumentality of this design for living. As a matter of history we know that party government has succeeded in those countries where environmental factors have provided the integration necessary to make political disagreement tolerable. If some interests use the institutions of party government to express their differences of opinion it is within a context unified by a wider public interest.

Ample evidence shows that the French are concerned with parties more as a "vehicle for registering their beliefs than for representing their interests." Political parties in France are significant largely on the plane of discussion. Their members do not expect extreme party doctrines to have any immediate practical effect, nor do candidates look to national party organizations as the most effective means of winning an election. It is said that "in practice the general policy of the country is dictated by certain regions," although it would be misleading to judge French political parties in terms of a struggle over economic issues. "Our democracy is Latin in origin," André Siegfried states, "and therefore unlike the Anglo-Saxon democracies where practical social accomplishments are the first consideration." [2]

The general tendency toward the left has made for an attitude of mind favorable to the accommodation of existing institutions to new needs and demands. The left provides a stimulus and a sense of direction, while vested interests stand ready to oppose radical action that goes too far or too fast. Notwithstanding the extremes that politicians may advocate in debate, the difference between this freedom of talk and the actual pace of radical policy has been sufficiently great to keep the French nation together while social legislation has progressed. Acceptance of this sense of direction has made up for the diversity found among blocs and parties.

Its multi-party system based on subtle diversities of belief does not mean that France has a form of government more representative than the American or the British. The French can avoid compromise no more than any other democracy. This process may be postponed but never eliminated. Under the French party system the proponents of special viewpoints come together in the Chamber of Deputies. The process of compromise tends to concentrate at this level. The formation of blocs is the first step. Then comes a coalition of blocs as the necessary support for any ministry. A Cabinet based upon such a condition is inevitably unstable. Postponing the adjustment of viewpoints until this belated stage means that the highest executive authority of the country rests upon a coalition of blocs. The theoretical justification for such a system lies in the desire to recognize many divisions of opinion and to base leadership upon a selection of the more influential views. A party system placing emphasis on the representation of principles and beliefs leads inevitably to such multiplicity. In practice it is necessary to secure a combination of those politicians who are capable of attracting among them a majority of the Chamber and thereby dominating all other dissenters.

Where a party's representative function is given first consideration, proportional representation is often offered as a way of overcoming the defects of a multi-party system. It is argued that if all elements are represented in proportion to their numerical strength, all will be well. Such a system, however, usually results either in a balance between various groups with power falling into the hands of a minority faction or in a coalition government with all the weaknesses of any multi-party arrangement. Proportional representation is simply another way of postponing compromise. Under this system the views of many different groups can be brought together in a representative assembly. Here these spokesmen at last are forced to adjust their views, since without compromise governmental action is impossible.

The multi-party system in France, while it brings a clear representation of diverse interests together, must inevitably blur these distinctions in composing a program for action. In this process personal bickering and logrolling arise. The instability of the Cabinet is the government's great weakness and the direct result of the party system.

"A Parliament detached from the Executive may provide these sects [blocs] with congenial battle-ground, but in the Parliament which controls the Executive, their feuds must be sufficiently composed to enable the Government to be carried on. That has been discovered in France, where the political groups are under a perpetual compulsion to find common ground for the support of a Government." [3]

We may conclude that French political parties serve primarily on the plane of discussion as agencies for representing different points of view. The integration of viewpoints in policy and action is left to the ministry and, even more important, to the bureaucracy. The integrating force of this latter institution is tremendous. "Alone of the major states of contemporary Continental Europe, the French Republic still remains faithful to the conception that a permanent administrative bureaucracy is compatible with responsible democratic government," Walter Sharp writes.[4] This continuity of the administrative organization joined with its highly centralized form adds greatly to its unifying power. Equally important is the great prestige enjoyed by the public service. "Throughout the nineteenth century French administration was the envy of the rest of the Continent. The 'glory' of service for the state was such as to impel every family throughout the land to attempt to place one or more of its sons in public employment." [5]

With a great bureaucracy, a strong military machine representing the nation in arms, a proud tradition of Republicanism, the wealth of empire and an intense love of the native soil, France has powerful impulses and interests promoting unity. Yet once writers saw the religious issue and the problem of social reorganization as questions capable of cutting the French public asunder. A party alignment based on such differences might prove fatal to popular government. French parties are electoral devices for deputies and loose groupings reflecting many shades of opinion.*

A bipartisan alignment would scarcely be fortunate for France. Where deep-seated differences exist it is more conducive to the adjustment of differences if there is no general alignment into two rival factions. Our readiness to take for granted the unity which modern democracies have enjoyed for the few decades of their existence is such that men often urge institutional expression in political parties for the deep potential differences within the community.

In contrast to the French, the British party system insures a high degree of responsibility and leadership. The representation of particularistic views has always been of less concern to the British. "It was above all owing to their dislike of being doctrinaire, of pushing ideas to extremes, that the spirit of com-

---

* "Critics of French institutions commonly start from the assumption that the two-party system is essential to the satisfactory working of Parliamentary government [Middleton has written]. The soundness of this doctrine has recently been questioned even in Great Britain, where it was for so long axiomatic. Certainly, France, with no fewer than seven presentable electoral organizations, would on this principle stand condemned. Some French politicians impressed by the example of the Mother of Parliaments, would indeed like to see in their country a concentration of the forces at present dispersed. In 1928 timid attempts were even made, by men on both sides, to promote a consolidation of Right and Left into two definite blocs. If the extreme admirers of the old British system found few to listen to them it was because, for one thing, they had taken too little account of the contrasting mentalities of two different races. British and French parties differ in temperament, in habit of life and manner of growth. Both are indeed always changing, gradually or suddenly, by internal evolution or by disruption. But processes of development which are natural in one system are not natural in the other." (W. L. Middleton, *The French Political System*, New York, E. P. Dutton & Co., 1933, page 16.)

promise for practical government established itself as the presiding genius of politics," Middleton states. "Progress occurred with the minimum of agitation. . . . But if the moulds of Liberalism and Conservatism remained unbroken, their contents suffered changes amounting in the sum to a revolution." [6] Internal changes within one or the other of these major party organizations met the need for new policies. It was not necessary to establish a new form in order to put forward a new idea. Loyalty to the Liberal or to the Conservative party as an institution did not erect serious barriers to changes in policy. The British were concerned more with meeting needs immediately and with getting things done than with stressing fine distinctions. In Great Britain the internal accommodation of the party organizations has prevented intransigence.

The conventional picture of the British system sets forth two clearly defined parties: the majority party, winning office and carrying through a program; and the loyal opposition, accepting defeat cheerfully and behaving as all good cricket men should. But this is an oversimplified picture.

We must reckon with the fact that Great Britain is an extraordinarily well-integrated society and until recent years was not disturbed by basically different social and political views from politically effective groups. As William Edward Hartpole Lecky has written, "Within wide limits the two parties move on the same lines, and are more like competitors in a race than adversaries in the field. The old ideal of conservative policy is indeed seldom likely to be realised except under a weak radical government confronted and controlled by a powerful opposition." [7]

At first glance the British government seems to contradict this view. Certainly a chasm separates the ideology of a Tory lord and that of an Independent Labour party trade unionist. If parliamentary government were forced to face directly the divergences illustrated by Tory versus radical Labourite, it probably could not function. In practice, however, a balance wheel of moderate opinion counteracts the extremists. Lecky has stated: "In practical politics there must always be much compromise and mutual concession; and, as Hallam long since said, the centrifugal and the centripetal forces, which correspond roughly to the rival party tendencies, are both needed to preserve the due balance of affairs." [8] Under democracy it is essential that we have a broad *mean* between extremes. The middle class is regarded as the influence that brings public policy closer to the needs of the community as a whole.[9] The great mass of voters tends to walk in the middle of the road. This has been the case irrespective of the extreme positions taken by partisan standard-bearers.

Parties could not function as they do in Great Britain unless a firmly integrated community made it safe for them to oppose each other strongly. The nature of British society has admitted of much apparent disagreement among those in control of the government, but government in Great Britain has been exercised to an extraordinary degree by a social class basically unified. The operation of British parties cannot be accurately considered apart from the society of which they are one expression. The British system has developed in a homogeneous nation where the responsibilities of empire, of industrialization, and of shipping stressed the importance of responsible leadership; along with an expanding Empire wherein direction from the center was only slowly relinquished; and with a gradually enlarged electorate that could be absorbed in an orderly fashion into two national party organizations. The representative aspect of government has been of less importance because an expanding economic order provided a common objective. The public interest has been identified with the increase of national wealth and power. Moreover, the monarchy has served as a strong integrating factor. The acceptance of class status and deference to rank and position have been stabilizing influences. Such attitudes have fortified the permanent civil service. The British Cabinet itself serves as an important integrating device. It is a supreme committee of adjustment in close touch with the dominant interests of the nation. Because of the completeness of party control, adjustment is channeled almost exclusively through the Cabinet. This may be defended as responsible government, but it also means highly centralized government.

Today the responsibility for adjustment and integration focused here is so great that some thoughtful Englishmen question whether their traditional form of government can cope with the conflicts they see impending. Harold Laski, for example, quotes Bagehot and Lord Balfour to show that, despite changes in Cabinets and partisan controversies, political parties in the past could bicker harmlessly since the nation was "fundamentally at one." Laski thinks that this is no longer the situation. "If the Labour Party means what its programme says, political parties now do differ about those foundations," he writes. He points out that "with the disappearance of fundamental unity, there goes also the ability to preserve that moderation of temper which is the secret of the ability to compromise. . . ." [10] This view ignores the margin of difference between what men say they must have and that with which they will be content. We have no good reason to think that the Labour party is an exception here. Moreover, men of conservative temper in the past have habitually exploded at radical generalities and then given way in the light of specific need and under determined pressure. Mutual concessions made extraordinary adjustments possible in nineteenth century Britain.

To predict the end of parliamentary government because of the incompatibility of the avowed program of the Labour party with the word pictures of the Conservative party is to overlook the difference between what men say (and often sincerely believe) and what they do in particular instances. It underestimates the compelling force of circumstance and the strength of habitual loyalties which bind men to the familiar. No *a priori* significance can confidently be given to the logically conceived programs of leaders. The meaning of their proposals will be determined step by step as specific issues are debated and the resultant statutes administered. We are hardly justified in discarding the machinery for compromise merely because some extremists say that the time for compromise is past. Public policy is never the pure logical product envisaged by partisan theorists. Laski's fears are justified only to the degree that voters and politicians can be rallied into two clearly opposed camps by the doctrinaire alarmists of the right and of the left. I see nothing inevitable about such an align-ment. Also, it is often overlooked that while they come out with definite programs, British parties have in practice been forced to ally with other factions or parties to hold power. The picture of clear party control is modified by the fact of coalition and minor-ity governments.

The success of a political party as an integrating device can be explained only with reference to attitudes and institutions that contribute to or obstruct the unification of society. Where inte-grating attitudes and institutions exhibit a traditional develop-ment they are usually accepted freely. Their effects may irk some, and insistent friction may result in modification. Their ac-ceptance, however, does not depend on political force or legal authority.

Totalitarian government has come as one answer in nations where the more natural social and economic ties of community have been broken. The disintegration of the community, the fail-ure of leadership, and the overdiversity of representation pre-pared the ground for a single-party system to weld the country together. A strong party imposed its will from above. In a dem-ocratic community the party system reflects diversities and cleav-ages that are yet not deep enough to threaten the social fabric itself. In contrast to the totalitarian state, democracy tries to re-tain both integration and liberty. To succeed under democracy, party government must achieve a working alliance of interests and bring support to leaders who desire both to control the gov-ernment and to tolerate a loyal opposition. These conditions may be met in different ways, depending largely upon varying insti-tutional forms. Fundamentally, however, government by parties means the control of government by alternating groups.

The theory of government by discussion assumes that by air-ing differences men may arrive at agreement. The party system aligns men into opposing camps only to seek a common ground for action. To survive, popular government must somewhere provide for an effective meeting of minds. If not through politi-cal parties, integration must come through other channels. The significance of this unifying activity should not be considered with reference to the party alone. Within any society some factors work for integration and others toward disintegration. Traditions of popular government often support and promote political integration through symbolic and even irrational means. Totalitarian governments must act more consciously in order to achieve similar ends. Propaganda is their substitute for traditionalism. Dictators must depend almost entirely upon disciplined party action, while the democratic leader is carried along by a wide variety of social institutions.

If party government is possible only within an integrated society, what are the forces making for such unity? For integration a society requires a core of faith common to most of the individuals within it, giving satisfaction to life and insuring acceptance of societal controls and co-operation in community objectives.

The point may be illustrated by recalling an anecdote of Confucius. Tsekung asked about government, and Confucius replied, "People must have sufficient to eat; there must be a sufficient army; and there must be confidence of the people in the ruler." "If you are forced to give up one of these three objectives, what would you go without first?" asked Tsekung. Confucius said, "I would go without the army first." "And if you were forced to go without one of the two remaining factors, what would you rather go without?" asked Tsekung again. "I would rather go without sufficient food for the people. There have always been deaths in every generation since man lived; but a nation cannot exist without confidence in its ruler." [11]

Translating this tale into modern terms, we might say that national safety and economic security are important, but that even more important is a nation's confidence that its political order holds meaning. The factors that maintain the confidence of a people in their rulers differ with times and cultures. In some civilizations, such as the Chinese, general poverty has been endured without effective challenge to the political order; cultural leaders persist even under the foreign oppressor's heel. So far as our own experience with democracy is concerned party government has grown up in nations that believed in being well armed and well fed. Our Western democracies have not had to face the choice put to Confucius. Confidence in democratic rule has been accompanied by two broad forces for integration, namely, nationalism and an expanding economic system.

Whether these conditions are indispensable to the continued confidence of a people in the democratic order we cannot foretell. I believe that the failure of party government in Italy and Germany is not conclusive either way. The conventional explanation points out that in Italy before the advent of Mussolini political conditions tended to "falsify the operation of the party system." The hostility of the Pope drew devout Catholics from participation in politics and coalesced them into an irreconcilable minority. Social and historic forces encouraged a feudalistic attitude on the part of the people. They supported their deputies in return for the favors which the deputies secured from the ministers as the price of parliamentary support. The ministers, for their part, were concerned in maintaining a support in the national legislature sufficient for carrying through their policies. Their strategy was to play one bloc against another, and this resulted often in the constructing of political programs on a basis of personal favors. Political parties tended to become gangs of henchmen rather than effective national organizations. These conditions reflect a pathology of parliamentarianism by no means confined to Italian politics. Indeed, they illustrate weaknesses that various democratic nations have had to face, though perhaps in less aggravated form.

The destruction of the economic basis of the middle class by the postwar inflation in Germany, the vacillating leadership of the Social Democratic party, and the feeling of national insecurity resulting from external pressure are often cited as forces undermining the foundations of democracy. It is agreed that these foundations were never very secure; in all of the countries now under a dictatorial form of government, the liberal democratic tradition had too little time to develop. The Nazis and the Italian fascists stressed the threat of communism as a justification for their totalitarian rule. They attracted the conservatives to their party in this way. Promising economic security and national strength, fascism appealed also to the "little man." The totalitarian state based its appeal upon its effectiveness in improving the economic condition of the populace and in gathering international prestige, but perhaps even more important was the insistence that all profess confidence in the ruler.

Germany and Italy were disintegrated. One-party systems developed to supply by artificial means the strength and unity sapped from the nation by war and internal disagreement. Internal conditions were sufficiently critical to enable dictatorial leaders to superimpose their ideologies and organizations. It is in these positive aspects of fascism that we must seek the explanation for its strength. The democratic myth ceased to make sense to nations unable to realize freedom, equality, or fraternity in the family of nations.

Most students of Germany and Italy seem agreed that fascism arose from "the unfulfilled promises of democracy." "In each of the phases of human organization in which the promises of democratic life have been more blatantly unfulfilled," it is argued, "germs of disintegration have multiplied around centers of infection which have combined in the general phenomenon called Fascism." [12] Existing institutions and interests, both social and economic, could not be brought into line with democratic ideals through the weak party system which was no stronger than the disparate elements for which it stood. The democratic way was rejected as a bourgeois invention when it failed to produce the economic welfare promised by its middle-class sponsors. The deflationary policy of the Bruening regime could not sustain popular faith in capitalism as an economic order. "The tenets, institutions and beliefs of the bourgeois order were . . . only accepted on the strength of their social promise and could only be maintained as long as the promise held good," Peter F. Drucker writes.[13] "The democratic system," he states, "which had no independent hold upon popular imagination, collapsed and the distintegration of the substance of the democratic order spread rapidly to the tenets, symbols, and institutions without encountering any resistance in the emotional or sentimental traditions of the routine mind." [14]

The masses could, however, fall back upon the nationalistic

tradition which the aristocratic leaders of the last century had created. As fate would have it, Hitler's clique hit upon a formula which shrewdly exploited loyalties to soil and blood. In the face of economic and international insecurity and the threat of social chaos, here was a myth to give a pattern to social relations. Even the nationalist myth, however, is too recent to be taken for granted; it is preached by the fascists with the fanaticism of the newly converted. National solidarity is believed to be endangered by middle-class loyalty to the democratic creed. Totalitarianism will not brook opposition since this would be regarded as a disintegrating force.

The one-party government that is postulated has to perform a function more difficult than that which befalls parties under a democratic regime. It must unify the nation. Totalitarianism asserts one creed and one hierarchy and denies the right of group interests to exist outside the party. The totalitarian state stands as the "completely political structure." "It is a prerequisite," one authority, E. B. Ashton, writes, "to any realization of the superior place which the state holds under the Fascist dogma that there should be no group structure existing beside, and independent of, and therefore incompatible with the state. The structure of society that does not fit the Fascist state must be removed." [15]

"The Fascist state . . . can more safely leave a lukewarm Fascist in an important government position than let a social organization remain uncoordinated, no matter how innocuous it may seem." [16] Fascist associations of civil servants, lawyers, actors, traveling salesmen, and the like are set up even in purely occupational groups. The state relies upon the party "to enforce communal interest and produce the essential collective unity of spirit." [17]

In Great Britain the acceptance of an ideal type in the "gentleman" has been a factor of no small importance in the furtherance of social integration.[18] The gentlemanly ideal was of slow and ancient growth. A German observer, Wilhelm Dibelius, has pointed out the significance of this social concept, making explicit a notion that most Britishers take for granted. The Nazis have recognized directly the importance of winning general social acceptance of an ideal type—the true Nazi party member. Their task is to substitute one type for the various class types of old Germany and their divergent loyalties. Whether an ideal type can be artificially created by party propaganda remains for fascists to discover. Fascist states are confronting the task of building a new view of the state, of citizenship, and even of society and of the individual. The individual must develop a "collective state of mind." Propaganda of necessity becomes a normal feature of government. New values are preached. The party is built on a new aristocracy composed, not of those persons outstanding in traditionally valued qualities, but of the most fascistic: an elite of the best disciplined and most collective-minded.

The fascists try to fit all interests into an orderly pattern. Strikes are prohibited, and a procedure for handling of labor disputes is provided. All interest groups are either given fascist coloration or obliterated. Even the churches have felt the challenge. The doctrine of a war economy comes as a crowning effort to co-ordinate the nation into an armed Leviathan. In Drucker's words, "the substance of Wehrwirtschaft is the attempt to make all social relationships conform to the model of the relationship between superior and subordinate officer, and between officer and men." [19]

In this connection the parallel between National Socialism in Germany today and the tactics of French Revolutionary leaders is striking, but the myth of popular sovereignty growing up with the myth of French nationalism produced results very different from the myth of nationalism which grew under Nazi auspices.* Democracy superimposed later on the myth of na-

* Carlton J. H. Hayes reminds us that

"It was the French Revolution, moreover, that elaborated the first general scheme of national elementary education, which should be state-supported and state-directed, compulsory and universal, and in which national patriotism and national duty should be taught equally with the three R's. It was the French Revolution, too, that adopted and gave effect to the principle of the 'nation in arms,' the principle that all able-bodied male citizens should be trained for war and liable to conscription for military or naval service. And, finally, it was the French Revolution that gave impetus and character to nationalist journalism, to the publication of newspapers, pamphlets, and magazines so cheap and so

tionalism in Germany and Italy did not take hold. Drucker states that "In England, France, Holland and in the Scandinavian countries . . . the experience and tradition . . . is that of the struggle for democracy. National unity had been achieved much earlier. . . ." [20] A vital distinction rests in the fact that the French preached the faith of the brotherhood of man and of popular sovereignty while the Germans assert the sanctity of race and the *Fuehrerprinzip*. National Socialism is the reassertion of a nationalism which was the product of the military and aristocratic tradition of Bismarck and reflects these influences in distorted form.

The great experience which attracted the emotional and sentimental attachment of the masses in Italy and Germany of the nineteenth century was the victory, not of a free bourgeois order, but of national unification. In Great Britain and in France the unity of the nation cannot be attributed solely to the extraordinary capacity of the people for self-government. Without attempting to decide relative strengths or priorities, it is enough to point out that the evolution of party government and the rise of nationalism were closely associated. Moreover, as Hayes notes, "the Industrial Revolution rendered possible and practical the permanent establishment and rapid extension of that national democracy which the French Revolution indicated as ideally desirable." [21] Another way of explaining nationalism and democracy is that these creeds made sense to the middle class which usually stood to gain by the working out of both doctrines. Liberal democrats were the leaders of the nationalist movement. Thus nationalism and democracy worked toward a high degree of harmony of ideals, interests, and institutions both in France and in Great Britain.

Where popular sovereignty has been a potent factor in the growth of nationalism, nationalistic sentiments have permeated

demagogic that they would appeal to the masses of the whole nation, to the half educated even more than to the well educated.

"From the days of the French Revolution to the present, the democratic dogma has proved a most helpful bolster for nationalism." (*Essays on Nationalism*, New York, The Macmillan Co., 1928, pages 47–48.)

the community. Here popular government has promoted the acceptance of national unity and the myths have been reciprocally strengthened. Where nationalism has preceded popular sovereignty, the coming of democratic institutions has entailed some disruption of interests and institutions that previously integrated the nation. This is illustrated by the identification of the bourgeoisie with liberal democratic parties opposing, on the one hand, national and conservative parties which drew their strength from the peasantry and the aristocracy and, on the other hand, communistic and internationalistic parties which were supported by radical intellectuals and class-conscious industrial workers. Party government in such terms ran counter to nationalism as an integrating force since it stressed class differences. The two myths became antagonistic instead of being complementary as in Great Britain and France. This conflict of loyalties weakened democracy. We do not have to argue that certain people are less capable of self-government than others or that democracy requires a long tradition. Democracy in Germany and Italy could not claim credit for establishing their respective people's awareness of their destiny as a nation. It had to prove itself as a competent governmental mechanism. Being on the defensive, it lacked the very unity requisite to its success. The myths of democracy and of nationalism function most smoothly when their assumptions pass unquestioned.

Government by alternating parties has been possible thus far only where the symbols both of nationalism and of democracy have been accepted without effective challenge. Also such government has flourished only under favorable economic conditions. Party government faces two potential cleavages which would threaten the nationalistic and capitalistic creeds under which it has developed. Conflict between employer and employee would split the nation internally, and dispute over foreign policy would divide men into factions urging isolation and autarchy and factions advocating collective security and economic co-operation. It is conceivable that these two areas of disagreement might serve to counteract each other. Threats from abroad unify a nation. On the other hand, international economic co-operation might well lead to an improvement of the conditions underlying internal industrial class conflict. This, however, must remain in the realm of speculation.

Democratic parties rely upon traditional loyalties to hold men together as a community and as a nation while party politicians engage in the luxury of debate. It takes a stable society bound by such implicit loyalties to enable men to enjoy the security of "agreeing to disagree." Democracy's first duty is the preservation of the conditions that permit this toleration of disagreement.

☆ 4 ☆

Leadership Under Party Government

"Who shall speak for the people?
who has the answers?
where is the sure interpreter?
who knows what to say?"
CARL SANDBURG

THOUGH adjustment is the goal of democratic politics leaders must decide whether this is attained better through programs stressing radical changes in relationships or through policies that guard the existing equilibrium of interests. The task of leadership is to bring the diversity of our society into a working harmony. Our system of political parties is designed to implement this purpose. Through such organizations the politician can contribute to the process of adjustment. The task is harder for the democratic leader than for the dictator. Both must win consent; but the latter has an official monopoly of the means of persuasion, while the democratic leader must compete for support.

Leaders standing for principles are effective in so far as their words give meaning to some pattern of interests. Would-be leaders of reform movements often fail because they do not distinguish between what men say they want and what prove to be their real desires. Thus, while in the area of belief and discussion voters declare themselves in favor of efficiency and impartiality in the administration of the law, they react quite differently when tagged for parking. The experienced politician is not disturbed by such inconsistencies. He takes life as he finds it. This is his value and his limitation.

What is the man in public life to do when his conscience forbids such an easy way out? The Adams family, as described by James Truslow Adams, illustrates one reaction to the choice.

"No Adams [he writes] has ever been a party man. Soon after his election, John Adams wrote to Richard Price saying that 'I have never sacrificed my judgment to kings, ministers, nor people, and I never will.' He certainly never did, nor has any Adams after him. This integrity of self, often demonstrated in face of the strongest temptation has been a continuing trait, but in an America demanding more and more that a man shall conform to the majority it is a trait that has more and more made it difficult if not impossible for the family to serve in elective office. As we look over the list of the early leaders of the republic, Washington, John Adams, Hamilton, and others, we discern that they were all men who insisted upon being themselves and who refused to truckle to the people. With each succeeding generation, the growing demand of the people that its elective officials shall not lead but merely register the popular will has steadily undermined the independence of those who derive their power from popular election." [1]

This implication that the highest form of statesmanship requires the leader to follow the dictates of his own personal standards is open to challenge. If the men of highest standards feel compelled to retreat from politics rather than compromise, they perforce leave their public duties to less worthy hands. The highest task of statesmanship is to preserve the democratic process—because it is through this process that we can best hope to foster and safeguard the integrity of the individual. Refusal to compromise with one's own principles may or may not be justified; the answer must depend on the effect of such intransigence on the governmental process. If the principles of high-minded individuals prevent their carrying their share of responsibility in community affairs for fear of contamination, they are in need of reeducation.

The true democratic leader seeks not simply to maintain his own power and personal integrity but also to offer policies that have most meaning for his followers. What is he to do if his supporters threaten to go off in what he sincerely regards as the wrong direction? *

The first responsibility of the statesman in a democracy is to make the system work. Undemocratic means cannot be justified for the attainment of a democratic end. A statesman of skill avoids such a dilemma. He carries his public along with him. He teaches them the need for action. The statesman must interpret public problems for his followers and explain how he proposes to direct social energies into fruitful channels. If he seeks more than a transitory victory, he must appeal to the intelligence of his followers. He must be an educator in the broadest sense of the term. The art of leadership embraces the methods of both the politician and the sage; and democracy makes the highest demands on both patience and determination.[2]

Granted that the democratic leader is willing to compromise with his own political beliefs in deference to a broader consensus, how is this consensus to be interpreted? Does the essence of

* Lindsay Rogers has asked:

"Should a statesman do precisely what he thinks the electorate wishes him to do, even though he is convinced that the electorate is wrong? Should he do what he thinks the electorate would wish him to do if the electorate had at its disposal the special information which he has? Or should he act as his own knowledge and conscience suggest that he act—should he play for a favorable page in the history of books, hoping that the electorate will support him, but prepared to pursue his course so long as he is not definitely checked by legislative veto or by popular criticism too strong and general to be resisted?"

The answers that Rogers suggests go to the heart of our problem:

"A public man probably acts at various times as if he were mindful of each of three considerations and were ignoring the others. In respect of some issues he may move on the basis of a combination of two or all three of the considerations. Some questions do not interest the public. On them he can determine his own course. Other issues stir up such passions that for the time being statesmanship may consist in following the popular will but in planning to modify the will. Selectivity is essential. The people may be willing to stand a number of things in succession but they may be unwilling to stand them all at once. The statesman must therefore pay a good deal of attention to the manner in which public support is to be secured and to the issues which it is desirable to put to the fore or which it is wise for the time being to subordinate. If a statesman wishes to lead he must educate so that the leadership will be understood and expected. He cannot step forth on one issue and expect to be followed when he has refused to commit himself on other issues. Leadership cannot be spasmodic." (Crisis Government, New York, W. W. Norton & Co., 1934, pages 94–95.)

democracy mean effectuating the majority will, or is it found in a free balance of interests maintained under constitutional safeguards? If we view democracy not conceptually as a logical system but pragmatically as a complex historical continuum, we find both viewpoints defended. Both tend to moderate purely subjective interpretations of what is "right" in politics. The majority concept dictates that personal judgment be subordinated to a broader will; the balance concept calls for modification of individual views for the sake of a larger unity.

Some leaders insist that the majority will must prevail; others stress the importance of preserving a balance through constitutional agreement. Both concepts have proved highly useful, depending for their maximum utility upon the conditions of a given time. When social conditions call for a rapid readaptation of government, insistence upon the validity of majority rule serves to justify changes greatly affecting minority rights. In a society cut through by sharp differences among groups of comparable strength, the attainment of balance through appeal to the authority of a constituent will must be the goal if discord and violence are to be avoided. It would be an oversimplification to argue that one kind of leader devotes his attention exclusively to integration and another kind is concerned with renovation, although there seem to be historical periods to which such distinctions might be applied. The relative emphasis to be placed upon these two lines of policy varies with the needs of different periods. Sometimes consolidating and integrating the diversity of society seems most important; at other times the impulses for change are felt most acutely, and the recognition of new forces pressing for change in the name of the majority is of primary value.

Leadership is as much the expression of underlying interests through an accepted channel as it is the dominance of an individual over his fellows. Thus the Puritan divine spoke with authority in a society built upon the values he expounded. Where a firm religious framework is established the moral law can be the guide for leader and followers. The aristocrat is accepted as the natural leader in a society constructed upon class distinctions.

When Benjamin Harrison set out for the First Continental Congress the plain people gathered about him. "You say there is something wrong?" they said in effect. "We have not felt its effects. But we trust you and leave you to do the right thing." [3] This is what Burke expected from the electors of Bristol. Henry Adams defined a statesman as one who tells the people what to think. Before the onslaught of Jacksonian democracy, leaders in the United States were drawn from the ruling gentry and expressed this institutional pattern and its supporting attitudes. With the growth of the nation and the clear development of sectionalism and class rivalries, a marked change took place.

At some points in our history we seem to enter dramatically upon a new phase. The party of Jefferson evolved into the party of Jackson and grew strong as a vehicle for the expression of democracy. The Federalist leaders did not adapt their organization to the broad forces about them. These great shifts were so fundamental that the Federalist party, failing to respond, died of atrophy. It has been said that Aaron Burr's pistolshot in killing Hamilton in 1804 blew out the brains of the Federalist party. A new party in time grew from the disintegration of the old. The Whig party arising in opposition to the party of Jacksonian democracy was united largely by dislike of "King Andrew." Less responsive to the effective pattern of political forces, the Whigs were significant chiefly for what they opposed. As the slave-owning oligarchy became entrenched in the Democratic party, the Whigs failed to find any lasting formula for constructive action. The slavocracy that took over the control of the federal government through the Democratic party machine was in time faced by a rising northern industrial elite.

The political issue of slavery was identified with regions and with ethical values of wide emotional appeal. Politicians of the time side-stepped the issues as long as possible, but no satisfactory *modus vivendi* was found. A conflict of interests became crystallized into a conflict of principles. The issue was, moreover, easily reduced to a contest between special interests in rival regions. The politicians as middlemen had little scope within which to operate. Since political power in this country lies in the control of regions and since slavery was identified with a region, the outcome of this issue raised the problem of which sections of the country were to rule the nation as a whole. The Kansas-Nebraska Act not only upset the existing sectional compromise but also aligned one section against the other. Classes with different ideas and social values dominated each region, and cleavages which party loyalty could not bridge were discovered. The tragic failures of the politics of democracy are such failures of adjustment. The great shifts in society, if unrecognized and pent up, may burst their bonds with a violence that causes deep suffering. The New Deal, whatever its faults, attempted to adjust the country to changes in the economy resulting from the great depression. This general process can be illustrated in more detail by a survey of several crucial phases in our national development.

Once the American Revolution had come to a termination, political leaders faced the task of consolidating the states and building a federal union. It is not surprising then to find in the writings of George Washington, John Adams, and James Madison an assumption of national unity as the primary objective. Since the fact of diversity could not be ignored, the ideal of balance was brought in so that synthesis might be achieved. The two classic examples of this point of view are found in Washington's *Farewell Address* and in paper number ten of the *Federalist*.

The *Farewell Address* warned against the harmful effects of faction. Washington hoped to prevent differences and social cleavages by urging all good men to put their country's welfare first.

"The unity of government which constitutes you one people is also now dear to you. It is justly so, for it is a main pillar in the edifice of your real independence, the support of your tranquillity at home, your peace abroad, of your safety, of your prosperity, of that very liberty which you so highly prize. But as it is easy to foresee that from different causes and from different quarters much pains will be taken, many artifices employed, to weaken in your minds the conviction of this truth, . . . it is of infinite moment that you should properly estimate the immense value of your national union to your collective and individual happiness; . . . discountenancing whatever may suggest even a suspicion that it can in any event be abandoned, and indignantly frowning upon the first dawning of every attempt to alienate any portion of our country from the rest or to enfeeble the sacred ties which now link together the various parts.

"For this you have every inducement of sympathy and interest. . . ." [4]

In the light of such an ideal, Washington's comments on the dangers of party assumed a more emphatic tone:

"There is an opinion that parties in free countries are useful checks upon the administration of the government, and serve to keep alive the spirit of liberty. This within certain limits is probably true; and in governments of a monarchical cast patriotism may look with indulgence, if not with favor, upon the spirit of party. But in those of the popular character, in governments purely elective, it is a spirit not to be encouraged." [5]

Washington warned his countrymen "in the most solemn manner against the baneful effects of the spirit of party generally." He pointed out that, while the party spirit was present in all governments, "in those of popular form it is seen in its greatest rankness and is truly their worst enemy." [6]

In the *Federalist*, paper number ten, Madison pointed to the danger of factionalism and to the adoption of the Constitution as a means of guarding against it. "Complaints are everywhere heard that the public good is disregarded in the conflicts of rival parties, and the measures are too often decided by the superior force of an interested and overbearing majority," [7] he wrote. He felt that the representative system provided in the Constitution was broad enough and involved so many interests that it would make it difficult for an interested cabal to organize and put through their selfish aims. "Extend the sphere, and you take in a greater variety of parties and interests; you make it less probable that a majority of the whole will have a common motive to invade the rights of other citizens. . . . The influence of factious leaders may kindle a flame within their particular states, but will be unable to spread a general conflagration through the other states." Madison thought that the Constitution provided against the sudden overthrow of institutions by the majority's will. He feared government by "the superior force of an overwhelming majority." [8]

The obstacles that Madison lauded as protective measures are just those obstacles that the national parties have at times endeavored to surmount through elaborate extralegal organization. Although the Constitution made difficult concerted action for evil, it also hampered concerted action for good. With a large and heterogeneous population a working agreement among citizens can be achieved only by organization. Parties must be formed if this broader will is to be expressed. Underlying Madison's conception of rule is the notion that a group of public-spirited, disinterested patriots would carry on the government, would consider above everything else the good of the nation, and would form the bulwark against faction. Madison saw government as moderating, counteracting, and transcending the particular interests of the community. A group of "true statesmen" would respond to the true public interest. In exhorting men to abhor faction Madison placed less emphasis upon the fact that a popular government must respond to the demands made upon it.

John Adams saw government as faced with reconciling the interests of the one, the few, and the many. By giving each force its appropriate place within the government he hoped to secure the welfare of the state. He sought to provide through the machinery of government a means for counteracting faction. Balance would be achieved by representing the people in the lower chamber and the aristocracy in the upper house. The executive would act as a moderator between the two. This conception was not without point in a society of class distinctions.

Washington and Adams saw the need for national consolidation. Among the framers of the Constitution was felt a great fear of rule by the majority. The framers regarded Jefferson as a leader of the rabble. Rule by his party might result in a mass tyranny that would destroy the delicate balance established within the new government. This old Whig conception of balance would result in stalemate if literally applied. Nevertheless, the great contribution of the Federalists' policy must not be underestimated. Their theory applied aptly to Hamilton's program. Indeed, his policies greatly strengthened the effectiveness of the new government. Rule by commercial interests could not be easily justified by the majority theory, but the Federalists could rationalize their interests under the Constitution, which set limits on the federal government and left industry free to develop.

Beliefs in checks and balances and separation of powers taught that even very divergent social classes and economic interests might safely come together under an instrument of government that forestalled the danger of tyranny by the majority or by any one group. In view of this belief the concept of rule by one party was slow in gaining acceptance. Could men disagree on policy and still be true to the fundamentals upon which the system rested? The Federalists viewed as basic the preservation of the social and economic order they represented. Checks and balances would guard their interests from infringement by the less privileged. Government would protect the status quo. To admit that parties might alternately dominate the whole government would open the door to change. The influence of the mob must be counterbalanced by the wisdom of superior men through their assured place in the government.

With his theory justifying the existence of different parties and defending government by the party of the people, Jefferson provided a doctrine suited to the dynamic forces working for change. As the leader of a new party Jefferson had first to prove that in opposing the Federalists he was not disloyal to the Constitution. In his first inaugural address he declared against political intolerance, holding it capable of results as despotic, wicked, bitter, and bloody as religious intolerance. He said: ". . . every difference of opinion is not a difference of principle. We have called by different names, brethren of the same principle. We are all Republicans, we are all Federalists." [9] E. E. Robinson states:

"Jefferson's use of this simple statement . . . is excellent evidence of his still persisting thought that he and his party were as yet on the defensive in the United States; that is, on the defensive in existing as a party. Having in mind, as had his critics, the time of war when a division of the population had been between Whigs and Tories, and when the latter were properly considered disloyal to the governments of the several states, he pointed out that now under a common government all members of the electorate, whatever their party faith, were of one body." [10]

The social changes then taking place could not admit the ideals of balance and synthesis upheld by Washington and Adams. Adams and Washington were not thinking of party government in terms of a dynamic society. Jefferson looked to the forces gathering for change in the new country. The ideal of rule by a responsible party was gradually to supplant the impossible ideal, held by the Federalist leaders, of a government devoid of faction. Nevertheless, the theory of government by a party was not fully accepted until long after party government had been realized in practice.

By the time the rule of alternate parties could be taken for granted and without distrust the nation had found itself and proved the practicality of the constitutional structure of government. This was a matter of growth. Looking backward to the experience of previous ages, men of conservative bent such as Washington and Adams could see the dangers of discord with which every society was threatened. They could see the tyranny that resulted when those in power attempted to impose their will. Washington warned his countrymen of factional dangers; Adams hoped that the new government would provide for a counterbalancing of social forces. The theory of two broadly representative parties equally loyal to the general welfare and rivals only in their desire to assume the responsibility for political control was an idea slow in developing. Defenders of checks and balances for the protection of minority rights and the curbing of governmental authority were confronted with spokesmen for the right of a majority to assume control for the general interest.

Innovation and Conservatism

> "Innovation is the salient energy; Conservatism the pause on the last movement. 'That which is, was made by God,' saith Conservatism. 'He is leaving that, He is entering this other,' rejoins Innovation."
>
> RALPH WALDO EMERSON

BOTH innovation and conservatism have their place in politics. These attitudes, while usually treated as antagonistic, may indeed in practice serve as complementary forces. It is in political debate that the two points are posed most sharply in opposition. In actual fact, "innovation" is as much of a tradition in our thinking as "conservatism." B. F. Wright, in a very penetrating analysis of traditionalism in American political thought, calls attention to our distrust of placing power in the hands of government officials as one belief that has been paralleled by a reformist and progressive tradition. "In other words, our tradition," he states, "may be viewed as an almost continuous process of adjustment as between the forces making for reform and those reflecting, or at least speaking in terms of, the inherited fears that are implicit in our institutions." [1]

It is in discovering the balance between conservatism and innovation that the key to effective leadership lies. Both are part of our tradition. Jefferson talked of the dangers of extending governmental power, but he was also in fact one of the greatest innovators of his time.

Jefferson's theories provided a rationalization for the emerging forces that sought political expression in a way that Adams's could not. Under the ideology of popular government no realistic politician or theorist can advocate counterbalancing the power of the people by the influence of "the good, the wise, and the rich." Under democracy all parties must be parties of the people. The democratic theorists who divide the community into the party of the people and the party of the few are found always on the side of the people. Their analysis is propaganda for their side. Jefferson preached a doctrine that recognized the current trend and pointed toward the future.

Jefferson made clear his view that party differences are desirable and general in all countries and that the best basis of difference lies between those who speak for the people and those who stand for the aristocratic minority. To John Taylor he wrote in 1798: ". . . in every free and deliberating society there must, from the nature of man, be opposite parties, and violent dissensions and discords; and one of these, for the most part, must prevail over the other for a longer or shorter time" [2]

In September, 1804, Jefferson wrote to Mrs. John Adams:

"Both of our political parties, at least the honest part of them, agree conscientiously in the same object—the public good; but they differ essentially in what they deem the means of promoting that good. One side believes it best done by one composition of the governing powers; the other by a different one. One fears most the ignorance of the people; the other the selfishness of rulers independent of them. Which is right, time and experience will prove. We think that one side of this experiment has been long enough tried, and proved not to promote the good of the many; and that the other has not been fairly and sufficiently tried. Our opponents think the reverse. With whichever opinion the body of the nation concurs, that must prevail."

To Henry Lee, on August 10, 1824, Jefferson wrote the following:

"Men by their constitutions are naturally divided into two parties: 1. Those who fear and distrust the people and wish to draw all powers from them into the hands of the higher classes. 2. Those who identify themselves with the people, have confidence in them, cherish and consider them as the most honest and safe, although not the most wise depository of the public interests. In every country these two parties exist, and in every one where they are free to think, speak, and write, they will declare themselves. Call them, therefore, liberals and serviles, Jacobins and ultras, whigs and tories, republicans and federalists, aristocrats and democrats, or by whatever name you please, they are the same parties still, and pursue the same object. The last appellation of aristocrats and democrats is the true one expressing the essence of all." [3]

Jefferson's theories were significant as a rationale for the groups most desirous of change in the status quo. He thought and talked of "rule by the people," but what did he do and what was the nature of his party support? The facts are too well known for more than brief mention. Jefferson centralized and consolidated power to an extent that would have satisfied the Federalists themselves. Yet he condemned this party for previous tendencies toward increased federal authority on the ground that this led to an oligarchic form of control. As Henry J. Ford states:

"The Louisiana purchase was effected by an assumption of authority quite in Hamilton's style. . . . The embargo upon American commerce, which he [Jefferson] ingeniously conceived as a dignified retaliation for the insults and injuries which his policy encouraged England and France to inflict, carried national authority to logical extremities to which the Federalists would not have dared to go. The enforcement act passed to sustain the embargo was a greater interference with the ordinary privileges of citizens than would have been necessary in the exercise of war powers. . . . In its character the government was as aristocratic as before." [4]

This could be said not only of public policy but also of the extent to which the people actually participated in their government. One historian of the Democratic party states:

"Up to the Jackson election this party, which was based on belief in the capacity of the people to rule, had not been run by the people at all. The people had had singularly little to do with their Government or with the choice of the men who ran it. Largely, the party had been in the hands of the Jefferson-Madison-Monroe type of men, statesmen or politicians, as you choose, but almost without exception men of substance, education, breeding, background, and social station, who, no matter how deep their devotion to the people nor how firm their faith in the masses, were not themselves of the masses and were personally far removed from 'the people' as the phrase is now understood." [5]

Government must follow shifts and changes. A theory and a means are needed to accomplish this end. For this purpose Jefferson's rationale was highly significant. It provided an ideology which permitted the rising and expanding classes of the time to adjust themselves to existing institutions and peacefully to alter these institutional forms. This indeed was made possible largely because of another Jeffersonian inconsistency. Even while arguing that the least government was the best government, Jefferson laid the foundations of the invisible government of party organization.

"When Thomas Jefferson found himself in serious and protracted controversy with the administration of Washington, he encouraged the formation of Democratic Clubs to resist the encroachments of the central government upon local governments and upon personal liberties. These clubs were similar to the Jacobin Clubs in France and to the Patriot Societies in America. The supporters of the administration did not, to an extent, organize local societies to strengthen their policy. The result was that the Republicans or the party of Jefferson became locally organized throughout the land, while the Federal party never was thus locally organized. It was largely because of this local organization that the Republican party endured and the Federal party became extinct." [6]

If we turn from the actions of the party to the interests composing it, we see that these elements could hardly be described in the lofty language of democracy used by their party leader.

"Not all of Jefferson's ambiguous allies [Herbert Agar states] came from the Northern cities. The State of South Carolina also voted Republican in 1800, and South Carolina was an oligarchy, with political power in the hands of the gentry. The Scotch and Irish mountaineers of South Carolina were democratic in way of life, conservative in thought. But the lowland aristocracy, which ran the State, had no sympathy with democracy and no intention of permitting it to infect South Carolina. Yet this aristocracy voted for Jefferson, thereby completing the pattern which has plagued the Democratic Party to this day." [7]

In 1800 a party came into power representing a new sectional alignment and based on strong local machines. To what extent the "people" ruled is impossible to say. The importance of Jefferson's creed did not lie in its description of reality. The significant thing is that Jefferson provided a philosophy under which the social forces stirring at the time were justified in seeking expression. The party of Jefferson responded more readily than the Federalists to the general current of the time. The Alien and Sedition Acts expired by limitation, and the spirit they typified received no more encouragement. The United States Bank was tolerated and a compromise worked out. The Federalists passed away because they could not march with the expansion to the west, the broadening franchise, and the newer leaders of the day. Jefferson embodied in his administration the Federalist policy of consolidation. Meanwhile, he talked the language of democracy. The inconsistency here is of little importance, although it bothered Jefferson. Of real importance is the fact that Jefferson had discovered a formula which was in agreement with the Constitution but which also made possible peaceful transformation from a stable gentry-ruled society into an expanding democracy bent on the exploitation of a continent.

So long as one party is regarded as hostile to the people, the very loyalty of such a party is suspected. Party government, however, demands a "loyal opposition." In other words, for a loyal opposition to function and for parties to be accepted as salutary influences, there must be common acceptance of the procedures and institutions by which men are to struggle for political power. It is interesting to note how slow leaders were to accept the idea that two parties, each equally loyal to the republic and the Constitution, might properly compete for the control of the government. Although in Great Britain the conception of responsible cabinet government by alternate political parties was clearly set forth in Edmund Burke's *Thoughts on the Causes of the Present Discontents*, his arguments were not accepted by his contemporaries as a rationalization of party government. His analysis was received as a narrow partisan bid for power though in fact he foreshadowed in brilliant fashion the subsequent trends of British constitutional development. Political leaders in this country were also slow to sense the meaning of the trends about them.

As late as 1816, Andrew Jackson warned President-elect Monroe of the dangers of partisan consideration in appointments to the Cabinet.

"Pardon me, my dear sir, for the following remarks concerning the next presidential term; they are made with the sincerity and freedom of a friend. I can not doubt they will be received with feelings similar to those which have compelled me to make them. Everything depends on the selection of your ministry. In every selection party and party feeling should be avoided. Now is the time to exterminate the *monster* called party spirit. By selecting characters most conspicuous for their probity, virtue, capacity and firmness, without any regard to party, you will go far to, if not entirely, eradicate those feelings which, on former occasions, threw so many obstacles in the way of government; and perhaps have the pleasure and honor of uniting a people heretofore politically divided. The chief magistrate of a great and powerful nation should never indulge in party feelings. His conduct should be liberal and disinterested, always bearing in mind that he acts for the whole and not a part of the community. By this course you will exalt the national character, and acquire for yourself a name as imperishable as monumental marble. Consult no party in your choice: pursue the dictates of the unerring judgment which has so long and so often benefited our country and rendered conspicuous its rulers. These are the sentiments of a friend. They are the feelings—if I know my own heart—of an undissembled patriot." [8]

Monroe in a letter to Jackson, dated December 14, 1816, wrote:

"We have heretofore been divided into two great parties. That some of the leaders of the Federal party entertained principles unfriendly to our system of government I have been thoroughly convinced; and that they meant to work a change in it, by taking advantage of favorable circumstances, I am equally satisfied." [9]

Monroe then cited the aid given to the enemy by the sympathetic attitude of the Federalists in the War of 1812 and referred to the

Hartford convention: in sum, he considered the opposition party disloyal. The gradual disappearance of the opposition party, however, by no means meant the absence of dissent.

John Quincy Adams in his turn tried to consolidate political forces at the very time they were ready to undergo most extensive change. He refurbished the old ideal of national unity. Party differences were to be forgotten.

"Ten years of peace, at home and abroad, have assuaged the animosities of political contention and blended into harmony the most discordant elements of public opinion [he wrote in his inaugural address of March, 1825]. There still remains one effort of magnanimity, one sacrifice of prejudice and passion, to be made by the individuals throughout the nation who have heretofore followed the standards of political party. It is that of discarding every remnant of rancor against each other, of embracing as countrymen and friends, and of yielding to talents and virtue alone that confidence which in times of contention for principle was bestowed only upon those who bore the badge of party communion." [10]

With a directness that seems naïve Adams proposed to compose the government of his campaign rivals; with Calhoun vice-president Clay would be secretary of state, Jackson, secretary of war, and Crawford, secretary of the treasury. In the face of curt refusals the project was abandoned.

In the thought of John Quincy Adams we have the lingering concept of a government which brings together for the conduct of public business the varying interests of the community: by relying upon men of integrity guided by their own views rather than the demands of their constituents, party differences could be ignored and the general welfare advanced. Adams was not aware of the dynamic currents surrounding him. He came at the end of an era. The Virginia dynasty provided a line of presidential succession so long as rule by the gentry survived. James Truslow Adams argues that it was not by accident that John Quincy Adams was the last of the family to hold high elective office. Once national leadership in terms of the aristocratic tradition had passed, Jackson emerged as the man of the people.

The theory of rule by the majority party defended by Jefferson came to full acceptance under Jackson. Men were no longer mere spectators of the political scene, no longer mere supporters of aristocratic leaders. Newly enfranchised, confident in their power, jubilant over their leader, Old Hickory, they enjoyed a direct participation in politics like their membership in their church or in their neighborhood. Politics had come home. Party organization helped to make all this evident. We see party emerge as an organization of individuals acting together for the purpose of controlling government. The clash of personalities attracted the multitude's enthusiasm. Hope for a share of the spoils of office further quickened their interest.

"For many years political parties had been chaotic, vapory, and indefinite; and if the politics of the young Republic had not been drifting toward personal government, it had been partaking of the nature of government by cliques and classes. The first message of John Quincy Adams had made the definite division of the people into political parties inevitable—these parties standing for well-defined, antagonistic policies. . . . The Jackson Administration marks the beginning of political parties as we have known them for almost a century." [11]

A new period was ushered in. Out of Jackson's administration two new parties rose. Cleavage did not become complete and organized until 1834. The split that had started under Adams then became clear-cut with the organization of the Whig party.

Party government was the institutional response to the ideals of Jacksonian democracy. It reflected, likewise, the interest configuration of the country. Once the reign of King Andrew was over, no national figure appeared in the White House until the Civil War revealed the greatness of Lincoln.

"In the second period [James Bryce writes], from Jackson till the outbreak of the Civil War in 1861, the Presidents were either mere politicians, such as Van Buren, Polk, or Buchanan, or else successful soldiers, such as Harrison or Taylor, whom their party found useful as figure-heads. They were intellectual pigmies beside the real leaders of that generation—Clay, Calhoun, and Webster. . . ."

Bryce blames our structure of government and points to the superior machinery of Britain. He states that the "natural selection of the English Parliamentary system, even as modified by the aristocratic habits of the country, has more tendency to bring the highest gifts to the highest place than the more artificial selection of America." [12]

It seems to me that Bryce misses the really important factor. This interim period was marked by great sectional struggles, and this condition dictated the selection of negative candidates for the chief magistracy. The men who came forward as leaders were the men who stood for something. Clay, Calhoun, and Webster were the great exemplars of their respective regions. In the light of the strong sectional differences, which grew only too strong as time went on, the only candidates thought feasible for the presidency were available politicians or military heroes.

The political pattern of sectional interests had to be dealt with by the politics of democracy. Lord Charnwood, for example, says of Lincoln, that his choice was "not the result of merit; on the other hand, it was not the work of the ordinary wicked wire-puller, for what may be called the machine was working for Seward. The choice was made by plain representative Americans who set to themselves this question: 'With what candidate can we beat Douglas?'" [13] Lincoln was not the choice of a people seeking positive leadership. Seward, the obvious candidate, stood for too much. He was defeated, Charnwood says, "because he had spoken of an irrepressible conflict and a higher law than the Constitution." [14] The campaign raised the questions: Could the slavery issue be dodged? Was the Union an end in itself? How should the government respond to the growing forces in the North and the West?

Here again we have the problem of synthesis or dynamics. Could a new equilibrium of interests be achieved through methods short of violence? The theories of those limiting rapid readjustment in order to achieve synthesis could not win a wide response. Calhoun fearing the very development that later took place, would have limited federal power by setting up a plural executive and government by concurrent majority. Calhoun saw the growth of sectional party alignments and with it the expansion of federal and especially of executive power. The president, through patronage and influence, he believed, would get control of the party organization. The parties, he wrote,

"then would cease, virtually, to represent the people. Their responsibility would be, not to them, but to him; or to those who might control and use him as an instrument. The Executive, at this stage, would become absolute, so far as the party in power was concerned. It would control the action of the dominant party as effectually as would an hereditary chief-magistrate, if in possession of its powers,—if not more so; and the time would not be distant, when the President would cease to be elective; when a contested election, or the paid corruption and violence attending an election, would be made a pretext, by the occupant, or his party, for holding over after the expiration of his term." [15]

Calhoun feared that national destiny would be determined by the party capturing the White House. Then what would happen to the group that had lost control of the federal government? If control were kept in Congress rather than in the White House, sectional leaders might work out a synthesis of minority views. Did not the political combinations in the decades between Jackson and Lincoln result in a rough approximation of Calhoun's views? Is not bloc government rule by a concurrent majority? Calhoun's ideas failed to win final acceptance. Yet the violence that he foresaw took place.

The Republican party on the strength of winning the presidency felt authorized to use the full sanction of law in coercing large social elements holding to different values. Lincoln's political support, numerically a mere plurality, was entirely sectional and drew its strength from the westward expansion of free-soil farmers and the growth of protectionist industrialists. Did democratic government here dictate that a bare majority had the indisputable right to rule? If so, did this mean advancing the interests of the groups represented by their formal majority to the detriment of the minority? The minority did not think so. If this was the price of union, the price was too high.

The politics of democracy broke down. Adjustment through consent failed. The respective sides were unable to compromise. Two economic orders, two cultures, faced each other, and Civil War resulted. Whether this failure of democratic government was inescapable is an intriguing, if futile, question. The future was on the side of the North; in time the Democratic party of the slaveowners probably would have gone the way of the Federalists. Politicians on both sides were through with compromise, however. The emergent interests would not be delayed; the entrenched groups would not retreat. The give-and-take of political negotiation was succeeded by the give-and-take of the battlefields.

Shall we interpret democracy today as the preservation of government by discussion and compromises or as government in the name of the majority and in response to protest groups? Whether we choose constitutionalism or majority rule, the essence of democracy hinges largely upon our view of the community. Madison, when writing the *Federalist*, John Adams, George Washington, and Alexander Hamilton all pointed to the dangers of factions and the need to counterbalance this particularism. Jefferson and Jackson saw in the people a community of interest broad enough to ignore their differences. Faced with national disintegration, Lincoln was forced to fight in order to preserve the union and bring under the aegis of democracy a class whose rights had been denied.

A question for politicians, leaders, and citizens is whether we are facing a time when we have need of emphasizing innovation or of stressing conservatism. Is this the time to organize for change in the name of majority rule or to consolidate the present position in the name of constitutional government? Is the nation as a whole entering a new phase? Are the intransigent elements as inconsequential as the Federalists proved to be or have they the strength of resistance that the slavocracy demonstrated?

Insistence upon majority will could not compose the sectional rivalries that finally culminated in the Civil War. While it is conceivable that a more skillful use of our governmental institutions might have adjusted sectional differences, the "irrepressible conflict" swept on to bloody consummation. Today our leaders may win over all but an ineffective minority to the desirability of radical change in economic relationships. Some writers argue that "it is later than you think" and that we must quickly rally sufficient political strength in the name of the majority to readapt our economic institutions to human needs. Other writers and leaders are convinced that the greatest need is to consolidate the advances that have recently been made, since further movement toward the left would create irreconcilable groups: synthesis and harmony must be sought under constitutional checks and balances of power. The future alone can tell where wisdom lies. Democratic leaders will stress dynamics or synthesis, depending on their interpretation of the times. A wrong guess may mean the agony of revolution before equilibrium is restored.

Accepting synthesis as an objective might in practice bring reaction and fascism. The dynamics of majoritarianism might in practice mean boss rule in the name of communism. The significance of political philosophy for society lies not in the accuracy of its description of our institutions but rather in the use to which a given doctrine may be put. Thus in stressing the inevitable conflict of factions in the community and the need for government to balance these interests so that some general policy might emerge, John Adams and Madison described a process recognizable as the essence of government then and today. If these theories, however, are treated not as an observation of fact but as philosophies to stimulate action, their significance is quite different. They may be used as defenses of the status quo; their emphasis upon the need for balance may be interpreted to mean that the present state of equilibrium must be maintained at all costs. Communal life and government I picture as a moving equilibrium. Political leaders tend to stress the importance either of movement or of equilibrium. Where should the emphasis be put, and under what circumstances?

The task ever before us is to find the combination of ideals, institutions, and interests that will result in the optimum harmony of relationships. This problem is as old as Plato. Jeffersonianism led to an attitude of mind and a use of institutions more in accordance with the developing interest pattern of the nation than would have been possible under the ideology of Washington, Hamilton, and Adams. Realistically viewed, Jefferson's administration and the rule of the Virginia dynasty could not be called government by the people, but Jefferson's ideals were in accordance with the economic and social trends of the times. Here is an illustration of idea, institution, and interests falling into alignment. Jefferson contributed a symbolism; he helped also to set up the institutions suited to facilitating the acceptance of his ideas and new emerging interests. He prepared the way for the great readjustments made under the aegis of Jacksonian democracy. The nation was not so fortunate in the decade before the Civil War; men could not find a common creed or a way to solve their interest conflicts through existing institutions.

Democracy reduced to its essentials cannot be identified ultimately with any particular set of institutions, though experience would point to the urgency of maintaining certain forms long useful in the struggle for liberty. Democracy is not to be defined in terms of the interests of any group or combination of groups. Its vitality depends upon the free interplay of such forces. This rests in the last analysis upon the general acceptance of the idea that in the integrity of the individual lies the ultimate social good. Leadership under democracy must decide when the times call for consolidation and when they call for renovation to the end that we may advance together toward the good life. In such union is our strength; but in the desperate perplexity of making the right choice lies our gravest danger.

☆ 6 ☆

Banners of Belief

> "O I see flashing that this America is only you
> and me,
> Its power, weapons, testimony are you and me,
> Its crimes, lies, thefts, defections, are you and
> me,
> Its Congress is you and me, the officers, cap-
> itols, armies, ships, are you and me."
> WALT WHITMAN

THE psychological state reflected in Whitman's feeling "that this America is only you and me" can hardly be induced merely by poetic or by philosophic assertion. In the struggle of day to day the defections often stand out more clearly than our sense of unity. Nevertheless we continue to seek those banners of belief under which men may perceive a flashing intuition of their common interest.

Any policy formulated for the general welfare can be reduced to the welfare of some group or groups. Decision depends upon the segment of the population to be preferred. May, for instance, the consumer's interest be taken as the basic criterion? Even if this were entirely defensible from an economic viewpoint, it would be unrealistic for political analysis. Nor may the welfare of the community be identified with that of the taxpayer. More-over both taxpayer and consumer are notoriously weak in the political realm. The outcome is the identification with the general welfare of those social elements which happen to be most effective in their control of the political process. This identification, however, is seldom simple and direct. It is colored by the prevailing attitudes and prejudices and affected by the existing institutions and by the skills of rival politicians. Even though some particular group may, from an economic point of view, quite convincingly be identified with a broad public purpose, the prevalent political ideology and habits of thought often dictate a more circuitous approach.

As a psychological need society seems to require discussion in terms of a broad objective even when narrow ends are being served. Thus much economic and political theory is used for the defense or rationalization of a group interest in terms of the general welfare. One answer to our problem has been offered by George Boas in these words:

"The task of modern government is the reconciliation of conflicts between the different interests which support it. It is not the extermination of any one group nor its exploitation. It is, therefore, essentially a juridical function and nothing symbolizes it better than the word justice. I shall not attempt to prove this; it is very probably incapable of proof, being a fundamental assumption of political philosophy." [1]

While offering a symbol of perhaps widest acceptance—namely, the concept of justice—this philosophic assumption still leaves its realization entirely open. Justice has no concrete meaning except in operational terms. Justice is as justice does.

How is justice to be had? The direct responsibility lies upon the group that happens to be in power. That group has the best opportunity of responding to social need, although rulers have often proved shortsighted and inflexible. So long as the concept of juridical balance holds meaning for the ruling group, the possibility of adjustment continues. It is certainly open to question whether the continuity of our present order has been sufficiently threatened by reactionary forces to justify the fears of leftist critics. The gravity of the problem cannot be denied, however. Its essence was admirably stated by Walter Lippmann years ago, and his words are even more pertinent today:

"Social life has nothing whatever to fear from group interests so long as it doesn't try to play the ostrich in regard to them. So the burden of national crises is squarely upon the dominant classes who fight so foolishly against the emergent ones. That is what precipitates violence, that is what renders social co-operation impossible, that is what makes catastrophes the method of change.

"The wisest rulers see this. They know that the responsibility for insurrections rests in the last analysis upon the unimaginative greed and endless stupidity of the dominant classes. There is something pathetic in the blindness of powerful people when they face a social crisis. Fighting viciously every readjustment which a nation demands, they make their own overthrow inevitable. It is they who turn opposing interests into a class war. Confronted with the deep insurgency of labor what do capitalists and their spokesmen do? They resist every demand, submit only after a struggle, and prepare a condition of war to the death. When far-sighted men appear in the ruling classes—men who recognize the need of a civilized answer to this increasing restlessness, the rich and the powerful treat them to a scorn and a hatred that are incredibly bitter. The hostility against men like [Theodore] Roosevelt, La Follette, Bryan, Lloyd-George is enough to make an observer believe that the rich of today are as stupid as the nobles of France before the Revolution." [2]

Yet the objectives of these liberal leaders have by now won wide acceptance, and the line of attack has been pushed far ahead. The conservative is not a man of foresight and imagination; his strength lies in his common sense in practical matters. He tends to underestimate the forces pressing for change and so is usually circumvented. He has always been loath to accord serious recognition to protests. Edmund Burke has given this viewpoint classic statement:

"Because half a dozen grasshoppers under a fern make the field ring with their importunate chink, whilst thousands of great cattle . . . chew the cud and are silent, pray do not imagine that those who make the noise are the only inhabitants of the field; that of course, they are many in number; or that after all, they are other than the little shrivelled, meagre, hopping, though loud and troublesome, insects of the hour." [3]

This view assumes that the lowing herd will always wind slowly o'er the lea and leave the world to their betters; time enough for listening to bellows of discontent when they become resonant against empty bellies. Is society composed of the great mass, the wise leaders, and the grasshoppers? The representative must be free to use his own best judgment if popular government is to function properly. He may do well to ignore the agitated grasshoppers, but he must always be able to distinguish between a buzz and a bellow. Burke's ideal of representation is applicable to a community so harmonious that its politicians are unconscious exponents of its values.

Implicit in this view of Burke is the assumption that the ruler, whether administrator or representative, is divorced from the pressures of politics. He is thought of as an umpire free to see justice done. The more realistic attitude of James Madison is reflected in paper number ten of the *Federalist*.

"What are the different classes of legislators [he asks], but advocates and parties to the causes which they determine? Is a law proposed concerning private debts? It is a question to which the creditors are parties on one side and the debtors on the other. Justice ought to hold the balance between them. Yet the parties are, and must be, themselves the judges; and the most numerous party, or, in other words, the most powerful faction must be expected to prevail. Shall domestic manufactures be encouraged, and in what degree, by restrictions on foreign manufactures? are questions which would be differently decided by the landed and the manufacturing classes, and probably by neither with a sole regard to justice and the public good. . . . It is in vain to say that enlightened statesmen will be able to adjust these clashing interests, and render them all subservient to the public good." [4]

Statesmen have never been able to divorce themselves from the context within which they must operate. Baron Munchausen on one occasion pulled himself out of a bog by a strong upward tug at his beard. His performance remains unique.

Nevertheless statesmanship by definition calls for breadth and vision in the management of human affairs, the long view rather than the short—the wider interest of the nation as a whole rather than that of a narrow segment. All this is obvious. Perplexity arises in the selection of a theory of the state that will give form and substance to a noble purpose. Madison saw in the republican form of government and the wide extension of the new Constitution over the country a means of counterbalancing interests and counteracting the whims of a popular majority. He felt that "the public voice, pronounced by the representatives of the people, will be more consonant to the public good than if pronounced by the people themselves, convened for the purpose." [5] He distrusted the sheer expression of majority will. We are still confronted by the question of how best to obey the majority without infringing minority rights. The problem is chiefly one of emphasis. To which banner shall we turn?

The answer offered depends upon the assumptions made concerning human nature in politics. For example, the argument advanced by progressives is founded upon a deep faith in the reason and good will of mankind. In their view, men can be aroused by appeals to their intelligence to see the broader interest beyond the more immediate. Policy can then respond to the broad self-interest of the majority. Education through the press and the platform is the means to this greater self-realization. People can be aroused to a plan for action and it is the duty of their leaders to plot the course for the future. Intelligence points the way: eloquent and zealous writers and statesmen must unceasingly rally followers. They see above all the threat that minorities offer to the attainment of a broader purpose. In the name of the majority, a group of enlightened men must warn their followers of this danger. One consequence of this philosophy must be the concentration of power in those men who know the road and are ready to keep their followers in line in the name of orderly and secure progress.

On the other side we have those who see dangers in the unified control exerted by an oligarchy acting in the name of the majority. These thinkers emphasize the fact that men tend to be irrational and custom-bound; they see authority inevitably falling into the hands of a few. Power breeds corruption. Plans for governing human behavior have little meaning since their application entails drastic modifications in meeting the unforeseen. Intuitive familiarity gained through experience is a safer guide for action than *a priori* rational analysis. Political power is safest when limited and decentralized.

This duality of approach constitutes one of the most perplexing problems in representative government.

Even if we limit our assumptions to the maintenance of social continuity and peaceful adjustment as the fundamental objectives under the politics of democracy, we still need a theoretical justification to give impetus toward the changes that are fundamental to continuity itself. The concept of majority rule serves this tactical purpose. It sustains those individuals who take the offensive in pressing for a readjustment of interests. We cannot ascertain the limits of peaceful adjustment without radical leaders who are ready to demand more than they are likely to get. It is through their constant clamoring at the limits of tolerance that new ideas win acceptance and emerging interests gain recognition. A political philosophy based on the importance of protecting minority rights is a defensive doctrine. It fulfills a useful function in that it insists upon the toleration of minority protest movements and thereby guards the conditions essential to their existence. Under such negative auspices protest movements may survive to hammer at inertia and reaction and thus stimulate change.

The two doctrines of majority rule and of minority rights are both essential in our democratic continuum, but the respective champions of these two viewpoints can hardly be expected to stress their brotherhood.

If we assume that men are selfish and egotistic we may, as Thomas Hobbes argued, set up a form of government so powerful that the individual is left little scope. Or we may insist that the best protection then comes in a system that counterbalances rival selfish impulses, since the majority cannot be trusted. Conflicts must be kept decentralized and government power restricted. As a concept of government this philosophy stresses the protection of minority rights. On the other hand if this view is offered as a banner around which to gather political supporters it tends to serve as a rationalization for maintaining the status quo. J. C. Calhoun used such an argument to protect the southern planters from the rising industrialists of the North. Today Herbert Agar falls back upon a similar line as a defense of southern interests against eastern economic forces that he distrusts. He restates Calhoun's position as follows:

"The great lesson which a modern democrat can learn from the South Carolinian is that the unchecked rule of numerical majorities means that government will be taken over by the strongest economic group within the State. In one age this may mean government by big business. In another age it may mean government by organized labor. In every age it means that the dominant group will pass laws (or interpret the Constitution) in its own favor and that these laws (and these interpretations) will be oppressive to other groups. So it means that in every age democracy will be moving steadily toward the totalitarian or absolute state. And when it reaches the goal democracy will be dead. Calhoun suggested that this degeneration can be avoided if the decisions of the majority, in matters of economic policy, are checked by the concurring decisions of the major interest groups." [6]

Agar argues that a majority vote may be acceptable for the solution of minor problems but "the basic economic decisions upon which people's livelihoods depend, will not receive the consent of the governed if large minorities feel themselves the victims of discrimination." [7] Hence we find the representatives of business, agricultural, labor, and other groups gathered at state legislatures and before Congress to protect their interests where an unfriendly majority or coalition of groups may be in control. "The net result," Agar continues, "is to create a check (in addition to the checks imposed by the Constitution) on the actions of numerical majorities in Congress. This is a form of Calhoun's concurrent veto." [8]

Faced with the fact that the government has already advanced far into economic affairs, Agar advocates the abolition of the special privileges created by government followed by the gradual relinquishment of political intervention. A property system fostering inequalities must, Agar thinks, be altered and men left free to work out their salvation. Lobbies arise as defenses against the infringement of minority rights. Policy is not the product of free discussion but of executive control. This will lead on to dictatorship. A moral reawakening of the individual to his responsibilities as a citizen is the only way to preserve democracy.

How such a political theory can be translated into effective political support is far from clear. Viewed in operational terms, it remains nebulous. Calhoun could base his theoretical structure on the solid interests of the groups in control of the southern states.

By way of contrast with this position is the theory that democracy can be preserved only by rallying the interests of labor, agriculture, and consumer into an organized majority strong enough to override the minority groups in control of business and banking. As an eloquent spokesman for this view of government Max Lerner insists that "our task is to re-establish the conditions of social peace through a rational system of economic controls, and thereby to re-establish the possibility of party government." [9]

"Economic undermining" of business control becomes essential. This must be done by the ousting of the "economic oligarchy" through a militant democratic majority which will secure control and then plan for production. Once this is accomplished, tension will be relieved and party government can go forward. Lerner fears that business, which is dominant, renders impossible the changes that would better the economic conditions of the mass of the population. He assumes that industrialists have failed and that a new ruling group should take control of the means of production.

This theory of the state has certain obvious advantages as a doctrine. The appeal is addressed to men in terms of their economic interests. It promises a plan of action and a means of using existing political institutions. It assumes that the politics of democracy would be capable of making sweeping changes in property relations without encountering effective resistance from the groups affected. What the actual outcome would be is impossible to predict. Lerner apparently does not anticipate violent resistance, though Agar points to the Civil War as an instance of what happens when the strong minority interests are challenged in the name of the majority.

Agar stresses the concept of balance, Lerner that of dynamics. These two interpretations recall the dual viewpoints suggested in the preceding chapter. The question in a given instance is (a) whether forward movement means alienating segments of society essential to unity and harmony or (b) whether a balance means giving in to reactionary forces that will merely delay the dynamic adjustments vital to the community. This problem offers the supreme gamble of statesmanship in a democratic society.

Theorists contribute to the politics of democracy by clarifying trends and interpreting the forces about them. The formulations that they offer are but partial pictures of a reality that is in constant flux. There is evidence to show how selfish minorities may threaten to reduce government to barter and grab. Or, on the other hand, it can be argued that rule by a majority unrestricted by constitutional limitations may appear as mass tyranny ready to override the values cherished by civilized men. There is no objective answer that can be divorced from subjective values. All that the politics of democracy can offer is a process of adjustment. Faith in this process is sustained in part by tradition and inertia and in part by a confidence built on successful past and present performance. Whether forces for political action are rallied in defensive array under the banner of minority rule or are drawn up in battle formation upon the slogan of majority rule is inconsequential so long as both sides still admit loyalty to a higher unity: so long as they see "flashing that this America is only you and me" and that salvation lies in seeking for some working compromise.

One reason why we have made slower progress than Great Britain and the Scandinavian countries in accommodating ourselves to the changes brought by industrialism is the absence of a well-developed administrative service. We have left to campaign orators and legislators the task of adjustment. Such men are not in a position to furnish the technical, intricate, and continuous series of adjustments needed to carry an issue through to the administration of a policy. Mutual suspicions are generated in one election and then revived in the next. Our failure lies in not utilizing for the continuous quest of solutions in concrete instances the political interest aroused in campaigning. In Great Britain an able administrative corps has provided a stable and continuing means of integrating politics and policy. In Sweden the bureaucracy is so stable and so respected that it can even develop and sponsor its own policy recommendations without arousing public suspicions.

Our political contests recall at times the methods of ancient Chinese warfare, wherein each side tried by superior din and terror-inspiring banners and slogans to scare the others into surrender. When the dust of battle cleared away the carnage was usually found to be negligible. On the other hand, the participants were all the more confirmed in the righteousness of their respective causes.

A final question remains. In the light of the problems and trends before us, does the politics of democracy promise to continue as an acceptable concept? The final answer rests upon our skill in self-government; but, granting the requisite good will and intelligence, what of the adequacy of our ideals and institutions for coping with the currents of change about us?

One uniformity of human behavior is a tendency to seek a sanction for governmental authority beyond mere expediency. The Japanese find in their emperor's descent from the Sun Goddess good warrant for the reverence due him. Men desirous of the security that comes from a common loyalty reach out for personally significant concepts. A priestly caste may offer mysteries; philosophers may offer reasons. Both have proved effective. As the Aztec rulers used human sacrifices as a gory symbol of the price that must be paid for safety brought by authority, the *Great Leviathan* of Thomas Hobbes in rationalistic terms sacrificed individual liberty to political stability.

Democracy is still another justification of authority. To assay the "true" meaning of democracy would avail little. Its connotations of a common tradition and complex of emotional loyalties explain its hold on our society. It is deceptive to view as ultimate truth this conceptual scheme called democracy. In assessing it we are dealing with concepts having the nature of creeds, dogmas, even myths. Our problem of analysis is to note the relationship of its theoretical values to the pattern of interests and institutions existing at a given time. The word "myth" is used here not in a derogatory sense but rather to underscore the assertion that in speaking of democracy we are not dealing with final values or even with a systematic philosophy. We are faced rather with an attitude, a tradition, a set of ideas that have proved significant to a large number of men during a brief historical period.

In the name of this symbol "democracy" millions of men have been called to battle and many sent to their death. Such purposes may appear to some people as antithetic to the more idealistic phases of the democratic ideology, but the strength of a myth does not rest primarily in logical consistency. The Crusades were fought under the symbol of the Cross and the creed of Christianity based on brotherly love. Whether through fear, love, or rational conviction, a myth has meaning to the extent that it holds men's faith and moves them to action. The action may at times contradict the fundamentals of the faith (yet the church temporal continues to fulfill a useful function even though it inevitably falls short of the ideals of the church spiritual). The fact of central importance is that people profess belief in democracy. While we hold to this common faith, government by compromise is possible though far from inevitable.

Ten million unemployed are not likely to support indefinitely an economic system which denies them a place in the productive life of the nation. They have not been content with the rationalizations that prescribe the therapy of bankruptcy and deflation as the best cure. Fevered sufferers accept panaceas when science has no remedy in which confidence can repose. Although the Townsend movement is dismissed as economically "unsound," it has brought hope to frightened men and women. Fascism has preached nonsense about race, but it also has offered recompense to despairing masses. Men insist upon seeking order and direction in their surroundings. When the task is beyond their powers of reason, superstition comes to their aid. The theorists of discontent are a product of the very conditions against which they offer an *ex post facto* rationale for resistance.

There are times in history when ideals, institutions, and interests seem to fall into a harmonious relationship. Francis Delaisi notes that at such periods "equilibrium is established between private enterprise, institutions and ideas by an almost perfect process of adjustment, involving at the same time individual prosperity, power for the commonwealth and the most brilliant artistic development." [10] As examples of such periods he cites the Athens of Pericles, the Roman Empire under the Antonines, the Christian world of Innocent III, and the reign of Louis XIV.

In every such period, it is true, dislocations have occurred, corruption has appeared, and the golden age has waned. The faiths sustaining the city-state, the empire, the papacy, or absolute monarchy have faded, overthrown at last by the new demands they left unanswered. Yet man's hopes have persisted even in the face of disillusionment, and his hopes have not always been unfulfilled. A collapse of ideas, institutions, and interests has not been the invariable outcome of human endeavors. Two notable exceptions hold warrant that adaptability can forfend violence in social change and that a "moving equilibrium" of ideas, institutions, and interests is humanly possible. Delaisi cites the examples of the Roman Catholic Church and the British government. In both cases their leaders "had the courage to alter the basic principles of the social structure" [11] and so attain to a new balance of forces. I think it highly significant that these two institutions, the Roman Catholic Church and the British government, while often viewed as rigid and aristocratic, have both provided for the continual renewal of their ruling group: the British upper classes by admitting to the amenities of their circle the most effective individuals born to a lower social status, and the church by eliminating hereditary influences through a celibate clergy. Through this circulation of their elites, flexibility and awareness of the need for adjustment have been reconciled with a most extraordinary stability.

Democracy is the political creed which makes these consider-ations the central article of its faith. Policy must be formulated and institutions built up or torn down as the majority may de-sire, provided the security of the system itself is not disrupted by changes so radical as to alienate the minority. In such roughly defined fashion democracy attempts to reconcile men's desire for political change with their need for the security that comes through unity. As C. J. Friedrich has stated, "Constitutional de-mocracy is not founded on majority-rule alone, but on popular consent built upon a mutual regard for each other and each other's interests. Though this sounds like conservatism, it is the only truly progressive creed." [12]

Under myths standing for any philosophic values the great problem of statesmanship is to discover the optimum relation-ship between ideas, institutions, and interests. Even a sheer drive for power is aided by discovering the institutions and creating the ideas most harmonious with this goal. Leaders have ap-proached their task with quite different preconceptions and objectives. Peter the Hermit preached a compelling idea which ultimately wrought a tremendous change in feudal institutions and in the configuration of interests in the Middle Ages. Indus-trial leaders have more or less unconsciously warped political ideas, such as equality and fraternity, and social institutions, such as the church and the family, in the pursuit of certain immediate interests, such as high profits and cheap labor. The creed of popular sovereignty has hard sledding under these conditions. Nevertheless, democracy can safely rest its continuing validity on asserting the dogma that men have the right to readjust their ideals and institutions in response to their needs.

☆ 7 ☆

Standards for Judging the
American Party System

> " 'Well,' he says, 'I don't see no p'ints about
> that frog that's any better'n any other frog.'
> " 'Maybe you don't,' Smiley says. 'Maybe
> you understand frogs, and maybe you don't
> understand 'em; maybe you've had experience,
> and maybe you ain't only a amature, as it were.
> Anyways, I've got *my* opinion.' . . ."
>
> MARK TWAIN

THERE can be, of course, no one interpretation of the complexity of our politics. The points significant from one scheme of values do not hold when different standards of judgment are applied. A survey of the definitions offered by various authors shows how many ways there are of interpreting the nature and function of the political party in the United States. Some authorities stress the search for office as the primary function of the political party; others point to the traditions and principles professed by party members. Other writers define party as a device for promoting special interests. All these definitions call attention to observable phases of partisan activity, but no one aspect can be taken as the complete picture.

To define is to issue a fiat. Definition means abstracting certain aspects from a complex factual context with the purpose of presenting these selected aspects as of essential importance. Hence in facing human behavior as involved and contradictory as that which is observable in political parties, it is hazardous to select one or two aspects as definitive of the whole. The pernicious nature of definition lies not in its inescapably partial character but in the tendency to view such formulations as in themselves social objectives. Hence when we observe that our political parties do not behave in accordance with our definitions, we sometimes conclude that the reality rather than the definition is at fault. It is time that we asked whether our preconceptions, if put to the test, would function as well as the party system with all its faults.

In this country the whole ideology of party is still closely bound to Edmund Burke's definition of it—the view which regards a political party as a body of men united for promoting by their joint endeavor the national interest upon some particular principle in which they are all agreed. If this be our definition of political parties, something is very wrong with our system. The only bodies answering this description are the short-lived and ineffective third parties, fatally dedicated to forwarding limited interests or specific panaceas. Perhaps the chief reason for the prevalence of Burke's notion lies in the fact that the interpretation of American political institutions has been deeply affected by assumptions derived from a study of the British government. An interesting study in the transmigration of symbols and ideas might be attempted in noting the vast influence of James Bryce, A. Lawrence Lowell, and Woodrow Wilson, the three great figures largely responsible for the birth of political science and all deeply imbued with the English tradition. It is fair to say that the standards for judging party government in the United States have been based most persistently upon norms derived from studying the Mother of Parliaments.

Our party system is better tested not by traditional theoretical assumptions but rather in terms of its political environment in the United States. How does it meet the demands made by this environment?

Party government has operated within a society basically unified by a confidence in a system of free enterprise. We have proceeded on a gospel of trust in God and the devil take the hindmost. Planning and forethought, while necessary for private pursuits, have not been regarded as essential for public affairs.

The significance of our system lies not in the alignment of voters pro and con in purely intellectualistic terms but rather in the maintenance of institutions which keep political power contingent and provide alternative sets of rulers. It is well to repeat that in practice our major political parties are primarily concerned not with framing issues and drawing up distinctive programs but in trying to discover some way of bringing together into a reasonably harmonious relationship as large a proportion of the voters as possible. The methods employed to this end are dictated by the times, the circumstances, and the kind of men in control of the organization. Principles and issues must remain relative to these conditions.

Would the clear statement of differences of interest lead to readier adjustment? It should, between "reasonable" men whose personal stake in the settlement is sufficiently meager for them to accept an adverse decision without serious personal deprivation. Is this a realistic way to face issues as they affect masses of men? In many walks of life we accept without argument the thought that for men to live together, in a neighborly and harmonious fashion, caution, and even reticence, is wise when disagreements arise. In governmental affairs we think of society in terms of a debating club rather than as a family or a neighborhood.

Irrational party loyalty has normally been an essential element in successful party government under a democracy. Many persons who adhere to a party for such reasons do not associate the success or failure of their party with their own immediate interests. Their eyes are fixed upon principles, ideals, and traditions long associated with the party. They are an important stabilizing influence and provide politicians with a dependable following that facilitates the task of getting people to work together. These voters constitute a strong and significant element in our political parties. Party loyalty serves them as a refuge from the confusion of public affairs. These citizens align themselves with one party or another because they are attracted by the "game of politics." Party loyalties are frequently fixed at a very early age, with rational judgment playing little part. The individual may rationalize his party allegiance in later years, but the initial allegiance is likely to endure.

"If party action were an accurate reflection of the passions, animosities, and beliefs of the mass of individuals composing the party membership, politics would be as tenuous in their instability as ocean waves [Henry J. Ford has written], but party action being a social product is in organic connection with all the processes of thought and feeling which pertain to human nature, and is subject to the play of their influence. A typical result is that curious accumulation of traditions and tenets which give to party communion almost the sanctions of religious faith." [1]

Churches are based upon faith rather than reason. Family ties are not rational. In the whole range of human relationships it is difficult to find purely rational bonds that cause men to stand together. We recognize in most human relationships that reason is not the sole bond or even the primary factor. Why do we assume that there is something less good about a traditional loyalty when attached to a party? The rationalistic tradition in politics, going back at least to theories of the social contract, has established a criterion which is still applied to our parties. As organizations they have attained power and evoked loyalties upon the basis of emotional appeals. This fact stands forth in the focus of our attention if we try to examine parties as they have worked.

What our parties are is more important than what they profess to be. Political parties came into existence because the enlarged franchise necessitated organization among voters if the new privileges of citizenship were to be carried into effect. Organizations of voters grew in communities; politicians had to take the voters as they found them. "The origin of any particular party," Graham Wallas writes, "may be due to a deliberate intellectual process. . . . But when a party has once come into existence its fortunes depend upon facts of human nature of which deliberate thought is only one." Wallas regards the party as, in fact, "the most effective political entity in the modern state" and "the most vigorous attempt which has been made to adapt the form of our political institutions to the actual facts of human nature." As Wallas so well argues, the justification of parties lies in their response to man's needs. The citizen must have a focus for his political loyalties. Wallas points out that

"to each citizen, living as he does in the infinite stream of things, only a few of his ten million fellow-citizens could exist as separate objects of political thought or feeling, even if each one of them held only one opinion on one subject without change during his life. Something is required simpler and more permanent, something which can be loved and trusted, and which can be recognized at successive elections as being the same thing that was loved and trusted before; and a party is such a thing." [2]

Walter Edward Weyl also recognizes that the party meets this need. "A man had to cling to something, and in America, where traditions were weak and where men, following their social instincts, became 'joiners,' the temptation to cling to party became resistless. Nor was this in itself bad." Weyl goes further, however, and argues that the abuses of our system grow out of such irrational attitudes:

"This party loyalty found expression in a traditional voting, which obscured contemporaneous issues and enrolled men under banners which they could not read. The Civil War blazoned certain ideas upon the minds of men. The North 'waved the bloody shirt'; the South rallied to the cry of 'negro domination.' The party fanned these dying fires into flame, and appealed with skill to an enthusiasm which in other countries would have attached itself to state, king or army.

"The men who were in politics for money build upon this loyalty, which was their asset, as a farm, mine, or franchise is an asset." [3]

The implication is that if voters only were rational their interests would not be betrayed. Exhortation, however, cannot make men rational; and if the fate of party government rests on this alone, its fate is already sealed.

What are some of the consequences of emotional party loyalty? One result is the presence within the same national party organization of persons holding to widely divergent political views. Factional fights within our major parties are frequent, and at present each party seems to have a liberal and a conservative wing. It would be a gross overrationalization to conclude that this indicates an incipient party realignment along these lines, however.

It is not my purpose to urge a change in attitude or to suggest that more rational behavior would contribute to or detract from the solution of social problems through party machinery. It is enough to note that the continuance of party government does not seem to hinge upon the citizens acting in the mass as informed and reasoning voters. Intelligent men would like to see intelligent men in control of the party machinery, but it is a far cry from this to the populace tightly organized in two hostile camps bound to their respective principles and determined to make their respective creeds prevail.

Our party system tries to reconcile conservative elements with the forces making for change. Such reconciliation is achieved not by debate alone. Common loyalty to an organization is no small factor in bringing men of contrary interests together. This straddle presumably can stretch only so far; but before the breaking point is reached, concessions are often made out of loyalty to the organization which both sides value. Our present system does not mean the negation of policies because the parties seem so similar in viewpoint. There is ample room for positive programs, but our parties are not the channels best suited to their initiation. The real springs for policy occur without reference to the formal organization of parties and the legal framework of government.

Creative impulses resulting in the formulation of views or in plans for action necessarily arise in the mind of some individual. These positive elements of thought gather strength as they are accepted by other individuals and become of increasing significance as those in agreement clarify and expand their common purpose and formalize their relations for the realization of their goal. Hence special-aim organizations inevitably appear. The community bristles with the diversities arising from this basis, but in the name of orderly government another step must be added. To identify parties with such organizations would be simply to substitute bloc rule for party government.

It is here that the American political party takes its rightful place as providing an accepted form of order through which differences of viewpoint upon public questions may in large measure be either disregarded or compromised. As Walter Lippmann states: "It is not a system adapted to the execution of great controversial policies. Major policies can be carried out only with bipartisan co-operation. But it is a system under which the frictions of federalism are reduced to manageable proportions. And that may not be a small service to popular government." [4]

Faced with the necessity of holding together in one organization the many varied elements that go to make it up, the party leaders find it inexpedient and unwise to commit themselves in advance to a definite program. In the first place they might not get general support for the program, nor could they secure agreement upon its contents. This causes much head-wagging as to the meaninglessness and futility of our parties. Yet the very lack of agreement results in such a degree of personal freedom for the individual congressman as would be impossible were the party to sponsor a set of specific issues. The legislator may stand forth as the spokesman of the most powerful and aggressive elements within his constituency, or under the pressure from divergent interests he may take a conciliatory attitude. Whatever his reaction may be, he is seldom bound by the stand of the party.

This situation has prompted some to decry the influence of special minorities which are thus left free to make their power felt. It is protested that "Congress has become the tool of selfish interests." Yet in what more appropriate place than in Congress, pray, could such forces come forward with their demands? The conflict and confusion there are indicative of the vital character of this assembly. Our congressmen may at times appear as quarrelsome politicians, but this very independence protects them from becoming automatons. They retain a greater degree of personal political responsibility than do most lawmakers in other countries. It is their manifest duty as public representatives to weigh the forces of various interests according to their conception of the general welfare. That they are often unable to meet this responsibility is no reflection on the political party itself.

Little would be gained by shifting the struggle to a party conclave and compromising differences in private caucuses in order that the party might offer the appearance of solidarity. In a parliamentary government the ministers do this bargaining and commit their followers to a particular course of policy in the light of such arrangements. To say that a party has a program is to say that it has agreed upon a *modus operandi* with the social and economic interests that constitute the underlying power in political affairs.

The question today is whether our political ideals and institutions are adequate to the peaceful readjustment of current economic forces. National problems which must be faced with positive solutions are now arising. Yet in this period of transition we have a government based on a geographical mold and federal in character. With government now taking a larger role in all fields, the inadequacy of traditional institutions becomes apparent. Our governmental institutions do not provide any agency primarily designed to formulate and enact a national program. With governmental activity incidental to social and economic affairs, legislation has tended to be haphazard and sporadic. The party system developed in order to carry on the electoral process. If the political party is concerned chiefly with gaining office and if pressure groups devote their time to pursuing their special interests, how can we provide for the formulation of public policy so as to advance the welfare of all? Can we expect policy designed in the public interest to emerge from this diversity?

Our political system is characterized by: a federal structure based on a constitution of limited powers; a separation of powers between executive, legislative, and judicial branches, insuring an independent area for each of greater or less extent; a bicameral legislative system providing houses of about equal powers; national political parties built on a loose confederation of state organizations, which in turn are bound by sectional, cultural, racial, or traditional loyalties that may not react directly to economic motives; an administrative service which for a long time to come will be influenced in various agencies by partisan considerations; a basis of representation that necessitates the supplemental activities of private organizations for the defense or promotion of special interests; an electorate in general more concerned with family duties and individual concerns than with broad public problems; a spirit of localism that makes a representative or a senator dependent for his political career upon pleasing the constituents of one congressional district or of one state.

Congress itself is handicapped in acting as an agency entrusted with the formulation of national policy. First, the organization of its chambers makes control and responsibility exceedingly difficult. Authoritative leadership lacks a focal point. The only discipline which can be achieved comes through presidential control. Second, the operation of the seniority rule places in position of less influence representatives with the newest popular mandate, namely, the last election returns.

Institutional factors are, of course, man-created and susceptible to revision. This does not, however, mean that they are artificial establishments. They are now deeply rooted and intertwined. Tearing up any one would have such unpredictable consequences that we may well hesitate about altering drastically the system of government. Our government works as it does not entirely because the machinery is cumbersome but rather because the propelling power is sporadic and the load is heavy. For example, not all of the difficulties ascribed to federalism would disappear if we erased state lines. Sectional interests would remain; differences in economic development, cultural characteristics, and geographical conditions would attend to that. The rivalries of sections are at least isolated to some extent within the boundaries of our states. Local leaders are forced to compose the major part of their own quarrels. As a result of our federal system not all of the ultimate responsibility for decision making is focused in one place. This dispersion causes some delay. Although this does not appeal to men of strictly logical mind, it at least tempers the intensities of feeling that arise when the onus of decision making is centered upon one governing agency or even one individual.

Our system has the great virtue of keeping decentralized many of the conflicts within the community. At no one point could the whole government be endangered; hence no need for the concentration of governmental force exists. Our system places the greatest obstacles in the path of the man on horseback—the dictator, who would override legal restraints; it obstructs also the beggar on horseback, the minority organized to force large monetary concessions. A heavy price is exacted nonetheless for such "protection."

As Frank J. Goodnow states:

"Our formal governmental system makes no provision for the co-ordination of the functions of expressing and executing the will of the state through the instrumentalities of government. On the contrary, it is so formed as to make that coordination impossible. That is the work of the party is not completed when it has elected a legislature. It must elect a series of executive officers as well, not only for the nation and the state, but also for the localities. Further, the fact that the terms of these executive and legislative officers are not coincident makes it probable that even if one party has elected all the officers it can elect at a given election, such party does not have complete control of the government." [5]

Goodnow represents the traditional view of the problem when he argues that the lack of any formal provision for policy coordination within the government forces the political party into the role of unifier. "The political storm center in the United States," he says, "is therefore not in the government, but in the party."

There is but a partial answer to the problem of implementing political power. Political party activity covers only one area; bureaucracy, another; interest groups, another. Representative bodies fulfill their primary functions if they fairly mirror the needs and attitudes of the community. By calling attention to the problems requiring treatment they contribute greatly: this involves revealing both strength and weakness, hope and despair, reason and passion. Experts can be hired; representatives must come from the people.

The abuse so prevalent in party government during the

seventies and eighties of the last century was due to the enormous difficulties caused by deep sectional differences, and to the rapid industrial expansion with its attendant social shifts and changes. There is still another factor insufficiently recognized. The political party was the main line of communication from the voter to the government. When this line was controlled by an oligarchy of professional politicians and industrialists, the outsider was in a very disadvantageous position. It was during this period and under these conditions that the farmers and wage earners as outsiders finally saw the necessity of setting up their own organizations if they were to realize their own strength and win a hearing in Congress and the state legislatures. Thus a tendency toward political monopoly was weakened, and political parties became less significant as rival organizations grew.

This development has reached vast proportions today. It presents a vascular politics with an infinite number of arteries penetrating down into the community. Self-government demands a free circulation of individuals' impulses. This calls for a varied network throughout the social structure. Disciplined parties, clearly differentiated, result in a hardening of these arteries. The affliction would not be so severe as the atrophy of the individuals' political strength caused by a one-party system, but to urge government by two such parties is to ignore the inevitable rigidity of organization necessary if their programs are to be realized. Any such dichotomy is an oversimplification of our social and economic pattern.

The problem that we must face is how to work out public policy more deliberately and consciously. Are our political parties the agencies to be charged with this purpose? A political party must maintain its members and its official hierarchy. Its leaders have a will to power and an urge to continue its existence. From this viewpoint the emphasis is not upon the party in its concern with public issues or community problems but rather upon the party as an organization. In a word, the purposive side of party as such must be contrasted to the party used as the means to accomplish the purposes of other interests not directly identified with the party itself. Confusing these two views of party befogs clear judgment of the extent to which the party is accomplishing its ends. There are the factors which affect the party as a party, and there are the many other external purposes with which various interests try to associate the party.

Two aspects of the party become evident. The party may be viewed as an association concerned with attaining to office, rewarding its followers, adding to its power, and continuing its life; or the party may be regarded as a means through which the underlying interest groups may exploit this machine for forwarding their own affairs. In the first case, the concern is not with policy or principle; in the second, whatever identification with these social or economic groups is achieved depends on the dictates of political strategy and the shifting power of partisan leaders.

To survive, the organization must attract and hold the loyalty of members. If the party is accepted as a useful and responsible agency of government, allegiance to the organization as such is justified. The sponsorship of particular measures as a means of holding the membership and of winning support is not enough. Allegiance must be based upon a general recognition of the usefulness of the party as an association with a valid and independent purpose. The party organization has a place under our system. The abuses to which parties are prone are defects characteristic of any organization.

The meaning of a national party is not to be measured solely in terms of its ideology. Its accomplishments and the followers and leaders associated with the organization are more significant. Its program must be formulated out of the needs of the time. Any hard and fast line of policy would prove futile. At best all a party can hope to maintain is an attitude, a temper, or an approach.

Disgust with the irrational nature of party allegiance and with the prejudices and traditions of partisanship is found. Yet the question whether a rational basis of party can be discovered in the face of our sectionalism and particularism of interests might well be raised. What common ground is possible? Can anything more be obtained than a governance by special interests founded upon the temporary adjustment of their conflicts?

The electorate is cut through and through by a variety of allegiances. This makes the political party but one of many associations competing for the loyalty of the individual. Any party which declared for specific proposals would immediately find itself confronted with many associations opposing or forwarding these doctrines. Sponsoring a multiplicity of interests would lead to unavoidable contradictions. Again, what possible political division could, with any consistency, cut down through national politics, through state problems, and even into local affairs? The sectional, the cultural, and the racial factors that a national party would encounter in such a process would prove insuperable.

Parties cannot be pictured realistically as coming forward with a program, winning office, and then putting their platform into effect. This view is based on a mandate theory of government. The essence of democracy does not lie in the plebescite or even in the initiative and referendum. A recording of ayes and noes by uninformed persons cannot be justified by any scheme of government that values individual integrity and judgment. It is better for the voter to act upon limited empiric evidence than to base his judgment upon vague promises and to act upon fuzzy notions about broad public problems far beyond his experience and capacity for evaluation. In presidential elections the voter has usually been able to cast his ballot upon an estimate of the candidate's personality. A president may point to a great popular mandate, but this gesture is necessarily a political argument rather than authority for action on any specific issues.

Defenders of the popular mandate theory of democracy point to the British system as providing the means for a clear expression of opinion. "Elections in Great Britain," they say, "mean so much more. You know what you are voting for." This is not the view taken by Ivor Jennings, one of the most careful students of British institutions. He shows how time and again arguments have arisen as to "whether a mandate has been given and of what a mandate consists." Of the many issues put before the voters upon which must the government respond? Must both the principle and the form of legislation be passed upon by the people? Must a fresh mandate be obtained as new crises arise? Jennings concludes that

"the doctrine of the mandate is part of the political cant. It is a stick used by the Opposition to beat the Government. . . . The doctrine is, however, of importance. Though it must necessarily be vague and its operation a matter of dispute, it is recognized to exist. . . . It is a useful argument that the Government has used its majority to effect changes to which the electorate has been asked to consent. It suggests that the Government cannot be trusted and ought to be turned out. Honesty apart, it is politic for the Government to consider whether or not the argument can, in the future, be used against it with effect." [6]

Another student of British institutions, C. S. Emden, came to the conclusion that "it is easy to find examples of general elections in which a number of confused questions were placed before the people; but it is extremely difficult to find more than one or two elections in which a single issue or one or two clear issues have been raised." [7] The concept of the mandate is useful as an argument rather than as a description of fact.

If it is difficult under a responsible ministry in Great Britain to establish just what has been decided by an election, it is impossible to identify a clear line of policy with the voice of the people in this country. To commit a party to a long-term program is to discount the unpredictable. Politicians must face issues as they arise and in concrete terms. To do more is to invite debate on abstractions. The New Deal has carried forward a process of basic readjustments with a minimum of debate on final ends. Once such questions are posed sharply by opposing political camps the probability of peaceful change is reduced. Then men focus their eyes not on the task demanding attention but on more distant horizons. There is no point in fighting today to settle a question which you now assume will be pressing in the unpredictable future.

To have two distinctive parties, each determined to carry out its program, would necessitate a change in our form of government. Obviously such a system is not compatible with staggered elections for House and Senate and with an independent executive. Nor could we then tolerate having a majority of Congress and the president of different parties. Even more important would be the abolition of fixed terms of office. Under such a system the electorate must be able to throw out of office a party whose program no longer holds popular confidence. If all those wanting change were able to gang up and force through a sweeping party program, while all those of the party against change were expected to stand by until an election occurred two or four years hence, the pent-up feeling and the resulting clash would probably blow the dome off the Capitol.

An acceptable theory of party must take into full account the context within which our parties function. The development of new criteria rather than the repetition of old criticisms would make for a better understanding of political problems. This might serve to show the voter where and how to direct his attention to politics. The apathy of the citizen is due not to a lack of interest in public affairs but rather to a feeling of helplessness at the booming, buzzing confusion. Accordingly, any standards of judgment, if they are to prove usable, must be simple and understandable.

The achievement of harmony within the party suggests itself as an appropriate criterion. Has the party demonstrated its power to compromise the differences of its members coming from the various localities? During the course of one administration the unity or disunity within the party is sure to appear. Has the party developed among its followers a consciousness of party responsibility that stimulates a willingness to co-operate in the solution of public questions?

To what extent has rule by the party in the majority resulted in efficient administration? Accomplishments certainly provide a basis for judgment superior to promises. Viewed as an organization with a continuing life and a definite leadership and membership, the political party stands forth as a body that can be called to task for the standards of public conduct of the politicians enrolled; it can be demanded of the party that the candidates put forward in its name be honest and able public servants.

The party can be judged according to the quality of its personnel. What kind of men does the party offer? The public is quick to decide as to the personalities associated with the party. If stuffed shirts are placed in positions of authority and bosses left to connive in the background, the situation soon stirs common gossip. Is authority within the party exercised directly and openly or deviously and darkly? Politicians cannot depend upon the force of party discipline to guarantee control of the legislature. Has the party sponsored an executive official who has succeeded in winning wide support? Has the party picked a leader?

Having asked these questions of the party, one may question the candidate directly as to his stand on particular measures of concern to groups and individuals. To require the party to stand flatly on an issue is simply another way of demanding that a particular position be urged upon the elected representatives through the party leaders of the national organization. The contact had better be direct, since party discipline is far from dependable. For the proposal of policies and the responsibility of promises, individual statesmen alone can be held accountable. Commitments on specific issues demand clear and direct answerability.

Limitations upon the party as an expounder of principles and supporter of issues make the need of leadership in the presidential office all the more urgent at times when positive action is required. The chief executive is in a strategic position to initiate policy and gain national support for legislative measures. His is the only nation-wide constituency. Not only chief executive but often also national representative-at-large, he is capable of holding the strongest mandate from the electorate. With party lines providing little guidance to public policy, with control in the legislative body disparate and uncertain, the presidential will must be positive and clear if Congress is to carry through a consistent program.

For a statesman to secure a following in support of his measures it is not necessary or even always desirable to identify the party itself with these policies. Under our system, government has often been conducted on a personal rather than a partisan plane. The problem has been one of individual and not party leadership. The American political party has not adhered to a fixed set of doctrines for deciding specific policies. It has done little more than launch leaders selected for their availability and their capacity to attract political support.

The voter can judge the political party more clearly in terms of its leaders than by its promises. If the validity of appraising our party system in accordance with these standards were recognized, much artificial dissatisfaction with political parties might disappear. The political system could then be evaluated not by criteria removed from reality but by standards that are human, direct, and comprehensible to all.

Part II

☆ 8 ☆

Our Parties Take Their Stand

"He stood a spell on one foot fust,
Then stood a spell on t'other,
An' on which one he felt the wust
He couldn't ha' told ye nuther."
JAMES RUSSELL LOWELL

UPON what footing should a party take its stand? Our parties are in a difficult position. If they are to survive as democratic institutions they must be responsive to the main currents of opinion within the community, and yet they are insistently called upon to develop a distinctive program. It is little wonder that party leaders shift uneasily from one stand to the other. The professional politician prefers to avoid the dilemma by offering the public candidates who will attract support by the force of their personalities. The position that our parties occupy is, however, the result of a whole complex of social and economic factors rather than due to the pussyfooting of partisan leaders.

The task of economic development accounts largely for the peculiar nature of American politics. The economic exploitation of a rich continent became the unifying purpose of the nation. The fact that a heterogeneous people was busily developing a vast territory meant that broad terms of co-operation had to be discovered. Such terms by the very nature of affairs had to be determined by the common denominator that would create a working majority. This tended to subordinate the importance of debate over great issues by partisan organizations.

The sectional diversity of interests has determined the strategy of politicians. To find a working combination of regions continues to be their common problem. This explains why the two parties persistently tend toward likeness. Both can rely upon a nucleus of traditional supporters; but the major parties must seek to win doubtful states and attract the floating vote as well. The electoral votes of New York (47), Pennsylvania (36), Illinois (29), Ohio (26), Michigan (19), and Indiana (14) hold one key to national victory. In the last nine presidential races these doubtful states have gone with the nation in six elections. Sectionalism in American politics, while a fundamental cause for national diversity, serves to stimulate similarity between our major parties. Sectional loyalties provide each party with a nucleus of support upon which it can depend. With this as a start each party seeks to win the doubtful areas.

To the variety of sectional interests, we must add a variety of differing economy systems. David Cushman Coyle, for example, points out that we have (a) small competition business, (b) finance capitalism, (c) public services, (d) nonprofit activities, and (e) a co-operative movement. "The combination of these various systems is not an ism in any usual sense. It has no real 'Ideology.' . . . It draws upon different, even contradictory motives, skills, methods and resources. By the same quality of diversity it leaves room for freedom." [1] No neat formula covers this picture. Union through pragmatic adjustment remains the basic consideration of American politics.

The Constitution set up a structure of government stronger than the Articles of Confederation but still hedged about with limitations. It set up a government devised to respond but slowly and indirectly to current popular sentiment. In national affairs some of the most controversial issues were eliminated from partisan consideration.[2] Though the Constitution served as an act of settlement, its framers could, of course, not foresee the place the federal government would come to fill. The Constitution could give no final answer concerning the extent of federal governmental powers. The political party aided in making the government more responsive by counteracting the effects of checks and balances.

"When the constitution was signed and adopted and the docu-

APPEAL TO THE VOTERS

Political Meeting, a Detail from the Mural in the State House at Jefferson City, Mo., by Thomas Hart Benton.
(Courtesy *Art Digest*.)

APPEAL TO THE VOTERS

Stump Speaking, 1854, by George Caleb Bingham.

(Courtesy of the St. Louis Mercantile Library.)

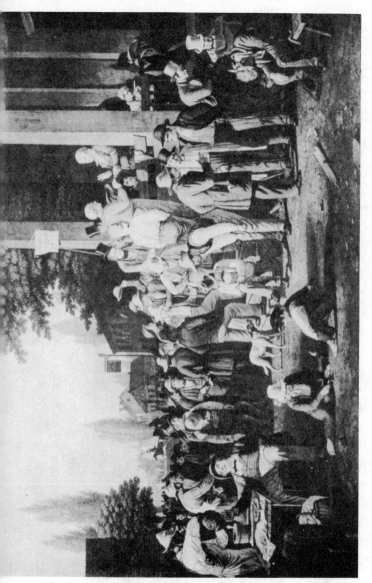

APPEAL TO THE VOTERS

County Election, 1851–52, by George Caleb Bingham.

(Courtesy of the St. Louis Mercantile Library.)

APPEAL TO THE VOTERS

Electioneering in the Rocky Mountains, from a Sketch by Alfred Mitchell, *Harper's Weekly,* September 29, 1888.

(Courtesy of the New York Public Library.)

APPEAL TO THE VOTERS

Getting Out the Good, Old, Honest Country Vote, by A. B. Frost, *Collier's Weekly,* 1907.

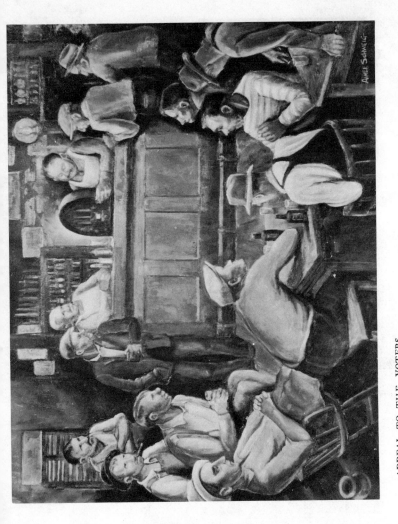

APPEAL TO THE VOTERS

The President's Fireside Chat, Exhibited in the Contemporary Art Show, N. Y. Wald Fair, 1939. Printed by Aimee Schweig, St. Louis, Mo.

APPEAL TO THE VOTERS

Trickery at the Polls, Election Night on the East Side, Painting by Don Freeman.

(Courtesy of the Artist.)

TALKING POLITICS

Politics in an Oyster-house, by Richard Cayton Woodville,
1848.

(Courtesy of the Metropolitan Museum of Art.)

TALKING POLITICS

Arguing the Point, Settling the Presidency, by A. F. Tait.

(Courtesy of the Bland Gallery, Inc.)

TALKING POLITICS

Canvassing for a Vote, by George Caleb Bingham.

(Courtesy of the Bland Gallery, Inc.)

TALKING POLITICS

Politics, by John Rogers, 1888.

(Courtesy of the New York Historical Society.)

TALKING POLITICS

Talking Politics, by A. B. Frost, *Collier's Weekly*, 1904.

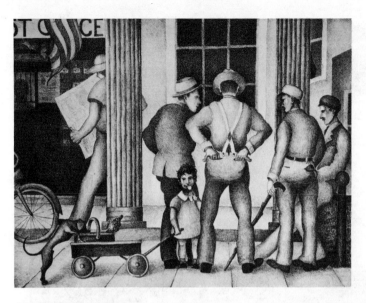

TALKING POLITICS

Politics, by Clarence Bolton.

(Courtesy of WPA Art Program, Federal Works Agency.)

TALKING POLITICS

Park Politicians, by LeRoy Flint.

(Courtesy of WPA Art Program, Federal Works Agency.)

VERDICT OF THE PEOPLE

Verdict of the People, by George Caleb Bingham.

VERDICT OF THE PEOPLE

Twenty Thousand Majority, by G. H. Story.
(Courtesy of the George Walter Vincent Smith Art
Gallery, Springfield, Mass.)

VERDICT OF THE PEOPLE

Election Night, by John Sloan.
(Courtesy of the Francis P. Garvan Estate and
Macbeth Galleries.)

VERDICT OF THE PEOPLE

Election Night Bonfire, by Glenn O. Coleman.
(Collection of the Whitney Museum, New York City.)

ment was safely locked away," writes A. C. McLaughlin, "there remained still unprovided for the two supreme jobs of democracy—the placing in office of the men whom the people wish to have in office and the transferring of the people's desires into legislation and administration." And he continues, "In any study of the party, we should see that the important thing is not in its principles, but the fact that it exists at all and that it is used as a means of conducting public affairs, of doing—or failing to do—the tremendously difficult job of carrying on popular government." [3]

Within the growing wilderness of conflict and confusion, our political parties have undertaken the task of keeping official government going. More than thirty years ago A. T. Hadley wrote:

"We see parties primarily arranged, not to promote certain measures of legislation, but to do the work of government. The party machine as an administrative body becomes the main thing; the legislative measures with which it is identified are only an incident. I believe this to have been the usual condition in the United States, especially in recent years. . . . Under ordinary circumstances the work of persuading the executive and legislature to work in harmony with each other under the somewhat strained conditions presented by the United States Constitution seems more important than the passing of any particular measure and that side of the party organization naturally comes to the front." [4]

Finer believes not only that the Constitution has limited the scope of partisanship, but also that "the geographical, economic and cultural features have gone further to reduce the number of political issues and therefore the spiritual vitality of parties."

In the federal sphere, our political parties are temporary alliances of local leaders held together by the hope of winning the presidency. These men know the temper of their supporters and they can guess shrewdly as to how far they can compromise with fellow politicians from other sections without endangering their own local following. Party leaders in this country count themselves fortunate if they can hold the allegiance of their followers to the party as an organization and hence do not endanger this loyalty by making undue demands. Moreover, it is questionable if those concerned would have the situation other than as it is. As John Dickinson has pointed out, "the various interests may be unwilling to put themselves so completely in the hands of a supreme board of adjustment responsible only to the electorate as a whole. This is doubtless true of the United States." [5]

The absence of a responsible ministry makes it very difficult for any one party to carry out a national partisan program. Power is placed in the hands of the voter rather than in a responsible ministry. The process of getting the government to respond more directly to the desires of the mass began with making the electoral college a farce, continued in the direct election of senators, and now is furthered by flooding the congressional mail with letters and telegrams and by other forms of pressure. This tendency grows as government comes close to the daily life of individuals, a tendency which in turn has added to the task of the party politician. Professionals were needed to organize the vast electorate and to fulfill the many responsibilities foisted upon the voter by the democratic creed. The system was supposed to run itself. It was not automatic, however, and yet no group was recognized as being charged with a direct responsibility.

Practical necessity demanded some degree of continuity and order in political affairs. Party organizations were not an entirely satisfactory solution, but they were the only means at hand. Boss rule was bad, but it was better than no rule. In our great cities government was often dominated by men who ignored ethical prescriptions but who nonetheless were tolerated by a citizenry too much concerned with private matters to think through the problems which gave rise to political abuses. The party machine tried to run the government in communities of indifferent citizens, divided by class prejudices. Where common purposes and mutual values were lacking, the party served at least to keep the institutions of government in operation. "When the public is as uncertain and obscure as it is today, and hence as remote from government," says John Dewey, "bosses with their political machines fill the void between government and the public." [6]

The political structure was too complicated for the average

voter. The electoral process was much too elaborate—too many candidates for too many offices. The privileges of the voter outstripped both his interest and his capacity for judgment. The doctrine of rotation in office aggravated this burden.

The reforms that were attempted proved abortive. The referendum and the direct primary further added to the burdens of the voter. Conversely, these changes often enhanced the power of the politician. Only a specialist could meet the burdens that the good citizen was supposed to carry. The tremendous rewards coming to men who developed the natural resources of the country offered counterattractions too great to be resisted. The state of political affairs was often deplored but seldom remedied.

There was little to stir the imagination of idealistic persons when they contemplated the day-to-day political scene. Since high-minded men were discouraged by the general public attiture from participating in the routine operations of government, the less fastidious grasped control. These men did not refuse to compromise or to sacrifice their theories in order to get things done. "Politics was business," Weyl writes, "but in America it was low-grade business like saloon keeping. Not offering the boundless opportunities of other enterprises, it attracted a poorer quality of man." [7]

The task was not done well, but the expanding economy of the nation was able to carry an enormous burden of dishonesty and inefficiency. The part played by government in the direction and control of life was relatively slight and the full effects of the spoils system were not felt because administrative work was simple. Disputes affecting daily life were more likely to arise between rival economic classes than between rival politicians. The latter engaged in conspiracies not against the people's liberties but rather against the public purse.

The party organization grew up around the formal structure of governments in cities and states. At best it helped bridge the separation of powers, linked the executive and legislative branches, and provided the leaders needed to conduct the agencies of government in a harmonious fashion. On those occasions when economic activity called for governmental aid, the party leader was the man approached. He stood for order and authority in a system inherently confused.

Since politics is sectional, we have not drawn together on a national scale except in the election of a president. The importance given the presidency by the Constitution plus the desire of the voters to vote directly for a president is one root of our national party system. A two-party system is needed for this purpose; otherwise the French bloc system would be more appropriate. Why did not a multi-party system develop? The answer lies in the constitutional provision for an independent executive and in the desire of the voters to determine his election. Under a multi-party system no one candidate would be likely to secure a majority of the electoral votes. Consequently, the election would be thrown into the House of Representatives and the chief magistrate selected through a coalition of blocs. This happened in the election of John Quincy Adams. Old Hickory, the people's choice, failed to enter the White House after the election of 1824 despite his plurality of electoral and popular votes. Was the will of the people to be contravened by a corrupt bargain among politicians in Congress!

The results of this affair displeased both political organizers and ardent democrats, so that they combined to support a system whereby such a miscarriage would be impossible again. Although its original raison d'être has been almost forgotten, the system has proved useful and adaptable to many other purposes. Since then several presidents have been elected although opponents received pluralities of popular votes, but the House of Representatives has not again been called upon to choose among several factional leaders as in 1824.

The popular contest over the presidency not only has fortified a two-party alignment over the country but also has acted as a nationalizing influence on the party system. The pioneers who went westward were absorbed in the conquest of a wilderness and the development of the natural resources that lay before them. The federal government was distant, and national policy meant little in their daily lives. Party loyalty supplemented loyalty to the nation, but the presidency was the great symbol of national union.

As Allen Johnson has said:

"The pioneers of the West were drawn out of their political isolation by membership in national parties. No doubt parties would not have become sectional if the union had not become so, but there is reason to believe that parties check the growth of sectionalism. And the best evidence of the beneficial influence in crises is the fact that the union did break up when parties lost their national character." [8]

Our party system grew out of the task of adapting a written constitution to the governance of a great continent. A politics of expediency, while lacking the vision of principle, has brought flexibility. We have seen the make-up of our parties change as the politicians in control have selected one line of policy in preference to another and thus have affected the group content of the party.

Underlying the sectionalism of our politics and the opportunism of our politicians has been the development of our national economy as a unifying force. Transcending state lines and ignoring gusts of political protest, industry and finance have consolidated our economy. This has gone so far now that writers find it important to call attention to its dangers.[9] Consolidation by the wealthy may lead to the exclusion of the have-nots from power. These hazards we must ponder, but at the same time we must not underestimate the tremendous solidity gained when economic self-interest is identified with a political structure.[10] This has been a central fact of American politics.

The liaison of business and politics has been a continuing thread through the fabric of our history. Capitalism and the party system grew up together. All went well so long as the economic sphere fulfilled the hopes of the citizens.

The Civil War left the Republicans in command of the federal government at a period when national policy was of great importance for industry. Manufacturers and financiers were embarked upon a period of rapid growth. In their train came an army of bondholders. All were intent upon business expansion.

To attain their objectives it was sometimes necessary to forestall political interference with their plans. Business could not afford to let the control of the federal government fall into hands unfriendly to its interests. William Allen White describes this situation as follows:

"Business organizations like railroads, insurance companies, and large financial houses, which concerns engaged in interstate commerce, owned the local state bosses: and these local state bosses assembling at national conventions of the party, took orders from Wall Street or, being proud, sometimes gave orders to Wall Street, like the nomination of a Vice-President or a pension plank in the platform. But the system was set and institutionalized. It was as respectable as the Constitution and the Constitution was held up before the eyes of innocent children as the inspiration and defense of the system. Money controlled caucuses; caucuses controlled conventions; conventions nominated candidates; candidates became officials; officials were controlled by politics; politics was owned by business." [11]

The resources of the nation were at the disposal of those controlling the federal government, and the Republican politicians had the wherewithal for developing a strong machine. The spoils of office were theirs despite the feeble beginnings of civil service reform. Their power was reflected in the temper of the Supreme Court and strongly represented by the Old Guard in the Senate.

The Democratic party also had business support, especially among those merchants and financiers concerned with foreign trade. Businessmen buying manufactured goods and supplies from abroad could not reconcile their interests with the high tariff policy of the Republican party. Industrialists as a class were not greatly concerned with a consistent partisan affiliation; they preferred to negotiate with the party dominant in their locality. As Henry O. Havemeyer once said, "The American Sugar Refining Company has no politics of any kind—only the Politics of Business." Contributions were made to both sides with fine impartiality. The Beards have pointed out that "in normal times, it made little or no difference to the Napoleons of business enterprise what party directorate commanded the field as long as the requirements of their political economy were met in a satis-factory manner." [12]

In the national field the party organization with the best chance of winning the presidency was the party for business. The Republican party was the best bet so long as it was able to hold the West in alliance with the industrial East. The stakes of in-dustry were too great for the businessman to risk being on the wrong side. The Beards write:

"The executive department was invested with a positive power of immense economic utility; if so disposed, it could operate the land office munificently, distribute the natural resources of the nation in a generous fashion, and manage foreign policy with reference to the demands of trade. It could also wield a negative authority; the Presi-dent had the legal right to veto acts of Congress; he nominated Su-preme Court justices who, in the grand manner of jurists, could set aside legislative measures. With respect both to action and negation the Senate of the United States likewise had its uses; as the upper House of Congress, its consent was necessary to the passage or defeat of any new legislation and to the confirmation of the President's nominees for important public offices, including the federal judiciary. Fortunately for business enterprise, the machine for electing the President was cumbersome and costly to move; Senators were chosen indirectly by state legislatures; and federal judges were selected by the President and the Senate for life." [13]

Businessmen were the leaders and exponents of the general environment. They expressed the ideals of the community, di-rected the accepted institutions, and stood for a firm combination of interests. In addition it was the common belief that the eco-nomic destiny of the nation was best achieved through private enterprise. This was the cause to which men gave their loyalty. Industry was to weld the nation together. Business was accepted as the force for integration and unity. To a nation believing in business setting the pattern for labor and agriculture, control of the party organization by successful businessmen raised no em-barrassing questions. Service to business characterized both parties.

By constitutional guarantees, the government was to protect

the civil rights of individuals. In the economic realm they were to seek their own salvation. The powers of the federal government were limited to the performance of certain definite functions. No unified executive authority was charged with the responsibility of carrying out a positive program. Yet the government might intervene at times to punish the immoral or to assist the more courageous by granting tariffs to protect infant industries or subsidies to establish new enterprises requiring large capital. In sporadic fashion, representatives from various sections reached agreements on particular pieces of legislation. Problems were met in this way. When discontent flared, concessions were made. Politicians wanted to keep peace in the family. With little popular disagreement upon central values, the general welfare would be promoted by leaving men to pursue their own best interests. Such objectives did not necessitate long-range planning or the responsible management of national affairs. Business was barter, and so was politics. Seeking political advantage meant higgling for votes. The customer could choose between competing politicians. So long as private business was successful, social objectives took care of themselves. Economic relationships were determined by negotiations between individuals. When the business of politics was identified with the politics of business, all went well.

With most people accepting the theory that through encouraging business the welfare of all would be promoted, the federal government favored the business class. Favors and subsidies to industry did not necessarily result in dissatisfaction in the working class. The workingman if he worked hard and was lucky might expect to be a businessman. The farmer might expect to reap riches if he worked hard and the weather was favorable. The extraordinary fluidity of social relations counteracted class consciousness among the have-nots.

Since men were able to move from one economic class to another and attain their aims through success in the business battle, they were not inclined to seek them through political channels. Recurring economic depressions, however, brought a lack of faith in the economic order. As the full implications of the economic system appeared, political differences became intensified. The party organization could not alienate its sources of revenue, nor could it ignore the pleas of men who asked more of parties than that they keep the governmental machinery going. The government was called upon to compensate for the shortcomings of the industrial system, to redress economic maladjustments. Prosperity must be restored through political action. The politician who promised relief and an increase of social opportunities attracted support.

Those who are confident that the economic order will give them what they want regard with suspicion those who seek such ends through governmental channels. The business of politics has become greatly enhanced. It is the business of politicians to respond to cries of distress from the voters. The politics of business is, however, logically opposed to governmental enterprise that may in any way compete with private activities. It is opposed to a high tax burden and to a large public deficit. It is opposed to strengthening labor unions. It would protect profits even at the cost of lowering productivity in a society where great numbers live near the subsistence level.[14]

Public policy has generally been posited on the assumption that the economic order could best meet our material needs. Thus democracy and capitalism would live together in happy wedlock. From the eighteen seventies to the present, however, sporadic conflicts between the politics of business and the business of politics have appeared. Farmers and workers have protested that the economic order was not working to their benefit. The business of politics, which is to retain control of government by securing popular support, runs counter to the politics of business. Many farmers refuse to identify their interests with those of the businessman. Politicians come forward to allay or exploit this disparity. The politician seeking a large following has generally found greatest advantage as a mediator or adjuster, and at times this aspect of politics has become an end in itself. It is the business of politics, however, to discover the terms upon which men will live together. But within what areas? The sphere of reconciliation serves as the basis upon which the politician will build his power. Thus building political support on local loyalties means that a less parochial politician must seek adjustments between local interests at a higher level.

In the past, protest has had a sectional basis. The Greenbackers, the Grangers, the Populists, and the cohorts of William Jennings Bryan were all manifestations of certain forces in the West and the South. This disrupting influence appeared as the Bull Moose movement in the Republican party in 1912 and found a spokesman in the elder Robert La Follette in 1924. The Republicans, better than their opponents, could afford to ignore this protest since they already had a dependable combination of sectional interests. The Democrats in casting about for a successful sectional alignment were forced to give heed, since their hope of victory lay in attracting voters away from the Republican party. The Democrats accordingly alternated between appeals to the liberals of the West and forays into the eastern regions where the Republicans were entrenched. Not until 1932 did the Democrats definitely break down the sectional alignment of the Republicans and ride to victory through a strategy combining West and South.

The New Deal in response to these new demands effected through political channels a distribution of wealth unattainable through the economic system. This process of distribution cannot be treated as a partisan doctrine, but rather as the necessary consequence of the functioning of popular government. Until recent years, under democracy as we have known it in this country the interests of property have been generally the basis for policy. At the same time we have been able to enjoy a relatively high degree of freedom of thought and of action. No serious conflict appeared so long as economic objectives squared with both these values. Economic issues seem to be fought out increasingly in political terms, and politicians may find it very difficult to please all. Yet democracy in the future must try to reconcile our political ideas and institutions with the conflict of interests engendered by our economic situation.

Following the Civil War the vision of building a great industrial system and exploiting our natural resources provided a common task. As in France and Great Britain, popular institutions grew and flourished in the United States under expanding trade and industry. As the United States had its western frontier, Great Britain had the frontiers of empire and France her immense colonial areas. Ours has been a politics of plenty. This has made men less likely to follow such myths and ambitions as those of Nazism and fascism offer. Our industrial order has provided a liberal margin for the vagaries of our politics. Social fluidity gave hope to all who glanced enviously at the top rung of the ladder of success. With business depression and less social mobility, protests have appeared from groups whose welfare was adversely affected. Faith in the theory of the inherent economic unity of all classes has weakened.

The present party system helps to preserve existing social institutions by blurring sharp issues and ignoring others. Party rule discourages the alignment of economic differences through political channels. Much of the impatience and even disgust with our existing parties stems from dissatisfaction with this tendency.

Economic conditions have discouraged partisan controversy over fundamentals, but a change now seems to be taking place. Up to now, geographic position has enabled us to take for granted the boon of national security. Even economic prosperity was largely assumed as the normal product of our community life until the rude shocks of recurrent depressions and industrial disputes forced many people to face prosperity as a condition calling for the exercise of thought, foresight, and some degree of planning.

Union has been and continues to be the underlying problem of American politics. This must be so in the government of a continental nation. A broad meeting of minds is necessary before democracy can adopt a policy. The object of representative government is not to represent men in all their divergencies but rather to establish freely their common grounds. From the Articles of Confederation through the framing of the Constitution, the agony of the Civil War, and the pushing back of the frontier, and now in the face of class and sectional differences, this goal remains. The activities of our politicians and the role of our political parties are understood most clearly in terms of the search for union. Democracy in this country can continue so long as such a working harmony is struck among the demands of various groups. The accomplishment of party government lies in its demonstrated ability for reducing warring interests and conflicting classes to co-operative terms. Parties try to establish a working accord to minimize dissension among their followers and to win a wide support. Our parties try to be as inclusive as possible.

Party government within a community of divided purposes cannot execute a definite program without imposing the will of one set of interests upon other groups. At best a party victory means a victory for a man supported by a combination of sectional and economic interests. The rule by such a combination must be freely accepted by the groups out of power if the party system is to work. This is axiomatic. The puzzling question concerns the degree of difference that is tolerable.

In the first place the victorious interests do not have carte blanche. For example, the president, in working out a program, calls upon party loyalties to support such adjustment of group demands as he deems wise. The interests do not set the terms. The policy pursued by party leaders, moreover, on those issues for which the party takes responsibility is not simply the product of abstract thought. The "must" legislation of President Roosevelt was guided by group demands and represented the compromise of special interests as compounded by the president and his advisers. Opposition came not so much from the Republicans as from those groups which were adversely affected by the New Deal policies.

Opposition in American politics is not necessarily expressed in partisan terms. Critics who bemoaned the overwhelming Democratic vote in the 1936 election interpreted the outcome to mean the abolition of any effective check because of the weakness of the opposition party. Such critics were unaware of the actual happenings of Congress. Their view was based on the assumption that legislative battles must be fought between partisan groups aligned pro and con on all important issues.

Most legislation, of course, is nonpartisan. Our parties do not take definite attitudes on all proposed legislation. Congressmen act in accordance with the needs of their localities or the demands of interest groups rather than in accordance with the dictates of party leaders.

In addition to the restraints imposed by the minority party, opposition within the majority party is a factor of great importance in keeping policy to a middle course. In recent years action demanded by New Deal theorists could not be taken until a substantial amount of support by more conservative Democratic congressmen accumulated and until modifications were made in the original proposals.

Since party loyalties are sentimental as well as economic, the battle of American politics has often been divorced from basic differences of interest. Parties which would align voters rigidly in accordance with their economic class differences would probably result in the breakdown of party government. No secession of class is possible. The problem of American politics today is the historic purpose of preserving the Union, but a union of economic interests rather than of sections. To obtain this objective it is necessary to preserve national parties based upon compromise. Yet if voters are to be kept loyal to the Union and to the values of liberalism they must be able to find through the federal government and through the tenets of democracy at least partial realization of the objectives dearest to them. The party system as a whole must respond to the broad drift of opinion. This drift in turn depends on common impulses of tolerance and co-operation, such as offset tendencies toward narrow class interest. This happy outcome is hardly to be taken for granted.

Our party system is best explained as a rivalry between two organizations each bent on presenting as its own a view of the public interest as widely acceptable as possible. The task of the party is to achieve a working combination of sections, of interests, and also of the liberals and the conservatives within its own ranks.

☆ 9 ☆

The Traditional Politician and the Service State

> "My perlitercal sentiments agree with yourn exactly. I know they do, becawz I never saw a man whoos didn't.
>
> Respectivelyyures,
> A. WARD
>
> P. S.—You scratch my back and Ile scratch your back."

THE politician has been traditionally lampooned as a persistent back-scratcher or logroller. His unconcern with principle is heartily condemned and his attitude sometimes ridiculed and habitually criticized. Actually, of course, the politician is seldom if ever found in such a "pure state"—but the attributes associated with this caricatured politician of fiction are observable in greater or less degree among men who succeed in public life under democratic institutions. In view of the increasing demands made on governments an examination of the function of the politician is pertinent.

Efforts at living together may arise from a common social need, but to continue amicably requires not only good will but also skillful supervision. Here lies the opportunity of the specialist in human relations, of the man who is concerned not with the one best way but rather with the paths that will prove acceptable to those who must tread them. William Ernest Hocking has defined the politician as "the man who deliberately faces both the certainty that men must live together, and the endless uncertainty on what terms they can live together, and who takes upon himself the task of proposing the terms, and so of transforming the unsuccessful human group into the successful group." [1] It is these "specialized inventors of settlements whom we term politicians." They seek not the ideal but terms of agreement that reduce the chances of violence or coercion.

"It is precisely that outcome of intergroup conflicts which the democratic politicians shield us from [writes T. V. Smith]. If they sometimes lie in the strenuous task, it is regrettable but understandable. If they sometimes truckle, that is despicable but tolerable. If they are sometimes bribed, that is more execrable but still not fatal. The vices of our politicians we must compare not with the virtues of the secluded individual but with the vices of dictators. In this context, almost beautiful things may be said of our politicians—by way of compensation, if not by way of extenuation, of whatever vices attend upon the arduous process of saving us from violence and murder. People elsewhere get killed in the conflicts of interest over which our politicians preside with vices short of crimes and with virtues not wholly unakin to magnanimity." [2]

A value so basic in the politics of democracy as to be taken for granted is preserved by men whose own careers depend upon their finding social adjustments short of violence acceptable enough to hold their fellows in the pursuit of common interests. This may not appear to the idealist as a function worthy of much attention. If men are assumed to be rational, mere knowledge of their own interests should dictate such a course. In fact, however, men are given to passion and greed. The period of government by discussion is but a tick in the clock of historical time. The skill exercised by those who seek a *via media* holds society together and gives others an opportunity to think and even to test the products of intelligence.

Neither the vision of the reformer nor the expertness of the technician can displace the peculiar contribution of the specialist in human relations. Whether the politician will use his talents to promote the good life is another matter. The same question may be asked about any reformer or technician. As an adjuster of human interests and passions, the politician has a positive role in the politics of democracy. His function is to stand for relativity in the struggle of absolute values and thus to promote continuity and cohesion in social relations. His task becomes greater, rather than less important, as governmental responsibilities increase.[3]

When blind forces of nature or inexorable economic laws were regarded as the determinants of human fates, man might pray or curse; but his first reaction in time of social stress was not to blame the government. Now with statesmen assuming responsibility for the business cycle, soil erosion, and public health, failures can be attributed to persons and politicians held accountable for social ills. The demagogue no less than the wise leader has a wider area within which to operate. The social environment changes; technology demands technicians; but human nature still sets conditions that must be met.

The problems raised by the presence of several racial groups in the community may serve as one example. Using a framework of government designed for a simple unified community wherein citizens might correctly be assumed as competent to deal with the commonweal, our politicians, particularly those in the city, had to cope with the new arrivals who were completely unacquainted with our ways and traditions of government. Our great cities have been racial jungles for generations. Various national groups have their own community life and tend to congregate in particular neighborhoods. (The story is told of a studious Chinese who took up his abode in the Polish section in the North Side of Chicago and applied himself assiduously to study Polish in the belief that the language which he heard on the streets must be the language of his new country.)

Tony Cermak built his political career upon the racial complexity of Chicago. He recognized that strength lay in polling the votes of racial groups. The party slates which he drew up included the names of Jews, Czechs, Poles, Germans, Italians, and Swedes, with perhaps a University of Chicago candidate and someone close to Hull House. With these components he built a powerful machine, and he defeated Big Bill Thompson. The latter directed his appeal chiefly to the Negro and the German elements and to the old Americans who could be rallied by the cry of "American first." [4] A threat to punch King George in the nose was effective showmanship, but its appeal was scarcely cosmopolitian enough for the racial mosaic of Chicago.[5]

Tammany Hall is the classic instance of a political organization that for decades skillfully manipulated the rivalries and demands of racial groups. As one writer states:

"The Tammany leader who picks men for merit would not last a year. When he prepares his ticket for November he must pro-rate his nominations with mathematical precision among the German, Jewish, Celtic, Italian, and African stocks. The Anglo-Saxons, a negligible and futile element, get a consolation prize now and then; so do those curious and amusing sectaries, the Protestants; but it would be fatal to a Tammany leader to give an office to John or Tom when it was the turn of Isadore, Aloysius, Heinrich, Salvatore, or George Washington. . . ." [6]

Only a well-entrenched political organization could superintend such a distribution. As long as the machine could curb the greed of its henchmen and satisfy the immediate desires of important groups, it continued undisturbed. The strength of Charles F. Murphy, boss of Tammany, lay in his moderation. It is said that he was able to enforce upon his subordinates "a sense of proportion that was almost as good as a conscience. His ideal was that of a fairly well-governed city, cheerfully yielding the amount of indirect tribute that was absolutely necessary to keep Tammany workers interested in their work." [7] For maintaining a tolerant community and in tending the melting pot of nationalities Tammany might be accorded much credit had not generous cash payments already been taken from the public till many times over.

Our politicians now, however, are faced with new problems. It is not enough for the organization to cast a sop to various racial groups in return for their support. Citizens one or two generations removed from their immigrant forebears are not so easily satisfied. In various parts of the country a political alignment between old stock and new stock offers a sharp challenge.

Thus in Massachusetts the Democratic party derives much of its strength from the Irish-Catholic element, while the Republican party is the stronghold of the Yankees. The presidential candidacy of Al Smith tended to consolidate the Catholics with the Democratic party. The party's stand against prohibition strengthened this alliance. The Yankees have been loath to share political power and social position with the Irish, and instead of bringing an amalgam politics has often embittered racial rivalry. Both parties seek the support of the "newest" racial groups. Yankee politicians have found positions at the bottom of the ticket for candidates of Irish, Italian, or French-Canadian extraction; but for those seeking higher office the Democratic party has proved the better channel. The politician as an adept in the art of handling men today succeeds to racial problems often much more difficult than those of his predecessor who shepherded the raw immigrants of a generation or two ago, and solving the problems posed by race is no less imperative now than then.

Economic as well as racial factors are creating problems requiring skilled political management. In the past, careers in machine politics have been built on Christmas baskets, buckets of coal, picnics, and excursions down the bay. Hinky-Dinky and Bathhouse John could vote their flophouse supporters en masse and reward their loyalty with plenty of beer. But the WPA has reduced the business of the flophouse, and the Workers' Alliance offers the worker on relief a means of voicing his wants. Today the voter is less dependent on the political boss. The laborer is being organized. The union organizer deals directly with the voter. Then in the name of his following he negotiates with men in public office, with party leaders, and with industrialists. Labor organizations have attractions to offer greater than a bucket of beer.

Mayor Frank Hague of Jersey City has been called the last of the bosses; and rightly so perhaps. He represents a kind of social organization distinct from the trends of today. He is bitterly jealous and fearful of another type of organization, the C.I.O., which threatens to meet him on his own ground. This organization promises wage earners higher wages and more security. The C.I.O. stretches down into the community, knocks at the voter's door, and provides a channel of expression in economic terms.

What meaning Hague has must be found in his "good works" rather than his roguery. The papers stress his ungrammatical speech and his attack on the Reds. This is part of his showmanship. To understand Hague we must note the $40,000,000 of federal funds secured for his county, his ball park built with $3,000,000 of WPA money, the $1,800,000 maternity hospital with an output of 500 babies per month, and his gift of the $50,000 altar in St. Aedan's Roman Catholic Church in a city three-fourths Catholic. His strength lies in his exemplification of dominant racial, religious, and social forces in Jersey City. Yet this personification is enforced by fear and intrigue. Mayor Hague may be a fearful figure to some today, but so was the dinosaur in its time.

The fate of Boss Pendergast of Kansas City, Missouri, offers another example. He has rightly been called an anachronism in the political scene of today. His methods recall the days of Boss Tweed in New York and his downfall came as an overthrow of unscrupulous power comparable in extent to the scandals of the past. The waning of boss rule is not to be interpreted simply as the victory of the righteous over the unrighteous but rather as a very important shift in the bases of political power.

That the public is becoming aware of this vital shift is well illustrated by the penetrating analysis offered by James A. Hagerty in the New York *Times*. He explains:

"It was the power of the State, acting through a legislative investigating committee, that produced the disclosures that led to the election and re-election of Mayor La Guardia in New York City and weakened the power of Tammany.

"It was the power of the Federal Government, acting through Federal income tax investigators and a United States Attorney, that brought about the downfall of Pendergast.

"There obviously must be some basic reasons why a push from the outside can throw Tammany from power in New York and send a boss like Pendergast to prison in Kansas City, and why bosses in other large cities have left no successors of their own caliber.

"Perhaps one of the reasons is the growing centralization of powers in the government at Washington. The Income Tax Law is a mighty weapon to prevent graft by city bosses and their followers whenever the Federal Government decides to use it.

"A local politician can hardly report income, illegally obtained, in his income tax report without making a record of criminality. If he does not report this illegally obtained income, he is, like Pendergast, subject to investigation and punishment.

"The extension of relief by the Federal Government has struck a blow at the big city machines and the remaining bosses. The best excuse for the existence of Tammany and similar organizations in the past has been the willingness of the local machine leaders to extend aid and lend money to the unfortunate. This charity received its return in votes.

"Now the Federal Government has assumed this function as a matter of duty to the underprivileged and to an extent many times greater than any political machine could afford." [8]

As the economic pattern of our society changes, the function of the old-fashioned politician will be altered. Rival organizations more directly representing the economic interests of the citizen will weaken the political machine. The "smalltime" politician who curries favor by doing favors will be superseded by leaders of groups better organized, more unified, and able to offer more in return for loyal support.

Changes of this sort bring a different type of men into positions of power. Graft in financial administration, fraudulence in voting, and petty favoritism are frowned upon. A higher moral tone will characterize the struggle for power. But the stakes of politics will be higher, and discovering the terms upon which men will live together will remain of prime importance. Our need will be all the greater for "social engineers," for artistry, adroitness, and even science in dealing with group conflicts and individual aspirations.

The very complexity of governmental jurisdictions has called forth politicians as guides through this jungle. They have provided informal lines of communication. Chicago offers an extreme example of such confusion. A tremendous variety of official agencies may be found within a 50-mile radius. There are 1,600 independent governments; four state lines are crossed; 203 cities are included as well as 116 townships. In Chicago itself, one finds six principal governmental bodies possessing independent taxing powers: the mayor and his council, the Board of Education, the Park Board, the Sanitary District, the Cook County Board, the Cook County Forest Preserve District. To a community cut through by the racial cleavages already mentioned is applied a governmental machinery which is uneven, confused, and overlapping in its jurisdictions.

The present tendency toward consolidation of local governmental authorities and the trend toward the reorganization of state government will make the politician less important as guide. Yet new and more urgent jurisdictional questions confront us. Regionalism and states' rights go to the very heart of our constitutional settlement. As local lines are broken down and simplified, great questions of federal-state relations and regional problems develop. The politician will have an increasingly important function to play in the adjustment of political questions which grow out of the relations between central and local governmental units. During the early days of the New Deal, many new federal agencies were set up to meet the responsibilities created by the depression. Although the politician has acted as an intermediary in securing federal assistance for local supporters, Harold F. Gosnell has found that

"The advances which have been made in the field of public welfare administration have made the social service activities of the precinct committeemen more and more unnecessary. There have been fewer occasions when the party officials can step in and mitigate the harshness of the law. The growth of such services as parole, probation, community case work, rehabilitation, and public employment bureaus has reduced the importance of the precinct captain as a community agent." [9]

The politician's grip will not be relinquished until his function is performed better by officials more adroit in human relations and more sympathetic to social needs. This would entail the disappearance of the traditional type but perpetuate his function in other hands.

As new administrative units establish direct lines of communication with their local clients the need for political intermediaries may diminish. Yet the political questions raised by grants-in-aid for public works, for relief, and for social security remain. They are not to be settled alone by considerations of sound fiscal policy or by application of pat formulae. Their human aspects remain of prime importance; they require the highest skill in meeting the conflict of wills engendered by such economic stakes. Likewise, regional developments, such as the TVA, as they impinge upon state governments and local communities, cannot be treated as problems simply of electrical power generation and transmission. Such developments involve the generation and distribution of political power as well. Local needs must be balanced against the requirements of national policy and development. This is a political problem of the first order.

In the area of social services also, broader considerations are replacing narrower ones. Consider by way of illustration the work of the Tammany district leader in the past. He would spend his evenings at the political club consoling the widow begging help, reassuring the shopkeeper who came with a court summons, relieving a businessman worried by a tax problem, performing a multitude of petty duties looming large in the lives of those affected. Here is a mother whose son the police have accused of truancy or theft; here is a laborer who wants an indoor job because of his rheumatism. The politician takes these human needs into consideration and busies himself in adjusting these demands. From his post in the city hall he telephones city politicians in the districts. At lunch he foregathers with his fellow officers and politicos. He is not concerned with the strict letter of the law or with a nice distinction between public and private affairs. He applies a rule of thumb. He treats men not as citizens but as human beings. In his contacts with the individuals coming for help he does not argue that since a matter is in another jurisdiction it is necessarily beyond reach.

In New York City the Democratic leader met problems concerning the income tax, veteran benefits, customs duties, and other national problems, even though the Republican party was in control at Washington. In settling these affairs he would treat with his Republican political friends who in turn asked for aid in city contracts, canceling of jury notices, violations of building codes, or infringements of zoning laws. Thus the politician in practice bridged the gap created by a formal separation of powers within the government and by the establishment of different administrative jurisdictions. Such lines have little meaning for the man who encounters the frightening force of the law and who comes seeking aid from the politicians.

These tasks of the politician are being obviated by an administrative service better aware of public relations problems. To meet the petty politician's favoritism and fixing, social agencies and social services are being improved and extended. These answers to problems in the social field raise even more serious problems in the field of fiscal policy. Social services cost vast sums. A sun tan at Jones Beach may be acquired free, but the hidden costs linger longer than the blisters and may sting more.

Political problems of adjustment going to the very basis of property relationships are the concomitant of greatly expanded governmental services. Adjusting our capitalist economy to the new demands on government calls for supreme skill in the management of social relations. The politician as a favormonger and petty grafter does not fit into this picture; but the political function of adjustment is basic in democratic government.

A politician's primary task is to please his supporters; if he fails too often, his political career is over. Where the content of public office is primarily political, as in the case of a representative, all goes well. When the office combines political elements with technical requirements, conflicts arise. An elective public health officer, for example, has two different sets of criteria for action. He must follow the canons of medicine in order to protect public health; he may lose his position altogether if he ignores the rules of politics. Such a man will act so as to retain his public support. He would be foolish, indeed, to undermine his own foundations. His standards for judgment are thus not only what is the most economical, or what is the most direct, or what is the most logical, moral, artistic, or sensible way to perform his public duties. He must also ask himself what is the way that will most please the people who maintain him in his office. If they are moral, logical, and alert, the behavior of public officials will tend to reflect this attitude. The politician succeeds only so long as he holds power—be it governmental or unofficial —and this power always has a base.

The differences within the community provide the strands with which the politician weaves a political fabric. If the product is often frayed and soiled, look to the threads as well as the fingers. Within the limits of his materials, the weaver can choose his pattern. His own standards may affect the design and the way it is handled, but he, too, is a child of his environment. Where social custom, religion, common racial origin, or economic status sets a communal pattern, there is less need for a specialist to seek the terms upon which men will live together. The politician's task is set for him by the environment. He must find a way to perform it. If this involves humbug, opprobrium cannot with justice be centered on him. Corruption is a faulty method in a virtuous society. Bribery is effective only where men will accept bribes.

Although because of the nature of his task the successful politician cannot rise above the highest level of his community, he yet has a reasonable range of activity between the highest and lowest standards prevailing. To be sure, compromise may take place at many levels; it need not be unenlightened by idealism if this has meaning in the community. The politician takes the pieces at hand, whether good, bad, or indifferent, and attempts to combine them in some sort of working relationship. His product is no better than his materials. The reformer seeking to build a party of the better elements may spend all his energies on collecting his materials, and even then he seldom gets enough pieces to complete his task. His effort is rewarded by public approval. The function of the politician, while usually rewarded in more tangible form, is nonetheless vital to the maintenance of a free community.

☆ 10 ☆

Community Standards and Political Ethics

"I'm givin' ye th' thruth whin I say that business ain't got a shade on pollyticks in th' matter iv honesty."

MR. DOOLEY

A DOUBLE code of ethics seems to hold for politics. We tend to judge men in public life by a higher standard than we apply to private affairs. The businessman, for example, is not expected to hold fast to abstract ideals; he is supposed to satisfy his customers. The politician must satisfy his constituents if he is to remain in business. Nevertheless, admiration goes generally to the man who stands by his principles. Though intransigence in politics may evoke approval, it may still leave immediate tasks unfulfilled. The conception of an inflexible justice is not helpful as a device for securing the co-operation of persons who remain unmoved by such idealism. The politician serves as an intermediary only too well aware of the frailties of mankind. He is confronted by men who are emotional, predatory, or irrational. His task is not to exalt reason and logic but to find some way whereby human beings with all their faults and weaknesses may be brought to support his purposes. He has treated government as a problem of mechanics rather than as a question of morals. From the idealism of the nineteenth century liberal tradition we have inherited a scorn of this matter-of-fact approach to politics. Men taking this attitude boldly have been denounced as bosses. Their function has not been regarded as respectable,

146

and hence men of lower personal integrity have performed the function of the politician. When bargaining is left to rogues the product is generally rascality. Yet where men of integrity withdraw from the barter of politics someone else must take up the burden. More often than not the very high-mindedness of our reforming element has played directly into the hands of the less scrupulous.

Reformers have sometimes failed to perceive that popular government in a community of diverse standards and interests must respond to this heterogeneity and that preaching the creed of unselfishness in public service is not enough in itself. By refusing to recognize the necessity of adjusting social differences in terms lower than their own private aspirations, idealists remove themselves from the field of action. They have to be content with the role of prophet. They forget that the word must be made flesh to dwell among us. The machine politician has exacted a high price for his services, but he cannot be regarded as entirely unworthy of his hire. We must not be blinded to his contribution by overemphasis on his weaknesses.

There are good politicians and bad—that is, skilled manipulators and clumsy. There are good politicians and bad—that is, those whose ethical values accord with our own and those who use different standards. Yet while communities have been able to grow under dishonest politicians, we have perhaps suffered most when well-intentioned but unskilled managers of human relations have held positions of public responsibility. Experience indicates that it is not enough to believe sincerely and to profess devoutly. We must act, and in a society of conflicting principles and policies action necessarily entails compromise. The politician is concerned not with what should be but with what can be. The man in public life must face the choice when his personal beliefs point one way and expediency points another. He must do either the expedient thing or retire from politics. If he retires he ceases to be a politician, and someone else must face the music.

Few men in public life, on the other hand, can be utter opportunists. There are lines beyond which as self-respecting personalities they will not retreat. Yet a wide spirit of give-and-take enables us to avoid the barricades of intransigence. Men willing to compromise so as to meet specific human needs contribute more to the politics of democracy than do those who are ready to die for such abstract principles as liberty, equality, and fraternity. The concessions of the former may forestall the sacrifices of the latter. Yet worthy of note is the tendency to eulogize the man of principle and to slight his pragmatic fellow.

Hence the successful reformer, while bound by circumstance as tightly as the practical politician, nevertheless can utilize lofty sentiments to advantage. He follows much the same course of action but uses different symbols. He does more than urge voters to become good citizens. He furnishes the organization needed to bring together an effective combination of interests. All this may be done in the language of the general welfare, clean government, and the like. The success of the reform movements in Milwaukee and in Cincinnati shows the importance of finding the right symbols while rallying and binding together effective interest groups. High-minded people elsewhere have suffered from too much reliance on language and too little attention to strategy. Many efforts at reform have been short-lived because the reformers have propounded a negative concept of government and differed with the professional politicians chiefly over whether the party should be dominated by men wearing clean collars or men wearing dirty collars.

If government is to perform only a few routine functions and if the tasks demanding intelligence and constructive imagination are left to private enterprise, the routinist and second-rater will be drawn to government service and the alert and intelligent will do elsewhere the really important work of the community. So long as inefficient government annoys but does not seriously interfere with the work of the community, we tolerate it even though the cost is high. In a recent study of Chicago, *Fortune* concludes that the Kelly machine succeeds because it meets the requirements of various influential groups of citizens. City finances suit the bankers because they find a sufficiently good market for city bonds and tax anticipation warrants. The great industries carrying on a national business are not hampered.

"The machine does not try to milk the city of Carl Sandburg's poem—the city of the big shoulders, stacker of wheat, nation's freight handler, hog-butcher for the world. Probably this is why such influential first citizens of Chicago—such as Robert J. Dunham, former Vice President of Armour & Co.—support Kelly unequivocally." [1]

The machine has not taken sides in labor disputes. Open-shop conditions prevail in the stockyards and steel mills. The strongly organized unions are able to manage their own political affairs. Occasionally the connection of union racketeers with the machine has provoked a scandal, but in general the machine has not intervened in labor problems. As a taxpayer the citizen finds the politician a useful intermediary. Under the antiquated Illinois Constitution of 1870, the tax burden rests upon real estate and personal property. It is said that the "honest citizen who declared all his worldly goods would soon find himself on the way to the poor house." Thus in the adjustment of tax assessments the political machine softens the impact of a constitution difficult to amend upon a modern community which has outgrown its provisions. To many citizens of strong moral scruples the present management comes as an improvement over the open town ruled by Big Bill Thompson. The success of the machine lies in granting a multitude of small favors which satisfy the desires of many individuals for privileged treatment at the hands of the law. The place of the Chicago machine is summed up as follows:

"In the final analysis, a machine is the inevitable political expression of a world of jostling desires and differing class interests. Its business is that of compromise. In the long run it cannot be 'reformed' in the interests of any one class this side of Fascism or Communism, for 'reform' demands allegiance to a fixed canon of value, and where differing groups have differing canons of value the 'corruption' of compromise is necessary. It can, however, be compelled to be more efficient and to work for a much smaller commission." [2]

The existence of a political machine is not due simply to indifference, ignorance, or apathy on the part of the voter. A machine survives upon its merits, upon the shrewdness, the understanding, and the moderation of its leaders. Conditions incidental to boss control are often confused with the underlying cause. The machine has been so often associated with corruption in city government that it is sometimes regarded as a purely urban phenomenon. The experience of Connecticut indicates that there is no essential connection between machine politics and metropolitan life. J. Henry Roraback, the Republican boss, rested his control upon the support of the substantial middle-class Yankee squirearchy of the small towns and rural districts.

There is certainly no essential connection between the presence of a large foreign-born population and corrupt politics. Fremont Older discovered in San Francisco that the greatest opposition to reform came from those of New England and southern antecedents, while the Irish and German-Americans supported change. Philadelphia, "corrupt and contented," has a very high percentage of native-born Americans, yet this has by no means meant the absence of graft. Boies Penrose, a leader in machine politics, was a scion of one of the "best families" in the city.

The heterogeneity of the American population and the absence of a tradition supporting an intellectual and social elite are two primary factors in explaining the nature of American politics. The experience of Brand Whitlock in Toledo illustrates our problem. He found that his difficulties arose from the many kinds of people with their differing standards, habits, and customs that he was called upon to confront in his day-to-day work.

"In Toledo something more than twenty languages and dialects are spoken every day, and as the mayor is addressed the chorus becomes a very babel, a confusion of tongues, all counseling him to his duty. The result is apt to be perplexing at times. The rights of 'business' in the streets and to the public property, the proper bounds within which strikers and strike breakers are to be confined, the limitation of the activities of pickets, the hours in which it is proper to drink beer, who in the community should gamble, whether Irishmen or Germans make the better policemen; the exact proportion of public jobs which Poles and Hungarians should hold; whether Socialists on their soap boxes are obstructing traffic or merely exercising the constitutional right of free speech, whether there are more Catholics than Protestants holding office; whether the East Side is receiving its due consideration in comparison with the West Side; whether boys have the right to play ball in the streets, and lovers to spoon in parks, and whose conceptions of morals is to prevail—these, like the sins of the Psalmist, are ever before him." [3]

It is against this background that the duties imposed upon our rulers and the men placed in official positions must be considered. Money, the solvent of so many socially irreconcilable elements, is all the more necessary under a political system that puts a premium upon consent and unity. Many persons coming to a new community find themselves bereft of those familiar stabilizing influences that constitute the bulwark of morality. The problems of adjustment are particularly difficult for persons belonging to a different literary tradition or possessing no literary tradition at all. Carl Schurz developed in America standards of political morality growing out of his experience as a young man in Germany; he found a place in the New World for his Old World convictions. The Chinese laundryman, however, is in a different predicament.

Much of the apparent corruption in political life reflects not only different standards but likewise different intensities of moral consciousness. Morality in politics differs in intensity in the various strata of society. As Professor Ford has said: "One of the first things which practical experience teaches is that the political ideals which receive literary expression have a closely limited range." Ideals thus limited do not penetrate very deeply into the community. Since moral judgments are dependent upon a philosophical formulation, and since this habitually harks back to some common literary presentation, such as the Bible or the Koran, such codes have been affected by the limitations of human communication. The pulpit has been a common device for reaching the moral man; but the preacher without communicants is without influence. Our means of communication today could reach a world-wide audience, but the congregations have trended in opposite directions. Sectarianism has grown into a tendency toward reliance upon individual moral judgments. A code of pragmatic morality tends to meet more closely the needs of those divorced from a familiar religious or philosophic tradition.

A general codification of moral standards and the development of an elite charged with the custody and interpretation of these standards are rendered all the more difficult by characteristics of American public life already discussed. The conflicts that have disturbed society have grown out of different cultural backgrounds and moral standards. It has been possible to treat much of this behavior as deviations from a generally accepted code. Thus political corruption is rotten to the extent of its deviation from what is regarded as the normal soundness of the rest of society.

Considerable talk about political skulduggery is by no means an indication that corruption is widespread. The frame of mind signalized in the expression "every politician has his price" is an attitude fostered by a sensational press and fed by the garrulity of politicians themselves concerning the misdemeanors of their rivals. Moreover, the absence of censorship in a democracy makes it possible to discuss and magnify the shortcomings of public men. In the uncertainty about what is right and wrong in the political field, rival leaders find ample opportunity to slander their opponents in the promotion of their aims.

It does not follow that the task of those concerned with higher moral standards is any the less important because of the divergency of the traditions and interests already noted. Yet frequent and exaggerated charges of political corruption may induce a general callousness toward dishonesty. The goal of good government under a democracy is assumed to be that of developing a harmonious community. The goal is to be found not necessarily in the triumph of any one standard but rather in a peaceful integration of various interests in such a manner as to promote that of the whole.

Much moral and social legislation differs widely from the standards accepted by important groups in the community. Since the police are unable to enforce a law rigidly when it is widely disregarded, they must use discretion in selecting victims. This opens the door to favoritism and results in the purchase of protection by certain groups. A respect for law may depend upon selecting for legal scrutiny those aspects of social life that may be appropriately handled through the courts and the police. The sanction of moral suasion has often been passed over and statutory wish fulfillment embraced.

In discussing the causes of corruption a distinction should be made between that due to dishonest administration and that arising from social maladjustments or economic inequalities. Often corruption is simply a term applied to cover an unresolved relationship, the product of a misunderstanding between those holding to different goods and seeing different evils. There are blind spots in the moral vision of everyone just as there are different levels of morality, different intensities of interest, and different areas of attention. In practice public morality inevitably tends toward the common denominator that can be reconciled with the diversity of codes prevailing. In this sense the level of morality in public affairs is lower than that reflected by some groups and higher than that of others. Unless we are willing to turn over the conduct of public affairs to a social group that we assume to act in accordance with a more exalted conception of the public interest, we must be content with a form of behavior reflecting the current moral standard of the community.

We must discount efforts to explain machine control in terms of the ignorant voter, the foreign elements, or absence of the right people from politics. None of these explanations is satisfactory. Where intelligent and well-fed men unite, the ignorant and the poor have little chance. Political organizations utilize the foreign vote, the ignorant vote, as well as that of the pusillanimous; but these are common conditions of boss rule rather than the explanation. Political machines are found in country districts as well as in city slums, and among the native born as well as among the foreign-born. They persist in communities where the churches are strong and where a reform element now and again throws the rascals out. Louisiana bayous, Chicago stockyards, Pittsburgh precincts, the sidewalks of New York, and the village greens of Connecticut have all known boss rule.

Where connection with government is immediate, as in the very small New England town meetings, the machine is of less importance; but even there, if political problems grow complex, if government is far separated from the influential men of the community, a small group will come forward as intermediaries, organize a following, and seek rewards for their services.

Any community must have a structure of relationships to integrate and direct social life. Under very simple conditions family ties are sometimes sufficient, or a church may perform this function. More often an industry or other business group controls. Where such an interest basis is in harmony with the prevailing ideology, all goes well. On the other hand, interest conflicts, as between employer and employee, may lead to a struggle over the control of political institutions, and sometimes bitter ideological battles ensue. Where integration does not follow naturally from social institutions or traditional forces, unofficial political organizations arise to supplement the relatively ineffective official government. Where the diversity is great, the common denominator of political agreement must inevitably be low.

The machine flourishes where we fail frankly to meet through official channels community needs for direction and integration. Contrasting actual political behavior with absolute ethical standards usually leads either to moral indignation or to cynical tolerance. But it may also lead to the hypothesis that men persistently maintain a margin between their ethical hopes and their powers of attaining any such level. As observers of political activity, we have no reason to become dismayed at the cleavage between performance and aspiration. That such difference is persistently present is, however, a point to watch. Such aspirations may at times play a significant part in shaping institutions and human reactions. Our concern is with such ideological factors in their relations to the institutions and interests about which men cluster. That man acts one way and talks another is an interesting fact to be observed in our analysis rather than a kind of hypocrisy to be condemned.

The responsibility of the politician does not lie in the enforcement of consistency. It is not his task to persuade men that they should act in accordance with abstract doctrines. If the institutions of government fail to accord with the demands of effective power-units, the politician does not insist that institutional forms are more important than human desires. If we examine the behavior of politicians in terms of an abstract ethical code of clear right and wrong we inevitably conclude that many of them are arrant rogues. This is no discovery. Nor is it of much significance in itself. Only the most naïve would expect men in public life to be different from men in private life. The interesting point to ascertain is not how far the politician diverges from an absolute ethical standard but rather how closely he follows the prevailing rate of honesty and unselfishness.

A parallel may be drawn between the businessman and the politician. The latter is to public life what the entrepreneur is to industrial life. Politician and practical businessman are usually thought of as poles apart. They appear so when the businessman discusses politics in terms of his picture world of what should be: public affairs apparently are not to be met in the same way that private problems are faced. The politician by ignoring this fancy has scandalized the less tough-minded. Both businessman and politician try to please the public, however. They try to sell a service. They take social relations as they find them; their purpose is to earn a living. To seek one's fortune through economic channels is the traditional American way. Our admiration goes out to the man who makes good in business even though his methods may be ruthless and he may keep within the letter rather than the spirit of the law. The same admiration does not go to the man who makes a full-time job of politics in an effort to win power and wealth. As a matter of fact, a political career often offers greater opportunities for advancement to the poor boy than would a career in industry. As Max Ascoli has written, politics as a career is "open to the active among the young men springing up from the lower classes even in an era when cultural qualifications and social manners are required everywhere, and bureaucracy looms in every social and economic form." [4]

If the politician is analyzed in the same terms that might be applied to the businessman, his relative security and income compare unfavorably. The politician has a heavy overhead. The upkeep of a political organization is always a severe strain. The cost of advertisement and salesmanship is great. If his campaigning activities are thought of in these terms, the risk of his undertaking is even greater. His success depends almost entirely upon public favor and the quality of the goods offered is much less tangible than in business. He needs a quick return on his investment, since terms of office are short and re-election is uncertain.

The politician cannot be paid directly and fully for his services because of preconceptions concerning unselfish public service. The need for pecuniary rewards is discounted or disregarded. It is difficult to secure wealth and security in politics without running counter to moral conceptions. The consequence is that our political elite is recruited for the most part either from men who can temporarily accept economic sacrifice since they regard a political career as incidental to their major occupation or from men who are not restrained by general moral precepts from seeking economic gain in politics. Pecuniary gain in political life must come indirectly if the gainer would appear respectable.

The British have taken a more realistic view. They recognize that "even the strictly honorable want honors" and that public office must be made attractive. Office carries salary, prestige, and perquisites appealing to leading citizens. Take, for example, Sir John Simon's comment on his experience as Lord Mayor of Manchester:

"The universal respect and consideration with which the Lord Mayor is treated is part of what might almost be an organized conspiracy to destroy his judgment by turning his head. In his first week of office he presides over meetings of the twenty standing committees of the Council for the purpose of electing chairmen for the ensuing year, makes twenty speeches, and receives twenty votes of thanks! And the votes of thanks go on all through the year. He has a most comfortable flat in the Town Hall, with free service, a larger private suite for dinners, and he controls the great reception rooms. In fact, he almost regards the Town Hall as his private residence! He has an elaborately uniformed attendant who has nothing to do but hover around, call out in a stentorian voice, 'Make way for the Lord Mayor,' fill his glass with champagne, and in season and out of season address him as 'My Lord'! He can send for anybody in Manchester at any moment. Everybody is extraordinarily polite and friendly and helpful. And every word he utters is reported at length in the Press as if it meant something." [5]

In the United States such perquisites of office would be denounced as graft and such respect as undemocratic.

Meanwhile the politician has carried on with too much attention to winning his immediate objective and too little to the beliefs, ideals, and symbols of the community. The different standards applied to business and government immediately appear. Much activity condemned in politicians is condoned in the business world. George Washington Plunkitt, of Tammany Hall, stands out from the common run of politicians more for his frankness than for his morality:

"Supposin' it's a new bridge they're goin' to build. I get tipped off and I buy as much property as I can that has to be taken for approaches. I sell at my own price later on and drop some more money in the bank.

"Wouldn't you? It's just like lookin' ahead in Wall Street or in the coffee or cotton market. It's honest graft, and I'm lookin' for it every day in the year." [6]

Few people are still so naïve as to insist that public business is inevitably shot through with graft while private business operates on a much higher plane. Some may question the conclusion of Harold Zink that "Altogether it seems quite certain that city barons make their money fully as honestly as their compatriots in the business world. . . ." [7] Yet the abundant evidence concerning the behavior of some businessmen turned up by the La Follette Committee and the busy official life of the Federal Trade Commission persuade one to the view that the old parallel between the scruples of Boss Tweed and of Jay Gould still remains between their modern counterparts. The social effects of some of the methods of private business may be fully as bad as those of public corruption. As William Anderson said of the twenties: "The peculations in public business, national, state and local probably do not approach in volume one single form of business dishonesty—the sale of fraudulent stocks and bonds." [8] Political malpractices may be compared with price-fixing, black-listing, illegal monopoly, the sale of impure food and drugs, deceptive advertising, *et cetera*. The politician cannot be shown as white by painting the businessman black, but both can be seen as products of the same environment.

The function of the politician is essential to common living. The more social interdependence and governmental activity, the more his importance increases. Under the politics of democracy the adjuster frankly operates as such. He has enjoyed little prestige; he has been forced to depend for power largely upon his own skill as a manipulator. All rulers must in some measure, through under different guises, perform this same function. The Nazi cannot rely wholly on fear or nationalist fervor, nor the aristocrat on the prestige accorded his position. Both must also at times become politicians in order to rule effectively. The party system in the United States has produced many politicians who are fixers and manipulators and little else beside. While subjectively we are irked by the unprincipled or contraprincipled attitude of many politicians, it does not follow that the function of adjustment as such should also be condemned. It is, in fact, a vital element in the politics of democracy. We can always use more politicians. Seers and men of high vision there must be, but the workaday world calls for a frequent shift in focus. The politician is no stargazer. As F. S. Oliver has put it, "His eyes are not fixed on the millennium nor yet precisely on the end of his own nose but somewhere between the two." [9]

☆ 11 ☆

Looking Forward

"Suppose you've no direction in you,
I don't see but you must continue
To use the gift you do possess,
And sway with reason more or less."
ROBERT FROST

OUR politicians by the nature of their task seldom have the opportunity of seriously pondering long-range objectives. The question that party leaders must consider is not: How distinctive shall party policy be? Rather it is: How far can the program develop without alienating the present loyal interests? For example, a choice said to lie before the Democrats during the second Roosevelt administration was whether to supplant the G.O.P. by wooing business or to develop into a strong national liberal party. From the viewpoint of sectional strategy, this latter course has several weaknesses. A persistently left-wing tendency on the part of the Democrats might break up the Solid South. The South was not always solid: the political alignment between Democrats and Whigs was based on economic differences in that area. A liberal Democratic party would hold together the sharecroppers of the South and the debtors of the West. Such political strategy would place chief reliance upon the poorest elements of society and those living in the least populous regions. Some New Dealers urged the Democratic party high command to appeal to farm and labor organizations, to the urban consumer masses, and to the northern Negroes. The difficulty of working out a consistent program to appeal simultaneously to consumer and farmer and to trade unionist and Negro laborer is obvious, though the political strength in these groups is equally clear.

If the Democrats can solidify their strength in the populous states once the stronghold of Republicanism, can they hold the position once occupied by the G.O.P.? Political strength can be more readily consolidated by a policy that attracts the electoral votes of such great states as New York, Pennsylvania, and Massachusetts. For the Democratic party to maintain a militantly liberal policy based on the sectional strength of populous states would require an increase in class consciousness among the urban industrial wage earners. This class consciousness would have to be strong enough to change the complexion of the sectional citadels of capitalism. If labor can see its strength as clearly identified with Democratic control of the federal government as capital did with Republican dominance, and if labor consequently swings the electoral votes of the industrial Northeast to the Democratic party, we might then enter upon a period of Democratic supremacy comparable to that of the Republicans in the decades after the Civil War.

This line of argument, though often used, stresses the special interest aspect of party make-up almost to the exclusion of factors which we have urged as of equal importance. Major parties can profit by left-wing strength without going all the way to the left. The future of a party lies, as we have argued, in its skill at compromise, synthesis, and manipulation. Business would tend, as it has in the past, to swing to those in political power. Yet traditional loyalties may be sufficient to keep many businessmen Republican, even though the Democrats undertake the deliberate task of winning over segments of business. Neither party can afford to alienate either business or labor. Both interests must be increasingly considered, since within the last decade or so questions of economic readjustment have come to the forefront of politics.*

* Lindsay Rogers suggests that

". . . the great question is whether politics will be competent to provide a tolerable economic life. The size of the country, great natural resources, a small

Never were the problems more perplexing nor economists more perplexed. Some economists today argue that "a basic change has come over the structure of American economy." They insist that the

"underlying factors of growth upon which our economic life has depended in the past are no longer operative. The rate of population growth has slackened, the new techniques developed today in many cases involve less capital investment than the older methods which they are displacing, and the process of pushing back frontiers is now nearly complete. It is largely because of these and other similar basic changes in our national life [these economists argue], rather than because the New Deal was 'disturbing to business confidence,' that private industry was unable to continue the recovery movement when the stimulus of government spending had been withdrawn." [1]

We are told the country is faced with a profound change in trend: private enterprise, even at its best, is unable to absorb the whole of the savings the country accumulates, and in the absence of supporting measures by the government, the result will be a collapse of economic activity and a decline in the national income to poverty levels. Hence a planned economy is the only alternative short of fascism. Reputable economic opinion may be cited, however, which holds forth a less drastic prospect. Alvin H. Hansen, for example, points out that even under conditions of economic stagnation, a period of increase in the real income of labor can occur, and an increase in productivity as well; he suggests that we may look forward to a standard of living in

per capita public debt, relatively low taxation and a rising standard of living have combined to muffle the creaks and strains of the governmental system. Moreover, as in Great Britain down to the advent of the Labour party, the United States down to the advent of Mr. Roosevelt had escaped political cleavages on any matter (save slavery) that was fundamental. Even now in the United States the cleavage is not between parties. Indeed, it may conceivably force a realignment of parties. Publicists frequently point out that governmental institutions as we have them—parliaments and executives—were set up in an age when governments dealt with problems that were largely political. Now governments must deal with a host of economic problems." (Lindsay Rogers, "The American Presidential System," in *The Political Quarterly*, VIII, No. 4, 1937, p. 529.)

the next decade or two higher than any heretofore known in this country. Further, he does not envisage, as an inevitable consequence of government spending, the disappearance of private enterprise as it is currently known.[2]

Whatever the course of economic trends may be, political differences of opinion promise to become much deeper in the future. A questioning of the adequacy of the Constitution may lead to an alignment for and against change. To amend or to rewrite the Constitution would raise issues long dormant. So long as the Constitution was generally accepted and the federal government was expected to play a minor role, partisan differences related to relatively superficial problems. Suppose, however, that the chief magistrate should decline to be hampered by the separation of power and should insist upon acting in thoroughgoing fashion as the head of a national party bent upon making great changes through political action. Basic questions of power must then arise.

Such problems of institutional change are closely related to economic relationships. In response to demands for relief, social security, and similar aids the New Deal used political channels to seek a distribution of wealth unattainable through the economic system. This process of distribution must be treated not as a partisan doctrine but rather as the inevitable consequence of the functioning of popular government. Under democracy as known in this country until recent years, the interests of property have generally been the basis for policy. At the same time we have been able to enjoy a relatively high degree of freedom of thought and of action. No serious conflict appeared so long as economic objectives squared with both these values. Economic issues arise to be fought out increasingly in political terms, and politicians may find it indeed difficult to please all. Yet democracy must try in the future to reconcile our political ideas and institutions with the conflict of interests engendered by our economic situation.

To this end the most fundamental movement is that of increased state activity. This means more deliberate political control and management. According to Wesley Clair Mitchell:

"It is most unlikely that this trend toward national economic planning will rise steadily. Its course will be diversified by accelerations and retardations, perhaps by some vigorous reactions toward *laissez faire.* But the indications seem to me fairly clear that in the long run men will try increasingly to use the power and resources of their government to solve their economic problems even in those nations that escape social revolutions." [3]

This basic trend involves greater use of the political process, namely, more conscious adjustment of group interests, more planning, increased importance of the expert, more public and less private management of business. All this entails more discipline and control, more thinking in national and less in purely local terms.

In the face of all this, what will happen to capitalism and democracy? If we regard these concepts as static, the prospect is gloomy indeed. If the social values associated with these words are identified with fixed economic and political institutions, conflict or crack-up seems inevitable. Yet nothing is static unless our thinking makes it so. Capitalism and democracy growing up together have enormously enriched our lives materially and spiritually. Their contribution came from the capacity of capitalism to release and reward initiative, while democracy kept the ultimate power in the community fluid and responsive. In our thought, at least, capitalism and democracy have occupied separate areas. We have seen no reason why economic institutions should not be free to go as their leaders may direct.

Under the freedom provided by popular government, fields of technical competence developed. The liberal regime witnessed great advances in the fields of medicine, engineering and the sciences as well as a rapid development in industry. All of these fields had their own peculiar elite. The standards and values of these groups had no deliberate connection with each other or with the standards of democracy itself. In fact, success in most fields was achieved in terms of standards that contradicted the equalitarian assumptions of democracy. However, whenever private enterprise reached a scope where it could no longer be left under the control of its own elite, a conflict of jurisdictions appeared. Bankers, for example, feel that they have certain responsibilities to their clients. They do not necessarily agree with the opinions of their functions held by politicians, debtors, and other outside interests. When critics point to their lack of responsibility, bankers look to their own group loyalties and values.[4] To permit such group leaders to control alone their field of work would endanger the fluidity of relationships essential to the democratic process. In the past they have used political parties or governmental agencies as adjuncts in the administration of their own affairs. Today the balance is shifting as more and more the government assumes a positive responsibility for the continuous adjustment of individual and group relationships.

The trend is illustrated in current economic theory. Irrespective of our current notions about the role of the law of supply and demand as an underlying regulation of economic activity, we no longer believe, as many once did, that the untrammeled operation of these forces automatically distributes economic resources in strict accord with widely held notions of justice. Whereas in the past it was assumed that the law of supply and demand would enforce a salutary balance in society, now it is recognized that deliberate control and management must play a greater part—whether that control is exercised by private business or public authority. Prices, for example, are not entirely determined by bargaining in the market place but are set in advance by businessmen who consider many other factors than what the traffic will bear. They have learned how to manage the market. Demand can be created; supply can be regulated. Hansen has raised the question "whether political democracy can in the end survive the disappearance of the automatic price system."[5]

The answer to such questions will come in terms of our skills in administration, both public and private. Traditionally democracy has denoted such a distribution of power as has given private administrators great scope. Only where their managerial activities have brought severe repercussions on society have governmental managers taken over their function. Business enterprise has been responsible for most of the management and adjustment of individual relationships. The great economic inequalities resulting have militated against the welfare of certain groups. These have vehemently protested against the operation of "economic laws" that placed them in a highly unfavorable position in relation to other economic groups. Dissatisfied with the consequences of private management, they strive to set up a rival set of managers within the government itself.

Private affairs have grown so great that their social repercussions cannot be ignored. When private management has impinged upon public problems, the state has been forced to intervene. This is an old story. The East India Company, for example, became too involved with questions of national policy to remain under private control. Even when it was a private company in name, it was a governmental agency in fact, in that it controlled the actions of a huge bureaucracy and administered affairs in India. Now that the state itself is deeply concerned with problems of management, many of our current political issues arise from conflicts between two sets of managers —those responsible to stockholders and those employed by taxpayers. The dispute over government regulation of industry is a battle of these bureaucracies. Neither side can claim a monopoly of enterprise or initiative.

Now, in order to protect and foster the initiative of free enterprise, the government is frequently called upon to ease rigidities in industrial organization and to eliminate bottlenecks in distribution. More than this, the state is "going into business" in many lines.* When the government turns entrepreneur, democ-

* As Copeland has argued:

"In a reaction against state interference it is tempting to think of the entrepreneur as being the driving force in economic progress. In all countries, even in the United States, governmental or semi-governmental bodies plan and carry out a substantial proportion of new development. In Australia it is much more than 50 per cent, and in Great Britain it is about 50 per cent. Public investment accounts for half the total new development. In some European countries the proportion is higher, culminating in nearly the whole of investment in Russia being under the direct control of the state. This is highly significant. The state has devised administrative machinery with which, in an increasing range of industries and services, it can and does perform the functions of the entrepreneur.

racy must face unique problems. Through political and administrative devices it is attempting to reach decisions affecting the welfare of the whole society.

To the extent that democracy has meaning, individuals may choose the values that each regards as fundamental, with some idea of what the choice entails. Technology tempts us to draw up a new bill of economic privileges. The resulting economic problem, according to the analysis of Douglas Berry Copeland, "is one of reconciling the authority of the state with the free play of individual enterprise in a wide though diminishing field of industry." Speaking of the situation in 1936, he continues: "The early enthusiasm of the New Dealers has perhaps obscured the view of this fundamental problem. It is well to start a steep climb in low gear. You have been in high gear for three years, and you may feel the need of relief from machine-gun legislation." [6] The question of pace is thus seen to be critical. In the course of this movement we have periods where consolidation seems of more importance than change. Our disputes arise over how fast and how far we shall go. Predictions of conflict come largely from leftist intellectuals who forecast an intransigent opposition from rightists intent upon maintenance of the status quo. Such prophets may be correct. Only time can tell. I believe that they underestimate the capacity of democratic governments to meet the basic needs of their citizens.

Our politicians have shown themselves averse to gambling upon the long view. Party leaders find themselves in a difficult position: they wish to alienate neither business support as a source of revenue nor the numerical support of the great mass of voters. The public man is expected to use the resources of society to re-

---

This is perhaps the most striking change that has taken place in the economic system in the present century. It has been accompanied by the development of administrative machinery by the state and by an increasing emphasis upon the social responsibilities of the entrepreneur. The rise of the state as entrepreneur is a direct challenge to individual enterprise and its methods." (Douglas Berry Copeland, "The State and the Entrepreneur," in *Authority and the Individual*, Harvard Tercentenary Publications, Harvard University Press, 1937, pages 48–49.)

lieve distress. He hopes to postpone more distant contingencies so long as he achieves this in the short run. Our party leaders refuse to anticipate the future. Beard writes

"In his refusal to cross bridges before he gets to them, President Roosevelt obeys an old and realistic tradition in American politics. Lincoln never adopted the system of unconditional emancipation. He understood it, but did not commit himself to it. That slavery was highly objectionable to him all informed persons knew at the time, but he was elected President on an almost minimum program. His act of emancipation, when it came, was shaped by the exigencies of the hour, by circumstances not of his own choosing." [7]

If we grant that the logic of events points toward an extension of social responsibility and control, this trend may take quite different forms. The insurgent element has been gaining in strength and now finds a higher degree of recognition than ever before in both parties. But only of recent years has it been "good politics" to reckon with this element. We have discovered that much change can take place without a formal alignment of parties. In politics we stress the importance of getting our fellows to profess loyalty to ideas. In the minds of some persons interested in the labor movement, for instance, this seems to be more important than the gaining of tangible ends. The attention of most labor leaders has been focused upon finding ways for advancing the strength of their unions by gaining wage and hour concessions than in preaching loyalty to a conceptual picture of what kind of social order would be best in the future. Over a long period a new class basis may win general acceptance. In the meantime, if violence is to be avoided, compromise is inevitable.

The democratic process does not demand that men seek compromise, but it does require that they do not violently repudiate such halfway measures. For example, if we take what actually occurs in Congress, compromise appears the inescapable product of our system. Nothing would be more misleading than to regard this function of the political parties as a negative one. Compromise need not be sheer opportunism. Agreement may be established upon a new and higher common ground. The adjusting of human affairs can be accomplished only by dealing with one concrete situation as it impinges upon another. Our party system is significant not as a way of clarifying differences but as an institution for seeking broad terms of agreement.

☆ 12 ☆

Class Cleavage and Party Loyalties

> "—that problem, the labor question, beginning to open like a yawning gulf, rapidly widening every year—what prospect have we? We sail a dangerous sea of seething currents, cross and under-currents, vortices,—all so dark and untried."
>
> WALT WHITMAN

THE labor movement in the United States has not been led by men who think in terms of class struggle, nationalization of wealth, and the like. Labor leaders have focused on ways and means. The movement has need of all of its intelligence and skill to attain tangible gains for wage earners; it has conjured up no imaginary ideological battles, thereby creating unnecessary arguments and frightening men into two camps. In a world of uncertainties labor in the United States has paid scant heed to the soothsayer.

The politics of democracy provides a means of accepting labor as an emerging interest without disruptive effect. This transition depends in large part upon labor leaders playing the game of politics in a way that will enable the party politician to profit from labor support. To this end Labor's Non-Partisan League is well suited. Philip Taft has described the League as "an independent political party operating in the primaries instead of in the final election." [1] In various states the League is attempting to build its organization from the precincts upward. Its leaders believe that only through favorable governmental policy can the economic interests of labor be protected. Since public policy may shift away from the line desired by labor leaders, a strong organization is essential. Party politicians must remain convinced that supporting the League policy is good politics. The League likewise tries to get nominated men of strong labor sympathies. They recognize that the product of compromise is colored by the nature of the compromisers. On the other hand, League leaders are not attracted to independent political action for its own sake. They have worked for immediate and concrete advantages.* In view of the striking adjustments in employer-employee relations made within recent years, one need not assume that a distinctive militant organization will replace the present tactics of compromise.

Is any one class sufficiently large to serve as a base for a national party? If its leaders seek political power as a party, they will confront the old problem of party strategy in this country. To attain the necessary support they would have to appeal to farm and middle-class elements. The election of 1936 disclosed more than 29,000,000 voters supporting Franklin D. Roosevelt and more than 18,000,000 behind Alf M. Landon. Organized labor is not strong enough to succeed without a wide public support. The strength of union labor is estimated at about 7,500,000. How many of these union members are party workers or can be relied upon to vote as their unions dictate it is impossible to predict.

The immediate task of labor leaders is to promote unity among the wage earners themselves. Labor is divided by issues both economic and psychological. Before labor can be successfully organized and its purposes envisaged, many psychological factors must be taken into account. So long as the rags-to-riches philosophy is

* R. R. R. Brooks comes to this conclusion:

"The correct form of political organization . . . can be determined only by reference to the exact social and economic conditions of a period. If a labor party is to have mass support, its objectives cannot deviate far from the objectives and ideologies of the mass. But in generalizing its objectives sufficiently to capture the mass, a labor party surrenders much if not most of what is valuable in its own specific political program. Whether labor should make this surrender in order to enter the political field depends upon the exigencies of the situation." (Robert R. R. Brooks, *When Labor Organizes*, New York, Yale University Press, 1938, pages 298–299.)

accepted, a class-conscious labor movement is impossible. Whether the worker will retain this point of view in the course of economic development seems highly doubtful. The need of finding objectives peculiar to labor is essential. A labor party's success would depend on increased class consciousness. Thus far organized labor has been opportunistic and chiefly concerned with concrete gains. It seems remote that employees, any more than employers, will discover a wide area of common interests.

To align workers into a fighting union is one thing; to direct a national political party is another. The labor leader stresses grievances, emphasizes rights, and fights the employer with all the resources at his command. The welfare of the consumer does not have to be regarded. The labor leader's goal is to promote the welfare of the worker. This has been expressed usually in terms of shorter hours, higher wages, and better working conditions. As a politician the labor leader would find his task more complex. He would have to consider not simply the wage earner but other groups as well. He would have to make good his promises to labor and yet devise a working compromise with other interests. Sectional alignment would be as embarrassing to a labor party as it has been to party leaders in the past. Unionists as well as politicians would have to seek support from doubtful states in terms which would appeal to marginal voters within those areas.

At its present stage of development organized American labor needs fighting spokesmen and single-minded champions. How can such men work most effectively? They have greater scope if they remain outside political parties. This envisages not nonpartisanship but rather aggressive bargaining with the dominant political party. The methods of politics in the United States suggest a division of labor between the professional party man and the special interest representative. The latter fills the useful functions of organizing and clarifying the views of persons having definite but limited common interests.

The difference between the Congress of Industrial Organizations and the American Federation of Labor involves primarily the rivalry of two leaders and their respective followings and an issue of tactics. The A. F. of L. derives its strength chiefly from craft unions—skilled workers forming the aristocracy of labor. There are conflicts of interest between such wage earners and their less skilled fellows. Through industrial unionization, which characterizes the program of the C.I.O., emphasis is placed not upon differences of skill but upon the common interest of all who work in the same great industry. Since this approach stresses the common interest of workers without regard to craft differences, its foundations are stronger and its promise of unity for labor greater.

If we assume the importance of clarifying and unifying group interests, we must accept industrial unionization as well promoting such an end. By its very nature craft unionism can never embrace the whole of the working class; and for the C.I.O. to win complete control of the labor movement would require not only time but also basic changes in the attitudes of many skilled workers. It would entail repudiation of many labor union officials among the conservative unions. Granting that labor can reach agreement within its own ranks and that the increase in wages and the upturn of the business cycle have a stimulating rather than a contrary effect upon unionization, it does not follow that a distinct labor party could succeed politically without compromise as the price of victory.

In terms of more immediate probabilities, can our present party system adjust itself to laborers' and farmers' demands for permanent places at the council table? As already noted the strategy of American politics has been to discover a formula for bringing together sectional interests. Sectional interests were based on local economic differences, but now economic groups of national, even international, scope arise. The federal government is expected to act positively on behalf of such groups. It is not enough to grant concessions and then lapse into repose. National policy must face the continuing adjustment of economic conflicts. In Grover Cleveland's day the federal government might invoke military force to settle a strike. Now, however, the problem is recognized as more than a question of law and order. Adjustment rather than coercion wins public commendation.

That government must meet such questions in constructive

terms is recognized by leaders in both major parties. No leader can prosper on a platform of denial. It is obvious that labor has become more class-conscious with the growth of capitalism. It is evident also that wage earners are becoming aware of common political interests rooted in their economic status. In the United States we face the question of how individuals who regard themselves primarily as employees may best express this interest in politics. Similarly the farmers associate their economic welfare with their influence on government.

Both the labor and the farm movements have long histories. As minority movements they have in the past reacted sporadically and intensely against the status quo. The present situation, however, is novel. It has greater significance, owing not to the isolated violent protests of the movements but rather to their scope and their spirit of quiet conviction. Farmers and wage earners in representative numbers now expect political leaders to treat them as the peers of industry. Labor leaders have been more widely accorded a respectable status, and the spokesmen for agriculture are generally accepted as sober middle-class citizens. These minority movements have come of age. Industry is on the defensive. The politics of business is no longer the major business of politics. The president and Congress must make the welfare of labor and of agriculture their concern. We have at least a tripartite interest basis to political power.

In the past, politics was a squabble over an economic surplus. Wage earners and farmers accepted positions of secondary importance. Employers were willing to concede that governmental aid to business promoted the general welfare; but they were not so ready to admit that the general welfare demanded concessions to labor, agriculture, and consumers at the expense of the entrepreneur. Now wage earners, farmers, and professional and white-collar workers in both parties see possibilities of achieving, through governmental channels, ends which they deem good and which they failed to achieve under private enterprise.

Much of our present expectation of governmental aid and relief is only traditionalism expressed in novel terms. There is no great alteration in fundamental attitudes. We had a politics of the handout—free land, mining concessions, shipping subsidies, tariff, and so on. A survey of the nineteenth century reveals continual demands for grants and subsidies. The demands of the little fellows can no longer be met by homesteads and similar concessions. A broader distribution is now demanded. The process, however, involves few niceties of theory or philosophy; it appears as opportunism faintly flavored with humanitarianism. We do not find the ideological conflict which aroused passions so hotly in European countries. In the United States social problems have seldom been related to systematic philosophies, nor has public policy been guided by an abstract formulation of values. Leaders of discontent talk in terms of concrete needs. In spite of theoretical talk of change, the general attitude toward politics today follows a traditional pattern.*

We have not a new radicalism but a form of traditionalism given a new turn by the fact that government can no longer bestow economic goods from nature's bounty but must take from Peter to placate Paul. Criticism has been centered on the profit motive, but with little persuasiveness. Rather we hold individuals

---

* As M. J. Bonn notes:

"The monetary conceptions embodied in Father Coughlin's or Dr. Townsend's plan were but the corollary of the national land policy. As Uncle Sam owns the land, so he should own the money. And as he gave away the land to deserving homesteaders for practically nothing, he should offer them the cash for running their farms on similar terms, so that they need not pay interest to blood-sucking banks. The issue of unlimited fiduciary money was always the ideal of the frontier, which depended on an unlimited supply of free land. Since its exhaustion, the need for free money is even greater.

"This attitude of Uncle Sam was by no means unsympathetic to the business men. It enabled them to get their lumber, their coal, their oil and their silver from him—just for the asking. And he has given generous protection to their industries by a tariff, the fiscal need for which had to be artificially created by setting up a scandalously wasteful pensions system. The American business man's rugged individualism did not prevent him from using Government intervention for profitable inroads on other people's income; but it must be kept from meddling with his own property. . . . The exhaustion of free land put an end to those limitless opportunities which dangled before the eyes of the American people, and which had made them callous to the wastage involved in the opening up of the West. They had gone before the War, but the great boom had prevented the nation from realizing the change." (M. J. Bonn, "The Making of a National State," *The Political Quarterly*, London, Macmillan and Co., Ltd., III, 4, 1937, pages 589 and 592.)

responsible. We believe that the system itself is not to blame, and that leaders more representative of the people will put matters to rights. This is an oversimplification of a complex reaction, but the nondoctrinaire character of the response to present problems is generally observable.

Many theories as to what should be done are advanced, but those securing official sanction and widespread support are those which celebrate temporizing, moderate alterations. Although John L. Lewis is regarded by some people as a radical, he nonetheless talks the language of a traditional democrat. He assumes that our economy is one of plenty and that the people, if denied, have but to make their demands in sterner tones. Thus in the New York *Times* in August, 1936, he warned that

"when the people once become convinced that the economic and financial masters of America have no intention in logic or morality or reason to make reasonable concessions and accord fair treatment to those who make it possible for them to assemble that wealth, then it is a safe assumption that when the burden becomes too great and human agony reaches its limit, the people of the country will do something about it."

The record of the New Deal has been an effort "to save business from its worst faults," to preserve democracy and the existing order. Our accepted political institutions fortify this moderate policy. Noteworthy at this juncture is the relative unimportance of new creeds, ideas, or slogans based on a mental picture of society radically different from the one currently and widely entertained. This means that political power will seek expression not in the vindication of a new ideology but rather in the manipulation and rearrangement of group forces and the readaptation of old institutions.

The unresolved question is how these economic forces will interact politically. Our major parties are criticized as the "tools of corporate interests which use them impartially to serve their selfish purposes." It is upon these familiar lines that the necessity for reinstituting our party system has been urged so as to align political forces into two clearly distinguished camps.

Critics insist that our parties "stand for something," and by that something is meant either a definite legislative program or at least a set of principles. It is assumed that two distinctive parties are essential to the functioning of the American party system; the likeness between the Democratic and the Republican parties makes a new party essential, it was argued before the New Deal arrived. "An opposition party must arise," the League for Independent Political Action then asserted.

"The building of this new party will demand great sacrifice and probably years of labor, but it must be done. Critical constructive opposition is our greatest political need. Progress is always made by the conflict of ideas. Today in the United States there is no vital political party of opposition. Democrats in the election of 1928 revealed the fact that they have not one fundamental economic issue to distinguish them from Republicans." [2]

The arguments in favor of a party realignment are still heard. On the one hand, it is urged that parties should be based upon economic and class distinctions; on the other, that they should be founded upon a collection of issues generally denominated as liberal, progressive, socialist, and the like. Implicit in this view is a conception of the political party as an organization based primarily upon principles and concerned with policies. A disciplined party which "stands for something" is not impossible under our system of government. The Old Guard Republicans at the turn of the century and the Radical Republicans in the post Civil War years demonstrated how effectively a well-disciplined group may control our governmental institutions. One can imagine a party's developing, under provocation sufficiently great, through skillful use of propaganda and complete local organization, a unified following for a definite program.

Political adjustment can be effected through (a) a recombination and reshuffling of interest groups, (b) a change of existing personnel in control of an existing organization, and (c) changes in the party creed. Scrapping the old party names and loyalties is wasteful and is justified only when these symbols are a hindrance out of proportion to the strength they represent. A party realignment consists in the substitution of one oligarchy for another. A political party is not to be judged simply by what it says. As A. L. Rowse writes: "A party is at bottom a complex of group-interests; it may have also an historical tradition and a programme. And it is essential if one is to understand its policy and actions, to realize what classes its interests are bound up with and what precisely it represents in the community." [3]

The demand for party realignment may mark the failure of the oligarchy in command to move with the times; it may signal the outmoding of the party ideology, or indicate the rise of potent new interests demanding recognition. As we have noted, the Federalist leaders lost power when they failed to adjust themselves to changed conditions. If party leaders are intransigent, they will break up their own party and lay the ground for an entirely new organization. Parties must do the expedient thing in order to survive.

Yet there is always the possibility that entrenched organizations may prefer to resist change through violence, or that rising organizations, impatient at delay, may renounce persuasion for force. A strong pragmatic temper focusing political action on concrete and immediate problems seems the only way to avoid the dangerous extremism of left or right during a period of transition.

The policy of the Democratic party during the first Roosevelt administration brought about a realignment of economic interests. This meant that the policy of such organizations as the League for Independent Political Action became the program of the New Deal. The great potentialities of the policies advertised by left-wing organizations were realized in the experiments of the Roosevelt administration. A leader demonstrated that he could forestall a party realignment by changing the character of his own party.

Important political battles are fought within the political party. The essential question is whether the leaders controlling the party machinery will continue to have sufficient foresight to adjust to the times. This is not a prophecy that a party realignment will not occur. It is, of course, conceivable that shortsighted leadership and an uncompromising attitude on salient issues may result in the breakdown of our major parties as agencies of compromise. Yet once set in operation, the succeeding organizations would be called upon to take up the very burdens now borne by the major parties. No party realignment can dispose of the party as an agency for compromise under the politics of democracy. This procedure is based squarely on the thought that half a loaf is better than no bread.

Our parties are the exponents of the total social environment rather than of the viewpoints held by either reactionary or radical doctrinaires. When a competitive capitalistic order set the pattern of American life, the business of politics was to respond to the demands of this system. Now, since the social pattern is becoming marked by other emerging interests, it is the business of politics to reflect this change. If this is impossible, then clearly government by compromise and discussion cannot continue under our Constitution. The tactical problem is to discover for labor and agriculture the course that is most compatible with the politics of democracy.

☆ 13 ☆

The Significance of Third Party Activities

"They yelling mix tag, hide-and-seek, hop-
    scotch,
And leap frog in each other's way,—all's well.
Let newspapers profess to fear the worst!
Nothing's portentous, I am reassured."

ROBERT FROST

THE high-jinks of third party activities have called attention to new ideas to be examined for their future promise rather than feared as radical dangers. The rise of a third party to any position of influence would be a portent of serious rigidities in our political system. It would not indicate a movement to be frowned upon but would suggest rather that our party leaders had failed in their task of harmonizing and adjusting the economic and social forces of their communities.

The political awakening of the trade union movement in Great Britain to the need for a distinctive labor party arose from the intransigence of the existing political parties. The Labour party was the end product of a series of repressive acts. Not until the existing parties had clearly indicated a stubborn refusal to compromise with trade union leaders did the latter turn to independent political action. Through harsh experience the British workmen were driven to the conclusion that, as one editor expressed it, "the difference between Liberal and Tory is pretty much that between upper and nether millstone." The unfriendly attitude of the courts in the crippling Taff Vale decision and in the Osborne judgment, which prohibited trade unions from using their funds for political purposes, aroused the unions to fight, and the refusal of the existing parties to aid them forced independent action. The Webbs state: "It is not easy to sum up the whole effect of the legal assault upon Trade Unionism between 1901 and 1913. Politically, the result was to exasperate the active-minded workmen, and greatly to promote, though with some delay, the growth of an independent Labour Party in the House of Commons. . . ." [1]

If an independent labor party becomes established in this country it will be the product as much of the die-hards as of the radicals. British experience tells a story for all to hear. It was very largely the successive assaults on trade unionism itself that built up the Labour party; but the defeat of these assaults and achievement of the Trade Union Act of 1913 "did nothing to stay its progress." By contrast the flexibility of the American system in cushioning violent movements and gradually responding to labor's plea may be of the utmost significance. The conclusion seems warranted that a new party does not arise until the existing institutions have clearly proved their unreadiness to respond.

Minor parties in this country are essentially parties of belief and of class interest. They are also inevitable consequences of our party system. Yet so long as our major parties are controlled by shrewd and flexible politicians, minor parties will be unable to replace the existing parties.

Time and again groups of citizens have grown impatient with both major parties and have started third party movements. The system has appeared so unresponsive that ground swells of discontent have been virtually a secular movement in our political life. These efforts have been directed toward clarifying or even simplifying issues and aligning voters for the attainment of something more than office.

These third party movements give some indication of the degree to which the major parties have failed in responding to certain elements among the electorate. They call attention to maladjustments in the community. As Frederick E. Haynes states:

"The Greenback, Granger, Free Soil and Populist parties were the expression of repeated efforts on the part of the democratic citizens of the West to exert themselves against prevailing characteristics of the industrial and social development since the Civil War. . . . Their instincts opened their eyes to features in contemporary developments that were not discovered for many years by the people in the older parts of the country." [2]

A third party serves to show the strength of a point of view deemed too radical for the established parties but still demanding expression. By demonstrating a powerful support—a support strong enough to justify its being taken up by the established parties—the minor party has performed an important educational service. Inasmuch as it puts forward new ideas and stirs up the major parties, a third party is significant. It makes a mistake in trying to meet the major parties on their own ground, however. The major parties are conscious of their own limitations; the minor parties as a rule are not. The leaders of the minor parties have frequently been enthusiasts and crusaders—frequently out to convert the world to their point of view.

As formulators of issues minor parties have been in advance of the major parties. The Free Soil party, the Populists, and the Progressives developed issues later acted upon by one of the major parties. "It is a truism of American political history," says Haynes, "that minor parties ultimately write the platforms for all parties. . . . Looked at from the social point of view the chief function of third parties has been to bring new policies before the people: they force new policies upon the old parties and after accomplishing their work they pass away." [3] These statements bear the earmarks of *post hoc ergo propter hoc*.

As third parties have at times advocated ideas that have subsequently been accepted as generally sound, they have likewise made propositions now happily forgotten. For example, the Social Labor platform for 1892 advocated "the abolition of the presidency, the vice-presidency and the senate of the United States." [4] When, if ever, the rest of the country catches up with this proposal it may be that third parties will no longer be a problem.

The issues raised by the Anti-Masonic party and the Know Nothing party brought to the fore questions that were better ignored. These parties reflected forces that are still present in American politics; but they demonstrated at an early date the inexpediency of institutionalizing prejudice.

The techniques of the Prohibition party suggest that our minor parties have been swayed by expediency. The Prohibition party has been torn between adherence to its major issues and advocacy of an assortment of extraneous planks of a moralistic or economic character. The Prohibitionists found that they lost more through factional disagreement on points other than Prohibition than they gained through widening their appeal.

Most of our minor parties in recent decades have inclined strongly to the devil theory of history. Theirs is a nigger-in-the-woodpile politics. Plutocracy, they insist, is the cause of all evil. Their party platforms reiterate that "the dominant parties are arrayed against the people and are the abject tools of the corporate monopolies" (Greenback national platform, 1884), that "plutocracy has been enthroned upon the ruins of democracy" (People's platform, 1896), and that the old parties "have become the tools of corporate interests impartially to serve their selfish interests" (Progressive platform, 1924). The Farmer-Labor platform in 1912 stated that "wealth is monopolized by the few and people are kept in poverty." "The party promises to do righteous battle," it continued, "for democracy against its despoilers." The Independent platform of 1908 announced, "Our action is based upon a determination to wrest the conduct of affairs from the hands of selfish interests, political tricksters and corrupt politicians and to make the government an agency for the common good." The persistence of this viewpoint stresses the fact that although minor parties come and go a consistent attitude distinguishes their protests. They are aspects of a continuous rebellion against the empire of big business. Strangely enough, they are bred in prosperity as well as in depression.

Where third parties have discovered more ample support this has usually been sectional. "Let one section begin to feel that its interests are being permanently discriminated against by both old parties," says John D. Hicks, "and the time for a plain-spoken third party, organized mainly along sectional lines is ripe." [5]

The Locofocos centered in New England; the Anti-Masons in New York, Pennsylvania, and Vermont; the Free Soil party in the North; and the Greenback, Granger, and Populist parties in the West. A third party has been most successful where it has limited itself to the needs and desires of a given area. In such situations, it has provided one means of expression for voters dissatisfied with the major parties. Minor parties have relieved local tension and in such localities have had a salutary effect upon entrenched political interests. From the national point of view they have drawn off those forces threatening disruption to the major parties.

The minor party is by no means the only, and hardly the most effective, way of promoting an issue. Propaganda is necessary to convert public opinion to a favorable attitude, but the third party is not the most auspicious channel.

Predominantly agrarian and debtor, these movements have sought simple and direct expression. In trying to contest presidential elections with national parties, they have been foredoomed to failure. Our decentralized government makes it necessary for political parties to establish themselves locally before trying to bridge the gap between state and national jurisdictions. The system of electing our legislature by a plurality vote in single-member districts makes it difficult for minority groups to secure representation. Statutory requirements that parties have a certain minimum number of supporters, moreover, make it impossible for many minor parties to get on the ballot. Our system of government itself condemns the third party to a position of unimportance.

Minor parties in France may secure a cabinet portfolio in exchange for their support to the ministry in power. A third party in Great Britain may co-operate in the formation of a coalition government. In this country, however, a third party leader must usually remain an agitator. No regular way whereby he may enter into the governmental process is provided. A bloc in Congress may be organized without establishing a party; but even if a third party controls a bloc of votes in Congress the most it can hope for is an occasional opportunity to affect the balance of power. Furthermore the control of procedure in Congress by the dominant political party offers little opportunity for minor party representatives to exert any influence. They are placed at a grave disadvantage when it comes to influencing congressional committee action, and they have no way of participating in the election of the party leaders who, in turn, control procedure. The stability of the chief executive is not dependent on a coalition of parties. In fact the character of the chief magistracy is the greatest obstacle to a multi-party system. So great is the prestige of this office that no party can hope to attain wide popular support if it has no chance of sending its candidate to the White House.

When third parties enter national contests they are forced to fight for power rather than for principles. Their raison d'être lies in the vindication of a viewpoint or of a specific program. They tend to be doctrinaire; they are tempted to enter into the bargaining and the adjusting that are the essence of politics. If they refrain they are thrown back upon criticism and theorizing rather than seeking to create through legislation appropriate administrative devices for achieving their ends. The minor party, as one writer says of the Socialist party, "has the unique if somewhat gloomy prospect of being always a bridesmaid but never a bride in the matter of national policy. It is dead right about the fact that a marriage is taking place but it is never found in the double-bed of practical politics on election night." [6]

As regards political strategy, minor parties show many weaknesses. In attempting to win members from the major parties, they encounter those traditional irrational allegiances which are such a potent factor in American politics. The Populists, for example, met great difficulty in the South because a split in the Democratic party endangered control of local offices and raised the race issue. As one southern editor stated:

"The Democratic Party of the South is something more than a mere political organization striving to enforce an administrative policy. It is a white man's party, organized to maintain white supremacy and prevent a repetition of the destructive rule of ignorant negroes and unscrupulous whites. . . . The safety of the South . . . as well as the conservation of free institutions on these shores depends upon the strength, unity and perpetuity of the Democratic Party." [7]

Our major parties have adjusted themselves to the peculiar economic and social conditions of the country.

The appeal of minor parties must be more specific than that of the established parties. Positive propositions of a radical sort are their chief appeal. They have generally urged a very liberal interpretation of the Constitution ignoring the fact that proposed alterations of basic institutions, whether legislative or economic, do not make an appropriate partisan appeal. For example, to amend the Constitution would require such large majorities that no one party could well hope to muster sufficient support except in most unusual circumstances.

In view of the great diversity of sectional and economic interests in the United States, it is not surprising that third parties have flourished. Since 1872 there have been on the average six to eight parties with presidential candidates in the field. Yet in this period minor party candidates received electoral votes in only three presidential elections (1896, 1912, 1924). The Socialist party has perhaps been the most significant minor party since 1900. Its 1932 platform has on most counts been reflected in New Deal legislation. Yet no parallel can be drawn between its acceptance of such proposals and the popular support of the party. In 1900 Eugene V. Debs received .7 per cent of the total popular vote; in 1912 he received 6 per cent; in 1928 the vote for Norman Thomas was again .7 per cent. No progressive accretion of support is discernible behind our third parties. Their support fluctuates in accordance with current problems. The successes of the Bull Moose movement in 1912 and of La Follette in 1924 were mass protests rather than manifestations of institutional growth. Movements of protest, however, are not to be judged solely in terms of their strength at the national level.

Where solidly founded in their localities, third parties have been strong and effective over long periods of time. The story of the Farmer-Labor party in Minnesota is an excellent illustration. This party is an expression of its cultural, social, and economic environment. Its roots run back into the trade unions and the farmers' co-operatives of the state. It is an idea organization, but its interest-group basis is clear. In practice, however, its socialist creed has proved to be something of an embarrassment. As one friendly observer states:

"a party of this kind, based on trade unions and farmers' cooperatives, is by its nature dedicated implicitly to the task of making the conditions of collective bargaining favorable and farm prices reasonable, and this task implies that of making industry prosperous, since prosperous industry is more able and likely to concede wage demands and better working conditions than is depressed industry. And such an implication is of course exactly counter to the pursuit of any sort of socialist policy, for capitalist prosperity requires that the capitalists have confidence in government and its purposes." [8]

Since this party has never had full control of the state government, it has escaped the difficulty of trying to realize its complete program. It has used its influence on behalf of labor and agriculture by working toward concrete gains for the workers and farmers of the state. Its members have felt a close loyalty to an organization that they regard as their very own. They have not treated their socialist goals as immediate objectives. The Farmer-Labor party has not been able to spread into other states where different conditions hold, however. It does not follow that this is impossible; it is enough to record the fact that our most vigorous and long-lived third parties have had their being in states where they have reflected the local background. Thus the significance of the La Follette family must be sought in the "Wisconsin Movement." For all the talent and vigor of this remarkable political family, they have not succeeded in finding through the channel of a third party a national market for their wares. On the other hand, the influence of the La Follettes' viewpoint has not been limited by the ineffectiveness of third party movements.

Third parties in this country today have little of the structural strength of our major parties. They serve as promotional agencies for minority viewpoints. The third party fights where the pressure group bargains. Minor parties must remain on the outside; pressure groups on the other hand may hope to get on the inside and influence party policy. Through their lobbying activities they can participate in the task of adjusting conflicting interests and of constructing administrative devices for management. To be effective any group must participate in the process of management itself. The third party, however, is not a device well suited to achieve this end. Our minor parties are primarily concerned not with adjusting conflicts but rather with advertising a program. This may be attractive in itself, but it is seldom politically feasible. Although the New Deal brought forward objectives long sponsored by third parties, its chief task was to construct forms of management. Only in such terms can government become effective.

Since major party politicians are not bound by party discipline to follow a definite program, they have much freedom to bargain with interest groups. In this sense the fact that our major parties stand for so little makes minor parties all the more unnecessary. Through the formation of blocs in Congress sections and states win concessions from party leaders. Special interest organizations control votes that may affect the political life of Democrats or Republicans.

Once protest becomes institutionalized in a minor party, bargaining power with the major parties is weakened. Minor party candidates confront those of the major parties. This is seldom a battle of David and Goliath. The Townsend plan could not be ignored by politicians especially in the far western states, so long as it remained uncommitted to either party. As a pressure group, the movement was a force that might shift for or against the Democratic or Republican candidates. The Townsendite leaders went into primary contests seeking the nomination of men committed to their scheme. A victory challenging national attention occurred in the Third Michigan District, where the Townsendite [9] candidate defeated four rivals in the Republican primary by a two-to-one plurality. The district was traditionally Republican, and the party leaders dared not repudiate the nominee. Accordingly party leaders in the state, by contradictory statements on the Townsend plan, sufficiently beclouded the issue to divorce Republican support of the candidate from the program upon which he had won the primary. Thus the Republican State Committee denounced the Townsend plan but supported the nominee who had won on that issue. They rallied behind him as a Republican, not as a Townsendite. A third party candidate could not have caused so much concern.

During the 1936 campaign there was talk of a Union Party to bring together the Townsendites, Father Charles E. Coughlin's followers in the National Union for Social Justice, the vestige of the late Huey Long's Share-the-wealth movement, and Representative William Lemke's former Non-Partisan League members and radical farmers from the plains states. These groups soon found their leaders in disagreement. No internal basis for harmony existed except discontent with economic conditions. This President Roosevelt was able to turn to his own use through WPA and farm relief measures. Union party strength dwindled, and the old story of disarming third party strength by concessions from a major party was repeated.

Why cannot there be more direction and less confusion in our political life? Surveying the history of our parties, we find discord among their members and frequent evasion in their platforms. Our parties have generally side-stepped the issues that have divided the nation most deeply. Time and again the parties have failed to offer a significant choice. The exceptions are striking. William Jennings Bryan tried to give the Democratic party new content and emphasis. Woodrow Wilson offered a leadership for men of principles. Theodore Roosevelt and Franklin D. Roosevelt stand at the high points of their respective periods. The interesting question is how such tendencies came to fruition. We know that such periods of relative clarity and direction are few. The normal course of party activity is marked by confusion, internal dissension, and working at cross purposes. Such was the period from 1876 to 1896 and from the Harding administration through the days of Hoover. Bryan came forth in 1896 as the culmination of an accumulation of dissatisfactions, just as Theodore Roosevelt and Woodrow Wilson were a later and stronger expression of similar forces. The New Deal is an old alliance more widely supported and more ably directed.

Third party leaders are ready to face urgent problems in radical fashion. By their courage (or rashness) the support for a new point of view may be discovered. Third parties likewise tend to prevent the atrophy of our major parties by disclosing fresh sources for political strength. Fundamentally, however, third parties have a focus very different from that of the major parties. The former seek to stand for a definite program or interest. They try to be definite and forthright. This is not the way to gain majorities except perhaps in crisis situations, however. The major parties are dominated by their essential purpose—seeking majorities. They must pay the price that this entails. Leaders may at times inspire their followers with a broader vision, but the nature of this following ultimately colors the pennants of the standard-bearer. A dull and neutral shade is the inevitable consequence of mixing many clashing colors. Walter Lippmann illustrated this paradox years ago by pointing to what happened to Theodore Roosevelt in 1912 between the June Republican convention, which he bolted, and his Progressive Party convention the following August.

"As soon as Roosevelt had thrown off the burden of preserving a false harmony among irreconcilable Republicans, he issued a platform full of definiteness and square dealing with many issues. He was talking to a minority party. Roosevelt's genius was not that of group leadership. He longed for majorities. He set out to make the campaign a battle between the Progressives and the Democrats—the old discredited Republicans fell back into a rather dead conservative minority. No sooner did Roosevelt take the stump than the paradox loomed up before him. His speeches began to turn on platitudes—on his vague idealism and indisputable moralities of the Decalogue and the Sermon on the Mount. The fearlessness of the Chicago confession was melted down into a featureless alloy." [10]

In democratic politics we are bound to accept the validity of Emerson's dictum: men descend to meet. While one may deplore the fall from forward-looking programs, the effort to find a general meeting ground remains of transcendant importance. If third parties serve to make the public more critical of the programs of the majority parties, they have served a useful purpose. The narrowly based minor parties cannot, however, be a substitute for the broader and less articulate major parties. For all their avoidance of controversial issues, our major parties retain a meaning more fundamental than that drawn from specific promises on current issues. Henry Steele Commager, looking at our party system with the perspective of an historian, states:

"We have escaped, in this country, the strife which seems to result from parties which represent particular sections, particular classes, particular interests. We have not, as yet, a real labor party, a farmers' party, a business party, a party of the employed or of the unemployed, a party of the East or the West, the North or the South. We have but two major parties, and both represent cross-sections of American life. The experience of most European nations would indicate that this is a healthy situation." [11]

☆ 14 ☆

Left! Right! Left! Right!

"The last step taken found your heft
  Decidedly upon the left.
  One more would throw you on the right.
  Another still—you see your plight.
  You call this thinking, but it's walking."
                                    ROBERT FROST

TO survive in our dynamic society, parties must try to anticipate the broadest interest alignments of the nation. Their highest function is to readjust existing forces into more effective patterns for action. Parties do not contest with each other on basic questions of policy. Their real gamble is with the future. The fate of the party is determined by the skill with which it adjusts and coalesces these emergent economic and social forces. Hence our party system as a whole tends to go toward the left or toward the right. This is the characteristic pedestrian pace of democratic government. It distresses those who desire a system offering clear objectives.

We shall probably continue to demand parties based on principle or even on a class basis. The outcome will not be determined by such exhortations, however. The desire for clear-cut parties of principle probably has a foundation in the human desire to see an institution that reaffirms the individual's beliefs. The desire may not be unlike the human attitudes that support our churches. Where the practical consequences are not so great we seem better able to afford the luxury of fine theological distinction. The inevitable result is sectarianism. However, the immediacy of political goals and the pragmatic approach of the politician are factors militating against particularism in the political realm. Nevertheless, we must reckon with the aspirations for more meaningful parties as a persistent phenomenon.

"It puzzles me," Heywood Broun wrote in June, 1938, "that sincere conservatives should be so irate at any suggestion of a purge. We ought to have a liberal and a conservative party. The Virginia Reel has gone on so long that we are all mixed up. Let somebody blow a whistle and say choose your partners." [1]

This same point is made even more directly by Denis Brogan, who insists that in our party politics "the sections of the population who believe in giving the rich their head, should be on one side and those who disagree on the other." [2] To talk in these terms is to reveal a desire to put the "rich" out on a limb. Under institutions popularly controlled no party could afford to be jockeyed into such a position. Regardless of the cliques controlling them, both major parties must strive to appear as parties of the people. The confusion of American politics cannot be reduced to an alignment between liberal and conservative parties. No political party in this country can afford to be avowedly conservative unless the general climate of opinion favors a "return to normalcy." It is the liberals who want a conservative-liberal alignment, with all persons of progressive tendencies on their side. Such leaders strive to attract under their banner all those likely to support views more radical than the policies of the established party. But no party can corner the market on new and attractive ideas. Our parties must go with the current of opinion.

Our party system as a whole responds, though one party reacts faster than the other. Woodrow Wilson and Charles Evans Hughes were both hailed as liberals in 1916. James M. Cox and Warren G. Harding were colorless candidates from the same state. John W. Davis and Calvin Coolidge reflected a conservative viewpoint. Alfred Landon and F. D. Roosevelt vied in showing how to be liberal and conservative at the same time. No realistic politician is going to let any group of other politicians reap the whole harvest of a nation-wide swing to either left or right.

There is a strong tendency for both parties to take the same stand. Once a winning program is discovered, it is equally attractive to both parties. This is well illustrated by the appeal of Senator Arthur Vandenberg during the high tide of Democratic party success. He urged a liberalization of Republican party policy through support of unemployment insurance, retirement pensions, and minimum wage laws. He declared that "true and traditional Republican liberalism should save the country from the false liberalism of the Democratic party." He concluded with the thought that "as Lincoln said, we must 'lean upon the heart of the great mass of the people, satisfied to be moved by its mighty pulsations.'" [3] Republicans will not let Democrats have a monopoly of farmers, workers, and the middle class. Democrats are divided about the wisdom of alienating business. What is good for one party is also good for the other, the differences lying chiefly in matters of personnel, emphasis, and tempo rather than substance. The rivalry really comes down to who is going to manage the rearrangement and fix the terms.

Argument concerning a conservative-liberal alignment is generally nothing more than a battle of words, with neither side ready to champion outright conservatism. Reading the die-hards out of the party is an effective after-dinner motif for Jackson Day celebrations but hardly an analysis of what can be. When he used this argument, President Roosevelt was engaging in the game of politics and arguing for wider acceptance of his authority. What if our two parties do at times resemble Tweedledum and Tweedledee? The pacific relations between these two would-be warriors offer an example that is not without point in an age where there is more than enough conflict.

If we take the simple picture of conservatives as stand-patters and liberals as forgers-ahead, governments alternating between these extremes would seem hardly practicable. One party cannot afford to look to the past and the other to the future; one cannot openly represent entrenched wealth and the other the people. At the pain of death both parties must respond to the major current of the time. In the swing of the political pendulum both parties must be in accord with the underlying secular trend. Political parties have little to do with shaping these secular trends. Not by discussion are such conditions established. A conservative-liberal alignment is futile if this means that one party is to buck the basic trend while the other rides upon it. The conservatism of the Federalist party was suicidal. The conservatism of the Democratic party in 1850 brought homicidal consequences. There are many indications that the Republicans today are reading a lesson from history. Certainly many Republican leaders are matching the Democrats, promise for promise.

In an open letter to the Republican national committee, Governor George D. Aiken of Vermont urged that the party "accept in general the social aims which the opposing party has had the wisdom to adopt, but has lacked the ability to put into efficient operation." He demanded the purging of reactionary elements from the Republican party and the preparation of an affirmative program.

A further indication of the fact that no major party can ignore the symbols of "liberalism" is to be found in the American Institute of Public Opinion poll. A cross section of the people who supported Landon in 1936 were asked this question in 1938: "Would you like to see the Republican Party be more liberal or more conservative than it was in the presidential campaign of 1936?" The replies were as follows: more liberal, 56 per cent; more conservative, 15 per cent; about the same, 29 per cent. In commenting on these findings, Dr. George Gallup, director of the poll, stated:

"Many staunch Republicans have felt that the G.O.P. should become the conservative party in American politics, drawing a sharp line of distinction between itself and the Democrats so that the voters would have a clear choice between two points of view. But the survey vote indicates that this tactic is not at the present time popular with the G.O.P. rank and file. The reasons appear from the many hundreds of comments given by Republican voters in the poll. Typical is the sentiment expressed by a Republican civil engineer in West Virginia: 'The Republicans have to be more liberal if they ever expect to be revived. Reactionaries in the party have killed it.' Another comment typical of many was that of a New Jersey grocery store owner: 'The trend today is toward liberalism. The Republicans must go that way in order to be elected. It's their only chance of winning.' " [4]

The Gallup polls indicated a cleavage within the Democratic party of 72 per cent liberal and 28 per cent conservative.

I do not wish to underrate the value of the conservative-liberal concept as a convenient means of distinguishing political attitudes. On many specific issues the attitudes of individuals may readily be charted in terms of the degree of change that each is ready to advocate. To the duality previously offered between synthesis and dynamics, integration and revolution, consolidation and renovation, may be added conservative and liberal.

Underlying the discontent with the present party alignment is a question of the utmost importance. While I do not think that a conservative-liberal alignment offers a solution, the criticism is symptomatic of a fundamental problem. A dispute concerning the place of government in our society is under way. This finds expression in a conflict between leaders in the realm of private enterprise and those in public office. With an influential group in government antagonistic to business leadership, a conflict of wills is precipitated. This has been rationalized into a class conflict by some writers, or into a struggle between the champions of the people and the spokesmen of wealth, or a fight between champions of "the American way of life" and "a bunch of radicals." As an hypothesis, I suggest that our political differences are not to be explained in these terms, but rather that men tend to approach reality in two different ways. Some judge by their own limited experience and the evidence of specific observation; others take a more abstract and imaginative view. The first we might call pragmatists and the latter idealists or, better, "conceptualists."

The Communist party as of 1936, for example, approached problems in broad conceptual terms. The party would build up a "united peoples' front," win over 40,000,000 workers to a farmer-labor ticket, and sweep to victory. The eight-point program adopted by acclamation promised to put America back to work by providing jobs and a living wage for all; provide unemployment insurance, old-age pensions, and social security for all; save the young generation by providing educational and occupational opportunities for them; free the farmers from debts, unbearable tax burdens, and foreclosures by guaranteeing the land to those who till the soil; levy sharply graduated taxation upon incomes in excess of $5,000 a year; defend and extend democratic rights and civil liberties by curtailment of the power of the Supreme Court; obtain full and equal rights for the Negro people, and keep America out of war by keeping war out of the world.

Most men would agree with such objectives if they thought they could be realized in practice. A psychologist, G. W. Hartman, has discovered experimentally that "the parties which are committed to the establishment of a 'collectivist' society and the 'economy of abundance' (which the bulk of the voters evidently want when the details of such a program are presented) are the very ones to whose names an attitude of hostility or indifference is most marked." He concludes that "evidently, most of these voters want the specific things for which socialism stands, but they do not want to have them labelled that way." [5] The profound skepticism that men feel toward such party programs arises from their sense of the practical difficulties of actual administration. To the extent that men gamble on the validity of an elaborate scheme for change they must proportionately reduce their faith in things as they are.

A good example of conceptualist thought in politics in contrast to the pragmatic approach is offered by the Industrial Expansion Bill. This offers a plan for increasing industrial output by setting quotas, guaranteeing prices, and removing any surplus from the market. "This measure is designed," its proponents state, "to effect greater consumption of goods and services by providing the necessary purchasing power through productive employment at living wages of those now disemployed." [6]

The plan offers objectives of strong appeal. The bill, moreover, is being defended by skillful economists. Yet by the very scope of the problem, it must meet its full implications in administrative and political terms which are foreseeable. While many may refuse to support a scheme so far-reaching and unpredictable in practice this cannot be used as an argument against efforts at planning and constructive thinking. When men are faced with unpleasant conditions they construct a better world in imagination and seek from others support for their vision. In general we might say that some men are more often moved to action by these broad concepts, while others base their judgments upon particular concrete examples. Thus some men judge the WPA by the workmen they see resting on their shovels, while others are more impressed with the declaration of national policy that work must be provided for the unemployed. Perhaps the really significant difference in political viewpoint lies between those who think in terms of broad pictures of what should be and those who judge reality by the concrete, albeit limited, aspects that fall under their immediate observation.

Does thinking in those various terms have any bearing on political party alignments? I should hesitate to make any identification between such attitudes and parties in this country. Yet speculation is tempting. Do men of conservative temper tend to be more matter-of-fact and less concerned with voicing belief in broad general principles? Have they a keener sense of immediacy? Wilhelm Dibelius contends that this is true of the Conservatives in British politics:

"They have possessed the longer view of what is politically possible, the greater art in the management of men, and a capacity, impeded by no theorizings, of learning from their Liberal adversaries. Always the Liberals have had greater plenitude of political ideas, the Conservatives a greater art in directing the State. Further, the Conservatives are an intimate touch with the things that every Englishman in his heart of hearts adores, with the court, the Church and the nobility; hence, however often and for however long they are driven into opposition, they are, in the long run, politically the strongest element and the one that tends to attract the strongest political heads." [7]

A parallel between Dibelius's view of the British Conservative party and certain phases of Republican party leadership may occur to some readers. Certainly the New Deal has been distinguished by its "greater plenitude of political ideas," and its failures have been largely in the administrative realization. For party government to operate successfully, however, both sides must attract men of imagination and men of executive ability.

Why is the conceptualist approach so strong today? Many tendencies of our society so narrow the range of personal experience that men are forced into seeking a wider range, even if in imagination. Abstract thinking comes to the aid of limited observation in order to round out the picture of individual relationships. Thus the farmer today soon finds that factors far beyond his direct experience determine the price of his product. The industrial worker standing beside the assembly line must seek wider horizons if he is to explain to himself his own life. Unionization offers a means. When the businessman finds himself in a world of commerce in which his points of reference are obscured, he seeks comfort in what scraps of classical economic theory he can recall. In all three spheres the tests that can be made by actual experience are limited. Concrete experience is so circumscribed that abstract concepts are embraced.

Bookish men, however, rather than the men of action, find abstractions congenial. Empirical evidence points to a close connection between this bookishness and liberal political views. Thus Gardner Murphy and Rensis Likert found a rather high correlation between college scholarship and radicalism in tests that they conducted.

"The reason for this correlation may lie [they think] either (a) in a factor of general bookishness, i.e., respect for the printed page, which exposes one to radical trends in contemporary literature at the same time that it expresses itself through scholarly habits of mind, or (b) in a general serious-mindedness which makes one analyze the social scene critically at the same time that it makes one devote oneself to one's college work. Quite possibly these two explanations are not mutually exclusive." [8]

These investigators discovered also that the more radical-minded students expressed a preference for courses emphasizing wide reading as against those emphasizing laboratory work, mathematical calculation, or acquisition of practical skills. The difference is between "how to get things done" and "what should be." Both questions demand intelligence, but the first question means considering the specific and the second the general.

A political party holding power over a protracted period inevitably attracts to itself the loyalty of men who have a stake in the maintenance of the status quo and also those concerned with the practical task of how to get things done. To this extent such party adherents tend to react against changes that might disturb their position or interfere with their administrative work. They prefer to bear with evils they know rather than to change conditions and thereby perhaps meet with novel evils. To this extent their attitude is pragmatic. Its very simplicity confuses men of more doctrinaire minds. When business conditions are bad, businessmen want relief. When business improves, they want to be left alone. They are not guided by a clear philosophy of what should be; liberals accuse them of being inconsistent.

These critics call for a rational explanation of such apparent vacillations, and they receive a response in clichés. The negative character of the response wins the epithet "reactionary." The practitioner, lacking faith in mental pictures of what should be and challenged to present an alternative picture, is at a disadvantage. His genius does not lie in this direction. Lacking faith in what for him is the unpredictable future, he harks back to a picture of the past. Left to himself, he would not bother about abstract conceptions of reality whether past or future. Goaded into conceptual thinking, he places his faith in traditional values as reflected in established concepts which may appear to the liberal as infinitely less realistic than his own Utopias.

In 1938 many Republicans felt that they must project a program. It went contrary to their habits of thought to think in terms of Utopias. This habit of mind comes more easily to liberal leaders. Yet as an opposition party the Republicans felt the need for a picture of what should be. They hired a skilled worker in language, Glenn Frank, to tackle their problem. Many Republicans of conservative temper had little sympathy either for the search for a program or for the program committee. Yet when barred from action, the conservative is at a loss. The Republican leadership was faced with a situation which it was ill prepared to meet. Men of action and men with practical commitments, men with something to protect, had identified their interests with this party. They found themselves ousted from power.

The opposition, dominated by the other type of mentality, was called upon to act. Men of imagination and vision, utopian if you will, were given their chance. Weakness on the operational side was soon revealed. Plans for change exceeded the planners' administrative capacities. They responded to practical difficulties by conjuring up further schemes when many believed that it was not schemes they needed but managerial skills. Men of pragmatic temper struggled to get control of the party organization.

We need both elements within each party for a properly working system. The conceptualists must win over practical-minded partisans to their own camp. If we are to get government by alternative parties, we need both imagination and practicality in each party. This in fact is what we have, though in different proportions, depending on the opportunity offered by conditions within the party for men of different temperaments. Our various levels of government and numerous jurisdictions have given many men in both parties wide scope for developing their political capacities. Though our party system tends to blur issues, it provides ample opportunities for individuals to develop ideals and policies and to struggle for their concrete realization. This is due in large measure to the decentralization of power which results from our party structure.

Part III

Part III

☆ 15 ☆

The Structure of Our Party System

> "There was a most ingenious architect who
> had contrived a new method for building
> houses, by beginning at the roof, and working
> downwards to the foundation, which he justi-
> fied to me by the like practice of those two
> prudent insects, the bee and the spider."
>
> JONATHAN SWIFT, *Gulliver's Travels*

THE architecture of our party system seems at first glance ill
suited to the problems that the federal government is expected
to meet. Public policies are national and often international in
their implications; party politics is intensely local and often sectional. Direction from national headquarters is weak. Yet neither
democratic ideas nor common sense would sanction our building
a party structure from the top down. Can we build, then, from the
bottom upwards?

The most striking thing about our national party organizations
is the very tenuous and changing character of the various parts.
There is no machine in a strict sense. Lines of control do not run
down through a systematic hierarchy of committees. Although
an organization chart suggests a pyramid, the actual powers of
party agencies cannot be symmetrically presented. The national
committee has little internal strength. It has no power to dictate
to the state committees. The national party committee is an advisory agency and does not act in any locality without the con-
currence of the state organization. It meets every four years to

select a convention city and it directs the temporary organization of the party conclave. Once the presidential candidate is selected, the chairman chosen by the nominee becomes the dominant committee member. He acts under the candidate's directions. He may exercise great influence over the rank and file of the party workers. The distribution of campaign funds from national headquarters may be a very persuasive factor, but the strength of the chairman himself must not be overestimated.

The organization of the party on a national scale is most accurately envisaged in terms of a network of personal relations. Nothing is more misleading than to take the formal pyramidal arrangement of committees from precinct and ward to national headquarters as indicating the actual flow of authority. Obviously, impulses do not progress toward culminating force at the apex; nor is the national chairman able to send orders down to the rank and file with much confidence that his words will be followed. Our partisan power relationships are infinitely more complex. On practically all public policy matters the national chairman has nothing to say. His function is to find out from the party workers what the voters are thinking.

The chairman's strength lies in the friendships that he has established with key people over the country. This is not a matter of sentiment—although this factor is present—so much as a relationship built on common sympathies and interests. For example, certain state leaders play along with James A. Farley, Chairman of the National Democratic Committee. He helps them and they him. Jobs are pawns in the game, to be sure, but intangible values such as prestige are very important. To be one of the boys, to belong to the crowd in power, to be on the inside are urges satisfied by this relationship. The local leaders attractive to the national chairmen are those who command a substantial local following. Thus, if one tried to chart the lines from party headquarters to the real state leaders, official titles would not provide a true guide.*

* *Fortune* caught the shifting web of relationships in the following quotation, which serves as a graphic illustration not only of the situation then existing but even more significantly of the great alternations that have occurred since then:

On a national scale our party organizations have lacked continuity in direction and control. The national committee is a representative rather than an executive body. Its greatest activity, of course, is in connection with the presidential campaigns. The presidential candidate and his immediate following compose the national organization for all practical purposes. Once the campaign is over, the committee seldom meets until the next presidential election year, unless some emergency arises.

Through his supporters in various localities, Mr. Farley may work out informally a more unified organization than the formal structure of the party can hope to accomplish. Mr. Farley has his party within the party. Here is an effort to develop harmony

"A list of the real personnel of the Democratic machine of Mr. Roosevelt and Mr. Farley will somewhat surprise the newspaper reader. The gentlemen to whom the national headquarters of the party looks for final decisions in matters affecting the party in the various states—the persons, in other words, through whom it 'clears' matters of patronage and the like—are very infrequently the gentlemen named in the official records. They are, nevertheless—bosses and Senators, Governors and Congressmen—the gearwheels of the Roosevelt machine.

"In the Democratic states of the old South—exception made for Senator Long's Louisiana—Mr. Farley clears through the Democratic Senators. In Louisiana he clears through any Congressmen except Mr. Long's Maloney and Fernandez. Since Long is the only Democratic Senator in the region who is also National Committeeman the record of the National Committee is precisely zero.

"The opposite situation holds in California, Rhode Island, Tennessee, Wyoming, and Virginia where Senators McAdoo, Gerry, McKellar, O'Mahoney, and Byrd are also and incidentally National Committeemen. But it is because of the senatorial toga—or, in Senator Byrd's case, of the boss's grip—that the position is occupied. In California, for example, neither the old-line Democrats like Isidore Dockweiler nor the new-line EPICs like State Chairman Culbert L. Olson waste any love on Senator McAdoo. But Senator McAdoo and his horse-racing, lot-selling, social adjunct, Mr. Hamilton H. Cotton, run the state nevertheless. While in Rhode Island, where the Democrats have broken half a century of Republican monopoly of the Supreme Court by retiring the entire bench, the real power is not in the hands of the local leader, Governor Green, but in the hands of Senator Gerry.

"Elsewhere the feudal lords are men of many positions and many professions but rarely members of the National Committee. In a few states the Democratic machine is in the hands of the Governor. In Maine Governor Brann ranks slightly above Congressman Edward C. Moran, Jr. in the Washington estimation. In Pennsylvania the new, socially-registered Governor, George Earle, divides control with the ex-indictee, Senator Boss Joe Guffey who, as we have seen, deserves even more Rooseveltian gratitude for the Roosevelt nomination than James Aloysius himself. In Indiana Governor Paul McNutt has a slight lead over Senator Van Nuys and Dan Tobin, the President of the International and unity through encouraging personal loyalties and by using the persuasive power of patronage. Yet headquarters must work with those in control of the local situation. When our national party organization is considered with reference to the pattern of personal relationships and of allied interest groups, we see the artificial character of the formal national organization, the gap between the national committee and Congress, and the unstable position of the chairman. The confederate nature of the system and determinate importance of local machines cannot be overlooked.

Since the national party organization is built largely on personal relationships, it can very rapidly fall to pieces once presidential

---

Brotherhood of Teamsters. In Oregon Governor Martin conducts the Washington correspondence. In Oklahoma Governor E. W. Marland stands with Senators Thomas and Gore. In Kentucky Governor Ruby Laffoon exerts an ambiguous influence in opposition to Senator Barkley. In Wyoming when it is not Senator O'Mahoney it is Governor Leslie Miller. And in Massachusetts it is a tossup.

"Massachusetts deserves a paragraph to itself. In that state, in which Democratic pacification on the old Indian model is in full swing, a curiously Celtic backstairs duel within the party is also in progress. Governor Curley, who combines not only the political strength but many of the political qualities of such bosses as Tweed and Long, *is* to all intents and purposes the Democratic Party in Massachusetts. But he is not necessarily the representative of Massachusetts Democracy in Washington. In the first place, although Chairman Farley likes him personally, his political reputation is a bit strong for the formal approbation of Washington. And in the second place his rival for Washington recognition, Senator David I. Walsh, though a diehard Al Smith man at Chicago, polled three times as large a plurality in Massachusetts as Curley did and is known to have the respectable Catholic support which Curley for all his Roosevelt-before-Chicago orthodoxy notoriously lacks. So far Washington has dodged the issue. A showdown over the postmastership in Boston was avoided when Mr. Roosevelt threw the whole row into a civil-service examination. But sooner or later a decision will be made. When it is made the seemingly impregnable Democratic position in the state may show embarrassing fissures.

"The roll of ruling Governors would also include such ex-Governors as the deposed executive of North Dakota, Thomas Moodie, who still nudges State Chairman J. C. Eaton for dominance, and ex-Governor Ritchie of Maryland, who is still a power in spite of the fact that Senator Radcliffe was once Mr. Roosevelt's fellow vice-president in the insurance business: such defeated candidates as John Sullivan who is the outstanding figure in New Hampshire: and such unpredictable leaders as Governor C. Ben Ross of Idaho who ran ahead of his ticket by 17,000 in 1928 and behind it by 20,000 to 35,000 in 1934.

"There remains the more interesting if less admirable category of bosses—

leadership changes. The Republicans had ample opportunity to build organizational support after 1928. Herbert Hoover defeated Alfred E. Smith by 444 electoral votes to 87. Yet remember what happened to Hoover in 1932. So quickly did the Republican national organization disintegrate after Hoover's defeat that John D. M. Hamilton, the new national chairman, found a tremendous task before him in 1936. In an interview in the autumn of that year he stated,

"When we started this campaign we didn't start from scratch, we started from taw—way behind the line. The Republicans had their

---

politicians without official position who nevertheless run their states as Vincent Dailey, vice James Farley, *cum* Tammany Hall, now runs the state of New York. The greatest of these, within the pure definition of the word 'boss,' are Frank Hague, in the hollow of whose hand lies northern New Jersey, and Thomas J. Pendergast, to whom Missouri is as another man's vest pocket. But there are others of almost equal interest. Whitehaired, soft-spoken, goby-faced Patrick A. Nash runs, and *does* run, the ruthless and effective Illinois machine put together in 1931 by the late, not entirely great, Mayor Anton J. Cermak. Bruce Campbell in the southern part of the state, Ed Kelly, Mayor of Chicago, and Mike Igoe, Congressman-at-Large, assist. But Pat Nash directs. And Long's dominance in Louisiana, despite the opposition of Washington, is too obvious to require comment.

"The rest of the states fall under less spectacular and more pedestrian leadership, more or less effective. Vice President Garner and Senators Connally and Sheppard, with a bit of competition from Jesse Jones, run Texas. The crippled Michigan organization is loosely ruled by an anonymous group. The nonexistent Minnesota machine, living on Farmer-Labor suffrage, is split between the brewer-backed, Roosevelt group headed by Joseph Wolf, the National Committeeman, and the state committee dominated by former Congressman Einar Hoidale. The ruined Ohio engine is divided between Senator Vic Donahey, who is definitely in the ascendant, Senator Bulkley's group (including James M. Cox), Governor Martin Luther Davey, and the remnants of the following of ex-Governor George White. Connecticut is the province of Senators Maloney and Lonergan; Wisconsin of Senator Ryan Duffy and Editor Charles Broughton; South Dakota of W. W. Howes, First Assistant Postmaster General, and Senator Bulow; Kansas of Commissioner of Internal Revenue Guy Helvering and Senator McGill; Nebraska of Lobbyist Arthur Mullen; Nevada of Senator Pittman; New Mexico of Dennis Chavez, Congressman John J. Dempsey, and Senator Hatch; Washington of Senators Bone and Schwellenbach; Utah of Senators King and Thomas; Arizona of State Committeeman Charles Adams and Senators Ashurst and Hayden; Delaware, where the party is very weak, of John Biggs, Jr.; and Vermont, where the party curiously enough begins to show signs of life, of National Committeeman Frank Duffy." ("The Machine That Walks Like a Man," *Fortune*, April, 1935, page 67.)

tails between their legs. . . . So I decided that the only thing to do was to get the national committee closer to local affairs, to go around the country. . . . First I went to New England and then out West. In sixteen Western states I found that no national chairman had visited eight or nine of them in years. We went to work through the State chairmen to build up the local units. . . . You see, when we started this campaign many of our local leaders had died, or become discouraged, or, because they had been in power for twenty years, had become too old and cantankerous to be of much value. We had to find younger men, and we had to do so in every important Republican state." [1]

The task for the high command of either national party is to discover such a combination of local politicians as will insure the party the largest possible number of electoral votes. This is the primary concern of the national organization. After the rout of the Democrats in 1928 the organization of the party was demoralized. The national chairman, John J. Raskob, turned to the task of reviving the party. He provided a quarter of a million dollars over a three-year period, and he placed the responsibility for building up the organization in the hands of an experienced politician and a shrewd newspaperman. The national Democratic committtee itself remained in that state of suspended animation characteristic of such an organization between presidential campaigns. Jouett Shouse and Charles Michelson were for all practical purposes the national party organization. Their objective was to embarrass and criticize the Hoover administration as much as possible. Neither party had an affirmative program, but Democratic national headquarters proved able to put on a great show. Michelson directed timely darts at Herbert Hoover, and Shouse went about the country further to arouse the state leaders, who were already heartened by the sight of the presidential squirming. By the time of the Democratic national convention in 1932, the persistent attacks on the G.O.P. were showing results.

The candidate selected by the party, however, was one highly disliked by those in control of national party headquarters. The insignificance of such control was dramatically illustrated by Jim Farley. On his way to the Elks' convention in the summer of 1931 he stopped off at many points through the northwestern states and left behind him a large number of people who ever after called him by his first name. He had convinced local politicians in this region that Franklin D. Roosevelt would be a much better bet than Alfred E. Smith. The latter had various political handicaps that added to the burden of local politicians. There was much less to explain away in a candidate such as Roosevelt. We are not concerned here with what took place in the convention except to note that the party candidate was a man whom the Old Guard would not have selected. Roosevelt and his aides, however, were able to take over the party organization built up by Raskob. Michelson was as effective a publicity man under one leadership as another.[2]

Our party organization at the national level is temporary at best and held together by a cement that must be renewed every four years. Political success is the result not so much of constructing a strong national organization as of finding a formula for combining the interests of local and sectional politicians. Those who seek control must be able to outguess the leaders of rival factions within the party.

To many observers, our national party structure seems outmoded: it does not match the emerging national pattern of important economic problems. Yet under the present system there is no necessity to build up a new national organization in order to meet changes in public opinion. By a rearrangement of local or sectional support, a national party can reach new groups of voters or emphasize a different line of policy. In localities the political organization may effectively oppose change for a long period. Once entrenched, a machine is difficult to dislodge; but because of the wide differences of sections and the sharp rivalries of politicians, this is not likely to happen on the national stage.

There is greater stability of party organization in most states than in the national party structure. A. N. Holcombe writes:

"Politicians do not speak of the solid North or West as they do of the solid South, but the fact remains that there is a huge Republican following more or less concentrated in various sections of the North and West which offers little more encouragement for the Democrats than the solid South does for the Republicans." [3]

Even within the states, control of the party organization is contingent upon the guessing ability of local politicians. Thus the state committee must wait until the party primaries have determined the leadership. The party primaries make for factional disputes. Many party leaders are opposed to them for this reason. The leaders would greatly prefer the opportunities for negotiation and compromise provided by the party convention. Many political leaders bemoan the confusion of local politics. They can exert little discipline. Their power rests in their capacity to answer local demands. Their political fortunes need have no essential relationship to the policies of the national party or of the federal government. If these local feudatories can impress upon the national party officers their vote-controlling ability, they can secure concessions.

A basic difference between the British and the American situations is found in the almost unlimited powers centralized in the House of Commons. Parliament determines economic policies. Hence, political policies are worked out by national parties in national terms. Public policy in the United States is divided between at least forty-nine different governments. Hence, each of the major parties may have forty-nine different platforms.

More striking is the fact that our national party organization is a mechanism ill designed to support national policy. Today we face such problems with a political machinery based on local politics. Out of the narrow desires of city machine and state and county leaders we expect a national support to arise.

Our national party committees are removed from the present basis of strength in the United States today. They stand isolated except to the extent that the jollying and conniving of the national chairmen can establish ties with the communities. Localism is the inevitable result. The leader looks downward for what support he can muster. Opportunism becomes his creed. "My first job is to stay in Congress. I must watch my district." Thus frankly spoke one of the most sincere members of the Progressive bloc.

Congressmen must not think of national policy without considering the local interests that may be involved.

Our party structure is one product of our system of geographical representation. At best it is broadly sectional, at worst narrowly parochial. National economic policies are before us—their appropriate institutional support today comes through organizing the individuals along functional lines affected. More significant than the party as sources of policy are the trade association, the trade union, and the farmers' organizations. Policy can be worked out by experts trying to take a broad view and then passed along to the followers for criticism and support. Policy formulation in these terms is to be seen operating in federal agencies such as the Department of Agriculture and in nonofficial organizations as well. Unless we are ready to develop these avenues we are thrown back upon the necessity of building unified, disciplined national parties.

Disciplined national parties cannot be democratically reconciled with unity and leadership unless a national harmony exists. The diversity of the nation has been so great that nationally it has seldom been possible even for a *sub rosa* organization to assume control. Today, however, with the increase of national responsibilities the demand for national political control emerges, and we see—and condemn—the subterfuge created to meet the situation.

The demands made upon government may force political parties to attempt a more authoritative line. Carefully devising a program would be pointless unless the party leaders were determined to carry it through. This would entail central control, which in turn would entail sanctions to make such power effective. The easygoing, rough-and-tumble politics and compromise and barter would then give way to disciplined parties. The British have frankly recognized the necessity of demanding compliance from the rank and file if the party is to stand for a line of policy. They are willing to pay the price for more orderly politics. This entails such a concentration of power in the Central Office of the party as would be unthinkable in this country at present.

Professor James K. Pollock in a recent investigation finds that "today the Central Office is the keystone of the whole party organization. It is the focal point of party control, and its activities extend to every phase of party life. More and more does the whole party turn to the Central Office for guidance." [4]

The parties have their representative conventions designed to be policy-determining agencies. There are the National Union of Conservative and Unionist Associations, the National Liberal Federation, and the Annual Conference of the Labour Party; but real power lies elsewhere. The Central Office controls by several means. Campaigns are directed from headquarters. Indeed, the local associations of the Union go out of legal existence during an election. The Central Office may be very influential in the selection of candidates. Herman Finer writes:

"Local associations may insist upon their own candidates. Unless there is really serious reason why they should not be adopted, they are 'endorsed' by the central office. Endorsement means that the central office approves of the choice and will help that candidate during the campaign. The local association may have no person considered clever enough to meet its standard for a member of Parliament, or may lack the special qualities needed to win that particular constituency. If this is the case the central office is approached. This already has a long list of people who urgently aspire to election. Of these several are suggested to the local association. They are invited before the Nomination Committee or the Executive Committee of the local association. The Secretary of the Association, or its agent, interviews the candidates beforehand, and experience shows that his judgment has much to do with the final choice." [5]

Once the nominees are selected, the Central Office imposes its control over the policies and promises of the candidates. Pollock writes:

"Large staffs of trained Central Office workers are continually covering the country in systematic fashion performing the multitudinous tasks which a good party organization must perform. There are also provincial branches of the Conservative Central Office, for example, which really head up all the local party work. These provincial offices are not mere clearing houses of information. They assist with candidatures, with literature, with speakers, with money, and they exercise great control over the constituency organizations within their areas. Hundreds of full-time, paid workers, usually the most experienced ones, those who have proved unusually successful in local constituency affairs, are selected to do this work and they do it under Central Office guidance." [6]

Central Office staffs have increased in size and financial resources within recent years. Control by the rank and file of the party is crowded out:

"Just as the development of parliamentary government has carried with it the corollary of strong, centralized leadership in the Commons, so has the extension of suffrage necessitated the concentration in the Central Office of control over the party organization outside of Parliament." [7]

Under this system the member of Parliament becomes the creature of the party organization rather than being dependent entirely upon his constituents. The Central Office not only exercises crucial influence in the selection of candidates and the disbursement of campaign funds but also plays an important role in recommending persons for the honors list. It is very significant to note that "the larger part of the list is prepared by the Chairman of the Party Organization, who also collects most of the money for the running expenses of the organization." [8]

Pollock noted "the lessening influence of the local constituencies in the control not only of the party but of their own affairs." The member of Parliament is "much more the agent of his party than of his constituency." [9] The chairmanship of the party organization, a purely unofficial post, is of more importance than that of chief whip. The professional party worker is becoming more important.

"In theory English party organizations are quite democratic and anyone can fill even the highest offices. But in practice the higher positions are restricted. Through the maze of committees the discerning eye can see that the leader of the party holds the power and that the party is expected to follow his lead. The organization is his tool and it responds to his decisions." [10]

The detailed story of current trends inside British parties is well worth study. The points cited here merely serve to suggest the implications of strong national parties.

It is difficult to imagine transposing this into terms of American democracy. The closest parallel to our experience at the national level would be with the old caucus system, although even this was somewhat too representative for entirely smooth operation. As Marquis James writes, the caucus "made for party solidarity, and no other method yet devised has brought forward as nominees men of larger calibre. The caucus belonged to a day when the country was governed by leaders who imposed their will, rather than by popular men who must propitiate to preserve their prestige." [11] We have followed the latter path, at least, in national politics. In state and local governments the impact of party discipline has been too harsh for the electorate to experiment with its extension to national politics.

The traditional American attitude toward party control is one of grave distrust. Political corruption and machine domination are closely associated ideas. The abuses that arise under control by such political rings are best illustrated in our cities and states. The rigidity has become so great at times that men can best think of these political relationships as a machine. A classic example of such a system was the organization perfected by Boss Tom Platt in New York State.*

* As Harold F. Gosnell says:

"The mechanical elements of Platt's autocratic power were: first, control over the nomination and the election machinery through his cooperation with the state committee; second, control over the state legislature through his relations with the oligarchy ruling that body; third, control over the patronage through whatever influence he had with the president, governor, and the federal, state, and local administrative officers; fourth, his control over the party campaign funds through the relations which he maintained with the directors of certain corporations who were high in financial circles; and lastly, control over the minds of the voters through his intimate relations with party editors and men of influence in the business and political worlds. By checking off these levers one against the other he was able to play upon the habits, customs, traditions, ambitions, rivalries, gratitudes, greeds, and fears of those with whom he had dealings. He was a fit leader for a rivalrous, egotistic organization like the Republican machine in New York during the late nineties." (*Boss Platt and His New York Machine*, Chicago, University of Chicago Press, 1924, page 348.)

William Barnes, in telling Theodore Roosevelt of Platt's methods, said:

"You know yourself, Mr. Roosevelt, the Senator does not bully. He does not have to. That the man who went into politics and wanted to go ahead found out for himself that he could not get ahead if he didn't do what the organization, what the leader, what the boss wished. That it was not necessary to give orders; it was quite sufficient to have it understood by example that the man that stood by the organization benefited because the organization stood by him and that if he did not stand by the organization he got punished and that the ordinary man found this out for himself. If he declined to learn, then he got dropped; he failed to make a record, he could not satisfy his constituents, that his bills were not passed or his work failed in other ways, and that he did not get a renomination and he was eliminated." [12]

It is not always necessary to give orders and to insist upon personal obedience. There is the tacit understanding that the men who stand by the organization will receive their reward. Obvious coercion is not necessary here. Moral suasion is a weapon of great power in the armory of the boss.

Professional politicians know that their strength depends upon their control of the party organization. More important than public office is control of all party committees and chairmanships. The machinery is usually so contrived that control from the bottom is difficult. The party representative sent from the county committee must be *persona grata* to the chairman of the state committee if he is to serve on that body. The state party committee must be controlled by the professional politicians if they are to remain in power. Through this committee they can largely determine nominations for posts within the party. The disbursement of patronage and campaign funds is again a means of control within the party organization. Many of the links of power are not necessarily dependent upon victory at the polls. There have been instances when, rather than endanger his position as commander of the organization, a politician has been willing to have the opposite party win the election.

We cannot forget our experiences with strong and disciplined party organization in the United States. The strength of our local party organization is in marked contrast to the protean character of the party viewed nationally. We have escaped in this wider realm the rigidities that have made democracy a mockery in our cities. To call the roll of state and city bosses is to remind ourselves of the consequences that have followed from a concentration of power in the hands of unscrupulous men.

Is it enough to say that we must get better men? As we have already argued, the leaders who come to the top politically are one expression of the underlying pattern of interests. Our system can work successfully only when there is effective political support for leaders who follow the conventions imposed by belief in rule by law. Where bossism prevails, constitutional morality lags. An inner ring may so completely control the avenues for the expression of opinion that those out of power despair of gaining a chance to influence government through legal means. Assassination stopped Huey Long. His regime and that of Hitler might be called similar in kind if not in degree. In each case, party leaders place their will and purpose above the limits imposed by constitutional morality.

While this has happened here in the United States, our dictators have been local bosses tolerated by a citizenry too little disturbed to reassert the standards of justice and morality latent in the community. The diversity of the country has protected the preoccupied voter from the consequences of his own inattention to national politics. The common national interests of bankers and large industrialists offer a possible basis for dictatorship. It is conceivable that a highly class-conscious labor movement might provide a context favorable to national political control by a small clique.

A higher degree of party control from the top down to the precincts may be the price that we shall have to pay for more coherence and direction in national policy. It may be that the future of our national politics calls for a higher degree of centralized control from party headquarters. This cannot be made effective, however, without great changes in our laws and customs, in our attitude toward politics, and in the distribution of powers between the states and the federal government, between the legislative and the executive branches.

The Republican party is better viewed not as a national phenomenon but rather as an organization containing New England Republicans, prairie Republicans, and lily-white Republicans. The varied natures of their Republicanism result from their local traditions, loyalties, and economic and social conditions. There are Democrats of the cotton states, Tammany Democrats, New Deal Democrats, and Democrats who "take a walk." Concern with national party principles is ill suited to the task of compounding regional differences.

Highly indicative of the present difficulties in centralizing political control within our national party organizations has been the general failure to influence from Washington the nomination of members of Congress.

The 1938 congressional election and the primary preceding brought to the fore again the ever uncertain balance between presidential leadership and congressional independence. Congressmen may be ready to love and honor the chief executive, but they balk at the promise to obey beyond that honeymoon period of a new administration when political relationships rest upon an anticipatory quality found only in very young love.

It is a truism that politics makes strange bedfellows. Congress and the president must try to live together though their political bases and even their habits of thought are different.

The president tries to act for the nation—of which he is representative-at-large. The size of his constituency elevates his responsibilities to a plane higher than that of the average congressman.

Can he marshal a party following loyal to his leadership and ready to share the same picture as to what should be?

To expect such a response from Congress is like asking churchgoers to practice on Monday what they profess on Sunday. It may not be asking the impossible, but it means expecting a good deal. Congress reflects our workaday attitude toward government. It represents our local interests and the demands of special groups.

A congressman to keep his job must satisfy his more powerful constituents. This can rarely be done by holding to a general party program sponsored by the president. Only emergency brings such unity.

With factionalism and localism rife in Congress and with party leaders often lacking both expert knowledge and authority, the president has turned increasingly to his administrative advisers. Such men do not have to consider the immediate reception of their proposals in terms of a specific situation back home. They can think—and the president can talk—in Sunday terms of what should be. The congressman faces a weekday frame of mind, not of what would be best for all but of how a particular policy will affect individuals in his own district today.

Despite the talk of a rubber-stamp Congress, a scrutiny of President Roosevelt's relations with Capitol Hill shows more manipulation than control. Diplomacy, bargaining, intrigue, persuasion, cajolery, threats, promises, flattery—these have been his tools. Can the president bring together under the Democratic label in Congress "a group of men united for promoting by their joint endeavor the national interest upon some principles in which they are all agreed"?

The answer seems to be that while Congress sits on a hill by the Potomac the level of representation can rise no higher than the sources from which flows political support. The party purge was to bring about a clearer alignment along lines of common belief so that issues might be more coherently debated. The need arose in part from the great size of the 1936 Democratic majority. Coherence diminishes as numbers increase. The need was sharpened by the president's concern in carrying through a positive line of governmental policy.

At one end stand the idea men, the brain trusters, who want the government to do something; at the other extreme are the organization men, the party machinists, who want above all to hold power and maintain harmony in the ranks. Keep the boys satisfied but don't stir things up. The president makes use of both viewpoints.

It is when the president and Congress fail to see eye to eye that difficulties arise. When a president approaches the end of his second term he may or may not toy with the idea of a third, but certainly he ponders deeply the contribution that he may make to his country's future welfare and his own enduring fame. He tends to shift his eye from the middle distance to broader horizons.

Localism and factionalism are the twin demons the president must exorcise, and our presidents are reduced to using spells and incantations. They can make speeches and write letters; they can argue, appeal, exhort, and condemn. But what they can *do* is little. Federal funds and federal jobs are their most tangible means for control or support. We can leave to partisan conjecture the use and effectiveness of these tools. Though such methods have certainly been used, the results of the primaries in 1938 indicated that they are relatively ineffective.

When our presidents try to get their programs accepted, they face the separation of powers and a government designed to check and balance power. They must turn to party controls, but these are in the hands of men who place party solidarity above presidential programs.

Two decades ago the visions of Woodrow Wilson received a reversal which makes Roosevelt's setback in 1938 seem slight. Fired with a desire to bring the full weight of his influence into possible peace negotiations and faced with an election to determine the make-up of Congress in his last two years, Wilson intervened in various primary fights in 1918 as well as in the congressional November election. In the spring he tried unsuccessfully to prevent the election of Irvin Lenroot of Wisconsin. Later he opposed Senator Vardaman of Mississippi and Representative Slayden of Texas and Huddleston of Alabama.

The newspaper editorial writers indicated bewilderment then as they did later as to the basis upon which congressmen were selected for the party purge. The editorial comment of twenty years ago would need little refurbishing for the purge of 1938. The New York *Times* declared on August 15, 1918:

"It is only natural that the Democratic voters resent Executive interference, an attempt, in appearance if not in intention, of the Executive to pick out members of Congress. Moreover, no general rule can be deducted from the sporadic cases in which Mr. Wilson has been induced to express his opposition or support of particular members. Opposition to the Administration is not necessarily a crime, anyway; and a good many members in good and regular standing and high favor and at the head of great committees need to plead a statute of limitations." [13]

As the November election drew near, Wilson and his advisers discussed various schemes for bringing presidential influence to bear. Finally putting aside any elaborate strategy the president issued his eloquent appeal:

"My Fellow Countrymen: The Congressional elections are at hand. They occur in the most critical period our country has ever faced or is likely to face in our time. If you have approved of my leadership and wish me to continue to be your unembarrassed spokesman in affairs at home and abroad, I earnestly beg that you will express yourself unmistakably to that effect by returning a Democratic majority to both the Senate and the House of Representatives. I am your servant and will accept your judgment without cavil, but my power to administer the great trust assigned me by the Constitution would be seriously impaired should your judgment be adverse, and I must frankly tell you so because so many critical issues depend upon your verdict. No scruple of taste must in grim times like these be allowed to stand in the way of speaking the plain truth." [14]

Woodrow Wilson's request was based upon a view that made his office virtually equivalent to that of the prime minister in Great Britain. Wilson sought a vote of confidence that would give him a free hand for action. He regarded the presidential office as combining the titular headship of the state with majority party leadership.

The British king was once an independent executive and for a life term. Differences inevitably arose with Parliament. The British evolved the separate office of prime minister. We have invented the third term tradition and systematically discard our presidents after a relatively short time. A stable working relationship with Congress seems impossible under such circumstances.

The New York *Evening Post* accused Wilson of wanting a group in Congress comparable to George III's parliamentary following of the "King's Friends." One flaw in this parallel lies in the fact that George III frankly relied on honors, bribery, and concessions while our chief executive must depend largely on exhortation. He lacks the firm party discipline which the British prime minister can impose on his following.

Whatever one may think of Woodrow Wilson, none will deny that he was a man of vision. His strength lay in his aspirations and in his power of stating his ideals in noble language. His arguments could be denied only by pointing to human weaknesses. Our system seems to fortify the short rather than the long view. The world today may be reaping the tares sown in November, 1918. Localism in politics at home had its effect upon the discussion of world politics abroad. The voters in the districts and precincts could not focus upon distant horizons. As former Ambassador William E. Dodd has written, "Wilson's world leadership was broken in the Congressional elections of 1918, perhaps the most important of all the popular decisions of recent times." [15]

It is impossible to say how much Wilson's plea affected the party line-up. One conclusion seems inescapable: Under our system presidential intervention in local elections is not a workable way of securing a clear popular mandate. The election of 1918 returned a Republican Congress. Our national councils were divided.

Wilson in 1918, just as Roosevelt in 1938, felt confident that the inarticulate mass supported him. He said that he knew with an instinct that he could not doubt the faith of the people in him and in his interpretation of their desires.

During 1938 the report of the Gallup polls came to the aid of instinct in fortifying presidential confidence by showing a wide percentage of popularity. Yet Roosevelt played a cautious hand. The purge experiment showed the practical political limits to his popularity.

Many believe that the great question answered in the congressional campaign of 1938 was not who should be returned to

Congress and the Senate but how did the country feel about the occupant of the White House. Certainly the president wanted to know what the country thought in the sixth year of the New Deal. He wished to separate the sheep from the goats. He suggested that there were wolves in sheeps' clothing who had no place in his fold. Some of his fellow Democrats refused to be presidential sheep and resented with equal bitterness the role of scapegoat on the altar of party unity. The purge failed both as a disciplinary measure and as a device for clarifying opinion.

On September 20, 1938, the president stated that while as a matter of principle he would prefer the election of a liberal Republican to that of a conservative Democrat, as a practical matter he would keep hands off in the coming elections. Better not to look a Democratic donkey in the mouth!

Political behavior is often illogical. The New York *Times* reported that the state convention in Connecticut "overwhelmingly renominated Senator Lonergan while loudly cheering every mention of the name of President Roosevelt." In determining an election local conditions are more important than issues raised in Washington.

The papers reported maladroit handling of the purge in the Maryland and Georgia primaries. Ineptness on the part of New Deal stategists was suggested as one possible explanation. In any event they failed to cope adequately with local political forces. In Texas, Maury Maverick, the eloquent New Dealer, was defeated by the superior organization of his opponent. How are we to disentangle the effectiveness of the machine support given James H. Fay in New York from the voters' enthusiasms for presidential policies? It seems that issues must be settled through contests between organizations, and the group in Washington supporting the purge were not experienced organization men. They viewed the purge as a fight for principle and ideas. New Deal heretics were to be read out of the Democratic party. The way in which the purge bogged down points to the weakness of verbalism as a political tool and suggests the need for new political machinery for getting into local situations if national issues are to be tested.

Local leaders made strong efforts to prevent clear issues from being drawn in the primary fights. The purge was too erratic to make much sense. It may have been an experiment by Roosevelt to see if his popularity could be transformed into support for his followers. If so, he got his answer. A president cannot get a mandate for his administration simply by asking voters what they think of his friends.

The Hatch Act, passed in 1939, is a further indication of the strong forces working against a unification of our parties imposed from the top downwards. This law was regarded as a way "to 'defederalize' political influence and transfer to state leaders or bosses the fealty heretofore commanded by Washington by reason of patronage." [16] Ostensibly designed to "eliminate politics" from administrative offices and protect officials from solicitation of funds or support in campaigns, the measure actually goes to the core of national policy control. One Washington correspondent interprets its meaning as follows:

"An analysis of the Hatch bill shows that it seeks to remove the influence or interference of all Federal administrative officials who make policies of nation-wide application, from elections or nominating efforts for President, Vice President, or member of Congress. It also has 'teeth' designed to remove the relief worker as far from political exploitation as legal language can be employed to do.

"The administrative employes who come under the Hatch bill's terms are those just under the executive officers here, with the exception of those directly under the President, and heads of field offices and their immediate assistants, Federal district attorneys, marshals, collectors of internal revenue, postmasters and certain others whose status will have to be determined either by Executive order or by the courts.

"These officials number an estimated 5,000. All are expected to give allegiance to those who put them in office. As these officials start with those 'near the throne' and drop by tiers into 'respectable' jobs in the field, the effect of removing them from political activity conceivably would be so severe as to justify the bitter fight waged against the Hatch bill by the New Dealers in Congress, who would rather see Mr. Roosevelt the White House occupant after 1940 than anyone but themselves.

"Members of Congress and their employes are exempt from the

prohibition against political activity. Their campaigns will be affected somewhat by the bill, by reason of the removal of the influence of postmasters, district attorneys and collectors from participation. But in losing some support, or rather influence, of their appointees, they placed about them a measure of insurance against a repetition of the 'purge' attempts of last year.

"At the same time, members of Congress voted themselves a greater measure of control of the nominating conventions." [17]

Congressmen and senators are normally men of great influence in their states. The Hatch Act gives them a freer hand by eliminating as possible delegates to the national party conventions those federal officials such as postmasters, district attorneys, and collectors of internal revenue who are also strong figures in local politics. State leaders may thus hand-pick delegates who will be responsive to their wishes and have no loyalties to divide with Washington. The tie with national headquarters must come in terms of whatever personal influence the president or the chairman of the party national committee may have with individual state leaders.

In this way we return again to the traditional politics of persuasion, personal cajoling, and mutual assistance. For the time being at least the tendency toward building a political organization to implement national policy has been arrested. Eliminating the influence of federal officeholders from national conventions will accentuate the localism of these assemblies. Congressional representation among the delegations attending the conventions will probably be strong.

☆ 16 ☆

The Uses for National Conventions

> "The alligator waz made for sum usefull
> purpose, but like the muskeeter, the bedbugg
> and the kokroach, their usefullness haz been
> karephully hid from us."
>
> JOSH BILLINGS

THE usefulness of our national nominating conventions has at times seemed obscure. Most of the criticism of party conventions grows out of the belief that they are held to discuss policy as well as to nominate candidates. Such a belief misinterprets the structure of our party system as described in the preceding chapter. The behavior of any organization must be interpreted in the light of the elements that compose it if any understanding is to be achieved. To expect bands of local chieftains and their henchmen to come together and act as a deliberative national unit once every four years is to expect the impossible.

Our conventions could be orderly if they were the apex of a well-organized hierarchy. The most dignified, orderly, and impressive assembly for selecting an individual for a high office is the College of Cardinals. Even this august assembly is not without its political undercurrents, but it can function with its unexampled success because it is the final expression of a remarkably well-disciplined body. The Roman Catholic Church embraces members from all the races of the world. It may be tolerant of many human frailties, but on questions of dogma no deviation is permitted. Such ideological unity can develop harmonious internal controls that make organization smooth and efficient. At high moments of crisis its dignitaries may respond as exponents of their organization.

Our political parties are built not on the rock of faith but rather on the broad mud flats of popular desires and individual ambitions. The party convention is no better than the loose and undisciplined local and state organizations that send their delegates to bargain. If we cannot do much to change these underlying factors the question then is to consider anew what can be done with the materials at hand.

Judged as strictly rational and intellectual performances, these huge assemblies are flat failures; but are they to be measured by such standards?

Let us first hear some of the critics. No recent writer is more outspoken than Herbert Agar. He states that "the position of the average delegate at a national convention has neither dignity nor sense." "Never a wholly adequate device, the nominating convention," he says, "is now an anachronism." He deplores the absence of serious discussion of public problems and the "atmosphere of lightminded carousal." This comes in for heartiest condemnation. "The delegates even showed signs of being ashamed of their own immoderate antics. They wondered whether the way to run a great political party is to get drunk and ride donkeys into hotel lobbies. . . . They knew they ought to be doing serious work. Yet there was no serious work to do, so they took refuge in idiocy." The author quotes Milton on the noises of Hell and concludes that conventions are worse.[1] Agar's reaction is that of a cultured and sensitive man who evidently does not enjoy roughhousing. He would feel equally ill at ease at an American Legion convention or a conclave of the Elks.

Many of us would certainly prefer to see conventions less noisy, more thoughtful and "full of argument and heart-searching and high seriousness." My purpose here, however, is not to exhort delegates to be sober and meditative but rather to raise the question as to whether a convention is primarily an intellectual activity. The writers who carry these assumptions to our convention halls come away with a very unhappy impression. M. Ostrogorski, through thick lenses of moralistic and rational values, gained an impression comparable to Agar's. His eloquent description of this strange American scene concludes thus:

"In a fit of intoxication they [the delegates] yield to the most sudden impulses, dart in the most unexpected directions, and it is blind chance which has the last word. The name of the candidate for the Presidency of the Republic issues from the votes of the Convention like the number from a lottery. And all the followers of the party, from the Atlantic to the Pacific, are bound on pain of apostasy, to vote for the product of that lottery. Yet, when you carry your thoughts back from the scene which you have just witnessed, and review the line of Presidents, you find that if they have not all been great men—far from it—they were all honorable men; and you cannot help repeating the American saying: 'God takes care of drunkards, of little children, and of the United States.' " [2]

An analysis of political behavior that finds its ultimate explanation in these supernatural forces is going rather far afield. The emotional reaction of the author to emotionalism in politics serves to explain Ostrogorski, but it still leaves us to find the meaning of our convention. It is easy to ridicule these assemblies since they provide abundant material gratis to any observer. To play up the ludicrous is tempting but misleading. Moreover, a carnival always seems more attractive to the participant than to the mere onlooker. For James A. Farley "there is a carnival spirit, a touch of the sawdust and the side show, about a national convention that makes it unique among public gatherings. And we Democrats can always put a little more zest into it than our staid Republican brethren. While party conclaves may not always be successful, they are never dull." [3]

As to whether the atmosphere of high seriousness urged by Agar or the carnival spirit accepted by Farley should prevail, we need not take sides. An observer or a participant will find both attitudes at any convention. Our concern is not with what should be but with the interpretation of what is. The attention of commentators has been focused most eloquently on sins of omission. The following views of Lord Bryce serve as a classic critique upon the shortcomings of the party convention:

"It goes without saying that such a meeting is capable neither of discussing political questions and settling a political programme, nor of deliberately weighing the merits of rival aspirants for the nomination. Its programme must be presented to it cut and dry, and this is the work of a small committee. In choosing a candidate, it must follow a few leaders. And what sort of leaders do conventions tend to produce? Two sorts—the intriguer and the declaimer. . . . For men of wisdom and knowledge, not seconded by a commanding voice and presence, there is no demand, and little chance of usefulness, in these tempestuous halls. . . . Large popular gatherings . . . are excitable in virtue of their size. . . . A national convention . . . is the hugest mass meeting the world knows of. . . . The struggle in a convention is over men, not over principles." [4]

Such a sweeping denunciation hardly stands close scrutiny. The men influential in "these tempestuous halls" are the same men who serve as political leaders in Congress and the state governments. A huge mass meeting cannot be judged by its incapacity to perform tasks appropriate to a small committee. Unless we are to substitute for the convention a small executive council, we must accept the characteristics resulting from size. Moreover, its positive qualities are worthy of our respect. It is an indigenous institution and can be best evaluated with respect to our own peculiar needs.

What has our experience with national party conventions demonstrated their basic purpose to be? It is to find a man whom a majority of the voters will agree to support.

Farley has given us a perfect picture of the professional politician's attitude toward the selection of a candidate. On his way to the Elks' convention Farley called upon the national committeeman of South Dakota, Bill Howe. Farley relates:

". . . We sat in a lunchroom at Aberdeen on a roasting-hot day. Bill was a canny politician who had been in the game for years; he knew it backward and forward. We sat there for some time, exchanging generalities, without disclosing what either of us really had in mind. Just before it was time to go, Bill plumped his fat fist on the table and growled in a deep voice, 'Farley, I'm damn' tired of backing losers. In my opinion, Roosevelt can sweep the country, and I'm going to support him.' " [5]

The desire to find a winner and thereby help the ticket back home is a force of no small importance. The primary task of the delegates is to find a winning candidate. The convention is designed to unite diverse sections and rival leaders behind a man, and to whip up the enthusiasm of party workers to fight for his election. This involves not questions of public policy but problems of party strategy. In view of the rivalries, the frank self-seeking, and the bitter jealousies arising in our party conventions, the ultimate adjustment almost invariably reached is a triumph of popular government.

The value of the convention lies in its permitting the rank and file of the party to participate physically and emotionally in a common enterprise. Here are the men who must carry the brunt of the campaign. Here they have their chance to meet, to shout together, to act together, to feel together. The excitement and the turmoil of the convention fulfill a useful purpose. The relationship of follower and leader is seldom an intellectual bond. A common bond of sympathy, a common symbol, is easily grasped and equally binding.

The party convention places a premium on party harmony. It reveals in a beating glare of publicity any thin spots and holes in the party fabric. Hence the impetus of the whole procedure is toward agreement. Prolonged dispute is greatly feared. As William G. McAdoo explained to the 1932 convention, when shifting the California delegation to Roosevelt: "Sometimes in major operations, where skillful surgery is required, the life of the patient may be destroyed if there is unnecessary delay. We believe, therefore, that California should take a stand here tonight that will bring this contest to a swift and, we hope, satisfactory conclusion—a stand, we hope, which will be promotive of party harmony." [6] A convention must try to unify a party not inherently unified. Its purpose is not to examine intellectual differences but to seek terms of agreement. When differences cannot be reconciled, the politicians seek unity in the face of disagreement. A party convention offers them the opportunity to negotiate and human materials with which to work.

As just noted, the basic function of the convention is to focus national attention upon the task of selection that is going forward, and then to align the regular party politicians behind a man who will lead them to victory. To do this the methods must be such as to attract and hold the attention of the great mass of citizens. Experience indicates that prizefights, football games, and similar sporting spectacles have characteristics that please the populace. Debating societies have a more limited following. The intellectually inclined may view this as an unfortunate situation. If a political spectacle is the way to arouse public attention, that is reason enough for the average politician.[7]

The party convention may likewise be viewed as an excellent implement for compromise. Compromise in politics is not achieved simply through argumentation. The process entails bargaining and manipulation as well. There are various levels and types of compromise. To reach such peaceful adjustments of interest requires an area for movement and something with which to trade and barter. The party convention creates a human situation and provides scope under general rules of the game for elaborate interrelationships. Here concessions of many types can be made and victories in various terms are possible. The range of satisfactions is great, and disappointment on one count may be compensated for on another. There must be something wherewith to compromise.

The party platform, if solemnly regarded as a formulation of public policy, is perhaps almost as inane as it is painted. Can we let the matter rest here? If the true significance of this document remained here, it could hardly have survived the criticism of the commentators. "Ordinarily the framing of a party platform is regarded either as a joke or a nuisance," [8] one writer states.

To accept this view would force us to the conclusion that our politicians were either very earnest pranksters or very long-suffering traditionalists. The party platform may cause difficulties at times and laughter on occasion, but it is neither a joke nor a nuisance. It is far from trivial, and it serves an essential purpose; but its use does not lie in its forecasting of party policy over the next four years. Rather it discloses the pattern of purposes represented among the politicians who draw it up at the convention.

A party platform may be analyzed either as a reasoned statement of the party's stand on public problems or as an aspect of the political process. Viewed as an intellectual exercise, platforms are generally disappointing. As Edward M. Sait puts it,

"the platform, like any other commodity is manufactured in order to be sold. The skillful engineers who design it (for mass production) consult the popular taste and measure success in terms of votes on election day. . . . If Republican and Democratic platforms resemble each other, they do so primarily because they reflect the prevailing vulgar taste, as shrewd politicians interpret it. Such likeness is not due to a bi-partisan conspiracy of silence. Competing politicians, like competing manufacturers, are always sensitive to changes in taste and will give their products a distinctive equality whenever they have a good prospect of increasing the volume of sales." [9]

Platforms are framed undoubtedly with an eye to pleasing the public. It is this very effort to please everybody that is their undoing from the viewpoint of consistency. Lippmann writes:

"No party can represent a whole nation, although, with the exception of the socialists, all of them pretend to do just that. The reason is very simple: a platform is a list of performances that are possible within a few years. It is concerned with more or less immediate proposals and in a nation split up by class, sectional and racial interests, these proposals are sure to arouse hostility. No definite industrial and political platform, for example, can satisfy rich and poor, black and white, Eastern creditor and Western farmer. A party that tried to answer every conflicting interest would stand still because people were pulling in so many different directions. It would arouse the anger of every group and the approval of its framers. It would have no dynamic power because the forces would neutralize each other.

"One comprehensive party platform fusing every interest is impossible and undesirable." [10]

At rare intervals the platform rises above negativity. The Democratic party stand of 1896 marked such a time, but in the face of criticism from party conservatives. Harry Barnard states:

"The pronouncements on labor, on the courts, on injunctions, on civil and personal liberties and notably on that 'communistic' thing, the income tax—these were the items of the platform which indelibly stamped a new character upon the party. These were what the conservative minority had in mind in characterizing the platform 'extreme and revolutionary of the well recognized principles (hitherto) of the party.' " [11]

A distinctive party stand inevitably incurs the danger of internal and factional dispute. Class and regional differences cannot be denied though they are often ignored.

"Under these circumstances party platforms are inevitably reduced to their lowest common denominator [Siegfried believes]. Any interests or aspirations which cannot be fitted into this narrow framework or harmonized with the rigid views of the politicians must develop outside the party machine, which is expected only to furnish a practical means of achieving success. It is an indispensable tool and nothing more. . . . It is useless, therefore, to look in the parties for political ideals of underlying tendencies or even for a common outlook among their leaders." [12]

While party platforms seek to present an amalgam of views and sometimes result in stressing the lowest common factors, it by no means follows from this that parties are devoid of ideals or fail to reflect underlying tendencies or a common outlook. The party platform is not the place to look for such expressions, however. Let us grant that planks are often equivocal and that the platforms of both parties tend to likeness. Under our formal system of government the usefulness of the most definite set of promises would be of very doubtful value. Representative Robert Luce, who brings both learning and experience to our problem, has said that

"party platforms are futilities. No thoughtful legislator feels himself bound by the makeweights thrown in to catch a few stray votes. Knowing how platforms are made, he ought not to give himself much anxiety over their decorations. Were these to be taken too seriously, then the Committee on Resolutions of a party convention would in effect become the legislating body, enacting laws with none of the benefits found in legislative halls, such as the help of committee hearings, debates, and repeated consideration. Furthermore, if it should be attempted in a political convention to anticipate even a tithe of the work of a Legislature or Congress, unless the convention were dominated by autocrats it would break up in confusion and discord. Success could only come with the negation of representative government." [13]

Constitutional and procedural limitations restrict the legislative program for any party. None, however well intentioned, can through its platform commit itself in advance on problems which have not been adequately investigated, debated, or discussed. Lawmaking cannot be anticipated by platform framing. That party platforms are little more than political ballyhoo can no longer be seriously questioned. Perhaps the last word on this subject was that of the Pullman porter who explained to the politician loitering in the car vestibule that platforms were made not to stand on but to get in on. In practice it is impossible to guarantee definite accomplishment of campaign promises and usually politically inexpedient to make unequivocal commitments on controversial questions. A survey of the platforms of the minor parties of the past few decades demonstrates the error of such tactics.

Despite the evidence as to the limited value of platform pronouncements, politicians continue to fight over them. Yet agreement seems general that the final product is innocuous if not meaningless. John W. Davis has written:

"Except for the stout assertion that there is no health in the opposing party and that its works are evil, there is apt to be little on which the inquiring mind can fasten. Now, where mass action is desired, either at the polls, in a convention or in the smaller arena of a legislative hall, compromise is necessary of course to progress. But it ceases to be a virtue when it squeezes out of what is supposed to be an appeal to reason all force of meaning, leaving only the dry husks of empty and resounding words in its place." [14]

Do we not get a different slant on the platform if we consider as of chief significance not the words that are finally agreed upon but the process by which this end product is reached?

Politicians must bargain. Trade is impossible without something to exchange. Patronage is important here, but the recognition of ideas may be even more valued. Platform making is a process of psychological value. It provides a release for opinions and scope for the interplay of personalities. Platform making is one step more in the process of working out some kind of synthesis.

If the party platform means so little, why do politicians fight over it so hard? The words of the final version may mean little enough to the casual reader. But the meaning of the platform as a political instrument is to be found not in the words finally left to posterity but in the process whereby these words are agreed upon. In the first place the platform framers try to reflect the views of important leaders. This is by no means an easy task. These men hold to no uniform scheme of values, and their ideas concerning the relative importance of national issues vary greatly.

An analysis of party platforms reveals planks reflecting the views of various candidates and sections. The process of drawing up a platform is one of appeasement rather than of initiation. Planks reflect the views dominant among various segments within the party. For example, in the Democratic platform of 1932, the prohibition repeal plank was favored by Al Smith and Governor Albert Ritchie of Maryland and reflected the views of urban centers and populous states, particularly in the East. The proposal to rehabilitate silver while maintaining a "sound currency at all hazards" was an effort to meet the views of Alfalfa Bill Murray of Oklahoma and other silver politicians while at the same time reassuring the sound money people. The views of Senator Carter Glass and of Governor Harry Byrd of Virginia were indicated in the plank advocating the divorce of investment from commercial banking.

Mark Sullivan in commenting on the platform in the newspapers at the time stated that it fell "short of Roosevelt's presumed proclivities and short of the radicalism and near radicalism of those who have been regarded as conspicuous supporters of Roosevelt." There was, indeed, little in the platform to distinguish it from that of the opposite party. In Sullivan's opinion both old parties were at this time orthodox conservatives in so far as the platform pronouncements were concerned. He states that the "truth is and the explanation of everything is that the intenseness of the fight to stop Roosevelt caused everything else to be ignored by the delegates."

The platform is a compromise of sectional views, group interests, and the ideas of dominant leaders instead of the program of the candidate who is yet to be chosen.* In other words, the

* The way in which a platform is framed is well described by William Allen White:

"As a reporter of Conventions for a generation, I have observed enough to believe that the procedure is the same. It is something like this: In the late winter or early spring before the national political conventions meet in June of the quadrennium, small groups, representing opposing factions in both parties begin considering platforms. Often, but not always, the groups are assembled by Presidential candidates who desire to have their views embodied in the party platform if they win the nomination. With the growth of preconvention strength of candidates (or their failure), the platform writing group grows in strength, numbers and interest. Or the group fades as its candidate's prospects fade, or as the factional strength develops or wanes in the primaries. Generally two different platforms are in the making in the spring before each national party convention is to meet. Into each of these tentative platforms, factional leaders pour their ideas. If a partisan is interested in platform making in his party, it is easy to discover who is writing his kind of a platform. But to the public, it is more or less veiled in this stage.

"The platform in the opposing factions are written and rewritten—often half a score times. The faction that wins the control of the Convention organizes the Convention, names the Chairman of the Committee on Resolutions who, in turn, names the subcommittee on Resolutions—in which, of course, is minority representation, sometimes rather scant—and the members of the majority present to the subcommittee the platform they have drafted. It becomes the working model of the subcommittee. This tentative draft is never published in advance but after it is worked over—usually all one day and one night— often longer, the tentative draft which is remade by the subcommittee frequently leaks to the press when the subcommittee's revised and completed draft is presented to the general committee on Resolutions.

"There in the general committee on Resolutions, again the revised tentative draft of the subcommittee is worked over, phrase by phrase, plank by plank, subject by subject by the general Resolutions Committee. Minority opinion in both committees—the small committee and the full committee—has an opportunity to be heard. Moreover, before the subcommittee meets, it holds public hearings where all the pressure groups interested in various organized causes— labor, banks, prohibitionists, pacifists, medicine, the bar, the farmer, the preparedness groups—every organized interest—has a full hearing. But even more than that, while the minority and majority wings of the party are working over their various platform drafts, the platform writers become fairly well known to those deeply interested in various issues, questions and causes. These preliminary platform writers are overwhelmed with advice and counsel. More still than that, each of the factional platform drafts before a National Convention policy of the party is more clearly disclosed in the nominee's ultimate position than in the preliminary declaration of principle set forth in the platform.

Of course, the renomination of a president creates a different situation. Hoover could dictate the Republican platform in 1932 just as Roosevelt did the Democratic in 1936. When a new nominee is to be chosen in the convention, the process of platform framing must be considered as part of the strategy. It is the product of the group forces battling for recognition. The compromise reached on the platform may differ from the adjustment of interests reflected in the candidates later selected. While the views of conservatives determined the general tone of the Democratic platform in 1932, they could not control the attitude of the standard-bearer selected by the party.

With the party platform drawn up before the nominee of the party is finally selected, difficulties have ensued on more than one occasion. Al Smith in 1928, for example, came out for repeal despite his party's platform. According to White's account, the 1936 Republican platform committee had completed its work when word was received from Governor Landon concerning his stand on civil service reform and gold. The committee could not be reconvened in time for considering these changes. White had been given authority to commit the candidate, and Landon's telegram came as a surprise. It was thought by some that this was a strategic move on the part of the Landon managers to make their candidate appear as independent.

Would it be wiser to frame the platform after the candidate has been selected? This would obviate any conflict between the

---

meets has been mulled over by a hundred party leaders. Another hundred leaders of each faction knows something of its own leader's platform views while the Convention is in session. Scores of reporters know pretty definitely what is in the wind. Newspaper readers are never actually surprised at the stand taken by any platform. But before the reporters begin to speculate upon a party platform, probably several hundred responsible leaders of each faction know in a general way and in a pretty definite fashion what each factional platform draft contains. Platform making is not at all a secret process. A party platform is on the whole 'an open covenant openly arrived at' as those things go in American politics." (*What It's All About*, New York, The Macmillan Co., 1936, pages 25–28.)

views of the candidates and planks in the platform. It is argued that the platform would then mean more.

According to our view, the platform would mean less. Under our system of government it is impossible for a platform to be a prophecy of what the party will do. Human affairs cannot be administered by prophecy. The meaningful aspect of the platform is the process that it provides. Since the end of the whole process is agreement upon a man, the platform squabble is a serviceable preliminary. Conceding a plank in the platform offers a *quid pro quo* to groups who must be won over. Thus the building of the party platform provides an opportunity for the politicians to test their strength, to sample the strength of various blocs, to make concessions to each other, to jockey for position and thus prepare the way for the great and primary task of finding a winning candidate.

Describing the conclusion of the platform discussion, Farley wrote: "The ballyhoo period was ended: the time had come to cut out the theatricals, to throw away the stage props, and to set in grim earnestness about the business of nominating a presidential candidate." [15]

A scrutiny of the dispute in the 1932 Democratic convention over the election of the permanent chairman, the seating of contested delegates, and the abrogation of the two-thirds rule discloses in each case successive steps toward their culmination in Roosevelt's nomination. Viewed as parts of a larger strategy, these preliminary skirmishes fall into perspective.

No one would think of planning an industrial development, an army campaign, or an educational program by devices similar to a party convention. No one can accurately regard our conventions as deliberative or planning agencies. Our conventions are a romantic and flamboyant attempt to get a high degree of popular participation in the high drama of democracy. It is not an institution to be dismissed contemptuously because of its noise and apparent confusion. It is characteristic of our free political system; the Nazis have pageantry of a different sort. Those who prefer order will find it at Nuremberg.

There is much that is not heroic in our system. The heroic mold has seemed ill suited to the peaceful routine of minding one's own business and working for a living. If we are approaching more dangerous times we will have less use for negative candidates selected because they came from the tactically important states with large electoral votes. Our easygoing, rough-and-tumble politics of compromise and barter may give way to a more efficient and effective control from the top. The demands made upon government may force our political parties to attempt a more authoritarian line. There would be no point in carefully devising a program unless the party leaders were determined to carry it through. This would entail sanctions to make such power effective. Our party conventions have sought not the strongest or wisest candidate but rather the man who would best serve to unite the party and attract the voters. This is one consequence of treating the presidency as a symbol as well as a job.

A party convention is a parley of state bosses accompanied by their henchmen carrying with them local jealousies and favoritisms. A convention might possibly become a meeting dominated by a clique of politicians in command of a national machine. Instead of selecting a compromise candidate, they might decide to put before the country their strong man who would—through all the arts of persuasion—be sold to the public as the leader.

The party convention is not an inappropriate device for serving our present purposes. In fact, it is admirably suited to testing the talents of our politicians. It demands organizational skill and manipulative genius—both of which qualities are exceedingly useful in democratic government.

Other writers have suggested improvements that could be made in our nominating machinery.[16] The value of such suggestions should not be minimized. Yet in criticizing our political institutions we must be critical also of the standards of judgment that we apply. We cannot expect a plan of action for the next four years to emerge from a national party conclave. Public policies are too broad, intricate, and dynamic to be handled thus. Problems must be met as they arise; parties cannot be expected to penetrate the future.

Much more can and should be done to give men of reason and

knowledge a more strategic position within the party structure. Parties can aid in the political education of their own membership. Questions of public policy must now be thought of in national and even international terms. This means that the inadequacies of the local politician become more evident. Social and economic necessities push us forward in demanding more intelligence in the conduct of political affairs. Yet we would be shortsighted indeed if we placed our faith in the expert as the only man with the answer. The party convention is one institutional expression of human beings competing by their wits and emotions for some of the prizes available under popular government.

☆ 17 ☆

Channeling Intelligence into
Party Activities

"The problem is how much of mind to use,
How much of instinct. . . ."
EDGAR LEE MASTERS

EVEN though the circle of our understanding is restricted, we must perforce deal with the complexity of modern society through the best means that our wits may devise and our emotions tolerate. With respect to political parties, the task is to make best use of the opportunities open to intelligence and planning.

Our parties today contribute to policy by formulating statements so broad that a majority of their members will acquiesce and a minority modify their protests. Walter Lippmann has pointed out that "the grouping of the voters into two large herds costs a large price: it means that issues must be so simplified and selected that the real demands of the nation rise only now and then to the level of political discussion. The more people a party contains the less it expresses their needs." [1]

This is true if we insist that parties try to take a positive stand on debatable issues. The mass of their adherents will necessarily differ on such questions of policy. On the other hand, our parties may find opportunity for encouraging the study and discussion of public problems. In this way some appreciation of their intricacies may be brought home to the citizen. A challenge to seek answers is offered to intelligent citizens. Our major parties can be rivals in educating their own members and stimulating them to alertness in criticism and readiness to seek out and support competent leaders. In the strictly practical purposes of recruiting leaders and promoting discussion our parties can find fulfillment.

With these limitations in mind we may perhaps appraise our national party conventions with more sympathy. The task still remains, however, of developing devices other than national conventions for the consideration of policy.

Organizations built on belief punish heresy when possible. Tolerance goes along with a less rigid, less centrally controlled organization. Increased discipline is the price for more "meaningful" parties. Some argue that this cost would be justified by the coherence that would result. Disciplined parties, however, imposed on the present diversity of our society would be more likely to give an appearance of unity rather than the reality. On the other hand, the very fluidity of our national party organization offers an opportunity for intelligence to compete freely for a hearing.

Our problem is to find a strategic position within the political process for the man of ideas to contribute effectively.

A party council has appealed to some writers as a device well suited to the development of a program. It is also a device that would increase the influence of national party leaders. It is premised on the assumption that a higher degree of responsible leadership is desirable. Believing this, Woodrow Wilson sought the creation of a party council which would supplement his proposed system of presidential primaries. He envisaged a body that would ratify the nominations made in the primaries as well as formulate the party platform. This council, according to Wilson, would be composed of the candidates for presidency, vice-presidency, House, and Senate, and the senators whose terms had not expired, together with the members of a national committee to be elected in the primaries. In this way he hoped to place the responsibility for policy upon the particular leaders in power at any given time.

Charles Merriam has envisioned an annual council of about six hundred party leaders and officials.[2] He sees this council as an agency to promote discussion of public problems, to test candidates and policies, and to create a more unified leadership. Whether the powers of this council should be authoritative as well as educational and persuasive is debatable. Realistically viewed, what could such a council achieve? This agency might expose party dissensions, but certainly the existence of weaknesses in party conventions is perceived without difficulty. It could encourage greater dignity and decorum and more orderly discussion of party problems. Yet no better than a convention could it compose sectional and group differences, without imposing discipline and central control.

The developments within the Republican party suggest ways of promoting discussion and perhaps stimulating a more coherent party policy. One was the appearance of a research division in the national committee headquarters. The other was the program committee, sponsored by the national committee and other influential elements in the party. Both of these developments may serve better to acquaint factions within the party of the intricacies of public policy.

Research as a recognized party function appeared in 1919 when an advisory committee on policy and platform was set up, enlisting prominent Republicans and aided by a qualified staff. Its recommendations were placed before the 1920 convention's resolutions committee.[3] Although the 1920 convention provided for a continuation of similar efforts to guide future conventions, the function remained dormant until early 1936. At that time preparing propaganda in the campaign called for the collection of data. During the campaign the importance of this function was so impressed upon the party leadership as to secure its continuance on a permanent basis, with a competent staff and a definite program.

This research division has served Republican legislators in the preparation of speeches, supplying factual materials for use in dealing with questions from constituents and in legislative debate, and the like. It has aided also in preparing the agenda for conferences among congressmen, party leaders, and experts for the determination of the party stand on current issues. The division has served leaders of the national committee, laying the basis for views used in their contacts with party people throughout the country. The research division has facilitated the work of the publicity division of the committee also. The division prepares the *Republican Reporter*, loose-leaf pamphlets on topics of current political controversy (such as social security and labor relations) which go upon subscription to party workers over the country. These pamphlets set forth the brief history of issues, the historical Republican attitude, and the current party position as stated by its leaders.

To this extent the division may promote the co-ordination of party opinion on public issues. The results of its statements and analyses are available for those within the party who care to use them. However, its influence toward unified policy is limited first by the fact that its activities have been confined for the most part to issues of national scope, and second by its position as a purely advisory staff agency.

The program committee, set up as a compromise response to former President Hoover's demand for a 1937 party convention, was ostensibly to create a platform for party action. A committee of two hundred and eighty persons of a representative character was appointed, composed of party members rather than party officials, and broken down regionally and topically into subcommittees. These subcommittees met to sound out party sentiment, hear the evidence of experts and special interest representatives, and draw up by topics and regions a consensus which, when combined on the national scale, would show points of national agreement and difference and points requiring further exploration.

Irrespective of the utopian character of the ultimate objective —a self-consistent, significant platform—the process of gathering opinion, arguing over evidence, and formulating statements may serve to give to a wider party following a better understanding of the nature of self-government.

Commentators on the movement in the party have noted its fall to a place of relative obscurity; but the larger significance of this effort is not to be measured by the publicity received. If it has given a chance for more people to discuss policies and develop new areas of agreement, based on the analysis of factual materials, it has accomplished much. Through the mediation of party publicity of all forms, programs thus formulated can be brought to bear in the process of seeking an ever wider consensus. Through devices such as the program committee and the research division, the Republican party can make a contribution to the large task of increasing the number of persons who try to find the terms upon which citizens will co-operate and thus promote both the meeting of minds and the sharing of responsibility for decisions utimately ratified in statutory forms.[4]

Thus our political party organizations can educate their membership and their leaders as well. In this way the national committee offers one channel for increasing the influence of intelligence in politics. Nevertheless, the relative ineffectiveness of these efforts so far prompts the tentative conclusion that the localism and diversity of the party membership is too great for the national party committee to unify. Partisan power is factional and protean.

In considering political parties and public policy a distinction must at once be drawn between the party in power and the party out of power. Under the Roosevelt administration, for example, Democratic national party headquarters has had almost nothing to do with policy. Charles Michelson issued press releases, and Mrs. McAllister, in charge of the women's division, edited a magazine and conducted promotional work. This was merely interim campaigning.

The National Emergency Council was once described in Washington as the administration's propaganda ministry. Its duties were to co-ordinate to some extent official publicity and radio broadcasts as well as to review bills drawn up in the various departments. The Council has recently been reorganized as the Office of Government Reports. This is now a clearinghouse for information. But in so far as the national headquarters of the Democratic party are concerned officials there have never been expected to deal with public policy problems.

To lay down dicta about the kind of party system we should have is easy. To set forth the structure of our party system as it is supposed to be is even easier. To suggest reforms in structure and organization is not too difficult. Yet to attempt an accurate description of the confused complex and subtle pattern of relationships which exist in fact is a task that defies adequate treatment with the tools now available to the student of society. The anatomy of party institutions can be described in terms of an articulation of committees from precinct up to national headquarters. Even here the framework is unstable and far from symmetrical in actual operation. If we consider specifically the nervous system of our parties—their modes of communication, direction, and response—we face an infinite complexity, only the general nature of which can be discussed.

Viewed as channels for introducing intelligence into policy formulation, our parties are clearly open to criticism. Yet little is to be gained in berating these institutions on such a count. Our major parties do not draw their sustenance and dogged persistence from their intellectuality.

At the risk of oversimplification, a conceptual scheme is offered in this chapter simply as a means of suggesting the fact that political relationships are far from simple.

Our parties cannot be understood if approached as unified entities. As we have already argued, we have no national political party system but rather a loose confederation of state and local organizations. Any one of these party organizations might be diagrammed by drawing three concentric rings. The center ring would represent the oligarchy in control of the party organization. This is the aspect of party commonly referred to as the machine. Those associated with it are primarily concerned with securing their livelihood through the party organization whether as party officials or through public office. They are usually professional politicians.

Surrounding this inner group, which must control the party organization if the group is to survive, is a larger circle of persons bound to the party by ties of tradition and emotional loyalty. They think of the principles professed by the party. They are more concerned with its ideals and symbols than with the acts of of the professional party workers and leaders. As a rule, they do not participate in the conduct of elections, in campaigns, or in party conclaves. They are more likely to vote for the party ideal than for the party record.

Surrounding this second group is a third area, difficult to delimit but nonetheless vitally important. Here are found the interest groups and the individuals who see in the political party, with its political managers and its traditional supporters, a vehicle for the attainment of their own particular purposes. The party leaders, for their part, see in these groups and individuals the voters who must be won if the support necessary for victory is to be gained. The strategy of the politician is directed toward the discovery of the appeals that will swing to his side support from this periphery. The rival party is concerned in a similar undertaking. Which side will roll up about its circle of traditional supporters the largest mass of peripheral voters who are attracted by the party attitude on current issues is the question answered at elections.

The proportional strength of these three areas differs greatly in various localities and at various times. In actual practice our political parties may embrace these three elements so unevenly that one factor may often dominate the others. Democracy can function only when there is some degree of freedom for each.

Abuses may arise from each of these three functions. Politicians may become messiahs; traditionalists may insist that theirs are the only political ideals and that all persons doubting their values are traitors; special interests may become fanatical and threaten the whole system in a desire to attain their single goal.

Thus far our party system has met the challenge of keeping our governmental machinery going. It has provided leadership loyal to democratic ideas. For the mass of people who need a more personal representation of the state and who want to join with others in fulfilling common aims, it has provided an agent to achieve these desires. Again, the party acts as an agent for compromise between sharply defined economic groups.

In this threefold fashion political parties have protected the democratic process: through providing leaders loyal to the regime, whatever their other faults may be; through attracting the

emotional loyalty of citizens to the two or more parties essential
to democratic government; and through compromising and reconciling the claims of self-interested groups.

The apparent disagreement among writers with their various
definitions of party is due to their emphasis on these different
aspects of party behavior. Snapshots of the same reality taken
from various angles and at various times give us pictures that may
seem to differ substantially. We are concerned with a flux that
could be recorded only by a continuous moving-picture camera.

Because of the threefold aspect of party composition, the party
cannot be described solely in terms of either selfish machine direction, traditional partisan loyalty, or concern with current public policies. Government by the peaceful alternation of parties
has always taken place in a society where great masses of the
populace have already been committed to one side or the other.
This acceptance of the party institutions forestalls violent fluctua-
tions in party strength. We speak of landslides in the U. S.; except for Roosevelt's 1936 majority vote, A. N. Holcombe states,

"Neither party has ever gained for its presidential candidate the support of more than sixty per cent of the total popular vote. The record
was made by Harding in 1920 and has been closely approached only
by Hoover in 1928 and by Roosevelt in 1932. Ordinarily, the winning
candidate has received less than fifty-five per cent of the total vote." [5]

The close balance between our two parties is of the utmost significance. E. E. Robinson, in his study of the presidential vote
from 1896 to 1932, notes that "the percentages by sections show
that rarely does either party sink below twenty-five per cent in
any election; this is true of the Democrats in New England and
of the Republicans in the Old South." In the great majority of
counties over the country each major party had a chance. "The
problem for each was the addition of a sufficient number of voters
to lead the poll, and in those counties where it was a two-party
contest, to secure a majority. What would appeal to the 'marginal
voter'? And what would appeal to the 'stay-at-home vote'?" [6]

This question has tended to make our parties act as both a
stabilizing and a responding mechanism. A shift of 10 per cent

is frequently enough to change a traditional majority into a minority, and often the outcome hinges on less. It is such facts that keep power contingent and opposition healthy and hopeful. The odds against success are not too great; the politician can rely on a nucleus of loyal supporters and then seek to attract additional support.

This contest between organizations for the unattached vote is of the utmost significance. Frank Kent calls this the floating vote and argues that the party able to buy the floaters wins the election. This is an extreme oversimplification. Some voters are floaters, others might be called independents, still others special interest advocates. Whether such voters are intransigent, thoughtful, or merely aimless in their private motivation, their political significance lies in the fact that they are not committed to either party. They are the prize for the skilled politician who can best guess their temper and who can present his organization as the means best calculated to realize their aims.

The politician faces uncertainty about how these voters will act. They may swing the balance of power one way or another.

Our parties seek to be as inclusive as possible without actually crumbling because of the very incongruity of the constituent elements. Those working toward this inclusiveness are the professional politicians; those most repelled by such a tendency are intellectuals, idealists, and others whose mental processes rate high the value of consistency and planning in government. The latter need no defense, but we sometimes overlook the fact that the politician provides the conditions under which intelligence may freely make its contribution.

In a democracy the function of parties may be reduced to two basic aims: to prevent one-party rule through the mere fact of continuing to exist, and to provide leaders who can find a common basis for action in a system which tolerates differences of opinion. These are the minimum standards which must be met if party government under democracy is to continue.

To go back to our analysis of the threefold character of political parties, there is in each camp a group of professional politicians at the center. Surrounding these politicians is a group of traditional supporters. The two parties, with their intense loyalties and their self-seeking managers, are insulated from each other by the great mass of the public not directly affiliated with either side. Elections are determined by the way in which this mass supports one or the other party. Consequently both parties must appeal to the same general group. This often makes for likeness. It may even foster superficiality in confronting public questions. Yet it does force party leaders to search for a common basis of action.

If we chose to think of political parties not in terms of men or groups but in terms of beliefs and principles, we would turn to the party platforms, to speeches by acknowledged leaders, and to similar sources. There would be little point in offering here static snapshots of this flow of thought and words. The feast of reason must be ever renewed. The trouble arises from too many cooks seasoning the broth. The success of this cookery is judged by public taste and popular consumption. Each party has its favorite recipes and many voters prefer the same old food for thought. When it proves unpalatable, someone is always ready with a new concoction. When we face the complexity of our society we must rely upon men of good will as well as men of reason to help carry forward the peaceful adjustment of democratic government. Political problems cannot accurately be treated as pure exercises in logic. If reaching agreement were a purely cerebral operation, we might then consider the method suggested to Gulliver by a famous professor in Laputa:

"The method is this. You take a hundred leaders of each party, you dispose them into couples of such whose heads are nearest of a size; then let two nice operators saw off the occiput of each couple at the same time, in such a manner that the brain may be equally divided. Let the occiputs thus cut off be interchanged, applying each to the head of his opposite party-man. It seems indeed to be a work that requireth some exactness, but the professor assured us that if it were dexterously performed the cure would be infallible. For he argued thus: that the two half brains being left to debate the matter between themselves within the space of one skull, would soon come to a good understanding, and produce that moderation, as well as regularity of thinking, so much to be wished for in the heads of those who imagine they come into the world only to watch and govern its motion: and as to the difference of brains in quantity or quality among those who are directors in faction, the doctor assured us from his own knowledge that it was a perfect trifle." [7]

☆ 18 ☆

The Talk in Campaigns

> "Politics is, as it were, the gizzard of society, full of grit and gravel, and the two political parties are its opposite halves,—sometimes split into quarters, it may be, which grind on each other. Not only individuals, but states, have thus a confirmed dyspepsia, which expresses itself, you can imagine by what sort of eloquence."
>
> HENRY DAVID THOREAU

POLITICS may be likened to a gizzard, if you will, but Henry David Thoreau erred, despite his knowledge of nature, when he suggested that dyspepsia is inevitable in this digestive process. Our parties habitually do quite well in digesting very tough differences of opinion and feeding them into the body politic. Very much to the point, however, is the relationship between the tone of a political campaign and the success or the failure that parties may experience in assimilating political rivalries and developing public policy. What kind of talk proves effective in campaigning? The following excerpt, taken almost at random from a collection of speeches by former President Herbert Hoover, illustrates a common variety of political oratory:

"We must have emancipation from the creeping collectivism of dictated economy. We must take the government out of business in competition with the citizen. We must have freedom of business, labor and farmers from government dictation. We must grant genuine relief to farmers and restore the farmer's judgment in control of his business. We must have reform in the Labor Act to deal equal justice to all workers and all employers. We must have the only basis of liberalism, that is the rule of law and not of men.

"We must reform relief under the administration of non-partisan local committees. We must reform the old age pensions to make them just to the workers. We need to adopt real measures which enable people to obtain better housing. We must advance the whole question of medical attention to the indigent." [1]

Consider the following phrases: "creeping collectivism," "dictated economy," "government dictation," "equal justice," "rule of law and not of men"—what an arsenal of weighted words addressed to the emotions! How is the government to leave private enterprise unaffected while providing housing, medical care, old age pensions, and farm relief? And how are these objects to be realized without an appropriate extension of administrative discretion? Such contradictions lead many to fear that the worst despotism under popular government lies in the "tyranny of words."

Yet these words of Mr. Hoover are the common currency of political debate. Such a speech is to be evaluated in terms of its persuasive power rather than its analytical penetration. Successful political campaigners deal with man not as *homo sapiens* but as *homo volens*. They have long recognized that the voter is more likely to be a wishful thinker than a detached thinker. Modern psychology recognizes these irrational factors as part of the innate pattern of human behavior.

Despite the recognition of the irrational in man's conduct as a psychological fact, we are rather loath to accept its implications for democratic theory. Emotionalism is not to be condemned as bad in itself. Whether or not we prefer man to be rational, he does in fact sometimes act reasonably and sometimes emotionally. Hence it is more important to note the consequences of emotion than to condemn the irrational as dangerous in itself.

There are certain attitudes, emotional if you will, that are as vital to the continuance of democratic government as any cerebral reaction. One illustration is to be found in our reaction to the scandals circulated through whispering campaigns. Here is one of the most insidious methods and one of the most difficult to combat directly. The victim is left almost wholly at the mercy of his detractors unless the community itself reacts against the slanderers. This fortunately has been the case very often.

A Senate committee in 1936 succeeded in tracking to its source the rumor that President Roosevelt was insane. A wave of popular indignation engulfed the author of this lie.

The canards and scandals in our national campaigns seem to fall within a narrow range. The private lives of the leading candidates, their personal morality, their family ties, and their alleged physical or mental infirmities, are all too often the targets of attack. Drunkenness has been a frequent charge. Grover Cleveland was accused of beating his wife when in this condition. Ulysses S. Grant was accused of alcoholism. When whispers of the same sort against Theodore Roosevelt appeared in print, he successfully prosecuted the offender for libel. The race problem has been appealed to in several instances. It was rumored that Abraham Lincoln's running mate, Hannibal Hamlin, was of Negro extraction and that Warren G. Harding had Negro blood.

Religion has frequently been insinuated into campaigns. Al Smith was not the only candidate to suffer. The Catholicism of Mrs. Blaine was a distinct handicap to her husband. The godless have also suffered. Thomas Jefferson was accused not only of fathering a brood of mulattoes and seducing a highborn Virginia maiden but of atheism as well. William Jennings Bryan said of William Howard Taft that no man who did not believe in the divinity of Christ should occupy the White House. Several candidates have been accused of being Anglophiles, while Alf M. Landon is not the only one to be accused of anti-Semitic opinions.

James Truslow Adams, in commenting on whispering campaigns, has noted "the persistence of the same topics as subjects for the unfounded slander stories. For over a hundred and thirty years of campaigning these have been almost wholly confined to sexual relations, treatment of wives, drunkenness, and the alleged possession of Negro blood." Of most significance from our viewpoint is the relative ineffectiveness of such appeals. Adams notes that

"of the sixteen men against whom the whisperers directed their attacks, ten were elected to office, and four were defeated. But of these four, two were opposed to other men who were being similarly attacked in the same election. One, Arthur, was not nominated for the

Presidency after having served out Garfield's unexpired term. A Vice-President, however, succeeding to office does not usually receive the nomination in his own right, Roosevelt and Coolidge being the conspicuous examples of the contrary. We may, therefore, say that ten men subjected to the false calumnies of a whispering campaign were elected and only two defeated. Of course, the whispering campaign is only part of the triple one. It is impossible to say how much or how little influence in any election the whisperers have had. It would seem evident, however, from the figures just quoted that false slander is an extremely weak weapon against a candidate. Otherwise ten slandered candidates out of twelve could hardly have won." [2]

Apparently, scurrilous attacks are relatively ineffective. Accepting emotionalism as inescapable in politics as in other walks of life, we may focus attention on some of its implications. Are the emotions aroused in campaigning predominantly those of hate or of sympathy or of excitement in the face of a contest?

So persistent were the rumors in 1932 regarding Roosevelt's physical disability that pamphlets announcing that insurance companies regarded him as an unusually good risk were issued. (The opposition had suggested that the candidate's physical infirmities might mean that "a vote for Roosevelt is a vote for Garner and Garnerism, and probably a vote for Mrs. Garner." A public sense of decency and sportsmanship prevented such appeals from going very far.) Broadsides depicted Mr. Roosevelt surrounded by insurance policies advertising the fact that twenty-two insurance companies underwrote policies for Mr. Roosevelt to the amount of half a million. At the request of *Liberty Magazine*, three eminent doctors examined the candidate and reported that his health and powers of endurance were sufficient for all contingencies.

In an effort to emphasize the physical capacity of the Democratic candidate, history was combed for examples of great men who conquered despite physical difficulties. Thus one pamphlet read:

"Clemenceau, Edison and Eastman were diabetics to the end of their days, giving their public service by virtue of their self-denial and control. Andrew Jackson, one of the founders of the Democratic party, was dogged by tuberculosis through a lifetime. Hemorrhage after hemorrhage came to him, yet he lived through his two terms as President of the United States and until he was 78 years of age, to the enrichment of American history. Thaddeus Stevens, often called the founder of the Republican party—what a picture he makes as, when 76 years of age, having lost the use of his legs, he is being carried into the House of Representatives, of which he was the master for many years and he turns to the two men carrying him in his chair and says: 'Who will carry me in here when you two fellows are dead?' " [3]

More effective than reasoned denials in blighting such gossip is the sympathy aroused toward the victim. Frank Kent has stated that "the plea for sympathy, the appearance of making a fight against odds, are far more effective in starting the tide toward you than any argument or issue." [4] This is illustrated by the popular reaction to Cleveland's frank admission of his bastard son. Cleveland, like Alexander Hamilton, made a clean breast of this indiscretion of his youth. He brought the story into the open and confounded his critics by frankness.

Many campaign managers seem agreed that bitter personal criticism of an opponent is likely to do him more good than harm. A striking illustration is found in the gubernatorial campaign of 1926 when Al Smith made the most of Ogden Mills's charge that he could not be trusted either in public or in private life. In a reply to this accusation, Smith stated:

"Twenty-seven years ago I knelt before the altar . . . and in the presence of God Almighty promised to care for, honor, and protect the woman of my choice. And if I suddenly was ushered tonight before the Great White Throne I would be prepared to establish that I had kept that promise. Let the Congressman lay his private life alongside of mine." [5]

Smith thus won the sympathy of the public and forced his rival to retract.

The sympathetic response to the victim of an unfair attack is a factor of no small importance. Irrational elements in political campaigning are best judged not in terms of their substance but rather by the kind of emotional response they elicit. Likewise the strength of appeals made upon sentimental grounds, while far from admirable if judged by intellectual standards, is still reflective of a humane attitude. Ridicule has its therapeutic value, but popular government today in many places suffers from worse ills than sentimentality.

My purpose here is not to offer a serious defense of the intrinsically indefensible. Yet triviality and sentimentality can hardly be viewed as serious menaces in themselves. A greater danger lies in the excessive disgust with our electoral process engendered in persons who take these lesser manifestations of human weakness too seriously.

Why do we seem invariably to be shocked more by the realities of human nature in politics than by its manifestations in other walks of life? It is probably because our expectations of man's rationality are higher when we think of *homo sapiens* as a citizen and a voter. When man foregathers with his fellows in these roles, the mass represents such diversity that the lowest common denominator may be of scant intellectual content.

Irrationality will not be eliminated by urging men to be rational. It is a phenomenon to be understood and, if possible, evaluated. How effective is a given irrational appeal, what emotions does it arouse, and how do these reactions contribute to the basic problem of peacefully adjusting diverse human desires? These seem appropriate standards for judgment.

By its very nature campaigning is concerned not with the rational analysis of public problems but primarily with winning political support. From the standpoint of political analysis the important thing to note is the effectiveness of various campaign methods. If a certain appeal works, it is likely to be used even though frowned upon by those men of principle viewing the game of politics from the grandstand.

Thurman Arnold has said:

"The only realistic test of a political speech is its vote-getting effect. This is recognized by the tradesmen of politics but denied by political scholars and high-minded persons generally. Such persons judge political utterances by standards of sincerity and economic analysis. The idea of using words and prejudices as tools to push people into desired courses of conduct, without any particular anxiety as to the absolute truth of these ideas or prejudices, is one of those 'bad things' which a sufficient amount of preaching is supposed to cure." [6]

While this view discounts, perhaps unduly, the effect of rational criticism upon political behavior, it does stress an approach to campaigning worthy of attention. The man seeking office must by virtue of this function limit his appeals to those that will win votes. Political campaign methods illustrate most graphically that arguments are addressed to the heart and stomach more often than to the head. The irrational appeal often proves the more effective. Political campaigns, like religious revival meetings, college commencements, and the gatherings of fraternal orders, are addressed in large measure to the emotions of the participants. Without the stimulation of sympathy they would lack meaning. If we accept this as a persistent pattern of behavior, we shall not condemn campaigning methods simply because they make irrational appeals, but will rather examine them for the kind of emotional response they try to elicit.

The voter in the United States can treat our political campaigns as a great show. This attitude causes much dissatisfaction among certain serious observers. It is usual to speak with contempt of the bunkum in our political campaigns; but is not obvious bunkum preferable to the subtle manipulation of opinion? The fact that much political propaganda can be regarded as bunkum is a healthy condition for democracy. While present tendencies provide little occasion for complacency, still the mere crudity of political appeals is in itself a safeguard. We play the game of politics—but with tongue in cheek and fingers crossed.

If measured by the discussion engendered, campaigning would rate higher than if judged by its profundity. Discussion in itself may settle nothing, but it is important, nevertheless, if it stimulates interest in politics, spreads a common sense of responsibility, and causes people to feel that they are part of the process of rule. It is essential that the good faith of one's fellow citizens be recognized even though we may disagree with their opinions. Campaigns do mean something if they stimulate a common effort to think about a common problem.

The most honest campaigning is that which reveals the integrity, personality, and ability of the candidate and his experience and training for the job he seeks. A campaign fulfills its highest function under democratic government if it gets the voters to decide upon the personalities and the performance of the contestants rather than upon their promises and aspirations. The subtleties of propaganda will not sap the vitality of campaigning so long as the voter is free to make his own estimate of the candidate. Drew Pearson and Robert Allen have written:

"When you get away from the national arena, political campaigning gets right back to the old horse-and-buggy days. Of course, the candidate may promise jobs instead of passing out cigars. He may kiss babies instead of telling the coarse stories of fifty years ago. He may use electric flood-lights instead of the old torch-light processions. But fundamentally, nothing has changed. What really counts is the all-important ingredient of personal contact." [7]

Practical politicians will agree. James A. Farley has in his own career developed the technique of personal contact to great proportions, and yet no one who has dealt with Mr. Farley can doubt that his methods are firmly based on the real liking for his fellows.

"It doesn't hurt my feelings when some sophisticated gentlemen of the writing craft describes me as the kind of fellow who likes to go back to the old home town and salute the neighbors by their first names while they greet me in return with a hearty 'Hello, Jim.' . . . To my way of thinking, there is no substitute for the personal touch and there never will be, unless the Lord starts to make human beings different from the way he makes them now." [8]

In campaigning, ballyhoo is useful but it is useful more to keep up the morale and to fire the enthusiasm of party supporters than as a means for gaining the support of outsiders. In winning voters the more direct the appeal and personal the contact, the better. Farley believes the radio is important because it brings the candidate to the voter. It enables the citizen to make his choice on his estimate of the candidate's personality and appeal. "The voters want to see the candidate for office, and make their own estimate of his qualifications, before marking the ballots," Farley argues. Since the radio came into use in the 1924 campaign, presidential elections have been won by majorities of landslide proportions. This suggests to Farley "the determination and the ability of the individual voter to pick his own candidate, regardless of what he sees or hears to the contrary." [9] The radio approximates on a nation-wide scale the intimacy of candidate with voter—so essential if one human being is to make a shrewd estimate of any other.

Campaigns stir the interchange of ideas, the essence of the democratic process. If men are to find measures short of violence for ruling their social concerns, they must exert themselves in the process. They will react in accordance with their natures, and the appeals used by realistic politicians will be selected primarily for their persuasiveness.

Sixty years ago Horace Greeley argued that the most effective campaign was more "usually produced, so far as conviction is concerned, by a quiet protracted talk in a log school-house than by half-a-dozen tempestuous harangues to a gathering of excited thousands." [10] When the eloquence of the rabble-rouser becomes more convincing than the protracted argument between individuals it is time to look to the gizzard of politics for signs of sickness. There is a place for mass meetings and similar displays of political showmanship. Circuses and pageantry are common phenomena, and it is not surprising to find their trappings taken over by politicians. Speechmaking, parades, mass meetings, street corner harangues, and torchlight processions have been used for generations. In comparison with commercial advertising, political propaganda is still crude. The politician in this country has not taken advantage of these more subtle ways of manipulating public opinion.

Why is it that the politician has not availed himself of all the arts of the propagandist? One reason suggested by a professional public relations man, Edward L. Bernays, why the "politician today is slow to take up methods which are commonplace in business life" is because "he has such ready entry to the media of communication on which his power depends." [11] Whether refinements of manipulation are politically desirable is certainly open to question. The very flaws in the technique of the politician disclose his purpose. Political ballyhoo is discounted. In Germany and Italy the art of propaganda in the political field has been much more highly developed. All the arts of mass manipulation are applied. In societies insecure, fearful, and uncertain a show of solidarity becomes important. Great efforts to impress the populace and sway their judgment become political necessities.

Democracies are driven by no such need. The scope of the propagandist is restricted by the skepticism engendered under government of free discussion. Some professional propagandists, however, feel that our politicians are missing opportunities. Bernays believes that the public mind should be made receptive to the politician's ideas by arranging circumstances that will induce a favorable attitude without openly disclosing the relationship. This publicity man advocates expert propaganda working through the creation of circumstances, through the high-spotting of significant events, and through the dramatization of important issues. He concludes:

"It is essential for the campaign manager to educate the emotions in terms of groups. The public is not made up merely of Democrats and Republicans. People to-day are largely uninterested in politics and their interest in the issues of the campaign must be secured by coordinating it with their personal interests. The public is made up of interlocking groups—economic, social, religious, educational, cultural, racial, collegiate, local, sports, and hundreds of others." [12]

How are we to interpret such efforts to manufacture opinion? The purported influence of propaganda has been pushed so far as to challenge the very vitality of popular government.

Francis G. Wilson has written:

"The most damning charge of the realist is his insistence that propaganda really determines the content of public opinion. The democratic belief that individuals freely form opinions on the facts at hand and, when election time comes, cast their ballots accordingly becomes, for the realist, the democratic myth." [13]

The empirical value of the democratic myth is not destroyed merely because "realists" discover its irrational character. The implications of propaganda must, however, be faced.

☆ 19 ☆

Propaganda in Politics

"We must fetch the public sumhow. We must
wurk on their feelin's."
ARTEMUS WARD

"Fellow citizens, in what part of your anatomy
Do you hide your vote? Little bird inside the
human skin
Come forth: we have a worm for your beak:"
OSCAR WILLIAMS

PROPAGANDA may often lead many people astray on particular issues. It may foster hatred, misinformation, and emotional reactions. Yet unless it actually determines the climate of opinion, it can never invalidate government by public opinion. In a word, we need not suffer disillusionment with popular government as an ideal simply because propaganda does at times manufacture opinion. While some attitudes are as natural as wild flowers, most opinion today is probably under cultivation. We need not fear the cultivation so long as the gardeners continue to compete.

There is a tendency greatly to overestimate the effectiveness of propagandists. Public relations men have not been averse to confessing modestly their ability to mold opinion. Yet the very existence of such practitioners is a tribute to our general belief in public opinion. As organizations grow, their managers seem to become more alert to the importance of gaining the good will of their publics. They strive more consciously to harmonize their institutions with the thought and attitudes of the outside world.

Public relations counsels, although self-confessed Machiavellis, are really the children of the age of bigness. Like skyscrapers, great bureaucracies create environmental disruptions. Some attempt at adjustment is needed. Growths, huge, strange, new, and dynamic, must be related to the society within which they rapidly emerge.

The successful public relations counsel is a man of shrewdness and imagination. He tries to envisage his client's place in the general social milieu. Propaganda provides him with tools for attempting adjustments. Bernays states: "Propaganda takes account not merely of the individual, nor even of the mass mind alone, but also and especially of the anatomy of society, with its interlocking group formation and loyalties. It sees the individual not only as a cell in the social organism but as a cell organized into the social unit." [1]

Obviously the propagandist tries to manipulate society, although he also urges certain modifications on his client as well. Yet it may well be that the public relations man contributes to social order in a positive fashion through his efforts at opinion manipulation. Reform organizations, big business, industrial unions, all represent new upthrusts shocking to existing attitudes in the community. A two-way adjustment is essential. While the propagandist may overstep the bounds of current propriety in his manipulative zeal, an even greater obstacle to social development may be the inertia of traditionalism.

The menace of propaganda lies in its exploitation of prejudice and inertia to attain an end not frankly avowed. Since this can best be done by appealing to an accepted doctrine and then identifying a hidden selfish aim with this accepted end, opinion is befogged and a goal gained under false pretenses. Propaganda thus often leads people to do something that they would not do if approached directly and if they clearly saw the purpose of the persuader. Fortunately, certain factors set a limit to the effectiveness of propaganda. Frederick E. Lumley has suggested the following points: Propaganda can arouse, but it cannot always control or direct the opinion created; preoccupation or absorption in some work or interest often shelters people from exposure to outside influences; an emotional recoil from what is propagandized often occurs just because its virtues are so insistently urged; human beings stand only a limited amount of stimulation without all motivation being weakened or exhausted; negativistic defensive reactions, such as prejudice or suspicion of lies, intervene; hesitation or skepticism demands evidence, not slogans.[2]

The appeal of the propagandist is strongest and most effective when linked with strongly held prejudices.* In fact, the propagandist can hope to prevail best by manipulating prejudices, stereotypes, and assumptions and then turning these to his own ends. The propagandist draws his strength from the society of which he in turn is but one expression. Thus propaganda in wartime does not mean simply the deception of honest citizens by adroit official liars. Propaganda bureaus serve rather as an institutional response to a total social situation. There would be propaganda in wartime without a single paid propagandist. Men are ever ready to believe ill of their enemies and to embroider their fancies. Propaganda plays upon deep-seated and enduring human attitudes for its own special ends.

The strength of propaganda lies in its understanding of the composition of society and of the behavior of the individual. Propaganda has a wide scope in the manipulation of attitudes and group loyalties, but propaganda alone is not capable of establishing these attitudes and loyalties. Too much has been made of propaganda and its influence on public opinion. More basic social

*The following quotation from the New York *Times*, September 7, 1939, "Topics of The Times," is pertinent:

"But it is common knowledge in the newspaper offices, as for that matter it is in the world outside, that the average man is far from being the helpless recipient of propaganda dosage. He does not swallow everything he is told. The letters from readers which are an important part of every newspaper editorial page show on the part of the general public a debating capacity, a gift for marshaling evidence, a healthy skepticism in the face of the other fellow's evidence, which certainly do not correspond to the usual propaganda picture of the average man as a simpleton who believes what he is told.

"We are much nearer the truth in speaking of the average man as believing what he wants to believe. To read the letters to the editor, to listen to any debate on bus or subway, is to see that men are anything but empty pitchers for the propagandist to fill up. The average man has his native stock of ideas and emotions, and it will be a very subtle propaganda that will overcome the native attitude so conditioned."

forces enter into this conditioning. To be effective, propaganda must occur in a favorable environment. Where the surroundings make for receptivity, propaganda can hasten change by directing effort and forcing discussion. Viewed thus, propaganda falls into place in a broad theory of public opinion. According to Doob, ". . . propagandists appear to be successful when they are able· to exploit preexisting attitudes or—from the other point of view —when they possess a rather thorough knowledge of the culture in which they are carrying on their campaigns." [3]

Today politicians study more intensively than ever before the composition of the electorate and the attitude of the voter. Politicians are well aware of the necessity of treating the public as a complex of group interests. A well-organized campaign always directs appeals to the major nationality groups in the community. Labor unions, professional associations, churches, and the like are obvious points of approach. The shrewd campaigner goes beyond these obvious groupings and tries to find the focal points of loyalties and friendships among his constituents. Very important are the personal followings of various key persons. The campaigner, for local or state office, must find such individuals and enlist their support. On the national scale the great contribution of a James Farley is his capacity to align local party chieftains. Through organizational skill and indefatigable letter writing Farley has to an extraordinary extent worked his way back into the locality. Charles Michelson has described the 1936 situation thus: [4]

"Almost daily he received a report from every State chairman. The State chairmen did not guess—they had a similar daily report from every county chairman. The county chairman got his figures from the district and precinct captains—and so on until the ultimate unit was the very smallest political division. In those ultimate units, it was the job of the workers in charge to know, not to guess, what his neighbors had in mind.

"So Mr. Farley could not be wrong unless the local leader, with only a few hundred votes, was so inefficient that he failed in the first requisite of a politician—to know where his immediate bailiwick stood."

Campaigning cannot be understood as activity chiefly significant on the plane of discussion. It is a problem of interests and groups as well as of ideas and emotions. The recognition of this is illustrated by the care that both of the major parties have recently taken to compile information about the electoral districts. The credit for introducing systematic methods of analysis into the Democratic national committee belongs to Emil Hurja, who joined the staff in 1932.

". . . Mr. Hurja had served a term as mining analyst for Mr. Ben Smith, the Wall Street speculator, and he knew the Art of the Trend. It occurred to him that the Art of the Trend applied to the straw votes of the straw voters might produce interesting results. It did.

"The method was this. The Hearst newspapers' poll for Nebraska showed, in September, 1932, a 64.4 per cent vote for Roosevelt, on the basis of which the Hearst papers expected a 132,000 majority. Mr. Hurja however attacked the figures in a different way. He observed that 46 per cent of Mr. Hoover's 1928 voters were now, according to straw-vote figures, voting for Roosevelt while only 4.5 per cent of the 1928 Smith voters were swinging to Hoover. Applying these switch percentages to the 1928 total he arrived at the conclusion, which he reported to Mr. Farley, that 'there is every reason to believe that Nebraska will return a majority of from 150,000 to 200,000 for Governor Roosevelt in November.' The actual majority was 158,000. Other estimates were even closer. He missed the majorities in the eight mountain states by an average error of 564 votes, the majority in Oregon by 522, and the majority in Washington by less than 2,000. His only error was in the state of Pennsylvania.

"All this, of course, has a coldly scientific look. But the action taken on the basis of Mr. Hurja's findings was very far from cold or scientific. Acting upon the principle that success can do its own succeeding without help from anyone, the Democratic National Committee merely adapted its campaign expenditures to Mr. Hurja's figures. Down to 1932 political parties had largely used the scatter-gun method. A campaign chairman, with the evenhanded justice of a blinded divinity, would spill his funds equitably and inefficiently over an entire map. Armed with the Hurja prognostication Mr. Farley avoided such errors. He tempered the wind to the shorn lamb, turned the hose on the dry ground, and made his nickels last. It was wise. It had a mechanistic look. But it was not mechanical. Nothing perhaps was ever less mechanical than the strategy of that campaign." [5]

The Republicans have in their files at Washington a record of the following data for each congressional district:

Facts relating to the population and its composition:
Note: Estimated Increase for State Population from 1930–1936:
  (a) Total Population   Per Cent of Total
      Native White   Population
      Foreign-born White
      Colored
  (b) Leading Foreign-born
      in order of Importance
  (c) Population by Residence   Per Cent of Total
      Urban   Population
      Rural

Population of voting age (21 years or over) 1930
  (a) By Race   Per Cent of Voting
      Total Population   Population
      Native White
      Foreign-born
      Colored

	Per Cent of Total Voters	Per Cent of Urban Voters
(b) By residence		
Urban		
Native White		
Foreign-born		
Colored		

	Per Cent of Total Voters	Per Cent of Rural Voters
Rural		
Native White		
Foreign-born		
Colored		

Note: Foreign-born refers to foreign-born whites only.

Facts pertaining to agriculture (1935)
Note: Information given only if farm population comprises 10% or more of the total population.
  (a) Farm Population
      Per Cent of Total Population

Total	Farm Operators	Value of
Owners	by Tenure	Farms
Tenants		

(b) Farm Mortgage Indebtedness
  Number of Mortgages   Value of Mortgages
(c) Farm Production: Leading type farms in order of importance.

Facts relating to industry (1935)

Name	Number of Establishments	Wage Earners	Payroll in Thousands	Value added to Products by Manufacture

Number of radio receiving sets as of Jan. 1, 1936.

Besides this information is compiled the previous voting record for congressmen over a ten-year period together with percentages showing the trend toward support for Democrats or Republicans. On the basis of these records party leaders can estimate with a high degree of accuracy the districts where success seems likely. Thus in 1936 they grouped the districts on a percentage basis to discover where party support might best be focused. For example, they found thirty-one districts where they had 47 to 49 per cent of the voting strength; thirty-three districts with 47 to 45 per cent; twenty-four districts with 45 to 43 per cent, and so on.

In the Republican presidential campaign of 1936 professional advertising methods were applied to politics. The tactics were comparable to those used by great national advertisers. It was said that "the campaign was an intensive, subtle, highly organized salesmanship drive to 'unsell' President Roosevelt and his New Deal and to sell Governor Landon and his highly advertised 'common sense.'" Ralph Casey writes that "no political party has ever excelled the businesslike effectiveness of the Republicans in the distribution of their party propaganda. Here again the techniques of advertising and salesmanship were drawn upon." [6] An experienced direct-by-mail merchandising expert was hired. The radio was used not only to present the candidate to the public, but also to "sell the idea of the campaign." While the mistakes of the New Deal were reiterated, the party failed to reach a genuine agreement on major appeals. To the opposition the battle appeared as "a succession of efforts to deflect the struggle into side issues."

The Republicans failed to build up their candidate effectively. How much this was due to their man rather than to their methods is open to question. Observers, however, were of the opinion that tactical errors were a factor of importance. A lack of co-ordinated direction from headquarters weakened the party's work. The relations between the research and editorial department and the public relations department were not well defined.

While factors such as these doubtless contributed to the ineffectiveness of the Republican propaganda, a careful study of the 1936 experience casts grave doubt on the feasibility of promoting by the same general techniques the popularity of a presidential candidate and a cake of soap. Ralph Casey concludes that "the Public Relations Department unfamiliar with political behavior in a Presidential campaign, placed too much reliance upon techniques and merchandising ideas." The research and editorial department "talked too much about spending and taxation and not enough about its candidate." The party "recruited too many specialists unfamiliar with political behavior and preoccupied with promotional ideas successful in the commercial sphere." [7]

These advertising and publicity experts were apparently not aware of the political attitudes of the lower-income and wage-earning voters. Much Democratic support undoubtedly came from voters at an economic level well below the range included in the advertisers' buying public. It seems likely that, despite the mistakes made by the Republicans, the advertising business will be called upon increasingly in the future. The politician can learn much that would prove adaptable to his peculiar needs.

Publicity directors freely confess their rule-of-thumb approach. Mr. Michelson states:

"This business of political press agentry, contrary, perhaps, to the general impression, is neither inspirational nor deeply subtle. It is wholly opportunistic. Hence no all-embracing rules can be laid down, for every campaign presents a different front, and that front is likely to change from day to day." [8]

The campaign methods that will be used are those that prove their effectiveness. Political campaigning is concerned no more than commercial advertising with the plain unvarnished truth. Both politicians and business try to present their side of the picture. Let the consumer beware! The public spends millions that would be saved were buyers more rational, more discriminating, less sentimental, less swayed by slogans, by snobbery, by impulses to imitate, to emulate, or to use short cuts to beauty, wealth, popularity, health, and happiness. Political oratory and persuasion are but another aspect of the same human tendencies. A public that seeks panaceas in economic or social relations will not suddenly react more critically when offered political nostrums.

Whether more integrity adheres to political propaganda than to commercial promotion must remain a matter of individual judgment. Each side seems equally vulnerable, although business, with the aid of high-powered public relations counsels, often appears rather less disingenuous in contrast with the frank partisanship of the politician.

To condemn the democratic process because it is often highly irrational is to retreat to a philosophy of cynicism or to government by aristocracy. The former means futility and the latter brings in its train abuses more irksome than the weaknesses of popular government.

Moreover, such disillusionment is not widely shared by those having frequent contacts with the voters. No one has studied public opinion on so wide a scale as George Gallup, and his testimony is weighty. Gallup says:

"The sampling surveys of recent years have provided much evidence concerning the wisdom of the common people. Anyone is free to examine this evidence. And I think that the person who does examine it will come away believing as I do that, collectively, the American people have a remarkably high degree of common sense. These people may not be brilliant or intellectual or particularly well read, but they possess a quality of good sense which is manifested time and again in their expressions of opinion on present-day issues.

"Theodore Roosevelt once said that the 'majority of the plain people will day in and day out make fewer mistakes in governing themselves than any smaller class or body of men will make in trying to govern them.' Lord Bryce has added that public opinion in America is 'generally right in its aims and has tended to become wiser and more moderate with the march of years.' The findings of the opinion surveys tend to confirm in every respect the conclusions of these two men.

"It would of course be foolish to argue that the collective views of the common people always represent the most intelligent and most accurate answer to any question. But results of sampling referenda on hundreds of issues do indicate, in my opinion, that we can place great faith in the collective judgment or intelligence of the people." [9]

Much of the strength of popular government lies in the matter-of-fact attitude of the average citizen. So long as our elected officials are judged by the way in which their policies touch the lives of individuals, we shall have as stable a guide as we can hope for in an uncertain world.

Some students of propaganda look with misgivings to the growth of the radio and the spread of newspapers and periodicals.[10] They argue that "to an amazing extent these mediums have replaced the face-to-face discussion of issues in the twentieth century." If this is the fact, we may well be on our guard. But how can any such statement be proved? One can, on the contrary, point to the great popularity of the Town Hall of the Air, where the questioning and heckling of well-known speakers is broadcast. Adult education groups and discussion forums have been set up over the country. Observers find no lack of interest in current political affairs. In fact, the radio and the press while replacing the group around the cracker-barrels in the country stores as sources of information may well serve to stimulate a vast amount of well-informed discussion.[11]

Our campaigning methods contribute to the politics of democracy by stimulating wide interest and even excitement over the electoral process. We need not fear propagandists so long as our political system provides an opportunity for the mass of voters in the light of their own experience to pass judgment upon those who would rule them. The voter, with all his irrationalities and lack of technical knowledge, has nevertheless much to say when he speaks from the pains and pleasures of his own daily life. Such citizens are statesmen akin to Gulliver's King of Brobdingnag:

"He confined the knowledge of governing within very narrow bounds; to common sense and reason, to justice and lenity, to the speedy determination of civil and criminal causes; with some other obvious topics, which are not worth considering. And he gave it for his opinion, that whoever could make two ears of corn or two blades of grass to grow upon a spot of ground where only one grew before, would deserve better of mankind, and do more essential service to his country than the whole race of politicians put together." [12]

Thinking in abstractions is forced upon us when the limits of personal experience are reached. Our troubles multiply when the average citizen sets himself up as an amateur economist or political philosopher.

☆ 20 ☆

Doctrinaires and Demagogues

> "The American doctrinaire is the converse
> of the American demagogue, and in his way,
> is scarcely less injurious to the publick."
>
> JAMES FENIMORE COOPER

HUMAN affairs seldom follow consistently *a priori* philosophic concepts. A. Lawrence Lowell has called attention to the acceptance of the theories of Montesquieu and De Lolme as descriptive of the British Constitution at a time when developments quite contrary to these schematizations were well under way:

> "It may be stated of the makers of the British Parliamentary government, as has been said of Columbus, that when he started on his voyage he did not know where he was going, when he got there he did not know where he was, and when he got back he did not know where he had been; and yet he discovered America.
>
> "I think, therefore, the example of the British parliament system shows that with men, as with animals, a continual conscious adaptation to immediate objects may sometimes, if the conditions are favorable, lead to a fully self-consistent and harmonious system which to the authors is quite unforeseen and which is not only very different from, but even quite inconsistent with, the theories (or in the language of Pareto, the derivations) that they retain continuously throughout the process." [1]

Experience shows that human institutions develop not in accordance with the schemes of philosophers but out of the interplay of many forces. The ideals men profess are but one factor in determining social conduct. Some theorists go so far as vastly to restrict the role of deliberate thought. Karl Mannheim states:

"We must recognize that conscious reflection or the imaginative rehearsal of the situation that we call 'thinking' is not an indispensable part of every act. Indeed, it seems to be generally agreed among social psychologists that ideas are not spontaneously generated and that, despite the assertion of an antiquated psychology, the act comes before the thought." [2]

It may be that the pressure for decision in the face of rival claims is of the utmost importance in forcing conscious thought in politics. To take sides concerning the relative importance of free will and foresight in the direction of political affairs is not necessary. Observation makes clear that we have many different responses and attitudes of mind interacting in politics. It is not my purpose to recommend one kind of reaction to the exclusion of the rest, but rather to seek some understanding of the process.

The quest for the absolute is a uniformity of human behavior that cannot be ignored by the student of politics. Some men, of course, are more acutely conscious of this urge than others. I am tempted to believe that the man of letters is often more impressed with the need for absolutes than the man of affairs, but it may be rather that the former leaves a more articulate record of his thought. In any event the prevalent human desire to see the world as an orderly and normative set of interrelations does have direct political repercussions. This urge underlies the insistence that social relationships be determined by the clear statement of logical alternatives, a debate followed by a decision of the issue and its subsequent enforcement. That such a simple and direct procedure fails to operate according to formula, and falls back upon irrational appeals and connivance as the course dictated by expediency, does not serve to banish the hope that the more logical method will somehow, sometime prevail. This hope is doubtless a factor of importance in the maintenance of our political institutions. Hope for what might be is not, however, the attitude most appropriate for a critical scrutiny of what is.

Putting aside pictures of a desirable future while examining an undesired present does not necessarily imply the rejection of an idealist approach. There is certainly a tenable distinction between assuming a relativist position for purposes of analysis and an idealist position for personal orientation in this world or salvation in the next. Such a distinction need not impinge upon individual judgments of value or of ultimate ends. To separate these two functions need not entail denying the end for which either side stands.

If, however, data are selected, arranged, and judged in relation to one set of previously fixed canons, inquiry is hobbled. Different pictures of reality may be procured by ranging the data of experience in accordance with a number of different codes of ethics or standards of value. For the purposes of experimental inquiry we may have a variety of arrangements of data each the result of different preconceptions concerning what is significant and what is not. For the purpose of personal acceptance or support the particular view of truth held by the individual will determine his choice among alternatives. For himself he may say my choice alone is truth—all else is false. But he still might be willing to admit that he could obtain a fuller appreciation of his own position by comparing his conclusions with those reached by other men who may start with a different set of premises.

For example, the Marxist who interprets the behavior of industrialists in terms of profit seeking and class conflict reaches an estimate different in kind from the Freudian who searches his subconscious for the childhood inhibitions or frustrations that may explain his conduct as an adult. In absolute terms and in accordance with individual judgment you or I might say that the Marxian was right and the Freudian wrong, or vice versa. For purposes of political analysis this metaphysical problem may be ignored and we may agree that here are two methods having possibilities as experimental devices for arranging data in meaningful patterns. Choosing the pattern which we regard as true or as the basis for action is another matter and one that involves a declaration of allegiance to some scheme of values. Men have never agreed on any one scheme, nor can the expert hope to find such unanimity. In human experience we have never found universal agreement concerning the nature of truth, nor of beauty, nor of the good life. The nearest we have come is through some intuitive unity of feeling that here or there we can say of a flashing perception:

> "Beauty is truth, truth beauty,—that is all
> Ye know on earth, and all ye need to know."

If we set out to meet political struggles upon the assumption that such flashes can be prolonged into the dawn of a new day we are doomed to disappointment or frustration. We cannot rely upon an intuitive acceptance of absolutes as the way to political unity.

It is well also to be aware of the limitations of intellectual analysis as a way to truth. In any attempt to explain causal relations we cannot proceed without positing certain values as of more basic significance than others. Causation can be explained only by selecting certain factors as more meaningful than others. The consequences of this logical dilemma are graphically shown in an anecdote which I borrow with thanks from L. J. Henderson:

"A student who has just had three or four cocktails is shaving when his roommate slams a door. He drops his razor and cuts his toe, carelessly ties up the wound and goes to the theater. His toe becomes inflamed and he finally dies. What is the cause of his death?

"The following causes, among others, may be assigned by various persons: General septicemia, by the doctor; a streptococcus infection, by the bacteriologist; there was no one to take proper care of him, by the mother; the doctor's incompetency, by the father; the slamming of the door, by the roommate; lack of discipline in the boy's upbringing, by the uncle; the boy's neglect of the wound, by a timid and also by a methodical friend; the cocktails, by a prohibitionist." [3]

As Henderson points out, the rightness of any one explanation as against another can be premised only on assuming certain aspects of reality to be more important for certain purposes than others.

This problem of choice becomes acute when responsible officials must size up a situation before taking action. This means that consciously or not they choose to see certain aspects and to ignore others. Thus the economists may say that a given fiscal policy is sound, but the politicians may regard it as inexpedient. Churchmen may support it on ethical grounds, while officials condemn it as offering insuperable administrative difficulties.

Each may be right in that each may be able to defend his position rationally within his own terms of reference. Economic laws, for example, are not to be taken as ultimate guides to action. They are rather efforts at systematizing one aspect of experience. For the development of a science such efforts at rationalization are of prime importance, but we must distinguish between the growth of a science and the direction of public affairs. While economics may make a useful contribution to public policy, it cannot prescribe the course.

Those social scientists who are highly conscious of the inescapably partial nature of their analysis hesitate to offer their abstract formulations as authoritative guides to policy. Many others, however, are not so self-effacing. One economist writes of his brethren thus:

"Some economists, while working more or less successfully on improvement of the scientific apparatus and formulation of more realistic assumptions and selection of more reliable data are so strongly conscious of their own limitations that they either abstain from offering any advice at all or give it only on special, more or less technical matters.

"Some others feel compelled by their civil consciousness to take the common risk of making and advocating practical decisions without basing them on any conclusive piece of analysis; but just because their professional standing might lead the uninitiated to the belief that they actually 'know the answers,' these economists try to make it quite clear that their actual knowledge could not possibly influence these decisions one way or another.

"And finally there are men whose political temperament is stronger than their scientific skepticism (or should I say idealism?). They know that a plea supported by a 'scientific' argument however spurious carries further than one based on purely emotional appeal. They prefer to use a good theory—if one is available,—they are glad to introduce some minor or, if necessary, major, changes in order to adapt it better to the 'given' conclusions; but they feel that in any case a doubtful theory which leads to acceptable or desirable results is better than no theory at all. And doubtful theories in the field of economics are usually available for every purpose.

"Each of us is a composite of these three types, but the proportions in which the ingredients are mixed differ widely. In general I think the majority prefers and is able to make a good argument rather than a good piece of analysis." [4]

The comments of this economist may with equal justice be applied to other fields of inquiry. The social sciences by themselves can never set social ends. All the scientist can do is focus attention upon selected phases of reality and show the interrelations that operate within the framework of reference set by his initial assumptions. The scientific method can never be the sole channel for the application of intelligence, though it does offer a useful supplemental technique for analysis and experimentation. Basic to such an attitude of objectivity is a subjective social ideal. It is the belief that questioning and testing are a good thing, and hence that the political beliefs justifying such freedom for inquiry are worthy of continuance.

The role of the social scientist has often been that of a producer of theories concerning probable or desirable courses of social development. Such theories sometimes win acceptance as political objectives. However, all analysis is partial and selective. Deviation is bound to exist between any tidy theory and the contradictions of reality. Too much of our present-day confusion arises from the discovery that the world is not acting in accordance with the mental pictures we have as to what should be. The task of the social scientist is to note these differences and to alter his theories so as more accurately to analyze human behavior. When the social scientist turns from analysis to proposals for action he becomes a statesman or a propagandist.

All experts, when they turn from the limits of their discipline to recommendations for public policy, inescapably become the apologists for certain social values or group interests. They enter into the contest for power. We need not here engage in arguing whether social scientists should advise upon matters of public policy simply because the need is great and they are relatively better informed than laymen.

The rationalizations of the expert are often very persuasive even though to talk in scientifically objective terms of what is socially sound is to fly false colors. The expert is often unwilling to confess the subjectivity of the values that he would promote in the name of his science. Any approach to reality necessitates philosophical assumptions. In our thinking about government the metaphysical foundations are particularly important. The practical-minded man who is most contemptuous of theory is most inclined to leave his premises unconfessed.

With respect to public policy, the distinction between what may be socially desirable and what may be technically defensible is habitually confused. Erasmus long ago called attention to the consequences for government when the man of books loses touch with the vital human imponderables. A passage from *In Praise of Folly* is illustrative:

"Now then let Plato's fine sentence be cried up, that 'happy are those commonwealths where either philosophers are elected kings, or kings turn philosophers.' Alas, this is so far from being true, that if we consult all historians for an account of past ages, we shall find no princes more weak, nor any people more slavish and wretched, than where the administration of affairs fell on the shoulders of some learned bookish governor." [5]

The course that intelligent men may take and the values they are prepared to defend are conditioned by social factors. Political problems cannot be met simply by spurring the reasonable man into activity. The aspects of reality that impress various reasonable men as important are greatly determined by the values and background of each individual. Mannheim points out that

"ruling groups . . . become so intensively interest-bound to a situation that they are simply no longer able to see certain facts which would undermine their sense of domination. . . . The concept of *utopian* thinking reflects the opposite discovery of the political struggle, that certain oppressed groups are intellectually so strongly interested in the destruction and transformation of a given condition of society that they unwittingly see only those elements in the situation which tend to negate it." [6]

Men satisfied with the status quo, on the other hand, may be so absorbed with problems immediately before them that they lose a sense of perspective. Those who are most discontented with things as they are, are most likely to seek a well-rounded and complete world of things as they should be. If the doctrinaire approach means an attitude toward government divorced from what is possible and what is wanted by the mass of men in terms of their specific needs, then it becomes dangerous as a guide to action.

The continuance of democratic government is dependent upon providing tangible satisfactions in an environment that makes self-respect possible. Under such conditions the citizen has a real contribution to make. He can give a clean and clear reaction in terms of concrete experience. The intellectual characteristically reacts by expressing an opinion as to what should be. He provides broad rationalizations. He may seek to win support for abstract values. He may even preach a creed. He can try to modify existing stereotypes. Such services are all particularly important when old beliefs are challenged and new values sought. On the other hand emotional loyalties may contribute positively to getting men to co-operate for common goals. Democracy needs men of good will as well as men of good sense.

Under democracy all that we can hope to retain is a process for adjustment that admits of trial and error in response to the changing desires of men and the pressures generated by their association together in seeking particular ends. Our solution will lie in the skill, luck, and patience with which we succeed in finding ways of living together. Men have used loyalty to constitutionalism, rule by law, states' rights, individualism, and similar concepts as reasons for not supporting measures designed to meet immediate human wants. Such idealists are usually men of good will, but they prepare the way for men of violence who come bearing gifts.

This danger is made all the greater by the limitations placed on expertness when results of involved analysis must be explained to the public. Oversimplification and dramatization of issues seem in fact to be concomitants of popular government. The results of expert economic analysis are often too difficult for the public to grasp. The ramifications are too wide and rest too unevenly upon the lives of different people. The process of analysis is very difficult even for those most directly concerned. When we turn to the political manipulation of economic problems, we must submit to the limitations inherent in the means employed. To move men in the mass the art of generalization must be used. As Sir Henry Maine pointed out, this involves stressing certain facts and ignoring others. The facts stressed must be such as to form an attractive picture. It need have little resemblance to reality.

Economic relationships are usually complex and multifarious. Economists who spend all their time studying this complexity emerge with different theories concerning it. Theirs is not the stuff of politics. Their analyses are not intended to move men to action. The call to action must be simple, clear, and dynamic. It must arouse hope and enthusiasm. It must rest upon the faith that a new order will emerge or upon the belief that the old order is worth preserving. A survey of all the facts is not conducive to a confident pronouncement of what is right. The conclusions of science are always tentative; but the politician must feel sure of his ground if he is to convince others that he alone can lead them to better things.

When economic problems, therefore, are approached from the political angle, they undergo a metamorphosis. They are treated either in terms of what should be or in terms of what has been. The radical reformer offers a generalized program which he guarantees as a cure for the economic maladjustment causing pain in the body politic. His cure must be simple and straightforward if it is to be politically effective. If it cannot be grasped by the unsophisticated mind, it has little value for political purposes. If it is incapable of firing the imagination of its adherents, it is useless. It must have an emotional as well as a rational appeal.

Panaceas of this sort by their very nature differ from the situation they are intended to rectify, however. They are significant to the extent that they indicate that something is wrong. We cannot afford to ignore them as symptoms of a basic disorder. We cannot afford to embrace them as solutions for this discontent.

The existence of social discontent means that one group demands a change and that another fears alterations of the status quo. This latter group, however, can be as unrealistic as the former. In both groups there are individuals who, because of their special knowledge or strategic position, are able to see the full implications of a particular maladjustment; but such persons can never be sufficiently numerous to be politically effective without the support of great numbers, who must act upon faith rather than certain knowledge. To get the support of this great mass of the "inevitably ignorant," simplification is essential. Those of conservative temper tend to take a stand upon "fundamental principles." They are guided in their reaction by these accepted maxims rather than by an objective scrutiny of the new situation. The factors in the new situation are always so numerous, so elusive, and often so technical that it is impossible to construct a clear picture. Yet principles serve to bring order into this confusion. Both the panaceas of the reformers and the principles of the conservatives are symbolic. They represent a transfer of attention from the booming, buzzing confusion of reality to the solace of the simple and familiar. They do not, however, advance us very far toward the adjustment of the underlying social difficulties that were the occasion of this search for facile solutions.

It is when men of intelligence and ideals fail in answering social demands that the demagogue finds his chance.

In the nineties, economic problems of great complexity confronted the country. The most disputed questions related to the relative importance of industry, agriculture, and labor. The protests of the populace arose from conditions brought about by overproduction of agricultural products and by the problem of transporting these products and disposing of them in world markets. The maladjustment gave rise to hotly debated issues. There was then—and there is today—among thoughtful people, a great deal of indecision as to the way in which these difficulties might best be met. The farmers, suffering acutely, could not wait for some ultimate solution of their problems. They responded to the agitators urging them to raise less corn and more hell. They readily blamed their difficulties upon monopoly, protectionism, and an inelastic currency. Politicians found that they could not ignore the strength of the farm protest.

William Jennings Bryan, through his personal zeal and political skill, was able to rally these forces in the campaign of 1896. He dramatically simplified their discontents by urging the free coinage of silver at a fixed ratio to gold of 16 to 1. The fate of this stand graphically illustrates what happens when a simple, direct solution is offered for the problems of a highly complex situation. To a patient requiring all that surgery and protracted therapy could do, Dr. Bryan offered a pill accompanied by eloquent homilies.

In bimetalism, Bryan raised an issue that cut across party lines and that disclosed the cleavage between propertied and debtor groups. Never before in this country had class feeling been so deeply stirred. The campaign revealed in dramatic fashion the fissures that weakened the unity of the nation. Yet did the tactics of Bryan aid the farmers in their struggle for better economic conditions? The silver issue turned out to be but another red herring. Bryanism was significant as a symptom of ill health rather than as a cure for what was wrong. Bryan succeeded only too well in disclosing conflicts of interest in the United States. His efforts showed the extent of dissatisfaction rather than the means for allaying it.

The Spanish-American War has indeed been interpreted as a way of distracting attention from the embarrassing issues which Bryan had injected into national politics. The tariff had been debated as a party issue but it would no longer serve as a diversion from more basic economic questions. As Walter Millis remarks:

"The gentle preoccupations of tariff revision were an inadequate answer to the dread vistas which had been opened by the election. Three weeks after the election Mr. Roosevelt was reminding his friend, Mr. Lodge, that 'Bryanism' was still a 'real and ugly danger, and our hold on the forces that won the victory for us by no means too well assured.' . . . On all accounts it behooved the astute to look about them.[7]

"They did so; and almost at once they discovered that the Island of Cuba was still there."

President McKinley, however, was advised that war would be bad for business, and the policy of the party suddenly became one of moderation as a result. But, continues Millis:

". . . in this there lurked an obvious danger. The South and West—the strongholds of the free silver heresy—were less imperialistic than the Eastern jingoes, but much more deeply impressed with our Christian duty to right the wrongs of suffering Cuba. Their representatives in Congress had manifested an even more lurid bellicosity than the Republicans. If the Republicans now showed themselves lukewarm toward their platform pledges, the Democrats might use the martial enthusiasm of the populace to unhorse Mr. McKinley precisely as the Republicans had used them to unhorse Mr. Cleveland. It was something of a dilemma." [8]

Yet the war enthusiasm had been aroused to such a pitch that McKinley hesitated to make moves for peace for fear of affecting his party adversely.

The war served to banish from the election of 1900 the economic issues that had stirred the country four years before. Again Bryan injected a specific issue into the campaign: Imperialism, he declared, was the paramount issue. Authorities agree that there was little general interest in this issue. "Well, I guess we can stand it so long as hogs are twenty cents a hundred," one farmer remarked. Though Bryan insisted in reviving silver as a secondary issue, the shrewd Mark Hanna held up to the people the full dinner pail. Of the election, Williams declares:

"It is hardly too much to say that the issue of imperialism was a personal issue with Bryan. We do not mean to say that there would have been no issue had he not raised it, or that no one else would have been found fighting on his side of the question, because many able men took the same view but no outstanding American political leader took a stand upon the issue until Bryan had spoken; and he alone possessed the influence and driving power to accomplish what he did accomplish in the solution of this question." [9]

Bryan dramatized the discontent of the nation, and he undoubtedly stirred thoughtful men to hard thinking. It is impossible to say how much influence upon the course of events his preaching had. We know that his tactics proved disastrous to his party, that his silver plank was a slogan rather than a solution, and that his extreme positions led his opponents to extreme measures of resistance. His own party swung from one pole to the other in the selection of its presidential standard-bearers. Bryan brought disruption rather than adjustment. He demonstrated the influence that a single man may have in formulating issues for public consideration.

Bryan's ultimate influence is one of those imponderables that escape objective evaluation. But we know that the strategy by which the goal he sought was ultimately attained was different from the strategy used by the silver-tongued orator. It is arguable that Bryan was simply ahead of his time and that Theodore Roosevelt reaped what the Great Commoner had sown. I would argue that Theodore Roosevelt succeeded where Bryan failed. Roosevelt dealt with corporations and financial interests in a manner that would have scandalized Bryan. Henry F. Pringle reports of Roosevelt's 1904 campaign:

"Roosevelt had done his share to obtain their benedictions. He had softened his expression of wrath regarding greedy corporations. He offered to appoint Henry C. Frick of the United States Steel Corporation to the Isthmian Canal Commission. He submitted a draft of his third annual message to James Stillman, president of the National City Bank, and promised to make changes in the passages referring to the currency question. He even invited Morgan himself to the White House. . . ." [10]

The president, however, left records of substantial legislative adjustments toward regulating business and promoting national welfare even though he did not use the campaign for expounding specific plans.

Leaders of the Bryan type call attention to problems and stir the more sedate citizenry into action. Gerald Johnson writes:

"The Mad Mullah always loses in the long run for the simple reason that when he trumpets to the feeble-witted he rouses the intelligent; and even as the former flock to his standard, the latter take arms against him. I hold no brief for Bryanism, but it is evident to the dullest that

Bryanism compelled some of the hardest and keenest political thinking of the last generation; and out of the welter stirred up by Bryan emerged both Roosevelt and Wilson, each of whom helped himself liberally to Bryan's ideas, stripped most of the lunacy from them, and employed them to excellent advantage." [11]

It is to be expected that under a representative system mountebanks will have their day. Democracy need make no pretense of infallibility. Neither its idiocies nor its aspirations are censored by a ministry of propaganda and enlightenment before reaching the public. What are we to make of the Tom Heflins, the Jimmy Walkers, and the Alfalfa Bill Murrays? To mention these names is to conjure up figures reflective of the prejudices and foibles of particular regions. Our mountebanks are parochial. As Alva Johnston has written:

"The ordinary attention-catching tricks are boomerangs in Presidential politics. Voters delight in electing low-comedy types as Mayors, Congressmen, and Senators, but the political clown is seldom appreciated outside of his own city or state. New York has had Mayors Hyland and Walker, and loved them; but New York cannot understand how Chicago ever put up with Bill Thompson or how Louisiana stood for Huey Long.

". . . The rise of James Hamilton Lewis, for instance, was expedited in Illinois by the eccentric elegance of his dress and whiskers. . . . But the country would never allow in the White House a man whose whiskers have been a national jest for more than forty years. . . . 'Alfalfa' Bill Murray has profited in Oklahoma from his nickname and from his habit of wearing two pair of trousers at the same time, and standing on his head and arguing about religion; but these things undermine him in most of the other forty-seven states." [12]

The appeal of the showman—his strength at home—often spells his defeat further afield. The mountebank may or may not be sincere. The crudity of his appeal has no necessary relationship to his intentions, good or otherwise. His showmanship must be related to the mores of his community. Thus the real significance of Huey Long rested on the extent to which he reflected the southern middle-class mentality. In this lay his strength. His danger rested in the direction that he might have taken with this support. His campaign methods were effective because of the meaning they had for his particular kind of audience. One observer described Long thus:

"He is a political revivalist: a Democratic gospel shouter who transmutes ponderous abstractions into the idiom of the people with a glib plausibility that is uncanny. The difference between one of his rapid-fire political broadsides and the customary campaign rodomontade is precisely the difference between the polished discourse of the curate of St. Somebody's church, and an old-time Billy Sunday diatribe on the inherent depravity of phonograph records. The curate of St. Somebody's may excite the admiration of his hearers, but Billy Sunday brought his, sweating and frantic, along the sawdust trail to the mourners' bench." [13]

Long was cut off in his prime, but his success suggests a problem basic to our discussion of irrationality in politics. Thus far, strictly emotional appeals have been limited in presidential campaigns. Bryan had his great following, but he could not arouse the entire nation on a single evening. This is now a possibility. The radio brings the voice and the personality of the candidate into the home. It approximates on the widest possible scale a man-to-man relationship. The man of reason may also take to the air—but is he as likely to attract a huge audience?

Among our radical organizations, for example, it is not the groups with the most logically consistent economic criticisms that have the largest followings. The Communist party in 1936 had 40,000 enrolled members. During the campaign in 1936 Father Coughlin was able to gather 20,000 enthusiastic supporters in the Cleveland Stadium and to talk of delivering the vote of his 9,000,000 radio listeners. Whence come such great followings? An observer at the 1936 National Union of Social Justice convention stated:

"Everywhere was evidence that Coughlin's power comes altogether from the accumulated effect of his weekly broadcasts. Invariably, delegates began: 'I've been listening for four years.' Or it would be two years, or, shamefacedly, only six months. They were people to whom a $10 radio was their only luxury, their great comfort. Week after week, Coughlin has explained that their depression-born poverty is not their fault, that it has been caused by evil, mysterious forces, international bankers, the Rothschilds, the Communists. He has told them, crudely and flatly: 'God wants you to have more money.' " [14]

Despite the exaggerated claims made by the N.U.S.J. and the Townsend movement, the methods of Townsend and Coughlin illustrate strikingly how mass support can be aligned through the oversimplification of economic issues. It is this type of radicalism that is really dangerous since its theories can only lead to chaos. Yet politicians have pandered for such support. They are playing with depth bombs. Their purpose apparently is to remove the detonator and to use the powder for their own purposes.

The appeal of Coughlin and Townsend stands in contrast with that of the Marxians and Socialists. Their dissatisfaction with conditions is mutual, but their appeal is fundamentally different. The latter approach political questions as economic problems. They analyze. They reason. They proceed logically from assumptions which they are at great pains to justify and defend. Theirs is the intellectual approach. If they win support, it is despite the popular I.Q. In contrast, the rabble-rousers have their legions because they appeal to the great mental lowlands of the nation. They win power because they offer the public the hocus-pocus it demands. Their influence has fortunately stopped short of responsible control.

The political process today has need of all the skill and imagination that intelligence can offer in focusing on ways and means of adjusting present difficulties. Yet the more social questions are treated as political problems, the more are their answers influenced and even determined by the opinions of the mass who are less immediately concerned and less informed of the intricacies of any given question. The problem of how to get the most thoughtful consideration of public problems by party leaders raises broader questions too profound to admit of a ready answer but too pertinent to be ignored. Though we must beware of both the doctrinaire and the demagogue, we can find no way out by substituting the philosopher for the politician.

☆ 21 ☆

The Limitations of Debate

"Every year, if not every day, we have to wager our salvation upon some prophecy based upon imperfect knowledge."
JUSTICE OLIVER WENDELL HOLMES

A PUBLIC policy is both a prophecy and a gamble. It is an expression of faith and a plan for action based on this faith. Yet despite the fallibility of human knowledge and the imponderables of the future, such wagers must continually be made by statesmen faced with the responsibility for action.

In judging the way in which they discharge these duties we are apt to be very severe. Writers analyzing with the wisdom of hindsight and relieved of the burden of decision making can be highly critical. For example, Matthew Josephson in his interesting study, *Politicos 1865–1896*, has berated the fertility of professional politicians

"in raising Live Issues that provided escape from class conflict toward some tentative equilibrium between the privileged and the discontented. For the leaders of the great patronage parties the essence of tactics lay in the legerdemain of pretended compromise, whereby these uncanny political illusionists played for the moneyed support of one class and the votes of the other—so long as momentary points of common interest between the classes could be improvised and enduring differences ignored." [1]

Is such political activity to be dismissed as mere trickery? While the professional politician has often avoided the clarification of social divergences, his search for points of equilibrium is not without deeper meaning. His choice of issues is determined

288

for him by the strategic demands of the job before him. He must address himself to those issues, trivial or profound, around which voting strength can be rallied. Mr. Farley presents with great frankness the pertinent considerations in this connection:

". . . the choice of issues is decided upon only after the most careful and searching inquiry into the state of public opinion, into the attitude of industry, labor, and other vital groups; into the question of whether an issue has national or only local appeal, and above all others, into the question of guessing just where the foe should prove most vulnerable. It is easy to realize how a line of attack might fail to impress the public, or worse still, might rub public feeling the wrong way and in the end turn out to be a boomerang." [2]

No weapon holds more terror for the politician than the boomerang. The issues he brings to the fore are more likely to be selected for their safety and dependability in vote-winning appeal than for their intrinsic social importance. The disillusioned reaction of the voter seeking rational debate of the merits of public problems is understandable.

To most voters, however, politics is a game in which men struggle with each other for office. One's sympathies are attracted to the personalities of one or the other party. Is the candidate sincere? Does he seem honest and well-meaning? Will he keep his promises? Who are his friends? Are they trustworthy people? What will the candidate do for me? Is he "my kind"? Does he stand for the same general social values and traditions that I cherish? These are the crucial questions in any campaign. How they are answered will vastly affect current international, industrial, agricultural, and similar public matters. The voter assumes that by placing in office men who reflect his own standards and attitudes these questions will be treated much as he would have treated them were he in a position to act directly. But the voter does not approach these problems directly. They have to be presented in simple form so that he can make some sort of decision about the general trend along which they are to be solved.

The function of political parties in the United States has been to provide some means whereby an effective majority of the voters may lend their support to a group of leaders for a limited period. This has generally meant emphasizing personalities rather than issues. Institutional factors influence this tendency. Under a political system timed by the movement of celestial bodies rather than by that of social forces, little direct relation between election times and the rise of important issues can be fixed. A view of a party standing or falling on definite programs is hardly compatible with our system of fixed governmental elections.

This rigidity is a condition not easily put aside. Hence, under our system, issues must often be created to meet election needs. Public indifference is evidence of sound sense on many such occasions. Since we vote by the calendar rather than in accordance with the demands of current issues, there is an inescapable artificiality in much of our campaigning. Politicians must pretend that great issues are at stake, whether this is true or not. Candidate confronts candidate and the voter is asked to regard the combat as highly important.

Besides the tactical considerations and periodicity of election dates there is another factor that greatly affects the issues of a campaign: namely, the business cycle. From the investigations made by scholars there seems to be good empirical evidence for the assumption that prosperity helps the party in power and depression strengthens the minority. On the basis of careful statistical analysis one authority concludes:

"When elections occur during or just following periods of expansion, other things being equal, the party in power may expect a vote of confidence; while on the other hand, when an election occurs in a depression period, the majority party must expect to be shorn of its popularity and even in some cases turned out of office." [3]

The factors mentioned thus far militate against the rational debate of issues and the determination of public policy through a party program. Our purpose here is not to urge that voters mend their ways but rather to trace the path along which we actually stumble.

Let us consider some of the issues which have been of paramount importance since the Civil War. The first problem was to unify a people torn asunder by civil strife. Fast on the heels of this came the questions arising from rapid industrial growth and agricultural expansion with accompanying problems of tariff protection, labor relations, and credit facilities. How were these issues met?

Paul Buck, in his *Road to Reunion,* has analyzed the period of reconstruction in terms of the forces that in fact actually healed the scars of the Civil War. Reunion came not through political debate but through common human sympathies revived by poets and orators and stimulated into action by opportunities for mutual aid. For example, when a yellow fever epidemic developed in the Lower Mississippi Valley soon after the war, the North generously responded with liberal relief measures. A great burst of sympathy resulted. Much of it was sentimental in tone, but the episode promoted better feeling between the sections. Many other illustrations could be cited to emphasize the point that reunion came slowly over the years through an accumulation of incidents stimulating sympathy, good will, and forgiveness. Accompanying these emotional factors were important economic developments. The flow of northern capital into the South and the extension of railroad facilities helped weld sectional interests into a new unity. Educational developments carried the process further.

Ironically enough, churchmen in the North and South found reconciliation difficult. Despite expressions of fraternity, "the net result," Buck writes, "was that the churches remained sectional bodies, an antagonistic element in the integration of national life." [4]

Most marked was partisan antagonism. Never have our national parties been so clearly differentiated. As Buck has written:

"The practice of American politics in the years that followed the Civil War seemed based upon a theory that the two great parties were hostile armies in camps irreconcilably divided. Democrats were to Republicans, and Republicans were to Democrats, not opponents to be persuaded, but enemies to be remorselessly pursued and destroyed." [5]

Nevertheless, because the Democratic party had both a northern and a southern following, its interests dictated a truce to sectional hatreds. The Republicans, however, profited as long as waving the bloody shirt caused disruption of the opposition.

The basic political need of the country from the close of the Civil War through the two succeeding decades was to assuage the results of bloody conflict and become a united nation. This in fact was achieved not through debating differences and stressing ideological divergences but through the forces that built up common bonds of sympathy and economic interdependence. Many politicians contributed little to this process. Many persisted in exploiting sectional distrust as a means of forwarding their own careers.

On the other hand the broader self-interest of the Democratic party dictated a course of policy which ultimately brought it back into control of the federal government. That the old party of the Rebels and Copperheads could be entrusted again with the control of national affairs was a fact of the first importance. Yet some historians have tended to discount this in their indignation at the way in which the Democrats side-stepped issues. Harrison Thomas, for example, in discussing the return of the Democratic party to power in 1884, states:

"The control of both [parties] was in the hands of men who seemed determined to avoid all issues rather than to seek them. . . . The struggle between the parties became more and more merely a struggle for office.

"The Democrats felt . . . that as long as they were under suspicion of being disloyal they must try to avoid issues rather than make them. The ideal thing would have been for the leaders of both parties to forget the past and to attempt to work out a solution for the new problems before the nation. . . . The easy thing for the Democrats, when out of office, was to criticize the Republicans for their shortcomings, and when in, to copy their methods, to appeal to local prejudice with whatever political nostrum seemed likely to get votes, and to discard any really constructive policy on the plea of party harmony." [6]

Implicit in this comment is the assumption that if the Democrats had really tried they could have erased deep memories and united the nation on specific policies.

To demand that party politicians produce definite solutions is to treat the art of government as though it were a mathematical problem or an engineering job. Men are not governed by blueprints or formulae, and least of all are they self-governed by such devices. The politician must first of all win office and then work as best he can with the materials at hand. Evaluated in these terms, the victory of Grover Cleveland and the Democratic party in 1884 marked an event of great consequence for the future of party government. It meant restoring the Democratic party as an agency loyal to the Union and competent to offer an alternative to rule by the Republicans. This was no small service.

During Cleveland's time and in the years preceding, the national problem of first importance was to mollify the effects of sectionalism. Upon the heels of the Civil War came the possibility of class war. To blunt the impact of such serious differences meant the blurring of issues and a compromise with principles. Many politicians, undoubtedly motivated by a desire to preserve their own organization and their own political hides, exploited the situation.

If we look back upon this period not as a contest of politicians but as a readjustment of social forces, we see how relatively insignificant was the course of political discussion.

The general view is to argue that if we had farsighted leaders and if we were all reasonable men we could better meet our problems. This is a truism. We might better ask how popular government has worked at all with the fallible leadership that the system has produced under the irrational impulses of mankind. We can exhort men to use more penetration and more reason, but from what has been said thus far it should be clear that while we sympathize with such sentiments we must push the problem further if we would seek an understanding of the political process. The fact is that political issues must first be tactically feasible.

The maladjustments and social rivalries that give rise at times to "political issues" are problems that cannot be viewed simply as questions for a debate and then a vote. Issues are actually worked out step by step. Thus the conflict between capital and labor can be met only as the organization of these interests produces leaders and managers who in turn can meet with public officials empowered to seek a compromise of interests as presented in concrete terms. No solution to a fundamental public issue is likely to be found without a long series of adjustments.

The issues that come before Congress are problems that are formulated elsewhere. Legislation is written and debated outside of Congress. The legislature is a ratifying agency that acts toward the conclusion of the adjustment process. Indeed, significant party action on an issue must necessarily be a relatively late step in the procedure.

Party orators serve one useful purpose beyond relieving their own feelings and stirring those of their listeners: they may call attention to situations that require administrative treatment. But issues begin to be met only so soon as the groups in conflict are provided with the machinery through which to negotiate.

There are always more than two sides to any public question; yet the electorate can do no more than answer "yes" or "no." Such a response is not adaptable to problems that demand a more elaborate and complex consideration. Many issues cannot be disposed of by selecting a simple "either-or." Vital and complex economic differences, for example, necessitate some machinery for adjustment. This process must be continuous, and until an appropriate machinery is established, such conflicts will persist as political issues.

By statute a formula may be presented that is supposed to bring about a proper equilibrium between conflicting groups. Parties finding their legal rights infringed under this statute may appeal to the courts, or an administrative agency may be set up to conduct a continuous adjustment among conflicting interests. To the extent that issues are successfully adjusted through such procedures, they are retired from politics.

Mannheim has written that "politics as politics is possible only as long as the realm of the irrational still exists (where it disappears, 'administration' takes its place.)" [7] Issues may be use-fully raised if the purpose is to secure support for devising means of adequate management of the conflict in place of the friction creating the issue.

The tariff offers an interesting example of this process. Here is an issue that has long engaged the attention of politicians. It was brought forward by Cleveland in his tariff message of 1887 and discussed as the major question of the ensuing campaign. Through his personal influence, Cleveland was able to inject this issue into the campaign. His biographers agree that he would have won the election of 1888 had he not insisted upon forcing the issue. "I don't regret it," he stated. "It is better to be defeated battling for an honest principle than to win by a cowardly sub-terfuge. Some of my friends say we ought to have gone before the country on the clean administration we have given. I differ with them. We were defeated, it is true, but the principles of tariff reform will surely win in the end." [8]

Did Cleveland advance tariff reform by injecting it into the campaign? I think not. Allan Nevins states:

"It is always a misfortune when an issue which demands calm study, like the tariff in 1888 or the League of Nations in 1920, becomes en-tangled with the heated complexities of a presidential election. The two parties, in their eagerness for attack, are pushed into extreme posi-tions. They are excited into repudiating the saner doctrines they had professed only a few months earlier. The victorious side is then cer-tain to carry into practical legislation the unwise doctrines to which it has committed itself. Repeatedly it has been shown that no feature of American politics more effectually arouses passion and prevents compromise than the violent quadrennial collision, in a grim six-months' battle, of the two parties. It is conceivable that under a parliamentary system and with no presidential election of 1860, the United States might have settled the slavery question in some more civilized way than by war, and that without the bitter election of 1920, it might have placed itself, with moderate reservations, in the League. The tariff question of the eighties should have been decided in Congress, not in the dusty, overheated arena of a presidential contest; but to this arena it was now consigned." [9]

To Cleveland the tariff was a matter of principle; it was a moral issue that overtopped political considerations. He was ready to sacrifice his political career in order to promote what he thought was right. He felt that greedy manufacturers were promoting their own selfish interests at the expense of the consumer and under the protection of the federal government. He was ready to fight to the death for a tariff system that would promote the general interest. He was motivated undoubtedly by an ideal, but like many men of high principle he identified idealism with intransigence. By making the tariff a paramount issue, he defeated the very end which he held most important.

The issue was not only the cause of Cleveland's undoing in 1888, but also the occasion of much confusion in campaigns following. When Cleveland ran in 1892 the tariff was again the issue. It was used by politicians to distract attention from more fundamental questions demanding consideration. Economic rivalries between the western farmer and the eastern financial interests were becoming tense. The Homestead strike was symptomatic of a growing tension between employer and employee in many industrial centers. Cleveland apparently had little sympathy for or understanding of the causes that were behind the radical protests from the West and the South. He refused, for example, to follow advisers who urged that he write a letter of sympathy to the poor farmers of the South who were threatening to desert to the Populist party. The Democrats preferred to center attention upon the fraudulence and robbery of Republican protectionism.

Democratic party leaders might well be criticized for their lack of foresight in 1892. In nominating Cleveland for the third time they selected a candidate who was unable to cope with the gathering forces of discontent. The need for vindicating the loyalty of the Democratic party had been fulfilled. A new threat to social integration had arisen. The differences grew between the bankers and industrialists of the East and labor, together with agrarian discontent in the West and South.

The chances are that politicians would not have strengthened party government at the time by insisting upon an alignment on the basic economic questions before the country. They went further, however, and took a repressive labor line and a negative financial view. It is doubtful whether they would have advanced further toward their solution had these problems been made the main issues of the campaign. Economists and statesmen have struggled with these questions for the last fifty years, and we have yet to find a satisfactory form for meeting the conflicts of interests within these fields. Stressing the difference between labor and capital or arguing the merits of government regulation versus nonintervention in business as a campaign issue would hardly have led to a solution at that time. There is no clear public sentiment on these issues at the present time, and there was less in 1884.

Yet from the seventies on, the issue of labor's relation to the industrialist was of steadily increasing importance. Barnard writes:

"This question had simmered as a major problem ever since the riots of 1877. Specifically, it was concerned with wage scales, working conditions and the problem of mass displacement of manual workers by machines. But broadly it was a matter of adjusting a new economic system to American democratic ideals.

"Had there then existed in America men of statesmanship in places of political power, much could probably have been done with effect to forestall or cushion later explosions in the Capital versus Labor struggle. America then was in a position to examine the problem clearly. Men and groups had not yet taken definite stands. There was opportunity for free action of the national genius for democracy and fair play. And mass opinion, insofar as it can be reconstructed today, was all for applying American democratic standards to industry. But the best in statesmanship that the country had at that crucial period was Grover Cleveland, and his qualities must be put down even by admirers as largely negative." [10]

No leader took the farsighted view urged here. This may be because no man possessed both the power and the vision in sufficient degree. Yet prophets were not wanting, and the implication at least arises that the times cannot be fully explained in terms of weak leadership and political chicanery.

There is a world of difference between voicing a need and devising a means for its satisfaction. The author just cited argued that "adjusting a new economic system to American democratic ideals" was the basic political issue. Debate could aid in educating the public to the need of the time; but organizing the pros and cons would merely have intensified the struggle. What was most needed was some institutional device appropriate for negotiation between the groups in conflict. To invent and administer such organizational forms is quite a different matter from urging their creation. Men longed to fly for centuries before they discovered the means. But in political affairs we are much more impatient with experimentation through trial and error. We emphasize objectives and ideals rather than ways and means. Cleveland, not knowing what to do, did little that was constructive. He called out the troops when disorder threatened. There have been other politicians who, not knowing what to do, have been willing to try anything once.

We have approached the solution of problems raised by the issues of sound money versus free silver, free trade versus protection, and collective bargaining, not simply by talking about these questions in campaigns but by setting up administrative agencies competent to deal with the parties in conflict. Cleveland approached these complexities of economic relationship in the language of high principle. Sound money viewed in terms of practical consequences meant widespread suffering for the debtor elements; "protection of the United States Mails" meant the shooting of fellow citizens by the United States troops called to suppress the hungry strikers. The answers that we have evolved have not been the vindication of abstract ideas such as "sound money" but the establishment of organizations such as the Federal Reserve Board and the Farm Credit Administration. Employer-employee relations are being met through the growth of trade unions and administrative agencies such as the National Labor Relations Board.

Treating the tariff as a partisan political issue delayed our actually coming to grips with the real interests with a stake in the outcome. Free trade versus protection was debated at length. A tariff for revenue only was offered as a solution. A formula was sought. Not until administrative machinery was set up with the creation of the United States Tariff Commission in 1916 did we begin to approach the problem. Scientific tariff making was discussed at length, and the Tariff Commission was to be an expert body for applying in objective fashion a cost-of-production formula. After much disruption it became clear that the tariff as an issue could not be disposed of in this way. Experimentation with institutional devices continued. Under our system of reciprocal trade agreements we are feeling our way toward administrative machinery that now at last seems suited to the nature of the tariff problem.[11]

A tariff has always been a focal point for the interest of the manufacturers, of important exporters of a particular article, and of their respective governments. When a bargain is struck among the interested parties we can expect a relatively stable situation. The present reciprocal trade agreement is an effort to arrive at such a bargain. It marks an advance over "the stealthy parliamentary legerdemain of congressional committees and inter-party bargains," where only those most immediately concerned took part. The system of reciprocal agreements provides, instead, a method of negotiation at a level sufficiently high to include not only domestic interests but the foreign governments that are also affected. Efforts to clarify issues at the stage of platform and campaign may result in deadlock and aimless debate unless a means of adjusting specific needs of specific groups to specific lines of policy are also established.

Some conflicts may be resolved; other differences are but further aggravated by such treatment. Issues are of varying depth and complexity; they may divide the nation unevenly. Issues may be international, national, sectional, and local. They appear on many planes and are constantly debated and resolved.

In general the likelihood of adjustment is greater when considered in concrete and specific terms. Each side may have its broad blueprint concept to guide its bargaining, but it is not essential that as a preliminary to action one side impose upon the other its general set of values and picture of the universe. Circumstances may pose an issue which by its very terms stimulates an alignment pro and con. As Stuart Rice has explained:

"Every group is possessed of some common point or points of resemblance, whether it be a physical or social characteristic, a common
experience, or a similar state of mind concerning a political question.
So long as the stimuli playing upon individuals call attention to this
common character, those who possess it will constitute a group in ac-
tuality. But no two or more individuals are alike in all things. When
the stimuli change so that new points of resemblance among individuals
are brought into the center of social consciousness, there will be re-
grouping of these individuals. The old points of resemblance may still
exist, but the old groupings to which they gave rise are no longer actual
but only potential." [12]

Issues, if they are to be more than mere talk, must bear a direct
relationship to concrete interests. The protective tariff and free
silver were two blanket formulae indicative that certain groups
and sections wanted protection. The need of the time was to
face the needs of both debtors and creditors and of farmers and
manufacturers. The silver issue deepened the cleavage instead of
providing men and institutions for handling the complexities of
debtor-creditor relations.

Since political issues are symptoms of maladjustments among
certain groups, the problem is how to get down to these fundamentals. Conflicts of group interest persist while administrations
come and go. Political leaders attempt to formulate schemes for
adjusting group differences. Such formulae may be based upon
a close knowledge of the economic reality; often they are not.
Some political leaders attempt to clarify the differences, while
others either ignore them and attract attention to extraneous
matters or offer alternative proposals. Any popular election
means that a set of officials is designated to face the issues resulting from group differences. Since these groups remain before,
during, and after the election and since they are the source of
our political differences, an election in itself need not basically
alter the situation.

Our elected officials are themselves the product of various
group interests. Once in office they are limited by their general
economic context. Faced with the conflicting demands of em-

ployers, farmers, industrialists, veterans, and the unemployed, the politician can throw his weight to one group or the other. He can promote a combination of group interests, but he cannot greatly alter the materials with which he must work.

One set of administrative officials may have more sympathetic relations with certain group interests than with others. Such officials, too, can throw their weight one way or the other. They themselves also are the product of group forces. Officials cannot be entirely neutral: they too have loyalties and lines of support back to labor or business or agriculture.

Administrative reconciliation of economic differences must be in accordance with some declared public policy. Such a policy to prove workable, however, must be the product of experimentation and negotiation among the interests in conflict extending over a period of time. Sharp issues must be blunted during this period. Both sides must test their strength, discover leaders, and come to some internal agreement. On all highly controversial subjects there is a large percentage of persons who are undecided. The presence of a high degree of indecision means that the extreme elements must win the undecided to their side if a majority opinion is to develop. Partisan preoccupation with this latter group tends to lessen their conflict with each other.

Experience has frequently demonstrated that the political party is an inadequate device for bringing sufficient order into the changing social pattern. Thus our party battles are not to be interpreted simply as the conspiracies of capitalists acting through partisan henchmen to bewilder the public, but rather as the inevitable product of a period of growing industrialism and rapid change. Men were groping for a line of direction. They lacked a philosophical pattern suitable to bring order to the complexities before them. The political impulses of labor and the farmer lacked means of appropriate expression. The party machine was monopolized by professionals; the trade union movement was in its infancy and farmers were slowly becoming organized. The demands of these interests are now being met not because politicians have reformed or political debaters become more rational but because suitable organizations for the expression and negotiation of many group interests have arisen to compete with or direct the party machine.

Political issues arise from forces more basic than those represented by partisan contests, and political parties have not shown themselves as the agencies best suited for the attainment of social reforms. Hence much of the insistence upon more constructive party programs tends to overlook the course that social legislation has actually followed. British parties are so often cited as examples for our parties to emulate that Edward P. Cheyney's conclusions concerning the role of party in the process of reform in Great Britain seem very pertinent. He finds that the development of reforming legislation from the first of the last century to the World War followed "an inner law of its own."

"It has been largely independent of political parties. Although Whigs and Liberals have been on the whole rather more willing to pass reform measures than Tories and their successors, Conservatives and Unionists, these measures have been pretty equally attributable to both parties. . . . Social legislation has been largely a response to pressure from outside of Parliament and party organization, and whatever party was in power when this pressure became sufficiently strong has performed the work of placing it upon the statute book. For the ultimate and efficient causes of reform, search must be made deeper in society than the ups and downs in the strife of political parties." [13]

The notable part of the process is its empiric nature. Specific needs were dramatized; particular abuses uncovered. Change did not come about as an over-all reorganization of society that was to usher in a new and better world. One party cannot attempt to arrogate to itself the one true doctrine whereby the ills of the world should be treated. Change depends on the attitudes of men and the interplay of forces too complex and far-flung to be embraced and controlled by a party program. We must look rather to broader and often imponderable factors.

Part IV

☆ 22 ☆

Why Believe in Public Opinion?

> "The people move
> In a fine thin smoke,
> The people, yes."
> CARL SANDBURG

LIKE fog or smoke, public opinion is obvious in its larger manifestations, but intangible at closer view. Unlike our fatalistic acceptance of the weather, so much decried by Mark Twain, many try hard to do something about the climate of opinion when it proves unsatisfactory. Orators sometimes use hot air; propagandists set up smoke screens. Various methods of befogging the situation have been tried. Attempts at clarification are difficult. Nevertheless two aspects of public opinion are essential to the success of democratic politics.

Public opinion has vital importance as a symbol that need stand for no value other than directing human affairs through the consensus that emerges from discussion and persuasion. The validity of government by public opinion lies in the kind of social milieu it helps to establish and the attitude of mind that it encourages. Thus the concept, by referring to the "people" for the ultimate sanction of authority, retains flexibility and even uncertainty as to the focus of authority within our society. No ruling group can properly claim the sole right to speak for the people. Hitler apparently has mass support for his regime, but we must deny his right to claim the sanction of public opinion as we understand it under a democracy. Under our political creed power can never be crystallized in a final determinate human will. It rests rather upon an ever fresh interplay of forces.

There is the danger, to be sure, that under aggressive leadership and strong organization a large body of individuals will try to arrogate to themselves the sole right to act for the public. The result would be tyranny in the name of the mass. Men do not act as a mass without strong leadership, nor do they seek the fulfillment of a program without indoctrination; and these ends can be attained only through disciplined organization. Dissenters must be punished. Rule by public opinion implies no such continuity and agreement. It is protean by nature; and like Proteus it is mythical.

In a particular instance public opinion may be resolved into the control of institutions by individuals acting in concert. However, as an abstract belief, it does promote free discussion of ideas and adjustment of special interests—the essence of democracy. Belief in public opinion as a creed stimulates the interchange of thoughts and diffuses among individuals a sense of social responsibility.

The concept of public opinion embraces another characteristic of great importance. It sanctions the belief that even the opinions of people who are not direct participants in a process must not be ignored. In this sense public opinion is well described as "the views of those outside any given group which must be taken into account by those inside it, whether the group is an institution like the government, or a hospital board, or whether it is some unorganized elements such as spoilsmen of the countryside or slum landlords." [1] In other words belief in public opinion imposes a decent respect for the opinions and standards of one's fellows even though their interests may not be immediately affected by one's actions.

This concept may be interpreted in many other ways. Numerous definitions of public opinion are available. Scholars cannot agree on a precise definition, and there is no authority to fix a formula. Yet the concept is nonetheless useful as a point of departure for varied inquiries. It brings into focus the attitudes, the sentiments, and the more or less articulate views of men taken not as individuals but in multiples. The fact that the term is general does not rob it of meaning; but it does indicate the limitations upon the concept as a tool of analysis. While public opinion, as such, eludes analysis, the fact of our belief in the concept is highly important.

Treated frankly as a social myth, public opinion holds implications highly significant for our political process. The concept of dictatorship of the proletariat is no less important for Soviet Russia than rule by public opinion is for us. Yet it is perhaps easier for us to see through this former phrase as an inadequate description of fact than to note the comparable limitations on our own theory of popular government. In neither case, however, does the significance of the concept lie in its accurate description of human behavior. It lives in the realm of ideology, whence it exerts its influence on the minds of men. As with all symbols, meaning is not to be found in the thing itself as a logical concept but rather in its effectiveness for evoking loyalties and sanctioning rule. A symbol may appear irrational, mystical, even fantastic, yet it may nonetheless give meaning and form to life for those who accept it. Belief in miracles has undoubtedly fostered the spirituality of religious-minded men. An anthropologist studying the history of religion would note its value for this purpose. He might regard similarly our deep faith in the will of the people.

Difficulties appear if public opinion is treated as a reasoning mass intellect or an ethical oversoul. To some writers the problem is a moral one. The citizen must be aroused to his duties as a citizen if popular rule is to mean anything. Public opinion becomes the collective rational judgment of a large proportion of interested citizens. We must secure this participation if popular government is to mean anything. An excellent illustration of the wishful thinking of such political theorists is found in *Democracy and the Party System*, by M. Ostrogorski. The author calls upon his readers to improve the conditions of political life, and states:

"The task is a gigantic one: the citizen has to be reinvested with his power over the commonwealth, and the latter restored to its proper sphere; the separation between society at large and politics must

308 THE POLITICS OF DEMOCRACY

be ended, and the divorce between politics and morality annulled; civic indifference must give place to an alert and vigilant public spirit; the conscience of the citizen must be set free from the formalism which has enslaved it; those alike who confer and who hold power must be guided by the reason of things, and not by conventional words; superiority of character and of intelligence, that is to say real leadership, dethroned by the political mechanism, must be reinstated in the governance of the Republic; authority as well as liberty, now usurped and trafficked under the party flag and in the name of democracy, must be rehabilitated in the commonwealth." [2]

Throughout Ostrogorski's comments are underlying assumptions. He refers to a day when the actual control of the commonwealth rested in the hands of the citizen. He assumes that then politics and ethics were joined, that they have since been divorced, and that this divorce must now be annulled. He appeals to a hypothetical citizenry guided by a universal conscience which, if successfully evoked, would reform public life. He asserts that power must be guided by reason as though the word had objective content which merely needed extracting. He assumes that "character" once ruled and must now be reinstated.

The arguments that rule by public opinion demands high standards of reason and ethics signify in practice that the groups holding to such standards must increase their political activities. This involves a rearrangement of interest groups. In blunt terms, such pleas are directed to the tender consciences of nice people in the hope that they will be moved to exercise more influence in the governmental process. Most frequently this comes down to an appeal to the substantial middle class to reassert its power. I do not necessarily quarrel with this as a social aim. The meaning of rule by public opinion is not embraced by any one code of ethics or the interests of any particular set of people, however.

Francis G. Wilson thinks that "Any theory of opinion as such, without reference to a standard existing above it, must be in essence pragmatic. Democracy," he states, "has become pragmatic and flexible in its method of determining right conduct in government. What the people want is presumed to be the standard of right in social relations." ³ This assumption may be part of the mythology of public opinion, but I do not think that we need to treat the phrase as though it denoted a clear sum of a determinable majority of individual wills.

If we talk of what the "people" want, we reify an abstraction and accord it a moral conscience. Rightness or wrongness finds expression only through the individual. Whether a combination of individual judgments manifested as an expression of "public opinion" is right or wrong depends on the judgment of the individual. Political leaders may strive to strengthen their position by an ethical sanction of popular will. Such a sanction can be given only through a consensus of individual moral judgments.

To justify rule by the concept of public opinion does not require us to argue that public opinion is always ethically sound. We are not forced to argue that what the people want is right just because the people want it. This must remain a matter of subjective judgment.

Yet around the concept of public opinion an excrescence of unnecessary assumptions has gathered. Here we find shibboleths about the common will and the necessity that all good citizens participate in elections and hold opinions on public questions in order that this general-will concept be vindicated. The persistent failure of men to act in accordance with this picture merely stimulates the exhorters to greater efforts.

If the significance of public opinion were to be measured by such moral and rationalistic standards, the prospects for popular government would be discouraging. It is enough if we treat the concept of rule by public opinion as simply providing a milieu within which group opinions may compete. Belief in government by public opinion means belief in the validity of that process. It does not entail any assumptions as to the superior wisdom of mass opinion or the rationality of man. It is enough if we allow for the free interplay of opinion, the tolerance of opposition, and a widespread participation by interested citizens in the discussion of problems that touch them closely.

The Constitution is not premised on rule by enlightened public opinion. The framers had their doubts about the capacity of the masses for rule. Values other than popular responsiveness were provided for: stability, peace, toleration—values cherished by the thoughtful men of the eighteenth century. These values are no less important today, but attainment of them involves social and economic adjustments of the greatest difficulty.

Walter Lippmann has argued that while the public can do nothing directly to meet problems, it can vastly affect the outcome nonetheless. He reckons the public as divorced from executive action and incapable of it; the public can, however, hold the ring for the active participants. The selfishly interested parties are then free to fight out their battle but under the rules of the game.

"What the public does is not to express its opinions but to align itself for or against a proposal [Lippmann says]. If that theory is accepted, we must abandon the notion that democratic government can be the direct expression of the will of the people. We must abandon the notion that the people govern. Instead we must adopt the theory that by their occasional mobilization as a majority, people support or oppose the individuals who actually govern.

"We must say that the popular will does not direct continuously but that it intervenes occasionally." [4]

So we have the external public and the interested parties whose rights are affected. The public is inert and unable to judge of the merits of a case, but the public can insist upon full freedom of discussion and the opposing parties can then expose one another. The public can require that both sides lay their cards on the table.

While Lippmann draws a convincing picture of the impossibility of executive action by the public, he seems to underestimate the influence of public opinion when he argues that this is limited to occasional intervention. The significant influence comes not from active intervention but from the general temper of opinion under which the parties at interest must carry on their contests.

Public opinion treated as the attitudes generally prevailing at a given time seems to pass from one period to another. Actions tolerated at one time are discountenanced at another; reforms once thought impossible are later accepted with alacrity.

The interplay of individuals and interest groups at different times creates a milieu which encourages some forces and discourages others. The interest groups which draw support from the milieu because of their harmony with it may be said to have the sanction of public opinion. Public opinion is thus the name we give to the policies of those groups backed by a favorable climate of opinion. This is far from a negative concept. Interactions occur from group to community and vice versa. In fact, the general climate is but the end product of many contributing currents of opinion.

Historically, shifts of opinion can be demonstrated to operate with an extraordinary degree of regularity. Arthur M. Schlesinger has worked out the following chart of the change from periods of conservatism to those of liberalism, starring leftward swings: [5]

*(1)	1765–1787	(6)	1841–1861
(2)	1787–1801	*(7)	1861–1869
*(3)	1801–1816	(8)	1869–1901
(4)	1816–1829	*(9)	1901–1918
*(5)	1829–1841	(10)	1918–1931

These periods are based on an analysis of "the dominant national mood as expressed in effective governmental action (or inaction)." [6] These distinctive periods cannot be identified consistently with any one political party. Parties can clearly be ruled out as the primary energies for bringing about change. Both Democratic and Republican parties have known their periods of conservatism and of innovation. Both parties reflect the spirit of these deeper historical cycles. Parties are thus merely one vehicle for the public opinion of the time. This does not mean that all men are of the same opinion. As already noted, protest groups, especially among farmers and workers, have been a persistent element. Such forces are doubtless important in bringing about shifts from right to left; but other less ponderable forces are also at work. It is difficult to establish any correlations that readily explain these shifts. As Schlesinger is brought to conclude: "Apparently the electorate embarks on conservative policies until it is disillusioned or wearied or bored, and then attaches itself to liberal policies until a similar course is run." [7]

Each of these election upsets has marked a unique period of opinion. The times became favorable for a change of policy, for example, under Wilson's New Freedom and Roosevelt's New Deal. The intervening Harding-Coolidge-Hoover period provided a distinctive atmosphere but of quite a different sort. Thus we find in our history clearly distinguishable periods when accomplishments that at one time could not be attained are achieved under other conditions. The era of Jacksonian democracy had its force and flavor. The reconstruction period reflected a quite different general state of mind, as did also the Progressive era and the New Deal. The fact that such times have acquired their own names is indication enough of the general recognition given the characteristic quality of these periods. At these times the predominant attitudes were favorable to certain lines of policy and inimical to others.

Crane Brinton, in his *Anatomy of Revolution,* found the course of public feeling following phases comparable to the temperature curve on a fever chart. Power passed from the hands of the moderates to the extremists; the Terror was followed by the reaction of Thermidor and a cooling off of the political atmosphere.

To speculate upon why such changes occur would take us too far afield. Brinton suggests that "human beings can go only so far and so long under the stimulus of an ideal. The outsider in the crisis period is pushed to the limit of his endurance by interference with some of his most prized and intimate routines; the insider is held to a pitch of spiritual effort and excitement beyond his powers of endurance." [8] On the other hand a prolonged period of stability often brings rigidities and needs for adjustment. Vested interests stand in the way; protest accumulates. Change is welcomed. Even a highly diverse group of people while held together by their common discontent can co-operate in opposing what is. Agreement tends to diminish as concrete remedies are proposed. The concept of public opinion need not assume consistency or stability in the views of citizens. In fact, its great value lies in the fluidity that it sanctions.

"The truth appears to be that what we mean by common will

is that there shall be an available peaceful way by which law may be changed when it becomes irksome to enough powerful people who can make their will effective," [9] Judge Learned Hand has stated.

Life in this country is markedly different from that in totalitarian states. Yet the latter have secured greater mass expressions of opinion and probably a higher percentage of agreement than democratic countries have ever witnessed. Through the control of all avenues of expression and deep penetration into community life Hitler and Mussolini have well-nigh established through propaganda the attitudes and prejudices of the individual. They exploit to their own aims underlying currents of nationalism and economic insecurity. Their purpose is to develop a nationally unified opinion. They must create and instill one common will. Freedom demands diversity and fluidity.

Under democracy rule by public opinion provides those conditions whereby special interests are free to seek a working compromise harmonious with the values prevailing in the community. The interests most likely to be effective in the intergroup contest for power are those groups whose aims and impulses are most compatible with existing public attitudes. Those that are not may still work toward change. The policy that emerges is the product of many interactions and during this process the responsibility is distributed widely. John Dickinson writes:

"There thus emerges the advantage of government containing what we may call the democratic element—of government, that is, whereby the conflicting interests in a community will themselves be made to bear some part of the responsibility for reaching through political action the adjustments by which they are expected to abide." [10]

In this sense public opinion, though "impalpable as the wind," as Lord Bryce once described it, is yet the breath of life in the politics of democracy.

☆ 23 ☆

Consummating Reform:
Two Illustrations

"It is better to work on institutions by the
sun than by the wind."
RALPH WALDO EMERSON

AGITATION by a small group of enthusiasts may continue for
a long period with very meager results. Once it is fortified by
compatible basic economic and social trends, the movement is
vastly accelerated. Party support comes near the climax of political change. The consummation of reform is the result not simply
of agitation but also of underlying social and economic factors.
Propaganda organizations do little more than accelerate the
movements already under way, and if their proposals are not
based upon genuine needs legal victories are fruitless.

The process might be illustrated in many ways. Two examples
may demonstrate our generalizations. National prohibition was
but a single expression of a broader secular movement of moralistic opinion, consummated at a time when the climate of opinion
was favorable to restrictive measures. When prohibition finally
went into effect the nation was facing the World War, a war
undertaken as a great moral crusade. Prohibition sought national
fulfillment at a most opportune time.

The Anti-Saloon League was one manifestation of the temperance movement. By skillful direction it organized and accelerated
this development. Through their enthusiasm and skill its officers
took advantage of every opportunity for promoting their cause

before the public and the state legislatures. In 1913, when the League decided to work for a national prohibition amendment, thirty-one states with a population of twenty-six million already had local option, and nine states with more than fourteen and a half million people had state-wide dry laws. As Peter Odegard, the leading authority on the Anti-Saloon League, has stated:

"Prohibition laws in the United States did not spring fullblown from the Jovian brow of Wayne Wheeler and the Anti-Saloon League. A careful reading of the record demonstrates, if it demonstrates anything, that the Eighteenth Amendment was not 'put over' on the American people. The Anti-Saloon League did not, as many good people believe, come like a thief in the night to steal away our liberties. Nor was prohibition adopted in a fit of civic absent-mindedness. The step from school and church district remonstrances to a constitutional amendment outlawing the liquor traffic throughout the nation is too great to admit of so facile an explanation.

"In a very real sense national prohibition represents a growth, and a rather slow, deliberate growth at that. It is true that the political activities of the myrmidons of morality must account for a large measure of the success which has attended the temperance people. But it is not the sole explanation. Moral and economic beliefs are not crystallized into law without the backing of a considerable constituency and the existence of a pretty well-defined opinion. The most that can be said of the Anti-Saloon League is that it provided an organization through which this constituency made itself effective. In final analysis, its success depended not only upon its ability to make prohibition sentiment, but also upon its ability to build an effective political machine upon the basis of an already existing body of opinion." [1]

The League gave form and direction to profound sentiments strongly held by many Americans. Any definitive appraisal of its ultimate significance is impossible, but its influence has often been overestimated. The League supplied generalship, but it did not make the issue or create the attitude. Moral issues have always had great weight in American politics. Churchmen, educators, plus a large bloc of substantial citizens and reformers have joined to fight for temperance since the early part of the nineteenth century. The League, by the skillful use of propaganda, pointed to the abuse of the liquor traffic and sponsored a definite proposal of remedial action.

The Demon Rum, while guilty enough in his own right, was undoubtedly a convenient scapegoat for many economic defects and psychological ills. Prohibition was regarded as a panacea. The prohibitionists were little concerned with those economic or psychological maladjustments for which intemperance was the avenue of escape. Intemperance was a problem for the psychiatrist as much as for the moralist. Many discontents were drawn off on this wild booze chase.

The prohibitionists focused their attention upon the evil of drink. The way to temperance was the abolition of alcohol. Through organization and persistence they secured favorable action on this issue in the states and finally forced through the national prohibition amendment. Their strategy in Congress was undoubtedly effective. They forced candidates to commit themselves on the prohibition issue. They bargained with party leaders for support. They took advantage of wartime conditions to ban the use of grain for distilled liquors. Their lobbyist, Wayne B. Wheeler, insisted that the prohibition amendment be voted on before the congressional reapportionment of 1920. He knew that adjusting the basis of representation would bring forty new wet congressmen from the urban centers. Wheeler's code was Machiavellian. As his biographer [2] states, "he never believed in hitting below the belt unless it was absolutely necessary."

To such dry leaders, temperance was to be enforced by law rather than developed through education or improved social conditions. They gave little thought to the changes that were already weakening the attraction of the corner saloon. The growth of recreational facilities, the increase in movie-going, the growing interest in sports such as football and baseball, the mass production of the automobile and radio were all factors related to the liquor problem; but not in the minds of prohibitionists.

It is, of course, impossible to disentangle all the complex issues involved. No agreement as to the effects of prohibition will ever be reached, but it is suggested here that the Eighteenth Amendment had unfortunate effects on the growth of temperance. It accelerated unduly a reform that could not be attained through law alone. It distorted the liquor question. It ranged voters into wets and drys and challenged the former to exert their political independence by demonstrating their loyalty to liquor. It became a political issue upon which the parties were finally forced to take sides. The question of temperance was associated with entirely extraneous questions such as constitutionalism, states' rights, individual liberty, and natural law. By forcing a prohibition amendment, the Anti-Saloon League made an issue of a social problem too basic and too ramified to be disposed of through a simple legal enactment. The subsequent fate of the amendment suggests that although change can be hastened through propaganda, such efforts are futile unless accompanied by appropriate modifications making for a social acceptance of the new rule.

At the same time the League's success demonstrated in dramatic fashion the effectiveness of a single-aim organization in American politics. Its striking victory stressed the futility of the Prohibition party. The major parties hesitated to commit themselves on a controversial issue.

The Anti-Saloon League showed how effective propaganda may be when surrounding conditions are favorable. The broad shifts in attitude resulting from the reactions of the postwar period marked a change in opinion under which League propaganda proved futile. Subsequent events suggest, however, that this reform movement overlooked desires and drives that could not be eradicated by fiat. Political change to be lasting must bring about changes in habits and institutions. Mr. Dooley once wisely remarked: "Th' throuble with most iv us, Hinnissy, is we swallow pollytical idees befure they're ripe an' they don't agree with us."

The environment within which an issue is faced is of the utmost importance. Treatment for hysteria is no longer the ducking stool, nor the therapy for senile dementia, faggots and the stake. Mental and physical abnormalities giving rise to problems of social adjustments tend also to stimulate moral overtones. In response to this, bills can be passed outlawing the disliked abnormal behavior; but the problem of therapy remains. Whether this latter question can be approached in a dispassionate fashion is determined by the general level of values in the community itself. It seems doubtful today whether the opinion of "the outside public" would be sympathetic to the tactics of Wayne B. Wheeler or Carrie Nation. Awareness of the need for a more enlightened attitude toward the problem of alcoholism is reflected in this excerpt from a recent editorial in the *New England Journal of Medicine*:

"Tuberculosis, syphilis and alcoholism are three of the major problems in public health. Tuberculosis has long received the most attention both from the public-health agencies and the public. One may point with pride at the work accomplished in the last thirty years toward the goal of the complete eradication of tuberculosis. The attack on syphilis is now being pushed at an accelerated pace, thanks to the work of the United States Public Health Service, the state and local agencies, the newspapers and the public. The end is visualized, although much work is yet to be done. The world is waking up to the fact that it is possible to do away with both tuberculosis and syphilis. The treatment of alcoholism, as a public-health problem has fallen far behind the other two. The routine 'cure' of the alcoholic is far from satisfactory, and the best method to prevent alcoholism exists only as a vague idea in the minds of a few progressive physicians. . . . No attempt was made to study the patient as an individual, and psychiatric treatment, the basis for any hope of reclamation, was not available." [3]

The answer that science has to offer cannot be realized through crusades for restrictive laws but through psychiatric treatment designed to reach the causes. When an atmosphere of general appreciation of the scientific approach to alcoholism as a public health problem is reached the antics of the Anti-Saloon League will seem as barbaric as witch-hunting.

The woman suffrage movement parallels the prohibition battle on many counts. The agitation for women's rights goes back, like the temperance movement, to the early part of the last century. Both were consummated through amendments to the federal Constitution at about the same time. In both the fight was carried on in the states and shifted to the national scene in 1913. Organized groups were chiefly responsible for forcing congressional action.

On important counts the woman suffrage movement differs. The prohibitionists had votes with which to barter; the women started as a disfranchised class. The prohibition amendment has come and gone; the suffrage amendment was one expression of much more basic and continuing forces. The Anti-Saloon League was able to identify its issue with accepted stereotypes. Prohibition held a strong sentimental appeal for the protection of the home, the mother, and the child. It could speak the language of idealism. Men were urged to vote as they prayed, not as they drank. Strong economic arguments could be brought forward: but preachment could bring no cure. The campaign for woman suffrage encountered, in contrast, a generally unsympathetic public.

Before the women could hope to obtain their objective, a changed public opinion was necessary. A mass of totally irrelevant arguments against their exercise of the ballot had to be met and seriously considered and refuted. A tremendous social inertia had to be overcome. They faced a wall of male complacency buttressed by sentimentalism and chivalry. They encountered masculine protectiveness mingled with condescension. They tried to argue convincingly that they were an oppressed class. That they were discriminated against legally was only too clear. Statutory disabilities placed woman in an inferior position and made her dependent in her political status upon her relationship to husband, father, or guardian. This did not necessarily work to the advantage of the male.

At the outset of the suffrage agitation both legal and economic institutions added to the factors unfavorable to woman suffrage. The efforts of suffrage leaders were denounced from the pulpit and ridiculed by the press. Clergymen and editorial writers displayed a remarkable insight into the divine will concerning the place of woman. Of a women's rights convention in New York in 1853 James Gordon Bennett, writing in the *Herald*, stated:

"The assemblage of rampant women which convened at the tabernacle yesterday was an interesting phase in the comic history of the nineteenth century. A gathering of unsexed women all of them publicly propounding the doctrine that they should be allowed to step out of their appropriate sphere to the neglect of those duties which both human and divine law have assigned to them. Is the world to be depopulated?" [4]

When women arose to address the convention they were booed, hissed, and stamped down. Yet the women's rights movement was under way.

The first convention was called at Worcester in 1850. In 1869 the American Woman Suffrage Association was organized for promoting legislation in the states. The next year the National Woman Suffrage Association succeeded the Equal Rights Society and carried on the fight for federal action. As might be expected, the movement did not have the support of all women. A few years later a national association objecting to the extension of woman suffrage was established and protests were made to Congress against the granting of equal suffrage.

The struggle for woman suffrage was a long battle fought largely outside party lines and by the organized women themselves. It illustrates in striking fashion the process of carrying an issue through to legal consummation and the relation between parallel advances in the political realm and the economic sphere. In March, 1869, a resolution calling for an amendment to the Constitution abolishing sex as a basis for discrimination in the exercise of the franchise was introduced in Congress. It received no attention. Despite the fact that petitions were presented and organizations formed in the years following, nothing was done. The greatest encouragement they got from the major parties was the innocuous plank of the Republican party in 1872 declaring:

"The Republican party is mindful of its obligations to the loyal women of America for their noble devotion to the cause of freedom. Their admission to wider fields of usefulness is viewed with satisfaction, and the honest demand of any class of citizens for additional rights should be treated with respectful consideration." [5]

At the same time the Prohibition party came out with a more forthright statement saying:

"Resolved . . . That the right of suffrage rests on no mere circumstance of color, race, former social condition, sex or nationality, but inheres in the nature of man; and when from any cause it has been withheld from citizens of our country who are of suitable age and mentally and morally qualified for the discharge of its duties, it should be speedily restored by the people in their sovereign capacity." [6]

The linking of the equal rights movement with the prohibition cause was a source of weakness rather than of strength. The Anti-Saloon League was unwilling to concern itself with woman suffrage, and temperance reform occupied the time of many feminists. Many women looked upon the liquor traffic as the underhanded opponent of women's rights. The machines' control of the corrupt vote and the politicians' relations with the saloon might be threatened if women were given the vote. For this reason they argued that the brewers, saloonkeepers, and national politicians opposed their cause. They were sometimes told, "Wait until manhood suffrage has proved itself, money has been eliminated, and politics has become a fit place for women." Agitation for equal rights had been carried on since the first quarter of the century. The antislavery movement and the temperance cause had outstripped the equal rights crusade. In vain did the women protest. Their superior right to the franchise over the millions of illiterate Negroes given the vote by the Fourteenth Amendment was disregarded. They were told by the Supreme Court that citizenship did not carry with it the right to vote.

The fruits of years of agitation for the suffrage were meager. By 1896 states representing only 2 per cent of the population had granted the full franchise. State constitutions were difficult to amend, and the women had no means of coercing the politician.

Fundamental social changes were at work, however. Developments between 1870 and 1900 undermined the prejudices of centuries. "New elements, materialistic and spiritual, entered into the situation which made inevitable at the end of the period what was scarcely thinkable at its beginning," H. U. Faulkner notes.

New and powerful forces were gathering on the side of the women. During the early years of the twentieth century women found increased opportunities in economic affairs. Their wages were low, but their place in industry became a public problem. The National Women's Trade Union League was started in 1903, and the importance of protecting women in industry was stressed. Slowly the chief inequalities in legal status were undermined on many fronts. Modern tenement laws were enacted in many cities between 1900 and 1910. This period also witnessed investigations of prostitution in New York, Chicago, and Pittsburgh. The plight of prostitutes was called to public attention, and the Mann Act was passed in 1910. Margaret Sanger started her work about this time and organized the American Birth Control League in 1914. The National Congress for Uniform Divorce Laws had met in 1906.

All of these reform movements were symptomatic of social changes taking place. The housewife was affected by the invention of household conveniences, by the development of electricity, by changes in diet. Even simplifications of dress and style were not without their significance. The woman at home as well as the woman in industry found expanding opportunities. The wife and mother had more leisure time. Women's organizations increased, and their members directed their attention to civic improvement. The General Federation of Women's Clubs grew from fifty thousand members in 1898 to more than a million in 1914.[7]

The progressive spirit in American politics was reflected in the woman suffrage fight. In 1908 Theodore Roosevelt had declined to recommend woman suffrage to Congress. He urged a visiting deputation of suffragists to "go get another state." In 1910 the organized women sent Congress a petition signed by 404,000 supporters. In 1912 Taft and Wilson side-stepped the issue. The Progressive party platform, however, that year stated that the party, "believing that no people can justify claim to be a true democracy which denies political rights on account of sex, pledges itself to the task of securing equal suffrage to men and women alike."[8] Ensuing years saw rapid gains. During 1912 Arizona, Kansas, and Oregon joined the five states allowing women to vote, and Montana and Nevada were added to their number in 1914. In 1913 Illinois granted women the right to vote for presidential electors; but it was not until 1917 that victory in New York marked the first break in the East.

As the national committees of the major parties were led by this success to give the movement their support, victory was practically assured nationally. The Democratic platform of 1916 had already declared, "We recommend the extension of the franchise to the women of the country by the States upon the same terms as the men." [9] The Republicans likewise looked with favor upon state action.

The problem of tactics confronted the suffrage leaders directly at this time. Should they continue their fight state by state, or should they concentrate upon securing a federal amendment? In 1913 the leaders of the National Woman Suffrage Association decided upon an intensive national campaign to amend the Constitution. Alice Paul, the chairman of the congressional committee and the chief lobbyist of the organization, advocated militant tactics. Because of the split in the Republican pary in the 1912 election, the Democrats had complete control of the federal government. In England the party in power was held accountable, and the militants focused their attention upon it. The majority of the leaders of the National Woman Suffrage Association hesitated to adopt similar tactics, believing that they were not appropriate to conditions in the United States. Miss Paul, ousted from her place in the N.W.S.A., led the independent and aggressive Congressional Union. This group tried to arouse women in the suffrage states of the West against the Democratic party. They opposed Democratic candidates because they belonged to the party in power, which declined to support the amendment. Democratic supporters of woman suffrage in the eastern states were annoyed by such tactics.

The ardent suffragists went directly to President Wilson and asked him as head of his party to force through the amendment. To their pleas he responded,

"As the leader of a party my commands come from that party and not from private personal convictions. In this country as in every other self-governing country it is really through the instrumentality of party that things can be accomplished. They are not accomplished by the individual voice but by concerted action; and that action must come only so fast as you can concert it. I have done my best and shall continue to do my best to concert it in the interest of a cause in which I personally believe." [10]

Yet it is difficult to estimate the independent influence that the militant suffragists had in the passage of the amendment. The significance of Alice Paul's strategy lay in its publicity value. Despite the interest of the war news, the suffrage campaign was sufficiently dramatic to keep the issue before the public. Holding the president responsible undoubtedly influenced his action. By December, 1918, he had come around to the suffragist viewpoint. As Preston B. Slosson concludes, Miss Paul's work "helped force the Wilson administration to take a definite stand for woman suffrage." [11] This decision was influenced to a considerable extent by war and by the work the women did during the war. In a message to the Senate, Wilson stated:

"No disputable principle is involved but only a question of the method by which the suffrage is to be extended to women. There is and can be no party issue involved in it. Both of our national parties are pledged, explicitly pledged, to equality of suffrage for the women of the country.

". . . neither party, . . . can justify hesitation as to the method of obtaining it, can rightfully hesitate to substitute federal initiative for State initiative." [12]

This change marked a distinct revolution in the attitude for the party. Miss Doris Stevens, historian of the suffragists, was able to say, "For six full years, through three Congresses under President Wilson's power, the continual Democratic resistance, meandering, delays, deceits had left us still disfranchised." [13] This Democratic delay was the Republican party's opportunity. Attack on the president was an important factor in stimulating the opposition party into actually passing the amendment when they came into power.

Viewing the movement as a whole, we find the political parties responding to a broad shift of opinion favorable to increased opportunities for women. Special-aim organizations gave impetus and direction, but little more.

The interactions of political parties and pressure groups illustrate the thought that the success of propaganda for change depends upon the general attitude of mind predominant at the time. Political party activity then indeed seems superficial, skimming the surface of events and effective largely in the form and expression that may be imposed on the existing flow of events. Both the woman suffrage movement and our experience with national prohibition brought to the surface the many irrationalities, the wishful thinking, and the sentimentality that characterize much of public opinion. Yet the history of these movements also illustrates the ways in which economic and social forces, developing and changing, interact with the opinions and aspirations of various groups and provide conditions favorable to some and unfriendly to others. The outcome rests upon no one determinant authority.

Under the theory of public opinion as set forth in this chapter there is no common will or substantive mandate for a political party to carry into execution. The political process in a democracy lies not in the expression of a mythical popular will but in freedom for the group wills that press for expression.

"The task of government," John Dickinson writes, "and hence of democracy as a form of government, is not to express an imaginary popular will, but to effect adjustments among the various special wills and purposes which at any given time are pressing for realization." [14]

☆ 24 ☆

Roots of Consent

"The people," said a farmer's wife in a Minnesota country store while her husband
was buying a new post-hole digger,
"The people," she went on, "will stick around
a long time.
"The people run the works, only they don't
know it yet—you wait and see."

CARL SANDBURG

DEMOCRACY may assert that the people rule, but how can
the roots of this consent be tapped? Government deals with
limited phases of community activity. Democracy's roots must go
deeper and further if its full potentialities are to be realized.

Adjustment decentralized, widespread, and nongovernmental
is a process vital to democracy. Thus is a true community maintained. Unless there is a permeation of consent throughout
various levels of association the higher stages of adjustment lack
effectiveness. They are little more than rhetorical battles conducted on the plane of discussion and never penetrate to the
underlying social sources. The organization of group interests
may promote rigidities by freezing opinion in definite forms and
thereby postponing compromise until the legislative lobbies are
reached. Democracy has certainly been most firmly rooted where
the discussion of community problems has been the task of all
citizens. Yet democratic government may still maintain at least
the minimum conditions of freedom by merely tolerating the
differences among groups.

The objective of democratic politics is a free integration of
parts. Pressure politics involves the substitution of blocs for a

broader communal synthesis. It provides a means of expression in a society which has grown alien to many of its citizens. What social unity we possess is largely of our own conscious creation.

The vitality of democracy depends upon the freedom enjoyed by the individual in realizing his powers. Unless attempts to fulfill individual aims are to result in violence the community must be of a character conducive to their harmonious adjustment with the desires of other men. Adjustment at the top is thus important, but equally vital is adjustment both at a lower level and in non-state areas. If the full responsibility for these conditions devolves upon the state our chances of success are slim indeed. For the state is no super-entity divorced from the men and institutions that act in its name.

Integration cannot be superimposed. It must grow within the society. The contribution that a political party can make is limited. We must examine the whole texture of the society. What is the nature of the relationships between the employee and his boss, between the churchgoer and his fellows, between the workman and his union, between the professional man and his professional association? Citizenship cannot be left in isolation and the values of democracy applied only to the government. Political problems are not the only questions to be settled by discussion; to have meaning for a society the vote must be a usual device in the settlement of differences. True democratic government is possible only in a democratic society. We cannot look to our parties for salvation. A wider front is needed. The ideology of democracy must extend throughout the relationships of society if democratic beliefs are to be effective.

The general welfare is achieved by harmonizing and adjusting group interests. For example, the welfare of the banker, the businessman, the worker, and the farmer must be considered if economic rehabilitation is to result. Pressure groups representing the community broken up into its occupational and economic interests call attention to the forces that must be reconciled and the differences that must be compromised.

It is clear that each individual has certain particular interests with which his own welfare is identified. His job, his family, his church, his club, his union, his lodge—these are some of the ties which bind him to his fellows. Standing alone or immersed in the great mass of society, the individual is lost. It is as he associates with others holding to like interests that he is able to express his opinion in effective form and to discover the power to make his views articulate.

All governmental policies are concerned with special interests. The national welfare does not present a united front. It is advanced as particular projects are attended to—as the unemployed are found jobs, as the farmers are given relief, as the manufacturers are afforded credit facilities or tariff adjustments. It is these multifarious special interests of classes and individuals which demand attention from the government and which accordingly must be evaluated and reconciled if the general welfare is to be promoted.

Most public policies mean in fact promoting the welfare of certain concrete and observable elements. Special interests only too often talk of the general welfare for purposes of bolstering their own group interests or attacking opponents. The concept of the general welfare is thus useful for purposes of debate. As the group nature of society is clearly recognized, we are able to face more directly the problem of securing a greater degree of balance. The identification of the general welfare with the interests of business led to the excesses of monopoly and big business domination in the final decades of the last century. This same attitude is implicit in most of the present indignation of business leaders. On the other hand, the welfare of the "producing masses" cannot be our exclusive standard of public interest unless we wish to cast over the democratic ideology in favor of the communistic.

One corollary deduced from all this is that the concept of checks and balances is still significant for any system that refuses to be dogmatic in defining the general welfare. It may be that we must alter the forms of balance and modify checks that make for dangerous delay. Yet unless we check and balance divergent economic forces and conflicting philosophies of value, one band of true believers will demolish another band of true believers in the name of the general welfare.

If our major parties did not both profess to act in the public interest, what alternative would they have? The ideology of communism is one alternative with policy based on the urban industrial workers' welfare. Under democracy, while we talk in terms of the general welfare and of the public interest, we recognize at the same time that actually concessions are being made to special interests. Our fights are not over this but rather over giving each element its share. This may appear tawdry and may at times accentuate short-run objectives; it may also encourage organized minorities. Yet it does remain close to the direct satisfaction of the demands arising from the community. The public interest remains rooted in this public composed of many particular interests.

A most important and yet a most puzzling problem is how to secure the permeation of democratic values and practices throughout the community. Government by discussion and vote-taking is regarded as desirable in many joint efforts. In universities, churches, clubs, agricultural organizations, trade associations, and labor unions this is so.

The danger of pressure politics must be sought not simply in the relationship between government and pressure groups but also among the members of these latter entities. If the state is to be democratic, so must the smaller associations that bind men more intimately. If in the government of clubs, churches, labor unions, trade associations, universities, and comparable conjoint efforts the spirit of self-government and the habit of free compromise are not respected it is vain to expect that the government will mysteriously succeed in its much more difficult task.

A. D. Lindsay has stated:

"We cannot, I think, ever make our political government, considered in itself, really representative. The scale on which it has to operate is too vast—its units, the constituencies, are, if taken in themselves, too big and far too little informed by any public spirit to be really democratic. But if a vigorous non-political democratic life exists, the political machinery may harmonize and co-ordinate all that partial focussing of public opinion which the non-political associations perform. There can be, and there is increasingly coming to be, a vast deal of public discussion and political education focussed by universities, by churches, and by all kinds of cultural associations." [1]

The life led by the individual in these more intimate relationships provides much of the tone and color of his existence. These groups express desires and stand for interests too diverse or personal for the sterner or broader aims of the state. Within the solid framework of law and national security, innumerable impulses may flower into associational life and grow or wither as the responsiveness of men determines. Certainly the problem of democracy must be considered not merely in terms of the individual and the state, nor merely in terms of interest groups and the state, but also in terms of the individual and his activities in various social groupings.

Sumner Slichter has said: "Industry produces men as well as goods, and it can't produce the type of men which democracy needs unless civil rights exist within plants. It can't produce the type of men which democracy needs if each plant is a little Oriental despotism." [2] The course of labor legislation indicates an awareness of this viewpoint, though the approach is protective.

A group of officials in the Department of Agriculture have been thinking of democracy in promotive rather than protective terms. One result is the present network of farmers' committees acting as adjuncts to the administration of many of the Department of Agriculture duties. The political theory underlying this development has recently been set forth in a book called *Democracy Has Roots*, published under the signature of M. L. Wilson, Under Secretary of the Department of Agriculture. Quotations from this book are in order because it stresses in fresh terms a current view of a persistent democratic hope:

"In the thousands of localities which form the constituencies of the country, these different functional and occupational groups meet separately. Such meetings are indispensable, in order that the members of the group may have an informed understanding of their group interest and a policy for its furtherance. But the very success of their separate discussions may endanger the process of general policy-making unless there is local consultation, local cross-fertilization among the groups, going on at the same time as their functional activities. The tendency now is toward national federation of the local groups of each kind, toward the formation of pressure groups which move on Washington in blocs demanding that their interests be advanced. Congress and the President thus become practically the sole source of whatever concept of the general welfare receives attention. So far as the constituencies are concerned, the representative system becomes representation of special interests.

"The fault in the system is thus a local, not a national, fault. If sound democratic policy is to be made, it must be initiated in local discussions participated in by leaders of farm, industrial, labor and professional groups in their home towns. Where such discussion takes place, the give-and-take, the bargain, the compromise that is the characteristic mark of democracy, is continually going on in local arguments, local conversations. The process of moderation is continually minimizing what appear to be irreconcilable differences in interest. Where such discussion takes place, representatives in Congress have a concept of the general welfare to represent." [3]

The authors hope that democracy's answers will come from such a source. The task cannot be left to representatives exhorted to think first of the public interest and second of their chances for re-election. Representative government can be no better than its base. Unless men come together and face their divergent interests in terms of their own experience, the politics of democracy can have no meaning. The growth of interest groups has sometimes deferred a meeting of minds until lobbyists confronted legislators. Associational life may also bring the participation and the interchange of ideas that lead to the permeation of consent.

We should not make the comforting assumption that public policy usually emerges from discussions permeating deeply into the community. Often this fails to take place, and segments of opinion are crystallized in blocs difficult to reconcile. This may be due as much to the rigidity of the community as to the intransigence of the distinctive group itself. While adjustments are often made at a level removed from the mass of citizens, still discontent has seldom been allowed to accumulate to proportions endangering the existing means of compromise.

We have noted how the shortness of the life span of minor parties illustrates this. Minor parties and pressure groups are agencies of representation. Democracy itself is usually treated as a problem in representation. The reform of democracy has been approached in terms of the initiative and referendum, proportional representation, the direct primary, the direct election of senators, presidential primaries, and the popular election of the president. This emphasis would provide for the fullest scope of individual wills. The time has come to re-examine this stress upon representation. In practice our popular assemblies are only too responsive to the group interests of which they are composed.

The essential problem of finding some common ground remains. In this effort it is obvious that we cannot rely upon minor parties as appropriate organizational devices. As previously indicated, our major parties are not likely to become sufficiently disciplined and unified to be effective agencies. The problem is how to offset our political particularity with a more co-ordinated view of public policy. Lindsay Rogers argues that

"historically the function of a legislative assembly was to fight on behalf of the people against threatened dynastic or executive oppression. Now the function is two-fold—first . . . to adjust interests; and second to collaborate with an executive who is responsive to public opinion, and who needs legislation in order to perform his overwhelming administrative tasks. The function of parliament—and the fact is inadequately realized—is performed well in almost direct proportion to the strength and ability of the executive." [4]

A strong executive has from time to time provided in effective fashion an integrating force toward a broader view of the public interest. On the other hand the consequences of such leadership bring a reaction. The people have always been of two minds about the relative influence of the legislative and the executive branches.

We have followed neither tendency through and hence have never had to reckon with the discomfort of ultimate logical conclusions. The conflict remains, however. So long as this process of tightening and loosening of authority continues, we have room for adjustment. Experimentation is followed by consolidation.

When should particularism give way to unity? When is the time ripe to ease the pressure of authority so as to admit the efflorescence of varied and diverse group interests? These are questions ever before the statesmen. Should our machinery of government stress leadership, unity, centralization, or the principle of representation, diversity, and localism? This question of emphasis underlies the battle of words between conservative and liberal, or between the haves and have-nots, or individualism and collectivism. Hamilton and Jefferson appear and reappear in various disguises: the negativity of Coolidge and the assertiveness of Wilson; the swing continues.

While we cannot stem the force of particularism, we still hope for a greater degree of co-ordination and direction. There is no final answer as to the place of groups and the scope of pressure politics. Movement we must have, but at the same time we must have direction. The vitality of democracy lies in group life; its task is to reconcile unity with this diversity.

Yet underlying our modern polity is a long secular trend toward collective responsibility. This takes many different forms in the world today. It shows itself as absolutism in totalitarian countries. It is expressed through rigid party organization and cabinet dictatorship in Great Britain. It is marked by increased governmental regulation and the growth of bureaucracy in the United States. We are all pushed along this road by economic and social forces beyond our control and comprehension. Political theory is one element in a complex of forces and institutional growths leading in the same general direction. We have not been willing to accept for guidance a philosophy of collectivism even though this in practice seems to be the course plotted by pressure politics. The total effect of particular pressures for limited objectives has brought us far toward collectivism.

Interests have worked out a way; institutional changes have been slower in coming, but the philosophical justifications are still slower. The thought has followed the deed. Lippmann writes:

"In the real world the historic advance of democratic collectivism has not been directed by any such rationalized vision of a new society. It is true that visions of this sort have influenced the argument over specific measures, rousing many to action and breaking down resistance, and it would be difficult to exaggerate the practical influence on western society of these collectivists who call themselves social democrats, Fabian socialists, evolutionary or revisionist socialists, or merely progressives. . . . But though collectivists exercise a kind of intellectual monopoly and absolute authority over the assumptions of modern politics, they have not imbued the mass of the people with their own general conception of society as a whole. . . . Though exceptions could be cited, it is substantially true that, while the moral and intellectual justification for each measure is derived from the general ideology of collectivism, the initiative comes from organized interests. . . . Thus no serious historian of politics would imagine that he had accounted for the protective tariff or the system of bounties or subsidies, for the actual status of property rights, for agricultural or for labor policies, until he had gone behind the general claims and the abstract justification and had identified the specifically interested groups which promoted the specific law." [5]

Pressure politics in the long run seems to press toward increased state intervention. It grows by what it feeds upon. Groups seeking concessions go to the source of power and wealth. The state inevitably expands in power and scope under these forces. It may be that in time a unified ideology will win acceptance as a rationalization of this trend.

Although agreement about ideals or institutions cannot eliminate the conflict of interests, democracy can afford to accept these differences with less subterfuge than totalitarianism.

In a discussion of the many unofficial avenues through which new impulses within the community may seek outlets and through which interests freely compete for power, the legal foundation upon which all of this rests must not be overlooked. Pressure politics and third parties enhance the responsive aspect of popular government, but their freedom is based on our deep confidence in the underlying constitutional settlement. W. Y. Elliott is one philosopher who recognizes the vitality of group life at the same time that he stresses the need for "the integrating power of legal sovereignty, unified by judicial review in accordance with the constitutionally defined purpose of the State." This institutional framework and the ideology supporting it have prevented the rule of law from degenerating into a "battle-royal of interests." [6]

A high degree of political diversity is compatible with democratic methods only where a higher loyalty to the institutions and the ideals of democracy exists. That men hold to the belief in democracy as a way of conducting human relations is of fundamental significance. The fact that this method in its turn has been successful in adjusting social and economic forms to new human needs fortifies the original faith. As Elliott says, "constitutionalism is a 'myth' (in the sense of a social belief which stirs men to moral action) that has proved its claims to being true and worthy of continued acceptance." One evidence of the force of this norm is the anger with which men react when the tactics of pressure politics infringe the rules of our game of politics. Defections from democratic fair play are to be expected; it is the existence of the norms that is important. These standards are fortified by emotional loyalties and usually implemented through law.

In this broader sense whatever promotes the peaceful adjustment of social problems is germane to the politics of democracy. Our political system is highly intricate, with much that is irrational in its make-up. Under favorable conditions we need not ask for a simple picture of the values implicit within it. Yet when other systems become rivals and offer with deceptive simplicity creeds easily sold to the public, a true appreciation of our own working philosophy becomes virtually imperative. The importance of constantly re-educating the public to the philosophic values for which this system stands cannot be safely disregarded by our statesmen.

The practical political need for a wide basis of power impels the politician to seek a broader purpose. As a narrowly partisan objective this may mean no more than a search for an immediate working adjustment. Yet on the higher level of statesmanship it means educating the following to a clearer conception of state purpose. It is for lack of this higher consensus that we find pressure and propaganda in the guerrilla warfare of interest groups playing a determinant part in popular government. Democracy is a creed justifying a competitive quest for the Holy Grail of unity; but the Grail has meaning as an objective, not as a utensil. That man has seldom actually attained to harmony in public affairs does not make this goal any the less important.

☆ 25 ☆

Money as Political Currency

> "The first question is, Where do we raise the
> money, where is the cash coming from?
>
> "The mazuma, the jack, the shekels, the kale,
> The velvet, the you-know-what,
> The what-it-takes, a roll, a wad,
> Bring it home, boy.
> Bring home the bacon.
> Start on a shoestring if you have **to**.
> Then get your first million."
>
> CARL SANDBURG

DESPITE the diversity of groups within our democracy, we must get enough agreement to formulate policy and conduct the government. Money in politics is very helpful in this process. Its use may be condemned because it falls short of a more rational and idealistic appeal, but it may also be condoned as a method short of violence for securing acquiescence among men.

A differing but widely representative view of money in politics is set forth in the following excerpts from a speech by Senator Gerald P. Nye:

"There are various influences at work these days which threaten our representative form of government, but upon me there has grown a most determined conviction that the most dangerous of these influences is that of money in the conduct of political campaigns. To my mind, such use as is being made of money and the hugeness of contributions and spendings to win election to high public office affords the greatest and most pressing issue threatening our Government and challenging our people to-day." [1]

In short, of what use is the ballot if it is outweighed by the wallet?

The meaning of wealth under democracy must be analyzed if

336

we would understand the nature of our political system. Senator Nye admits that "there are proper uses for money in political campaigns." He knows that it is costly but essential to bring issues before the voters. "It is the money which does not enter into a proper and necessary use against which I argue," he states. It is just this question of what constitutes a proper and necessary use that lies at the heart of the problem. To the extent that a common moral basis of evaluation exists, we have no problem except one of law enforcement. Pirates and felons can be hunted down. Their status is clear; so also is that of voters who sell their votes or of politicians who promise legislation as a direct return for campaign contributions. The wrong is very clearly established in such cases. A broader view of the function of money in politics is required.[2] It would be unwise to underestimate the seriousness of the need for better control of campaign expenditures, but effective remedial treatment demands that the problem be related to its general social context. Senator Nye states his belief that

"there are three positive things that can be done. First, there should be a tightening up of our law governing the conduct of elections, both general and primary. Second, there should be stricter limitation by law of expenditures, and, finally, there should be an awakening on the part of people to rebellion against money holding such sway as it does in some States in influencing the result of elections.

"In conclusion, let me say the best and finest results in opposition to the influence of money in campaigns would be gained if the people of America would stand out and uncompromisingly and jealously rebel against and guard against the corrupting of our election system, and fight it whether its sponsors were Republican or Democratic leaders."[3]

The problem, however, is not quite so simple as that. Public indignation is undoubtedly a vital force in American life and not lightly gainsaid. Existent standards of public morality condemn corruption in elections; but men fall into disagreement over what political purposes and practices are corrupt.

We have been loath to think realistically of party financing. Instead of facing the fact that organization is as costly as it is necessary, some writers have pointed to money as the root of party deterioration. To Walter Weyl the party was

". . . a sturdy rogue without visible means of support, yet living riotously, and insisting that the world owed him a good living. Instead of taking the vow of poverty, as a popular party should, instead of being supported openly and democratically (as is to-day the Socialist party) by the pennies and nickels of its members, the party demanded, and received, an endowment from men willing to invest in political organization as they invested in railroads and timber lands." [4]

We get nowhere by calling the party a "sturdy rogue" and insisting that a truly popular party should live on the people's pence. It takes money and lots of it to run a party. No one knows exactly how much a presidential campaign costs, but probably as much as $25,000,000 has been expended in some campaigns.

Opinions differ as to whether political contributions generally involve a direct *quid pro quo*. Senator Nye, for example, challenges great wealth in election campaigns as unduly influential:

". . . men with selfish interests to be served through legislation find it profitable to contribute to the campaign funds of a party, and at times to both parties. Investments in the form of such contributions have been found to be productive of certain and positive returns—returns of such proportions as make ordinary investments seem silly. Campaign contributions are but political favors. To establish that this is true, may I offer the very concrete evidence afforded through the record of campaign contributions in 1924 and legislative returns enjoyed by these same contributors in 1926? In 1924, with a presidential and congressional election on, John D. Rockefeller, Andrew Mellon, Payne Whitney, the Marshall Field estate, George F. Baker, sr., George F. Baker, jr., Vincent Astor, J. B. Duke, Julius Fleischmann, Cyrus Curtis, and Joseph E. Widener, to name only a few men, made contributions to party campaign funds ranging from $5,000 to $25,000. In 1926 the parties to which they contributed became sponsors of a tax reduction bill, which was whipped through Congress by party leaders and which saved to these men each and every year sums ranging from $200,000 to nearly $3,000,000." [5]

If men were as rational as they are often assumed to be, we might take Senator Nye's fears more seriously. To treat the use of money in politics as if it were the serpent in the Garden of Eden is greatly to oversimplify the matter.

To find a parallel between the interests of a group of political supporters and the subsequent policy of the party they support is not an extraordinary discovery. It is the characteristic concomitant of representative government. To go further and interpret the motives of the contributors is to raise moral issues which escape attempts at objective analysis. The interpretations that one places upon the actions of his fellows hark back to the group interests of the observer and his psychological reactions. For in contrast to the view of Senator Nye, we find Simeon Strunsky arguing that candidates of promise attract

"the support of politicians, whether professional or amateur, and of money. The money will come from friends who like the man and believe in him; from executive individuals who like to have a finger in success; from politicians who think they can use the coming man in their business; from local pride in the home town boy; from sectional and regional pride; and, as he goes up, from the great mass of disinterested people who are drawn to a winner. The last of these factors is without doubt the greatest: it is the friendly unenvious American sense of democratic participation in individual good fortune. . . .

"People are always investing in rising young men and promising candidates, and no matter who carries away the prize it will be found that he has had financial backing." [6]

That sentiment rather than expectation of personal gain prompts some campaign contributors cannot be denied. While Strunsky's interpretation is as applicable to some situations as that of Senator Nye is to others, experience clearly indicates that different "men of promise" make different kinds of promises to various interests and that money does not adhere so generously to candidates whose policies are unsympathetic to the interests of wealthy men.

A most pertinent question is how much effect do men's contributions have on political success. It is easy to overestimate the effectiveness of the money spent in campaigns. In sensational instances extravagant expenditures have actually caused defeat.

The notion that elections are bought outright is likewise erroneous. Means of persuasion more subtle than purchase of votes at a going rate are now employed. Direct vote-buying was apparently quite prevalent in some sections a generation ago. Paul Ward, a critical observer of present-day politics, writes as follows:

". . . The money that counts is spent not on buying votes but on getting out the vote, and the rest is spent on propaganda. Enormous sums are spent on printing or broadcasting the output of the campaign committees' research and publicity divisions, and most of it is stupid, ineffectual stuff. At best the output of one division tends to do nothing more than cancel that of its rival; only the appeals to racial, religious, and class prejudice click in substantial fashion, and these must be handled not only gingerly but also subterraneously, for they cut both ways. The money that counts, the money spent on getting out the vote, goes for hiring cars to take voters to the polls and for hiring runners to see that the cars are kept busy and filled. Some of this money, and no inconsiderable part, goes into the pockets of ward-heelers and other professionals whose chief stock in trade is their ability to make friends with a controlling minority of the residents of their bailiwicks, and much of that money is spent in turn on cultivating these friendships by providing the residents of ward and precinct with sandwiches, cigars, free beer, and clubrooms in which to hide away from their families, play poker, and acquire the feeling of being wise and valued members of the community.

"The belief of those who lay out the dough in this manner is that the friendships so cultivated are transferable and that a substantial number of the citizenry who have enjoyed the hospitality and confidence of the precinct captain or ward boss automatically will mark their ballots for the candidates whom they have heard praised by their friend and benefactor. Sometimes the belief is baseless; it is less likely to be so if the professional leader has been more than a jolly host. If he has been able to get parking tickets torn up, a street paved, an alley repaired, a son freed from police clutches, or jobs for the faithful, the loyalty and size of his following are many times the capacity of his till to buy." [7]

The impression of this observer accords with the conclusions of careful students of campaign expenditures.[8]

Taking this point of view does not abolish the necessity of using large sums of money in legitimate ways in party campaigning.

The environmental factor most pertinent in an analysis of money in politics is the coloration given all phases of social behavior by the tenets of trade, of competition, and of the profit system. Where so much of the goods of society is for sale you never know the limits upon the power of money until you dicker. If the talents of the artist can be bought in the open market, why not those of the legislator? Where success is measured by wealth, what rewards of a nonmonetary nature can attract the public servant? Since questions of this sort can be raised, money in politics can be seen to exercise an imponderable influence. It becomes one avenue for the expression of social values. The influence of wealth permeates governmental as well as commercial relationships. Money is needed to run political parties, and the support of party politicians is often needed for success in business.

In a society wherein money talks, its voice is bound to be heard in politics whether or not we like its crude accent. Here is a language more universal than Esperanto and infinitely more eloquent. To use money in elections is to adopt the most common current means for defending or promoting subjective values in a society of materialistic standards. The danger to popular government lies not so much in the use of money itself as in the lack of balance between political groups of wealth and those of poverty. The use of money cannot be outlawed. Effective regulation of it is limited. As we achieve a more equitable social and economic balance within our society, money in elections will become of less importance.

Quick upsetting changes, which in turn arouse stubborn antagonism, are demanded; then the battle is on and the coffers are opened wide. The use of money in elections is a concomitant of the politics of transition to new economic institutions. During this century the trend of public policy has been more concerned with curbing business and eliminating abuses than with extending privileges to facilitate private economic development. Of course tariffs and subsidies exist along with regulations, but the businessman does not look to Washington with the expectant air that characterized the land speculator, railroad builder, and manufacturer in the past.

Certainly during the nineteenth century governmental favors were regarded as a stimulus to economic expansion. Although the nation professed faith in the free economic life which would be most effectively promoted by encouraging competition, monopolistic privileges were granted to men undertaking great new enterprises. Industries were granted tariffs liberally when voters were convinced that the growth of home industries should be encouraged in every way so that the nation might benefit all the sooner by the general prosperity thought sure to follow. The last few decades have brought many disillusionments on this as on other scores. The muckrakers' investigations showed with startling clarity the abuses resulting from the franchises granted to public utilities and monopolistic corporations protected from interference through the accretion of legal fictions.

Under such a system it was not surprising that some privileges would be purchased. But the idea of privilege itself was accorded general recognition. From our vantage point in the present, we look back upon the entrepreneurs who built the railroads through the West and the exploiters of the natural resources of the country and call them "robber barons." Emerson's writings remind us that "the agencies by which events so grand as the opening of California, of Texas, of Oregon, and the junction of the two oceans, are effected, are paltry—coarse selfishness, fraud, and conspiracy: and most of the great results of history are brought about by discreditable means." He discounts the benefits conferred by conscious reformers as "compared with the involuntary blessing wrought on nations by the selfish capitalists who built the Illinois, Michigan, and the network of the Mississippi valley roads, which have evoked not only all the wealth of the soil, but the energy of millions of men." [9]

It is pertinent to recall these views held by a noble soul when today men of good intent, though less exalted spirit, see the only road to salvation through state planning. We need not deny the value of this more careful procedure should it prove workable; but it is well to note that social benefits have not been solely the product of unselfishness and foresight. If this were so who can say how far from the cave mankind would have ventured?

It does not follow that we should condone such abuses or that today we should tolerate the continued use of these same tactics which brought expansion at so fabulous a cost. It is unimportant whether we approve of the tactics of these entrepreneurs; such tactics may better be considered in relation to the standards of their time, and to the concrete results produced. These men acted in accordance with the theories then predominant; they carried current assumptions to their logical extremes. They demonstrated the *reductio ad absurdum* of the theories of a free competitive system. They took literally the existing moral codes and applied fully the opportunities offered both by laissez faire and legal concessions. They helped to disclose the shortcomings of these canons when thus applied. If we have learned that free enterprise may result in freebooting, we can thank the robber barons, who exhibited the shortcomings in our theories, and face the new problem of establishing a better relationship between business and government.

The problem confronting us today was developed by the activities of these industrialists. Their ways of doing things proved more effective than the methods of their competitors. They succeeded where others failed; and if their success has left us with battle-scarred conceptions, it has likewise given us a more highly developed industrial system. Their significance, however, is not that they acted wrongly in the light of subsequent developments but that they acted at all.

With regard to the problem of this chapter, the favorable line of policy accorded industry served to fortify a position that its beneficiaries have not been ready to relinquish without a struggle. The first great battle was fought in 1896. Though William McKinley was the standard-bearer, Mark Hanna was the quartermaster general. He requisitioned supplies for the campaign in a systematic fashion theretofore unknown. Contributions were made in much the same spirit as men at a later date bought Liberty Bonds. Yet despite the skill of the Mark Hannas, the politics of democracy has wrought great changes since 1900. The "revolutionary" changes that men feared in Bryanism have for the most part already been made—and yet the day of victory over the "economic royalists" remains unfulfilled! The very language of debate today reflects the belligerent spirit of the group conflicts involved.

Doubtless the tactics needed to counteract the human reluctance to alter established patterns account for these extreme statements. The immediate job is to reduce privilege where privilege blocks necessary adjustments and to eliminate practices generally regarded as abuses. To do so would involve the disturbance of vested interests. On our success in this manipulative process will depend the nature and scope of the further problems that will thus be created. Party politics of the future will have to face a problem more perplexing than that of mere control of campaign expenditures and the punishment of rogues who bribe and deceive. The great task of directing the distribution and even the creation of wealth is looming as a political responsibility. The financing of politics is growing into the politicizing of finance. This trend offers a new challenge to democratic government.

It is an absurd oversimplification to identify the creation and the preservation of property with the preservation of any status quo rigidly conceived. Economic advance has come about through great changes in things as they were. Wealth in an industrial system is the product of a dynamic economic order. Even policies which may result in great changes in economic relationships may be introduced in a fashion that does not arouse the opposition of existing interests. For example, the stamp system [10] of distributing surplus commodities among relief recipients, recently set up in Rochester, Dayton, and other cities, is receiving the cordial support of local businessmen and chambers of commerce.

We witness potential institutional changes of great magnitude growing up under the aegis of vested interests. When the government, as in Great Britain, collects and spends on a conservative estimate about a quarter of the total national income, the legions of wealth cannot be pictured as standing across the way of change. The "owners" of capital are for the most part holders of paper. Their certificates may indicate that their property is administered in the name of the "people" or of a corporation. So long as they can clip their coupons, what difference does it make? The great army of bondholders are not necessarily fixed in their loyalties. As Swiss mercenaries sought the highest bidder, our stipendiaries are looking for the safest.

The use of great sums of money in political campaigns may be interpreted as a sign that efforts at rapid change involving high stakes are under way. Under a more closely integrated system the need for such artificial and blatant means is less. Money is necessary in a society where frictions develop because of a loose and shifting social structure.

Money is a normal channel of expression in any commercial society; but it is of less importance where other channels are open. It would be misleading to suggest that the British do not spend large sums in campaigning, but here again their characteristic way of meeting the problem offers an interesting contrast to our own. As indicated in a previous chapter, funds are centrally administered and in the Labour party the financing is provided by the trade unions. This is a deviation from what has been the traditional method.

The process of British party finance, however, is cloaked with a genteel reticence. Activity in many branches of British public life could be encircled by the motto "Honi soit qui mal y pense." As J. A. Spender writes, with unusual frankness, "To speak above a whisper about party funds is thought barely polite in British political circles." The prime minister or the leader of the Opposition has no knowledge of the details about who contributes, or how much. "This may not be generally believed," Spender notes, "but there was in fact no more rigid etiquette among Chief Whips of the old school than that the Prime Minister should know nothing about these things." Secrecy was likewise thought desirable lest the opposite party gain advantage. Nor could the dignity—and hence the very vitality—of the House of Lords be impugned by such sordid considerations. Yet money must be raised, and wealthy donors are not lacking.

"The older British parties have generally obtained this money from wealthy supporters and rewarded them with 'honours,' i. e. with knighthoods, baronetcies, and peerages in an ascending scale according to their contributions," Spender continues. The system worked well so long as its managers acted with restraint and discretion. "It was just possible to keep it going without scandal when the parties had their turns successively; but when both were in power together, and both were drawing simultaneously upon the same fountain of honour, the discredit and the scandal became too flagrant."

Spender defends the system, pointing out that while rewards were given for party generosity all such transactions were final. Gifts were unconditional:

"An ennobled donor who complained that his money was being misapplied or that it had been given under a misapprehension would have been sharply reminded that having got his peerage he had exhausted his right to speak. . . . So long as it was played under these rules, the game was simply that of exploiting the human weakness for titles, and it kept the *political* influence of money at a minimum. It might be trivial and foolish, but it could not be called corrupt."

Our system is based on an idealism less intimately related to human reactions than is the British. The way in which the British have adapted to the needs of modern party government their traditional feudal ranking is seldom accorded the recognition it deserves. We have not enlisted on the side of "good government" the strength of snobbery and the force of social emulation. Spender admits that "human nature may require these concessions, but there is no question that they may be a very real debasement of the standards of judgment and an active encouragement to a trivial kind of snobbery." [11]

The British system of honors by frankly rewarding political support and loyalty has eliminated much of the sub rosa element that characterizes the spoils system in this country. We are not without our system of honors, however. At best the list is limited and the tasks are not entirely honorific. Ambassadorships, for example, while highly useful as rewards for favors rendered, also require men of ability. Generosity alone is far from being the optimum qualification for a diplomatic career! That we have been able to reward campaign contributors with diplomatic appointments is one commentary on the relative unimportance often accorded our foreign relations in the past. The rise of a career service is indicative of a change of attitude.

Each society must provide in its own terms for the desires of ambitious men. If money is of less importance where other channels of reward and persuasion are open, it is of no political or social significance in a community where no monetary values rule. On a remote island in the South Seas the breeding of pigs with curled tusks is the great aim of the ambitious savage. He seeks neither wealth nor office: spiral-toothed porkers are his life's ambition. When he has collected a suitable number, a festival is held, the hogs are slaughtered, and their owner plays host at a community barbecue. Power and prestige can be attained only through this sacrifice.

From some points of view this pig economy has peculiar advantages. To advance in the social scale each aspirant must spend for the benefit of his community the worldly goods that make him eligible for such honors. Thus the dangers of economic inequality are counteracted, while at the same time strong social incentives to enjoy community respect are provided.[12]

Contrariwise, in our competitive commercial society kudos goes to the man able to "bring home the bacon." Our politicians likewise use the pork barrel, but to less broadly social ends. Our failure successfully to reconcile the inequalities of private wealth with democratic doctrines of political equality is reflected in campaign abuses, corrupt practices in politics, and the unsatisfactory tone of public life. It is part of the price we pay for our dynamic, diversified, and unstable civilization.

Difficulty occurs today when vested interests obstruct programs toward balance. These efforts can be met only in positive terms. The Corrupt Practices Act can do no more than discourage some of the rogues in their more blatant activities. If we accept the blunt fact that men support those in office from whose policies they expect to benefit, labor unions and large corporations may be classed together. The influence of wealth as a selfish force is being met by the organization of the have-nots. The answer to the Liberty League comes from the C.I.O. and the Workers' Alliance. The increasing political strength of labor has expressed itself in financial fashion. Thus in November, 1936, Labor's Non-Partisan League reported that it had spent $156,240.38 in support of President Roosevelt. The United Mine Workers aided the Democratic 1936 war chest to the extent of almost half a million dollars.

The influence of large contributions cannot be met simply by efforts at regulating campaign expenses. A better economic balance within the community itself is necessary in order to reach the real cause. Antagonistic groups will use whatever weapons are available. Public morality may outlaw certain practices; phases of the battle may even be driven underground. Yet peace will not ensue so long as maladjustments remain.

☆ 26 ☆

The Struggle with Spoils

"Tar-Baby say nothin'—Mr. Fox lay low.
Brer Rabbit, he butted ez hard ez he could,
An' his head it stuck, let 'im do what he
would."

JOEL CHANDLER HARRIS

THE spoils system is the tar baby of American politics. It cannot be handled by reformers with the clean dispatch which undoubtedly characterized St. George's attack on the dragon. Although the battle has been going on for a long time, we are still stuck with the problem.

Viewed from a broad sociological angle, our difficulties over patronage parallel the questions raised by money in politics. Appointments to office have been used as a means to enlist or reward political support; but just as excessive campaign expenditures suggest a maladjustment of political relationships, so abuses in the civil service may reflect deeper causes that need attention. Nevertheless, jobs as political inducements remain a part of the present scheme just as money in elections continues as an essential in campaigning.

What to do for the rank and file of party workers is a persistently embarrassing question. There can never be enough jobs to go around. The very brashness of the question repels high-minded men and drives much political activity into sub rosa channels. Since we do not face this need frankly, political life remains precarious.

The difficulty is aggravated by the negative and nonprincipled character of our parties. Few but professional politicians are

349

stimulated to an active interest. Why should anyone else give an unswerving party loyalty to an organization that stands for little but traditionalism and emotionalism? Party loyalty would be futile indeed were it not rescued from time to time by loyalty to a striking personality.

"What strikes one mainly on looking into the facts is the extreme poverty and precariousness of the rewards which keep the American machine running," Spender writes.[1] Certainly the aim of government should not be to eliminate rewards for party service but rather to reconcile such rewards with the demands of good administration.[2] This the British have in large measure achieved.

The British have not ruled out self-seeking in politics; they have simply made it respectable. The distribution of rewards and honors has finally fallen into responsible hands. Britain's free trade policy was no small factor in the gradual reform of the civil service: it militated against subsidies, quotas, and tariffs and thus reduced the opportunities for graft.

"The progressive removal of customs duties reduced the reservoir of jobs for needy relatives and the number of officials capable of being bribed, and at the same time prevented the development of lobbying and pressure groups," Jennings writes. "It made easier, too, the unification of the governmental machine." [3]

The growth in importance of the prime minister joined with the enlightened policy of a succession of notable incumbents brought about a series of reforms. By 1866 patronage was largely eliminated except in the church and the law. Lord Melbourne might exclaim, "Damn it, another bishop dead!" in expressing his annoyance at the pressure for preferment that would ensue, but in time merit won recognition even in church appointments. Under clear ministerial responsibility and central leadership a tradition of incorruptibility grew.

Jennings writes:

"Gladstone made the Treasury predominant by raising the Chancellor of the Exchequer to the rank of second minister. Peel created the convention that the Prime Minister must be consulted on all major appointments, and Gladstone insisted that the needs of the Budget must dominate public expenditure. Moreover, the machinery for effective control was created. The power of initial appointment to the civil service was gradually transferred to the Civil Service Commissioners after 1855. Effective Treasury control became possible when, as a result of the Select Committee on Public Monies in 1857, the Public Accounts Committee was established in 1861 and the Exchequer and Audit Departments Act passed in 1866. After 1866 the Prime Minister, the Treasury, the Public Accounts Committee, and the Comptroller and Auditor General acted jointly and severally to complete the destruction of 'Old Corruption.' Even Disraeli could not recall the snows of yester-year." [4]

The prime minister had wide discretion, but accountability curbed the abuse of power. The system, while far from perfect, provided a way of removing petty favoritism and partisan manipulation. The British were willing to enforce party discipline by the ministerial threat of dissolution and thereby eradicate dependence on bribery or places as the price of parliamentary support. They did not worry about opening competition for administrative offices among the general public. The more intelligent sons, drawn from the higher social strata and educated at Oxford or Cambridge, were good enough competitors.

The progress of civil service reform in Great Britain was paralleled by ever more centrally controlled and disciplined party organizations. The British king and the prime minister in the eighteenth century found the bribing and placating of individual members of Parliament necessary, since they could not rely upon a strong party organization for support. Today in Great Britain the candidate for Parliament depends largely upon party headquarters for aid, direction, and funds. Often he is sent by his party chiefs to stand for a particular constituency. Even in cases where the candidate "nurses" his constituency by gifts to local charities and benefactions to individuals and organizations, he remains to most voters a cipher whereby they register their approval or disapproval of the government in office. Where party discipline is slack patronage is of more importance.

The British have not succeeded where we have failed. Theirs

has been a different problem, met in a different way. In the United States we have tried to meet the great human problem of staffing public agencies by trying to set up a mechanism that would reduce personal judgment to a minimum. We have tried to rate the diverse capacities of applicants without denying equalitarian and democratic assumptions. We have feared to center responsibility. Our parties, seeking some sanction for responsible control, fell back on patronage as one means of holding their followers in line. Reformers have been unwilling that so high a price be paid for party cohesion, and yet they had no clear practicable alternative.

Today we face in both directions. Some patronage seems necessary as a weapon for leadership, though spoils of office cannot be tolerated if gross inefficiency is the consequence. Hence, while civil service reformers strive for the elimination of partisan political factors in personnel administration, partisan politicians strive for better spoils administration. If party influence is to remain, it must in many instances support appropriate standards of technical competence in public office. Hence we find an interesting growth of a more efficient spoils system. When the New Deal took over, Mr. Farley was besieged by job seekers. Under the terrific pressure he attempted to systematize the distribution of jobs.

Job seekers came to the offices of the Democratic national committee in the National Press Building in Washington. They were interviewed by an assistant, and records of their names, occupations, and political endorsers were made. The theory was that each applicant could then be recommended for the positions that might be available. All applicants for government jobs were to "clear" through the committee. Ideally, political clearance meant that the applicant was to have the endorsement of his county chairman as well as of his congressman or senator.

Emil Hurja, when with the Democratic national committee, hoped to work out an equitable distribution of patronage. One Washington correspondent described his system thus:

"He has calculated a system of quotas. Out of every 1,000 jobs, for instance, New York is entitled to 101 and Arizona to 4. He has another chart based on the total salaries. By watching these charts no State ever gets far out of line or has for long a complaint that it is not receiving its share. A similar record is kept of all the Democratic members of Congress. During sessions a record of Aye and No votes has been made at times, and those members who stood by the New Deal have had their rewards increased while the backsliders were punished. In order to avoid placing applicants in positions for which they are not fitted, all seekers for routine jobs are required to fill out an extensive questionnaire giving their qualifications and experience. To see that square pegs are not put in round holes the Postmaster General and his assistant, Mr. Hurja, have their own representative in practically every bureau and department to handle patronage matters." [5]

Thus Julian Friant passed upon the unclassified personnel in the Department of Agriculture. Technical and scientific positions were left alone; attention was confined to the relatively unskilled jobs. Friant tried to apportion positions roughly among the states and to check on political recommendations. Many congressmen are very undiscriminating in handing out endorsements. The patronage official is valuable as a buffer between the administrative services and the vagaries of congressmen. A congressman's interest in patronage is usually a reflection of the demand for jobs made in his home district. Where the voters are often in need of work, the demand for public jobs is insistent. Many congressmen in other sorts of districts do not have to meet such a demand and can hence devote themselves to the study of legislation. If a congressman wants jobs for his constituents, he must hunt for them. If he spends enough time and energy, he can usually persuade administrators to find a place for his supporters.

From the viewpoint of party headquarters factional strife over patronage questions is a danger to be carefully watched. Hence the emphasis on system. The extent to which Mr. Farley went in his efforts to prevent misunderstanding is illustrated by the following written agreement between the Texas delegation in Congress and the postmaster general concerning the sharing of spoils:

"The two senators are to control the following patronage: District and appellate judges, district attorneys, United States marshals, internal revenue collectors, custom officers, postmasters in their respective home cities, all state-wide appointments, and all appointments requiring confirmation of Senate.

"The Congressman in each district is to control, subject to above, all postmasters in his district, all appointees in his district to be made by Mr. Morgenthau, the Reconstruction Finance Corporation, the Census Bureau, the Agricultural Department, the Treasury Department, and other appointments in his district not state-wide." [6]

This letter was signed by the entire Texas delegation and approved by Farley.

One task of the national chairman is to use patronage to strengthen his organization. He defeats his own ends if in this effort he discredits his party through sponsoring ill-qualified men. *Fortune* has stated that "few of the Farley-Hurja appointments have been bad: some, like the appointment of Robert H. Jackson [now attorney general] as chief counsel to the Bureau of Internal Revenue, have even been excellent." [7] There is no inherent reason why able appointments cannot be combined with partisan endorsement. Much depends on the level of partisan leadership and the quality of loyal party supporters. Jim Farley compares with Mark Hanna in his ability as a party builder. Hanna and McKinley were able to use patronage to good effect.

"They not only selected for the higher offices efficient public servants, but by virtue of an unusually clear understanding of individuals and local political conditions, they made leading Republicans feel, in spite of certain individual grievances, that the offices were being distributed for the best interests of the whole party.

"So far as Mr. Hanna was concerned, this success was due to his unusual ability in partially systematizing and organizing the distribution of offices, while at the same time giving life to the system by tact and good judgment in dealing with individuals and with exceptional cases." [8]

Mark Hanna gave particular attention to the South. With the hope of making the fight for Congress more attractive to southern Republicans, these invariably defeated candidates were given control of appointments to local federal offices. A board of referees composed of the gubernatorial candidate, the chairman of the state committee, and the state representative on the Republican national committee made recommendations for the higher federal posts. Mark Hanna's biographer states:

"To a large extent the system worked automatically all over the Union, but of course any such method goes to pieces, in so far as conflicting individual or factional claims are intruded. It was in dealing with these exceptional cases that Mr. McKinley's tact was useful as well as Mr. Hanna's gift of understanding other men, of getting their confidence and of bending or persuading them to his will." [9]

Hanna's powers of persuasion were worthy of note. The chairman of the national party committee must rely in large measure upon his skill in handling men. The national chairman possesses no secret reserve of power or influence. His sanctions are limited. Patronage and the power to command publicity are his chief weapons.

Party leaders are easily put on the defensive by the mention of patronage. They tend to belittle its importance. Typical is the reaction of Senator Joseph C. O'Mahoney of Wyoming, who, when asked by the League of Women Voters if parties could live without patronage, replied:

"The question rather assumes as a major premise, that political parties really exist for the purpose of patronage. If I were to say nothing else tonight, I should want to say that the history of our country proves this to be an assumption without basis. Principles, not patronage, have always constituted the living force of our political system. Those parties which have been uncertain in their philosophy even though they wielded the power of patronage without restraint have never been able to preserve themselves from defeat when fundamental issues affecting the public welfare have had to be decided."

Some political scientists take a more hard-boiled view. For example, C. J. Friedrich states:

"Civil service reform, by removing the patronage, proposes to dynamite the solid rock upon which the edifice of the American party system so securely rested. And indeed there has grown up in more recent years an appreciation of a causal connection between effective party organization and a limited amount of patronage which the early reformers used to overlook in their enthusiasm. . . . A way must, therefore, be found to mark out for patronage such positions as do not require special knowledge—and the postmasterships, for example, seem to offer a good opportunity—in order to enable the parties to carry on." [10]

M. J. Bonn goes further:

"The imposition of Civil Service rules (competitive conditions) on all appointees would paralyse the present political machinery. For the army of political 'volunteers' who do the party work are attracted by the hope of spoils. The influence of Assemblymen and Senators is partly based on their 'right' to propose worthy adherents for spoils. And the President's hold on Congress depends to a considerable degree on his power to grant or to withhold spoils to or from applicants, though lately public works have taken the place of spoils as means of exercising pressure of recalcitrants in Congress and State governments. The application of Civil Service rules to all appointments would shift the centre of the stage to impersonal spoils, which consists of legislative benefits voted to well-organized groups. Lobbying and log-rolling will become even more important than at present. Personal may disappear in favor of impersonal corruption; political parties may be converted into economic blocs. The moralist may triumph, but the economist may well weep." [11]

It is difficult to predict what effect a thorough application of the merit system would have upon the political parties. According to Ernest K. Lindley:

"Most of the reform groups undervalue the advantage of patronage, especially its uses as a cohesive in preserving the party system and as between the executive and legislative.

"But the establishment of a permanent merit system has a long way to go before it imperils those advantages." [12]

This is a conservative summary of the present situation. Certainly a great many more positions could be brought under the classified civil service without any deleterious effect upon the operation of party government.

Politics in appointments cannot be treated like Sir Hiram Maxim's aching tooth. When he could stand the annoyance no longer he had the tooth extracted and then with great satisfaction watched it ache and ache and ache. Not all evil lies embodied in the spoils system. It may be a sympton of corruption; but politics can never be extracted by a simple twist of the wrist so long as men are mortal. Selfish partisanship is no basis for appointments, but we have learned from experience that to extend the merit system is not enough. Political favoritism can invade any civil service system, no matter what its formal structure.

It is bad politics to defend political patronage, but it is often the best politics to use it. Today politicians in the struggle for better government personnel are all on the side of the angels. Few, indeed, are the men in public life willing to champion the practice of awarding office to the members of the winning party; but fewer still are those who entirely refrain from thus rewarding their supporters.

A man running for public office must have support. To get such support he must either build an organization for himself or depend upon an existing organization. He cannot get a dependable following unless he has something to offer the individuals who give their time and energy to his cause. Congressmen often emphasize the great nuisance caused by patronage. With ten applicants for one office, they say, a political appointment creates nine enemies and one ingrate. They complain that much valuable time is wasted in seeking positions for constituents; but they admit, when pressed, that such efforts are not without value.

Patronage is the most direct means whereby a politician may develop an organization for himself. The importance of professional full-time workers cannot be overestimated. As in any other walk of life, the professional worker is more effective than the amateur. Control over forty or fifty positions provides a congressman with the means of building a staunch personal following. Here is the nucleus for an organization to aid in campaigning and in meeting the demands of constituents. With a small band of dependable supporters a congressman can enlist scores of voluntary workers and develop an effective organization. We have yet to find a substitute for party patronage viewed as the cement for constructing effective political support.

In this country parties are loose confederations. We are a continental people living under a federal government. Political issues are much less clearly drawn. Our political problem is the compromise of sectional and class interests. Our politicians are identified with localities. The most effective way to reduce the hazards of a career in elective office is to develop strong party organizations. Today the political career of a man in elective office is very narrowly based. Why the great bitterness against politics in relief? One reason is the fact that the WPA in politics means federal interference in local situations. The home politicians resent steps toward building up a national political machine.

Political careers depend upon the support of these home communities. Sometimes, as in the 1936 election, candidates can ride into office on the coattails of the president as party leader. If a man hopes for a long political career, however, he must build himself into his locality. He may do this in various ways. He may identify himself with the business community; he may ally himself with labor; he may depend chiefly upon the farmers for his support. In these cases his political machine grows out of organizations such as local business associations, labor unions, and the farmers' grange. Except in agricultural districts, a politician can rarely serve a single occupational group. If he is to win the votes he needs, he must draw from various groups. The chances are that a man with such a diversified following is more representative of the whole community.

As a politician grows less dependent upon any one group, he stands in greater need of an organization of his own. Here patronage enters the picture. It is all very well to talk of an interested citizenry, but a candidate needs dependable subordinates ready to answer his commands and attend to dull routine. If the candidate relies upon organizations such as labor unions, chambers of commerce, reform organizations, or public utilities, he is committed to representing their interests. Patronage, by providing a representative with an organization of his own, often enables him to take a more independent attitude in the face of the many special interest groups with which he must deal. Much criticism of the evils of the spoils system comes from such special interests. If the representative can add the support of the float-ing voter to that of the traditional party follower, he is not forced to make concessions to the single-aim voters.

Admittedly one of the most disturbing developments threat-ening democratic government is the ease with which organized minorities have forced our legislatures to grant appropriations or other concessions. Such associations have a place in our repre-sentative system, but they have no right to coerce our representa-tives. Single-aim voters may be as great a menace to democracy as indifferent citizens or machine voters. Popular government depends upon a willingness to compromise, and the single-aim mentality is intransigent.

A representative must feel free to compromise. Legislation is impossible, otherwise. Yet leadership is also essential if support is sought for a program designed in the general welfare. Recent sessions of Congress suggest that a substantial number of federal positions for presidential distribution greatly facilitates leader-ship. By limiting his patronage, civil service reform would cer-tainly cut down the chief executive's powers of persuasion. On the other hand, if the president is able to retain a powerful pop-ular following by skillful use of the radio, the need for using henchmen in local communities and rewarding them with jobs is lessened. Moreover, if the federal government centralizes more and more functions in Washington and local officials de-crease in number, patronage becomes of less interest to the con-gressman. He may try to have his friends appointed to posts in the capital, but at best such appointees cannot help him greatly in fighting his local battles.

In the long run the persistence of patronage depends on the need for a local party machine. The machine will disappear when agencies better equipped to perform its functions appear. The importance of the machine as a charitable institution is an in-dictment of the inadequacy of existing relief facilities. As gov-ernmental employment bureaus are extended and as old age and sickness insurance is provided, the machine will be undermined. Changes such as these will undermine partisan patronage by robbing it of its function. As long as patronage is politically useful, it will remain.

The true significance of any subject is found in its strengths rather than in its weaknesses. For example, the real importance of Nazism lies in its capacity for uniting and strengthening the German nation. We may deplore its methods, but its strength lies in its accomplishments rather than in its abuses; and hence we must understand its positive qualities. Similarly the constructive aspects of patronage explain its continuance.

The quest of American politics must be unity and agreement. To attain these aims strong leadership and discipline may be necessary. We have preferred to approach these two goals indirectly. In our governmental structure and in our constitutional theories, we discount such aims. Unofficial devices have been resorted to when the pressure of circumstances has outweighed contradictory principles. Patronage has provided political leaders with one means of attracting and rewarding their followers. It is a faulty means, but they have regarded it as better than nothing at all.

In the long run patronage in terms of jobs will ultimately be overwhelmed by much more important demands of the citizenry, demands that can be realized only through thoroughly efficient administration.

Partisan jobbery as we have known it is on its way out, but a growth of national bureaucracy brings new problems. In the past our politics has been sectional because the economic interests of a great continent have inevitably been diversified. We have distrusted a strong central government and feared bureaucracy even more than we have abhorred corruption and favoritism in public office. Washington seemed far away. The control of the local situation was of first importance to the politician. He could best gain power by controlling appointments to local office.

If the administration at Washington increases the number of federal employees under the control of the Civil Service Commission, it reduces the available materials with which the congressman can build his own machine. Deprived of jobs to distribute, the local politician becomes more dependent on the favors that he can procure for his home constituency from the Washington bureaucrats. In lieu of patronage, the representative must rely upon grants for public works, upon generous relief allotments, and upon various loans.

One of the most striking attributes of the Roosevelt administration is the enormous variety of facilities set up to aid various classes. The federal government has now extended its bounty to the cities, and our mayors have discovered a generous Uncle Samuel to tide them over their difficulties. The direct aid to the farmers, to homeowners, to the unemployed, need only be mentioned. Even more important is the active role that the federal government has assumed on behalf of labor.

The hand of the president is felt in innumerable local affairs, while his voice comes into the home directly at strategic intervals. Vast regions such as the Tennessee Valley are being changed under direction from the nation's capital. Local politicians seem little more than puppets as they watch this work progress. These activities are all familiar enough in themselves, but their full political significance becomes clearer if considered in relation to the patronage problem.

The present concern over broad national issues that affect the average citizen in his daily life means that the localism of our political life is becoming of less importance. If such issues hold the center of the stage and if national elections turn upon the voters' opinions concerning these problems, then lobbying and patronage will have less reason for being. Economic clashes will be compromised in the public forum rather than through secret bargaining. The voter will have a greater stake in an election than the securing of a job as postmaster. As issues transcending locality arise, special organizations to represent these interests arise. The manufacturers develop their associations and labor its federations. Bankers seek national organization, as do all the economic interests of the nation. Patronage is one of the direct consequences of the localism and sectionalism of American politics. As national affairs become more important, petty jobbery becomes of less significance. What is the outcome likely to be?

Social agencies may bring a better balance of services than parties can offer. The state has been able to perform favors for great commercial and banking interests. It had little to offer to the little man. Complete loyalty was expected for a paltry favor or two. Now the citizen is demanding and receiving many tangible social and economic benefits. Here are the factors that will make for a basic change in the civil service. We face a transition period. Party patronage still fulfills a useful function, but its end seems inevitable. In the meantime we can control some of its abuses. We can demand that political appointees be technically qualified. We can win over various areas of administration and insist that proper standards be applied there.

Evidence shows that many men today realize how closely their own interests interlock with the efficient administration of national affairs. The recent campaign for better government personnel conducted by the National League of Women Voters is a good example. The public spirit of this organization is beyond question. Their programs are determined after wide consultation and some study. In the past their interests have ranged over a great variety of public questions. Their better government personnel program may be just another issue that will be discussed in women's gatherings and then put aside, or it may have a deeper significance which will keep it before the League for many years.

Does the concern of the League of Women Voters in this personnel issue mean that they recognize in it a direct economic and social interest? Does it imply that this great organization sees the meaning that a career civil service may have for their children and for themselves? Do they see the effect that maladministration may have upon their own affairs? An identification of such a group interest with the reform movement may well leave a lasting impress. It may result in bringing into public life a higher proportion of those young men and women who have enjoyed the social and educational opportunities of the prosperous middle class. Members of this class have not heretofore competed strongly for places in the governmental service. The interest of the National League of Women Voters in a better government personnel suggests that a change of attitude may be under way within an important area of opinion. If this results in the increased prestige of public service, the gain will be great.

Few deliberate moves to render service in the federal government more attractive to college men have been made in the last few years. Yet as a class they have become immensely interested. Is this a temporary enthusiasm born of the depression with subsequent lack of opportunities in private business? This is hardly an adequate explanation. The increased sphere of government activity and the positive nature of its work have fired the imagination and aroused the ambition of these young men. If government is to be as important as recent trends suggest, then it will attract the ambitious and the intelligent.

Here are fundamental factors working toward reform. Likewise, as a result of its technical nature, only the trained can fill certain governmental jobs. This in itself has a restraining effect upon the spoilsmen. Another very important result is that men within the government service are forced to consider ways of improving the personnel. Perhaps the strongest impulse for reform at the present time comes from such officials.

Moreover, many powerful groups are selfishly interested in improving the caliber of government employees. These forces do not argue in generalities. They have limited and definite objectives. They want efficient work from the officials with whom they must deal. Civil service reform to them is the practical question of how to get better men in the government service. Thus organized shippers want the Interstate Commerce Commission to have employees able to argue effectively with spokesmen for the railroads. Through their national association the shippers send persuasive lawyers to urge large appropriations from Congress. In similar fashion, the American Bankers' Association has long urged the nonpartisan appointment of bank examiners. Many similar examples might be cited.

Another factor is the influence of government employee unions. Through organizations such as the National Federation of Federal Employees, pressure has been brought to bear upon Congress and remedial legislation carried to enactment. The Welsh Reclassification Act was pushed through largely because of the efforts of organized employees.

Civil service reformers are only one factor in the extension of the merit system and the improvement of government personnel. The protests of public-spirited citizens by no means fully account for the extension of civil service status and protected tenure.

In the future the issue will not be drawn simply between petty politicians seeking jobs and nonpartisans seeking good government. The battle lines are becoming more varied. Important social classes, such as organized labor, regulated business, ambitious college men, have entered the lists.

Thus we find the interests of various politically potent groups identified with the movement for eliminating the spoilsman. Government is extending its scope beyond the performance of its routine duties. Safe, easy jobs have been the political plums of the past. Now the government's task is becoming more creative. The government can offer real careers to men of constructive imagination. It is undertaking functions that will vitally benefit social groups, sections, and occupations as never before. The administration in power will then have more than loaves and fishes to distribute. Patronage will be far outweighed by the influence of large appropriations, the extension of government credit, and the development of huge regions and great natural resources. Politicians will have higher stakes than jobs over which to quarrel. The powerful interests served will demand that they be efficiently served by trained officials.

Most important of all is the growing tendency not to protect ourselves against government but rather to use governmental agencies for protecting ourselves against certain consequences of our social and economic institutions. To attain this end, we set up compensatory devices such as the Reconstruction Finance Corporation, the Commodity Credit Corporation, and the Agricultural Adjustment Administration, and regulatory agencies such as the Securities and Exchange Commission.

One solution lies in the realization by party leaders that high personnel standards must be maintained and that their parties cannot afford to give jobs to stupid persons. The party programs cannot be achieved if ineffective men are charged with the execution thereof. Failure in administration will mean failure at the polls; therefore, at times it is good politics to appoint good nonpartisan men; at other times, it may be better politics to appoint a good partisan. Such questions cannot be met in *a priori* fashion.

In assuming the greater responsibilities thrust upon it, government has need of the best the community can offer in all branches—administrative, judicial, and legislative. Civil service reform is just one aspect of this larger problem. We shall not get far if all attention is focused on better administration. To be effective, administrators must have the support of elected representatives who cherish the same values. We cannot think of well-trained officials seeking to serve the public but held in bondage by politicians drawn from machines supported by ignorant voters. This view is fanciful; as a matter of fact, no such situation is possible. Representative assemblies are not going to create an administrative corps differing greatly from their own image. There will always be a parallel between the kind of men in elective office and the caliber of those in administrative posts. Legislators who value education and training for the public service are likely to have such qualifications themselves.

When voters feel the need for ability and expert knowledge in public office, whether legislative or administrative, we shall be likely to find more men with such qualities recruited for government positions. Civil service reform must be considered along with the reform of politicians in policy-determining positions. This is not to fall back upon the old bromide that every advance depends upon public opinion. We need not wait for this popular spontaneous combustion. The sheer importance of the personnel problem will make its neglect impossible. Basic forces are working toward this objective. A variety of contradictory factors explains our present personnel system. The classified civil service is not a prize that good men have snatched from bad politicians. It is the product of group forces—some altruistic, some narrowly greedy, some working with enlightened self-interest. Bringing needed talent into the public service does not necessitate a frontal attack on the politicians.

The task of improving government personnel will not be fulfilled either by merely trying to eliminate the spoilsman or by advocating a technically perfect system of administration. These efforts are contributory but not conclusive. The final solution will be determined by the way in which our parties develop and by the needs that the federal government is made to meet. The elimination of partisan appointments entails changes more basic than cleaning up corruption and increasing efficiency. Patronage is not an extraneous abuse; it is still a part of our political system, though there are many indications today that it is on the way out.

If this is so, we cannot relax with the comforting assurance that from now on all will be well. No sooner is one problem met than another treads on its heels. History offers a hint. The civil service reforms of the eighties meant a loss in revenue to the party in control of the federal government. If political leaders could no longer sell offices or assess officeholders, where was the money to come from? Of this quandary Matthew Josephson writes:

"Momentous transformations, far more important than the tariff struggle, were taking place under the surface. These changes, which flowed from the very reform of the party institution itself, resulted in the end in the marked strengthening of the reorganized machines, which came to be wholly, rather than partially, devoted to the service of the large corporations in their regions that required political privileges." [13]

In other words, politicians have habitually taken their support where it was offered. The more they are cut off from patronage the more they are thrown for help upon the organizations in the community strong enough to provide dollars or votes or both. Labor unions and other interest groups as well as corporate wealth hold possibilities. If strong national parties are to be built, their strength will be drawn from such sources. It may be that centrally controlled and disciplined parties will prove the only means of holding an able and powerful bureaucracy to account. Organization will attempt to balance organization.

One alternative to these tendencies seems possible. If our present parties remain decentralized and flexible we may be able to influence administrative growth along responsive and representative lines.

☆ 27 ☆

A Democratic Bureaucracy

"The Secretaries act in their bureaus for you,
not you here for them. . . ."
WALT WHITMAN

THE realization of a democratic bureaucracy rests upon the relationship maintained between officialdom and the citizen. The various forms that it may take can scarcely be foreseen. Useful theoretical objectives are best formulated by considering tendencies already discoverable in the flux of contemporary political action. My thesis comes to this: that in view of the changing and uncertain relationships between government and the economic system, no uniform pattern of bureaucratic development is feasible. An experimental and diversified approach is best suited to the nature of the problem. Under present conditions no one formula holds the answer.

Bureaucracy will be impelled to adjust to the demands which the public makes upon it now and in the future. One result of that adjustment will be to face the problem of efficiency in public office. The very demands of the modern state dictate the employment of public officials technically competent to do their jobs. Trends already apparent in our public service point in this direction. The growth of the administrative establishment is another observable trend. We do not need to argue the point here that great size is an inevitable result of social pressures. Nor need we defend the service from criticism directed at magnitude alone. In responding to the demands of the community, government must employ enough officials to do the work required and try to meet the problems of organization and centralization incident to size and complexity.

More difficult and critical for democracy are the concepts that give character to the public service, the interests that will be represented, and the forms that will provide for both responsiveness and responsibility. In an authoritarian state, wherein the ideological framework of public service is built upon loyalty to a prince or dictator, the problem is simpler. In a democracy, where administrative institutions must be founded on allegiance to the public, the voice of the master is not so precise. The public speaks with many tongues and many voices. Thus the problem of building and sustaining, within the limitations imposed by popular institutions, a public service which will be adequate to its tasks is a matter of peculiar complexity.

The great problem of bureaucracy in our society is how to recruit the administrative service. We cannot profitably consider this problem out of its historical context. Popular government has not necessarily resulted either in control by good men or in guidance by wise men. It has resulted rather in a regime under which mutual toleration of differing viewpoints and conflicting wills has permitted a temporary combination of interests to govern society in accordance with certain generally accepted rules of the game.

The values of this process must not be lost. One unfortunate element of our experience has been the spoils system, the scars of which are deep. We have suffered not alone from mere incompetence in office resulting from unfortunate partisan appointments. We have suffered much more seriously from the insidious effects upon administration of the cynical and suspicious attitude with which a public brought up in the spoils tradition has regarded government service. For the past fifty years the primary efforts toward reform of public personnel have been directed to eliminating the abuses of that system and its concomitants. Civil service commissions, state and federal, were set up initially to keep incompetent rogues and party henchmen off the public pay roll.

The emerging responsibilities of public service, joined with the uncertainties of possible public reactions, intensify the difficulties of meeting present needs in a forthright fashion. The problem now is not so much one of keeping incompetents out as it is one of getting competent personnel in, although current difficulties with spoilsmen in both federal and state jurisdictions make it impossible for personnel agencies as yet to relinquish their traditional task of policing. For the future, however, attention will be centered increasingly upon building an able officialdom trained to carry on the growing tasks of government.

Qualitative change in the functions of government, along with a merely quantitative increase in duties, makes it necessary for government to employ persons of high ability and rigorous special training. The changing character of governmental responsibilities puts a premium on such adaptable, imaginative, resourceful personnel as will be capable of adjusting itself and governmental programs to new conditions. It may be that the very preservation of any culture depends upon the guarding of its symbols and ideals by a limited number of its more intelligent and economically secure individuals. At any rate the duties of administering the modern state call for men able to see their activities in a broad social context and competent to deal effectively with the technological and human environment in which they live.

As these growing requirements for public personnel have become apparent to students and practitioners, a number of expedients to meet the needs have been put forward. Prominent in this connection has been the suggestion that we remodel our public service according to the brilliantly successful British plan.

Certain seldom mentioned aspects of the British service should, however, be clarified. It is admitted, of course, that the British have developed admirable public servants—". . . a type self-motivated, possessed of personal standards of a high order, independent of political influence, imbued with the sense of obligation to the *res publica* which has been a notable characteristic of the governing class from which they were drawn." [1] Leonard White here refers incidentally to the major premise which is so often passed over in evaluating the British civil servant. The career official in Great Britain is the product of the class structure peculiar to British society.

Harold J. Laski has pointed out that the basic assumptions of the British civil servant "are the same as those of the men who own the instruments of production in our society." He suggests that the notion of the neutrality of the British civil service may have developed because "the neutrality of the civil service has not yet been tested by the need to support a policy which like that of a socialist party, might well challenge the traditional ideas for which it stood." [2] He calls attention to the fact that "all the leading figures in the public services, whether the civil service or the defense forces come, in fact, from an extraordinarily narrow class within the community."

The British are ruled by an elite—a class rule accepted because of social tradition and sustained in part because of skill and restraint and largely because of the fact that tasks of empire have accorded with the talents of this class. This served very well when a homogeneous class of conscious or unconscious empire builders was riding the crest of capitalist expansion. The needs of empire gave rise to organizations which set the pattern for English administrative institutions. The British civil service grew out of the Indian civil service. As C. J. Friedrich has written:

"It was a question (so far as the Indian Civil Service was concerned) of securing representatives of a 'ruling nation,' and the graduates of Oxford and Cambridge Universities seemed best fitted for that purpose. Their ancient traditions of literary and classical scholarship, combined with a proud *esprit de corps* characteristic of such a highly selective group as their student body, helped to secure the kind of man who would with equanimity shoulder the 'white man's burden' in India. When this system was also applied to the home services, it escaped the attention of a good many people that there was just the tinge of a suggestion that what might be termed the 'white-collared men's burden' was the essential objective." [3]

The growth of empire, the aristocratic tradition, the tacit acceptance of the gentleman and the system of honors all tie in together to form more than a partial explanation of the British service—conditions that obviously cannot be reproduced in the United States.

We in this country have never regarded administration as the prerogative of any one social class. Just as the acceptance of a ruling class explains much of the efficiency of the British government, so the bitterness and corruption of our municipal politics are due in large part to the class cleavages that underlie local political alignments. Here substantial citizens, by withdrawing from politics, leave duties they should share to those with whom they find association distasteful. In England there has been a traditional acceptance of the natural superiority of the governing class and a correlative acceptance of responsibility to govern on the part of that elite.

The homogeneity of their society and the relative stability of social values have made possible the development of a corps of men devoted to the public service. Yet devotion to public affairs by administrators cannot be sustained in the face of bitter dispute as to the proper scope for governmental action. Whether the British administrative class can meet the challenge of newly arising governmental responsibilities is an open question in Great Britain itself. Here in the United States we do not possess—nor may we soon hope for—the homogeneity which the British appear to some at least to be losing.

Laski is one Englishman who realizes that much of the British success in administration has been due to the basic similarity of viewpoint between the political minister and his administrative subordinates. Laski has emphasized that the administrative mind is something more than a tool ready to advance every purpose of the minister. He is aware that "it is one thing to put through a policy the assumptions of which you accept. It is a very different thing to put through efficiently a policy the very foundations of which you believe to be disastrous." [4] He recognizes that permanent civil servants develop their own line of policy. When a minister attempts a change, resistance on the part of permanent officials is not unknown. Indeed, it is said that the policy of British bureaucrats frequently outweighs that of the political ministers.

In a nation undergoing the profound changes now witnessed

in the United States, it is unrealistic indeed to take the British pattern of public service as a guide. The British have evolved a notable service, but their problems, as Friedrich has noted, are very different from ours:

"We have neither an empire nor an aristocracy in the United States, and we therefore do not conceive the problem of our governmental services as that of 'ruling,' but as that of 'administering.' Therefore we should be exceedingly cautious in drawing any lessons from English 'experience.' An exhaustive analysis of the conditions from which the experience arose should certainly precede any such proposals." [5]

Thus the administrative service developed under the conditions peculiar to Great Britain during the last few decades has no final answer for our problems.

A career service for American public officials has also been suggested at numerous times and in various guises as a major reform required by new conditions of public service. Recruitment at an early age and a prospect of life tenure, with opportunity for promotion to the top, are suggested as necessary inducements to secure persons of first-class ability for government posts.

While it is true that a longer tenure for many administrative officers would tend to increase efficiency in the public service, the personnel problem before democratic governments is a more basic one than one of building a career service for men of good will and intelligence. Some students of public personnel administration on the federal level are of the opinion that the federal government already gets its full share of general ability. They believe that the real problem is to provide for the utilization of ability already available to the government. One important part of the task is not so much the tempting of more able people into the government as it is the avoidance of overhiring, and fitting abilities to the requirements of the great bulk of none-too-exacting positions.[6]

Moreover we tend to underestimate our success in attracting able people into governmental employ. In Laski's opinion,

"The [Roosevelt] administration . . . brought a remarkable host of able men to Washington. I know the British Civil Service pretty thoroughly; I am measuring my words carefully when I say that there are half a hundred men in Washington who would compare with the best it produces in imagination, resourcefulness and integrity. It is notable that they are mostly young; it is also notable that they are mostly lawyers. They have been (as the Cabinet has never been) the effective foundation of the New Deal. They have brought to it qualities that make their work of outstanding significance. For they have demonstrated that if ever the United States can be persuaded to rationalize its civil service, the quality and effectiveness of its administration will be second to none in the world." [7]

Getting more able men into government may help to solve administrative problems, but intelligence is not in itself an abstract force necessarily operating for good. It is rather an instrument used more or less effectively by members of particular groups for the advancement of those values which they conceive to be worth furthering. Witness, for example, the contempt heaped on the "bright young men" of the New Deal. Whether a public service composed of carefully selected members of the well-educated minority will be successful in meeting our governmental problems depends more upon the unity of the population as a whole and upon the harmony of purposes between the community and the bureaucracy than upon the mere presence in the administration of large numbers of high I.Q.'s.

Another movement in the direction of reform is the struggle to achieve the merit system. This is an ideal still remote from realization and fraught even today with political difficulties. It is an effective slogan rather than a clear and immediate objective. Even among able administrators, opinions on this issue differ. Some believe that the predominance of permanent civil servants in departments has had an arid effect upon new lines of policy. Flexibility is more difficult to secure under such circumstances. Moreover, our federal departments are federations of bureaus, and numerous staff officers loyal to the secretary are needed in order to create and maintain a consistent policy within the bureaus. To carry to fruition new national policies requires the vigor and enthusiasm of personal conviction on the part of administrators.

State officials protest that civil service appointments are often directed not toward potential capability but rather toward facility in the performance of immediate specific duties. This is due in part to the fear examiners have of criticism from unsuccessful applicants or from politicians who might accuse them of asking irrelevant questions if they tried to test for broad and general capacities. The clumsy procedure for dismissal in many state civil service systems undermines the authority of responsible officers and makes the exercise of discretion in examining applicants or greater latitude in testing and selecting those on the civil service list an unpleasant or futile business.

This criticism of the merit system as now constituted is offered not as a defense of patronage but rather as a protest against the complacent acceptance of a simple reform program as the solution to our personnel problems. No one can object to appointments based on merit. The difficulty lies in devising means to this end. The task of improving the civil service cannot be met by placing the blame on the politician and urging the creation of a system that will automatically insure the selection of able men.

In any reaction from the partisan control of public servants it will not be enough to establish a corps of officials trained for their jobs and secure in their tenure. A career service is not an end in itself. Present abuses obviously must be eliminated, but not at the cost of flexibility. Careers in public office should be made possible, but not if this encourages a bureaucratic type recruited from a narrow range of society and limited in social experience.

Public service reform which includes merely a borrowing from British experience, an application of the career principle, and an extension of the merit system is not broad enough in itself to encompass the bureaucracy problem which we must face in a democracy. The trends of healthy development of our public service may include these elements or parts of them; they must also include much more.

The place of public administration in a democratic society cannot be understood unless the broad interrelations of the bureaucracy and the community are analyzed. An administration which is merely efficient, one which carries out the law thoroughly, is insufficient as an objective. In the days to come the civil service will have to carry not only the burdens thrust upon it by legislators but also take an active part in maintaining a balance among the ever changing forces seeking government support. To this end, public confidence in the integrity and vision of officials furnishes the strongest support.

In Great Britain this need is met in part by traditional respect for the ruling class. In this country, bureaucracy must slowly build its own foundations upon existing social and political institutions. This broad basis of public confidence is likely to result when officials are drawn from every stratum of society and every section of the nation. Such diversity makes our public servants more representative in character. Possibly some degree of specialized training may well be sacrificed to recruitment from a broader social base, with gain rather than loss in future stability of governmental institutions. Furthermore, as Arnold Brecht writes, "Careful blending is the prerequisite of a well-balanced civil service, the members of which will not unite in the interest of one class but will exercise a salutary check and countercheck on one another in the realm of bureaucracy." [8]

The kind of a bureaucracy we want and the means by which we are to control it depend especially upon the general range and character of the demands laid by the body politic upon it. As Graham Wallas has pointed out, "a negative government requires only courage and consistency in its officials; but a positive government requires a constant supply of invention and suggestion." [9] Recent events in this country suggest that implicit assumptions as to the positive responsibilities of the state are widely held. The government is being called upon to integrate those tendencies which, left alone, have made individualism, competition, and the division of labor destructive forces in our industrial order.

Our bureaucracy must meet the varying demands of labor, industry, and agriculture without being split internally or growing into a sect apart in an effort to be impartial and professional. Successful administration also depends upon directing current conflicts of interest into a broader public purpose. Here officialdom is called upon to shoulder a heavy responsibility.

Most officials have certain common problems. If he is to be effective, the administrator must do more than find sound solutions for his problems; he must also be able to convince others of their soundness. The administrator must not only be master of the technical aspects of his job; he must be able to explain his program to the legislator so as to secure fair consideration in the matter of appropriations. He must be able to win support from persons who count politically. He must spend his appropriations in such fashion as to meet legal accounting requirements. He must be able to plan expenditures, recruit a staff, and win loyal response from his subordinates. Finally, he must report to the public and to politicians on the work accomplished. The factor of stewardship thus colors all the activities of officialdom.

☆ 28 ☆

Can Officials Be Neutral?

"Miniver thought, and thought and thought,
And thought about it."
EDWIN ARLINGTON ROBINSON

THE average officeholder, who simply has a job to do—collect taxes, extinguish fires, guard the public health—is supported by a well-recognized community purpose. The public interest in his case is clear. There are other areas, however, where notions of the public interest are confused or ·in conflict, where the administrator is expected to do more than perform services. He must champion a policy and fight for its realization.[1]

Neutrality seems feasible only in fields thoroughly accepted and understood by the public. For example, in public utility regulation or in administering the TVA, officials must take a positive line to be effective. Here are creative tasks which require efforts of the entire staff to realize public policy. Our bureaucracy has varied and vital responsibilities that must be continued despite the momentary ebb and flow of popular opinion. To expect a demeanor of official neutrality is to hope for an attitude hardly compatible with the nature of many administrative duties.

Where public policy is vaguely defined, aggressiveness, energy, and imagination are needed to bring about its realization. Officials may be called upon to act as leaders, as crusaders, as champions. They must believe fully and act vigorously. Of course they must not violate accepted canons of fair play. This does not mean that they must adopt the traditional role of the judge as impartial arbiter between contentious parties. This latter role is better suited to the functions of the bench than to the administration of relief, the development of natural resources, and the regulation of industry. Officials charged with these responsibilities must be impregnated with the purpose of their particular agency. The coonskin cap of the frontiersman becomes them better than the judicial ermine.

The relations of the administrator to political parties require re-examination. According to the usual theory, the administrator is to follow the policy of the party in power. This view fails to fit the facts. In the first place, many of the most important regulatory functions have been removed from partisan influence and placed under quasi-judicial tribunals. These commissions develop policy within the broad forms of the statutes under which they operate. Such officials have a wide area of discretion within fields where partisan politics provide no guide. In the second place, the elimination of partisanship is supposed to result in a neutral bureaucracy. Our bureaucracy cannot be neutral in the sense that its officials are persons with views and personalities as colorless as possible. This is scarcely the type needed to carry out the positive purposes of the modern state. We may take official neutrality to mean impartiality as between partisan politicians. This concept is tenable in so far as party loyalty means personal favoritism. Loyalty to the broad social purpose to which the country seems to be committed by its choice of certain political leaders seems essential for the effective application of the ends legislatively declared, however.

We can thus envisage our civil servants as nonpartisan, but we can hardly view them as nonpolitical in this broader sense. They cannot be neutral as between parties or other groups when charged with finding ways and means to realize pioneer public policies in new fields of social control.

What are the relationships of these administrators to the legislative branch? Sumner Slichter predicts

". . . that the policy of economic control will create a more or less perpetual controversy over how far the political branch of the government should go in giving detailed orders to the administrative agencies. No sharp dividing line between the spheres of the two branches of the government can be drawn, but the results of the policy of control will depend in large measure upon the balance that is worked out between the authority of the political branch and the discretion of the administrative agencies." [2]

Congress must remain the agency for the scrutiny of bills; but if the great burden of initiating and drafting acts is unloaded upon the legislature, the practical consequence is to bring organized interest groups into a position of greater influence. Busy politicians with thousands of constituents to cajole and satisfy cannot give the time and study required for the preparation of legislation, even assuming that they possess the necessary technical competence and grasp of special problems. A bureaucracy can be held free of narrow partisan control, but to fulfill the needs of the day our public officials will continue to contribute generously in the framing of public policy.

To face government in terms of a theoretical separation of powers is to ignore present actualities. Congress is far from being the sole source of policy, and further still are our political parties. It seems in the nature of modern government that administrators play a leading role in the determination and development of national policy. Secretary of Agriculture Henry A. Wallace writes:

"The alarming thing in Washington is not that there are so many special pressure groups but that there are so few people who are concerned solely with looking at the picture from the broad, national angle. Most Congressmen and Senators, it seems, are of necessity special pleaders for a particular region. It is, therefore, up to the executive branch of the Government to consider the national interest." [3]

Many think it not chimerical to hope that an able administrative service can do much toward building a more integrated community. Officials are strategically placed and wield great authority. They have actually formulated much of the policy upon which Congress has placed its seal of approval. This was dramatically illustrated in connection with the public utilities holding company bill and the undistributed profits tax. This process characterizes also the normal functions of such bureaus as the Forest Service, the Bureau of Agriculture Economics, the Corps of Engineers. This explains the genesis of much current legislation. Officials understand the substantive problems within their field, and they possess the tools of analysis essential to this end.

Many governmental problems are too technical for the legislator to handle understandingly. The legislator must turn to the bureaucrat for suggestions as to what to do and how to do it. Many of these men are studying economic trends to be ready with adequate factual data pertinent to legislative problems. For example, in attempting to regulate chain stores Congress needs information on price structure and related economic questions. Administrators attempt to be fully conversant with the economic effects of the legislation they administer. If, for example, they may become involved in disputes between business and labor over working hours, it is their duty to learn the viewpoints of both sides. However else can consequences be noted and improvements devised?

The government lawyer, if he is to do his whole job, must not only draft bills but also seek to understand the full intent of legislative policy and even anticipate questions that may arise after the bill has become law. His concern is with both the legal implications of a measure and the administrative problems that may arise later. The administrator cannot make useful recommendations to his superiors or to Congress, or explain the purpose of legislation to the public without a broad understanding of the whole program that he is called upon to execute. The nature of the official's position demands that he consider what to do in meeting the heavy burdens placed upon government.

A realistic approach to problems of modern administration requires a re-examination of our assumptions concerning the proper sphere of the permanent administrative service. As the responsibilities of government point more directly toward the direction and regulation of economic activity, the criteria by which we judge our civil servants must also be revised. A theoretical distinction is usually made between policy and nonpolicy positions. Anyone familiar with the actual operation of governmental offices knows that many officials in relatively subordinate positions contribute their mite to policy problems. It is commonly assumed that the duty of permanent officials is, as Lucius Wil-merding's words indicate, merely "first, to present fully and fairly to the head of the department all material facts and con-siderations which bear upon any issue which he is called on to decide; second, themselves to decide such issues as are delegated to them by the head of the department." [4] This assumes that permanent officials occupy a well-defined area that is adminis-trative and nonpolitical.

A fiction convenient for protecting the permanent official is the distinction drawn between the formulating of policies and the actual decision to follow a given line of action. The fact, of course, is that permanent officials may exercise a great influence in the determination of policies, even though they are not held personally accountable. Whether such a subtle masking of the facts can hold, in highly dynamic situations marked by militant interest conflicts, is open to question. It is probably most useful in a mature administrative service wherein the distinction has become crystallized by traditional observance. Yet it remains a fiction, for in fact politics envelops government just as the at-mosphere does nature.

While party loyalty as such may offer little trouble because it creates few demands, policy loyalty, on the contrary, may be of vast importance. Public policy may be set forth by the legislature in broad outline, but the meaning of the public interest must be spelled out by administrative rules and regulations and by a mul-titude of personal judgments in particular cases. Perforce the official falls back upon his subjective judgment when other guides are lacking. To serve the public is assumed to be his basic loyalty. This requires a broad understanding of the objectives of legislators, the realities of economic, institutional, and political forces, and the relation of his governmental agency to them.

In these terms an administrator stands forth as one whose actions are concerned with the development and realization of public policy. He is asked to translate social needs into efficient and democratic governmental action. He needs technical compe-tence for his particular duty, but this must be conditioned by an extraordinary breadth of view if his activities are to reach optimum effectiveness. This means a shift of emphasis away from mere specialization. Officials today seem acutely aware of the need for broader knowledge and better insight into their responsibilities.

Public administrators are expected to promote the general welfare. This is their peculiar responsibility. They should see the relevance of their activities for the country as a whole. Often they may lack such vision. They have, however, one virtually ubiquitous check. They cannot function in a vacuum, because their decisions are constantly being tested by the reactions of those affected. They remain in close touch with reality, however recondite their problem or specialized their process. They must deal with men speaking different tongues, whether of techniques or of social values. They may not speak their language, but communicate with them they must.

These broader functions of the administrative service may lead to a new emphasis on the functions of the congressman with respect to the administrative branch. More and more will the senator, and even more especially the representative, come to serve as a mediator between his constituency and the operations of government within it. He is in a strategic position to observe how governmental functions actually impinge upon his constituents. He is in a position to advise his constituents how to receive maximum benefits from what the government stands ready to give them and how to make their views felt about desirable fields for governmental action. He is in a position to discover areas where governmental activity should be withdrawn or modified. He is in a position to advise administrative officials how their actions affect the people of his district. Such advice may come as a welcome supplement to the information the administrator receives from his subordinates, from field reports, or from personal inspection, affected as they are by the interests, aspirations, and limitations of the persons making them.

The administrator dealing with such basic problems as social security, relief, industrial relations, fiscal policy, and the public regulation of business must be not only a technician but also at least something of a student of society. As Laski says, "the issue is the acquisition of those habits of mind which, in a period of rapid change, are capable of going back without fear to the foundations of tradition, and being able in the light of their examination, to see the full significance of the need for innovation." [5]

Basic differences of interest can hardly be eliminated by administrators, however expert. Most of our federal bureaus are concerned either with collecting facts about various interests in the community or with acting as arbitrators between various groups. To the extent that this work is done with intelligence and reason, the dangers of emotional attitudes and misunderstandings are reduced. An improved bureaucracy will not in itself solve our governmental problems, but it may assist the process by improving the conditions of negotiation. Through discussion and the airing of grievances, they can often reduce the intensity of conflict to manageable terms.

Secretary Wallace has recognized the need and the opportunity most clearly:

"In order to build the ideal democracy [he writes], we need more people who know and are willing to pay the price that must be paid to bring about the harmonious relationship between this nation and other nations externally; and between the parts of this nation internally.

"Thousands of civil servants of the Federal Government grasp this attitude instinctively because of the objective position in which they have been placed. But the special pleaders of agriculture, labor, and business continue to cry and contend for special favors. The ideal of understanding allegiance to a common end service has taken as yet but faint hold upon the American imagination." [6]

Such a public conception of common purpose would enable our administrative corps to function with great effectiveness.

An able administrative service is most likely to provide us with the integration needed by a society of increasing interdependence. This closer relationship requires the full contribution of the technician. Our community is held together not simply by ties of blood and sentiment but by cables and steel rails and high-voltage wires as well. Though technical skill in many fields is essential, it alone is not sufficient. The conduct of public business in treating social problems entails the co-operation of many specialists. The greater the division of function, the greater becomes the burden of general management. Administrative difficulties increase with the appearance of more technical specialties and the subsequent need for further co-ordination of function. Men speaking the technical tongues of their various professions must work side by side. Here stands our modern Tower of Babel.

Expertness alone does not guarantee impartiality. On the contrary, one often finds the expert closely associated with a particular interest by the very force of his training. Thus the agricultural economist tends to stress the farmer's viewpoint more than that of the consumer. This is not unimportant where the economist is working, for example, on a milk control board. In such a situation the employee appointed for party reasons may bring a higher degree of neutrality to his work.

A conflict of loyalties becomes acute only in those instances in which the official finds no underlying social purpose upon which to stand in dealing with conflicting interests. Our officialdom will reflect the divergencies and even the contradictions of purpose within the society it serves. This need occasion no misgivings so long as the bureaucratic pattern approximates the general contours of the community.

Democratic administration is a goal for democracy as basic as the representative process itself. Our administrative service has developed in response to the needs of particular groups. This has tended to make it responsive and representative. It has great fluidity. The best example of this is the great readjustment brought about by the New Deal.

The development of the Brain Trust shows the considerable flexibility and responsiveness of our system, under which men can be used and then pass from view. There are fewer questions of what to do than with a minister whose usefulness is over but who cannot be discredited by outright dismissal. President Roosevelt's freedom in choosing his advisers has enabled him rapidly to meet problems as they arise. A kitchen cabinet is a recurrent feature under our system. Whether enough would be gained to warrant the institutionalizing of this relationship remains to be seen. The present arrangement is often costly.

One takes note of the frequent interchange of personnel and of views between public and private business, the political control of many positions in the newer agencies of government, and the widespread recruitment of public employees from many social classes, economic interests, and geographic regions. These may signify that we are maintaining in this fashion such elements of responsiveness and representation as are important for a developing bureaucracy, even as are strict canons of efficiency. This variety within the public service is healthful if officials are thus kept in close touch with the public. This means that we cannot depend upon over-all planning or the concentration of power as a mode of administrative action or as a pattern in solving governmental problems. What we do need is a clarification of special interests. Thus the growth of unionism and the organization of agriculture and of industrialists indicate that these interests may be better able to understand their own problems.

This does not mean self-regulation; the limitations of this approach are only too well known. Yet there can be a closer relationship between group leaders and administrators. One authority, Louis L. Jaffe, stresses quite properly that

"Participation in law-making by private groups under explicit statutory 'delegation' does not stand then in absolute contradiction to the traditional process and conditions of law-making. . . . It exposes and brings into the open, it institutionalizes a factor in law-making that we have, eagerly in fact, attempted to obscure." [7]

Developments of the utmost significance for democracy and administration are the rooting of governmental agencies in the community and the establishing of many ancillary lines for consultation, adjustment, and control. Many illustrations of how officialdom can be kept close to those it serves could be cited. We have already shown much ingenuity and inventiveness in devising administrative forms for this purpose. For example, the Farm Credit Administration has apparently been successful in setting up a system wherein decision making is decentralized.

This approach to the political and the administrative aspects of fiscal policy seems promising for the future. Under the FCA "the local association and the district units are operated as business corporations. Consequently, their receipts are income from which is paid the costs of making the loans and other operating expenses." [8] Borrowers share in the control and ownership of the lending institution and participate in any earnings. It is contemplated that farmer borrowers will eventually acquire full ownership.

The FCA is a co-ordinating agency that grew to meet a definite need. Four or five agencies were already extending credit to the farmers. Co-ordination was clearly needed, since activities in the same field had to be related to one another. The FCA took over this task. Co-ordination and co-operation thus grew from the limited to the more general, developing from the needs of those served. They in turn are gradually to assume an increasing responsibility. This is evolutionary and pragmatic administration.

Another example is the Federal Reserve System. In an economy such as ours a strong credit structure is needed. Yet there has also been a persistent distrust of centralized financial power. Under the pressure of Jacksonian politics, the charter of the Bank of the United States was not renewed. The federal government was not subsequently trusted to set up a new bank. Business was left to develop its own integration through finance capitalism. The banking system has been torn between the public need of Wall Street and the public fear of Wall Street. Over a long period the nation has attempted to develop a monetary authority expert in nature and removed from the more direct influence of those seeking limited and immediate objectives. The Federal Reserve System, the resulting compromise, has a relatively independent and flexible organizational form. Here is a skillfully contrived interrelation between the private banking system and government officials. It has evolved to its present form in the face of a public unwilling to sanction in organized form the power of money joined with the power of government. Yet the social need for such a service was too strong to be denied.

Individual inventiveness has a vast field in the devising of administrative techniques suitable to new situations. The curse of bigness lies not so much in sheer size as in the awkwardness, the remoteness, and the unresponsiveness often found in institutions imperfectly contrived. The co-ordination and integration essential for social action today must come through far-flung nets of control and operation. This does not necessarily mean apoplexy at the center and anemia at the extremities. Functional devolution has great possibilities. Grants-in-aid can sanction standards of performance. County control associations, as developed by the AAA, suggest one device. Regionalism under the TVA pattern offers another approach. The public corporation has demonstrated its importance as a device competent to carry heavy administrative tasks while at the same time entirely compatible with a democratic environment. The scope for future experimentation and invention is wide and varied.

Bureaucracy, as such, need hold no peril if it is kept close to the people. Within our civil service we find represented the vital forces of our society, though not always in the same proportion. Thus the consumer is unavoidably at a disadvantage in an economy built on the producer interest. To some extent the administrative service might counteract this tendency. Public policy need not be the product of lobbying alone. Political leaders and administrative officials can exert pressure for the less articulate interests. There are many levels of social control and political perspective. Thus the official in the Department of Agriculture at least is in a position to take a somewhat broader view of policy than the lobbyist entirely dependent under the farmer members of his organization. On the other hand, danger to popular government would lie in a unified administrative service dedicated to realizing its own conception of the public interest.

We have attempted to analyze the problems that must be faced in developing an administrative service appropriate to the politics of democracy. Granting that a large bureaucracy is inevitable and assuming that technical services will engender social pressures for efficient performance, we note the further fact that administrators play a highly influential role in policy making. In this sense they cannot be neutral. If all these developments are to be kept harmonious with democratic values, it follows that the administrative hierarchy must be kept highly responsive and close to the people. On the other hand, the public service can function as an integrating force. The common loyalty of officials and their common task give them a mutual bond that exists on no comparable scale among the rest of society.

Developing this tendency is more a future potentiality than a present fact. The justification for such a development lies in the need for efficiency in public business in a government constantly under pressure to extend its activities for the benefit or regulation of one group or another. There can be no question of the need for developing the public service if democracy is to continue.

The political debate of the future will rage not over the spoils system as against the merit system but rather over the viewpoints and values reflected by our administrative servants. Such conflict cannot be side-stepped through the attempt to create a neutral bureaucracy. The function of any such instrument will be too vital and too close to the firing line of social problems for it to escape the consequences of its own importance.

The growth of big business and the expansion of the governmental services may develop into a rivalry of great bureaucracies. Upthrusts of power, hierarchic in form, cast their shadows over individuals working in smaller aggregations. A pattern of our society is suggested by the pictured city of the future with its great towering piles competing in their skyward reach. How can the individual hope to maintain his integrity?

The answer, if answer there is, lies in keeping ultimate power contingent. A loyal opposition will remain of essential importance, but this is not enough. The politics of democracy would also dictate that the process of compromise permeate down through the power-units of our society. This is not a pipe dream. As we have noted, provisions for discussion and wide participation in policy formulating are not incompatible with bureaucratic growth.

Under a well-developed administrative service, representative and widely recruited, we can work out a satisfactory future more in line with the democratic tradition than if we adopt the expedient of disciplined national parties. It should be clear by now that government by meaningful national parties, each with its distinctive program based on rival class interests, would necessitate a high degree of party discipline and a large party bureaucracy. If partisan distinctiveness were developed to a degree making its crystallization possible, political adjustment would have to be postponed until a program of changes could be put through at the national party level. On the other hand, if the process of adjustment and compromise permeates government and administration throughout its many levels, the end products of grievances and unresolved problems are likely to be few.

As a logical proposition it may be argued that a party realignment resulting in two rationally unified partisan organizations would take over the direction of public policy now performed in part by the president, independent commissions, bureau chiefs, pressure groups, and so on. Our concern is with this latter factual situation rather than the former suggested alternative.

It is essential in the politics of democracy that the responsibility for formulating and executing policy remain decentralized.[9] This process is too broad, too complex, and too fluid for any one national political organization to dominate. Yet our political parties can take an active role. They can select and sponsor the statesmen most acceptable to the voters. No alignment of national interests under our two-party system can give such continuing, imaginative, and expert concern for public policy as is the normal function of an alert administrative service. The political party makes its supreme contribution to democratic government by implementing changes in political leadership and selecting from the many competitors for office those most able and most likely to win the loyal support of free citizens.

The balance among power groups shifts and changes. In this lies a great protection. Power is nowhere ultimately fixed. Our parties, with all their weakness, keep authority contingent upon popular support. Our system leaves the door open to experimentation.

☆ 29 ☆

The Impact of Economic Inequality on Politics

"They both act pooty much alike, an' push an'
    scrouge an' cus;
They're like two pickpockets in league fer
    Uncle Samwell's pus;
Each takes a side, an' then they squeeze the
    old man in between 'em,
Turn all his pockets wrong side out an' quick
    ez lightnin' clean 'em."
          JAMES RUSSELL LOWELL

THE fact of economic inequality and the theory of political
equality present a paradox that must be faced. In a completely
orderly world such inconsistencies could not be tolerated. Some
may argue that the only answer can lie in banishing economic
inequalities, but unfortunately we would still be confronted with
inescapable differences between men, though posed in different
terms. This is not to argue on the one hand that we are to accept
fatalistically the injustices arising from the present economic
system nor on the other to deny the validity of equalitarianism
as a useful dogma.

This latter belief does not draw its significance from its strict
accordance with the observable character of men. We know that
men are not equal in ability, but we find it convenient in politics
to overlook this fact. To set up political institutions subtly at-
tuned to human differences in capacity is impossible; the inevitable artificiality of a caste system has been found less tolerable
than the fiction of political equality. As Jacques Barzun has
written:

"the political idea of assuming *a priori* equality relieves us of all the irrelevant questions which in present society form the greatest single obstacle to a better life. It is this same assumption of equality which in ordinary intercourse makes life not only pleasant but possible. If friends at my table were to be rationed according to their intelligence or moral worth, we should come to blows and never eat." [1]

As a practical political problem we need not argue the paradox of political inequality and democratic equality so long as through our governmental machinery we can get for all citizens that minimum of substance and security which will keep them content with the imperfect world within which they find themselves. In these terms the danger need not be sought in the excessive demands of the underprivileged so much as in the shortsighted resistance of the overprivileged. Thus far in our history the impact of economic inequality that has been felt most has come from wealth rather than from poverty. It is against this background that we can best consider the fears of those who see the aged and the unemployed threatening our system.

What is to happen if our representatives in Congress are judged by voters on the basis largely of their readiness to vote funds for relief, for the veterans, for the aged, and so on?

All "sound" men have assumed that an unbalanced budget is a bad thing and should be rectified. All "humanitarian" men seem agreed that an unbalanced economy is a bad thing and should be rectified. The latter argue that where there is food and where men are hungry the devices that will satisfy the need should be used. The sound men do not weaken their position, however, by discarding the will-of-the-people concept. Just as the humanitarians try to keep the balanced-budget symbol by indirection, so do the sound men continue to adhere to the democratic creed. The danger, they say, lies in governmental response to the wrong people; the unproductive unemployed voters are the ones to fear.

George Sokolsky writes:

"The peril to democracy is that this body of men and women may succeed in imposing their will upon those in control of government so that the government will not be able to free itself of the incubus of supporting an increasingly large body of non-productive citizens. . . . No democracy can withstand the corrosive effects of such an acid. It will eat into the vitals of government finance. It will destroy free capital by exorbitant taxation. It places a premium upon idleness and vagrancy. It makes a fool of the orderly, productive citizen." [2]

Writers of Sokolsky's sort find a moral distinction between the idle and the productive citizens. They disregard for purposes of their analysis the unmoral economic forces which transformed productive citizens into vagrants without regard to personal merit.

Those who would protect democratic government against its own evil nature conjure up a further danger. What happens when millions of voters become dependent for their sustenance upon the federal treasury? "May there not be a temptation to those in control of government to utilize this vast force to perpetuate themselves in office?" [3] Ogden Mills believed that the Roosevelt administration had early succumbed to this. The use of federal funds to control votes and elections was only too evident to him. "By this I do not necessarily mean the actual purchase of votes," he stated. "I mean that a political party which has dedicated itself to a policy of lavish spending of public moneys, for the sake of spending, almost inevitably sets up a whole series of vested interests in its continuance in office—an interest that is totally unrelated to its general administration of the country's affairs." [4]

The Mills argument is based upon the assumption that certain sound interests should be in charge of the general administration of the country's affairs. Efforts to administer the country's affairs in the name of other interests apparently are undemocratic, especially when these interests are attracted by a fiscal policy of lavish spending. A distinction is drawn between the vested interest of the citizen who has an established place in the economic order of society and the mass of citizens who are less fortunate.

Yet we can hardly deny the citizen the right to cast his vote as he pleases. We can urge that representatives be considered on their record as a whole; but if labor policy or taxation or any other single policy is the issue of foremost importance to the voter, representative government has little meaning unless he acts upon this conviction.

The question of what a policy should be, although posed on the discussion plane in terms of the general welfare, is usually answered as a political issue on the level of what particular groups demand. The politician is, of course, not limited merely to such demands in the formulation of policy; but reckon with them he must. They form the substance from which new policy is chiefly wrought.

Before predicting that democratic government means siphoning the Treasury empty, the popular reaction to spending policies should be considered. A *Fortune* poll disclosed the following results:

"If you were a member of the incoming Congress, would you vote yes or no on a bill to reduce federal spending to the point where the national budget is balanced?

	Yes	No	Don't Know
Total	61.3%	17.4%	21.3%
Prosperous	76.3	11.1	12.6
Upper middle class	67.1	17.8	15.1
Lower middle class	62.2	17.8	20.0
Poor	54.8	18.3	26.9
Negroes	40.2	19.5	40.3"

These findings combined with other tabulations brought *Fortune* to contradict the theory that "you can't beat five billion dollars." In fact, *Fortune* concluded in March, 1939, that "Roosevelt seems to remain popular in spite of his spending policy rather than because of it." [5]

Even though a balanced budget is accepted in principle and disregarded by special interests in their own specific demands, nevertheless their proposals must fight for attention in a climate of opinion traditionally unfavorable to deficit financing and increasing public debt. Their political demands must be related to this general pattern of values accepted by the community. Harmony with well-established attitudes vastly strengthens a new proposal; departures from traditions face a heavy weight of inertia. Yet in the field of fiscal policy traditional attitudes as well as established interests have been shaken by forces reaching far beyond political control.

The business cycle has played an important part in the process of political adjustment. Severe economic depressions not only cause wide suffering but also stimulate a distrust of the persons associated with the direction of political and business affairs. One aspect of this dissatisfaction is illustrated in the losses sustained by the political party in power. Certain aspects of this correlation have already been commented upon, but another angle to this diminution of political power prompts speculation.

Business depression means that existing economic controls are shifted. The wealthy are affected adversely from both the political and the economic side. Could it not be argued that such conditions of instability further social adjustments through governmental channels to meet the new conditions? For example, the undermining of real estate values makes slum clearance projects feasible. Land once tightly held is relinquished at a low price. Elaborate private residences are sold to churches, to schools, or to other private groups, and landed estates may be broken up for sale to small homeowners.

A depression as severe as that of 1929 and after results in a demoralization among those hitherto composing the elite. New men rise to positions of influence. Business leadership becomes of less social significance. The social worker, the labor organizer, the public administrator face new responsibilities and gain new prestige. The business cycle can hardly be welcomed as a social tonic to be desired for its medicinal qualities. Its price is too great for all concerned. Yet we have been protected from political rigidities through the changes in economic power forced upon the community by business ups and downs. Downswings of the business cycle serve to offset the contradictions in a system of political equality and of economic inequality.

More deliberate, if not more deliberative, efforts toward basic change in distribution of economic wealth through taxation, spending, relief, and a heavy public debt have been made in recent years. Through the political process reordering of economic interests is being brought about. Wall Street is of less importance, and Washington of more. Government bondholders become a huge vested interest; as public utility stocks become less remunerative, shrewd investors look elsewhere. Stockholders become attracted to government ownership of utilities that are unprofitable in private hands. The government enters further and further into investment. Individual savings are drawn off into government channels whether by taxation or borrowing. Opportunities for young men of imagination, drive, and ability are reduced in private employment, with a corresponding opening for their abilities in the public administrative services.

It is over such a wide field of social and economic life that adjustments are made. The issues of noisy campaigns and the rhetoric of sweating orators are at best but symptoms of further-reaching movements. Whether, as a matter of subjective judgment, the individual citizen views these trends as good or bad depends on his own group loyalties and philosophic values.

Alvin H. Hansen is one of the forward-looking economists who sees no necessary incompatibility between "the survival of private capitalism and a generous admixture of public investment." [6] There is no sound economic reason why government intervention cannot proceed to penetrate further into the economy, if such continued intervention is indicated as a means of preserving social stability and customary levels of economic activity. The practical political question raised by a decision to adopt this course is how to carry on the process without so disrupting business confidence that the objectives of government spending are defeated and private enterprise is frightened from areas unsuited to government activity, with the result that the total volume of economic activity is reduced. The related psychological and political considerations are thus as germane to the success of the entire process as is the economic logic of it.

Any view of public policy can be reduced to a combination of group interests which, after being identified with the public interest, are offered as the basis for governmental action. Our political debates arise over differences about which parts of the social whole we are to identify with the common welfare. Perhaps one can get a more detached view by taking an example from British experience. The tendency to identify one set of special interests with the general welfare is illustrated in the report of the British Committee on Expenditures. This committee, composed of distinguished public men, studied the fiscal problems facing the British government and attempted to make recommendations. The group split into two irreconcilable parts. The majority criticized the postwar tendency of electing to Parliament candidates pledged to expenditure schemes. The committee stated:

"The electoral programme of each successive party in power, particularly where it was formerly in opposition, has usually been prepared with more regard to attracting electoral support than a careful balancing of national interests. When the time comes to put that programme into force, matters which had formerly appeared easy and attractive are found to involve such grave questions as whether the proposals are administratively possible, whether they will have the desired results, whether the country can bear the cost; whether, in short, they are really in the national interest." [7]

By what standards should a government attempt this "careful balancing of national interests"? The substantive meaning of these words is more clearly revealed in the concrete recommendations of the report. "The first thing needful is to secure a return to general prosperity," argued the committee. Government action had in effect added to the economic burdens of the nation. Hence, the national welfare would be best promoted by the curtailment of governmental activities. Those of most "rapid and recent growth" should be selected for reduction. The committee offered three reasons:

"First, the older commitments of the state have stood the test of many attacks and in the main have proved that they are unavoidable even in years of depression. Secondly, the longer expenditure has been running, the more rights and vested interests have grown up around it. Thirdly, it is a powerful argument in regard to any service to say that the nation did without it a few years ago, therefore it cannot be essential." [8]

No qualitative distinctions of social utility are offered as a guide to retrenchment by this expert committee. Social services are described as "privileges or benefits for particular classes at the cost of the general taxpayer." It thus appears that the committee's "careful balancing of national interests" meant relieving the taxpayer and reducing services even in the face of popular demand for such governmental functions. The economic argument of the majority report was a justification for limiting state action for the purpose of easing the taxpayer's burden and thereby restoring prosperity.

The arguments advanced by the committee minority were based on a different set of value judgments. This group believed that government should be highly responsive. It criticized the majority report as describing

"a condition of financial irresponsibilities which in fact do not exist. . . . So far as their strictures concern the principle of ultimate financial responsibility, what they regard as 'undesirable,' we view as consistent with the right and proper course of democratic government and progress. How otherwise shall the people obtain legislative redress of social and economic injustice except through those who seek their suffrage?

"Moreover, we consider that many of the recommendations of our colleagues would in their operation impose an unfair measure of sacrifice upon certain large sections of the community, many of whom are already feeling with considerable and growing severity the effects of what has graphically been described as the 'economic blizzard,' but would fail to lay under any comparable contribution others more favourably situated, many of whom are enjoying, to the extent of their fixed income, effortless benefits from the increased value of money due to falling prices." [9]

How are the interests of the taxpayers, the persons with fixed incomes, and those possessed of money claims protected by contract to be balanced in any objective fashion with the welfare of those persons whose income is too small for the income tax, who work for wages and possess no money claims? To criticize a fiscal policy because it "attracts votes" is pointless unless this argument in itself is likely to win political support for those advancing it. On the other hand, the Committee on Expenditures argued that

"at election times those desiring increased expenditure on particular objects, are usually far better organized, far more active and vocal than those who favor the vague and uninspiring course of strict economy; and as a result candidates not infrequently find themselves returned to Parliament committed, on a one-sided presentation of a case, to a course which on fuller knowledge they see to be opposed to the national interest."

The concept of a fiscal policy designed to promote the economic welfare of the public as a whole is badly shaken when the incidence of a given policy is faced in terms of the groups actually affected. The general-welfare concept is of little if any value as a tool of analysis; it is most effective as an instrument of exhortation. As a battle cry for rallying sympathy and support to a given proposal, it belongs with "justice," "equity," and "fairness."

On the other hand, fiscal policy need not necessarily represent the partial, immediate, and selfish view of narrow groups. Granted the exercise of reason, restraint, and co-operation on the part of participants working through an appropriate governmental mechanism, a line of public policy might be established that would advance the wealth and happiness of a very large proportion of the population. Although the general-welfare concept is often abused, it may still be worth while to seek policies benefiting a broader rather than a narrower alignment of interests. A given fiscal policy must relate to the economic welfare of, for example, bankers or brokers or investors or farmers. One policy may embrace several of these interests, but no policy can embrace all group interests unless we assume that there is latent somewhere in our society an inner unity capable of harmonizing all apparent differences. We assume that the degree of social unity which makes communal life possible is of little aid in settling current policy problems.

Equity in taxation and expenditures for the public interest are thus concepts that must be analyzed in terms of the groups affected if we are to discover what factual content these phrases may have. It is not that these terms are devoid of meaning but rather that they have many meanings.

The formulation of fiscal policy lies at the dead center of democratic government. It is the very essence into which is distilled the conflict between the haves and the have-nots. It represents the terms of compromise between powerful economic forces in the community. Utterly divergent economic forces are seeking to use the financial machinery of the government to promote their own ends.

The essence of the problem comes to this: that fiscal policy necessarily issues from a complex of political forces. What will be the standard for guiding policy if we discard the general-welfare concept as offering little practical aid except for oratorical purposes? Secretary of Agriculture Henry A. Wallace has considered this problem. In his book, *New Frontiers,* he propounds a faith in a society wherein a continuing balance of interests supervised by an able bureaucracy will advance "the good life." What does this philosophy mean, however, when removed from the discussion plane of high principle? What are his guides for framing fiscal policy?

Striking a balance denotes that various people are to get their just due and that someone is to determine the distribution. Order, good will, and reason all contribute to making the transaction smooth and pleasant. But who gets what, and why? Basically, the actual content of Wallace's theories are most baldly stated by him in the following excerpt from recent Senate committee hearings:

"I think as long as government has given certain advantages to corporations, to organized farm groups, to organized labor groups, that it should use some of its powers to see that the unorganized people at the bottom of the pile are not too hopelessly discriminated against by the forces of modern society. If we are to have true democracy these people must get into position to exercise their part. They should be in position to earn more money." [10]

Here at last is a clear statement of his objective: the public interest calls for more money in the pockets of the people at the bottom of the pile. In the final analysis Secretary Wallace's views seem to result in belief that through governmental intervention our national economy can be so altered as to enable the bottom third of the population to earn more money, particularly the bottom third of farmers.

Secretary Wallace has a definite base for fiscal policy formulation. His task as a politician, however, is to develop the theory and the formulae that will make his proposals harmonious with accepted values. It has long been assumed in some quarters that if the top third of the economic heap determined fiscal policy, the benefits would trickle down. Secretary Wallace would reverse the situation. He may anticipate quite a long discussion.

The prevailing ideology is of vast importance in any effort to analyze political change. It is the very atmosphere that interest groups must breathe. In considering the politics of fiscal policy, therefore, the attitude of people toward their government is an ideological factor of transcendent importance.

From the political point of view the fact must also be accepted that man in the mass responds to symbols and embraces simple formulae. If he were other that what he is, the political problem would also be different. But to the student of government an essential bit of datum is the emotional response of the public to the clichés surrounding economic problems and the public's inability to grasp the refinements of economic analysis.

There is, I think, a law of political distortion under which economic facts, as soon as they are used in political debate, lose their original form and are shaped and oversimplified to achieve some predetermined end. Hence, fiscal policy is discussed rather in terms consistent with accepted ideology than with actual facts. A government which undertakes to manipulate the economic affairs of the nation employs symbols and slogans of the general welfare even though its action really deprives one group of something for the benefit of another. Much of reality is too complex to be widely understood, but in most fields the direction of activity is not dependent upon the approval of a mass of uninformed individuals.

Business organizations work in an atmosphere encouraging

initiative and frank profit seeking; government organizations are surrounded by social attitudes imposing responsibility for action and restraining the use of discretion. Through the fiction of corporate personality private business enables directors to handle other people's money as though it belonged to this personality whose mere organs they are assumed to be. Directors are the five senses of a legally created "person." Officials are always thought of as handling other people's money, and hence they have to be watched. Democratic government is not regarded as a great Leviathan representing the whole community in organic form. Yet when we wish to criticize governmental finance we revive the personal view of the state and point to the need for the government to balance its own budget as though it were a household.

The government today is using its control of monetary policy, of taxation, of borrowing, and of lending, to intervene in the whole economy of the nation. The consequences of this interference are not fully reflected in the mere income and outgo of the Treasury, for we are without a balance sheet that shows us the total result of current fiscal policy. These fiscal operations transcend the housekeeping of the nation. We see a huge deficit in dollars and cents. But these figures do not give a complete picture of national finance. It is not enough to know that we have spent more money than we have taken in. Unless we know the consequences of federal spending and the incidence of various taxes, we cannot tell whether the populace is better or worse off as a result of what the government has done.

When the government uses its legal controls of economic affairs in order to attain certain social ends, purely financial standards are inadequate. We use a fiscal term to cloak a social end. This cloak may appear bright red as a deficit in the budget, but the narrow bookkeeper's view distorts the reality. Understressed is the fact that taxation and public expenditures may contribute positively to the wealth and well-being of the nation. Taxes may discourage antisocial behavior and bring about a distribution of economic goods that actually promotes productivity. When taxation is not used primarily for raising revenue, the importance of the tax cannot be judged in terms of the moneys brought in.

For example, if the power to tax is used as the power to destroy, destruction becomes our criterion. If regulation is attempted through a tax levy, our first concern must be with the extent of regulation resulting and only incidentally with the amount of money raised.

In expenditures for public works or in loans to industry the social consequence of these policies is the significant question. The activity called "governmental spending" is often treated as an abstract concept and closely associated with the words "recklessness" and "extravagance." Sometimes these epithets describe the operation and sometimes not. Public expenditures are made for the attainment of such diverse ends that no one set of standards can be applied *in toto*, least of all narrowly financial criteria. Thus, the vast sums allotted to national defense must ultimately be justified by the imponderables of national policy and international relations. Fiscal policies such as the tariff, or subsidies, preferential or regulatory taxes, stem back to considerations of social control and a political balancing of interests. Public expenditures may mean investments yielding returns for generations. Millions spent for flood control may result not only in billions saved in property values but also millions saved from flood insurance charges.

Public spending has no meaning in itself; its significance lies in the standards applied. In the dispute over social aims contestants attempt to discredit spending in general. The popular distrust resulting makes the actual administration of fiscal policy unnecessarily difficult. A more forthright facing of social objectives, if substituted for emotional aversion to the abstract concepts such as "reckless expenditures" and "unbalanced budgets," would make possible the more effective management of governmental finance.

Suppose the government broadened its "capital structure" base; we should call it increasing the national debt. But why not more debt if it increases national income? In governmental affairs budget balancing is thought of usually in terms of economy. On the other hand, a business can often choose either retrenchment or expansion. Advertising to draw business may be the best way to balance its budget. No *a priori* assumptions settle the issue. The tendency to think of public finance in terms of personal expenses is, perhaps, a partial explanation, since for most individuals greater economy is the only immediately available way of keeping outgo within income. The excess of outgo over income is the fact that appears most clearly in the public budget— the causes are too confused for the public to grasp. The simplest explanation is to argue that selfish forces raid the Treasury and the government is unable to say them nay.

"The demand for an immediate budget balance as an essential preliminary to further business recovery" Professor Haig regards as "somewhat disingenuous." "This is really a symbol," he states—"a protest against waste and a plea for the elimination of unnecessary uncertainties." [11] Professor Haig's analysis seems to come closer to the kernel of our problem. He eschews the balanced-budget formula. It is the uncertainty that impedes business: the fear of making plans because of the upset that may be caused by change in the price structure or the exchange rate. But a balanced budget may or may not reflect a condition of stability.

Much argumentation is based upon the conception of state action as being essentially restrictive, negative, regulatory, and unproductive. What would happen if a more exact and realistic analysis were made of the assets resulting from governmental spending? Our governmental accounting system treats social services of vast public benefit as heavy charges against the community. This means that a one-sided picture is obtained which fosters the unfavorable attitude toward government expenditures.

As a formal bookkeeping matter it would, of course, be exceedingly difficult to assess the value of crime prevention or fire protection. Such computations have, however, been attempted. The economic value of educational and recreational facilities is still more elusive but nonetheless real. Our present trend toward collectivism is evaluated by the narrow bookkeeping of an individualistic economy. It may be that the social cost of this trend is greater than its returns. My only point is that our present system of evaluation throws little light on the matter one way or the other. Hence, the way in which public finance is treated, plus the stake that most people feel in it, makes the matter too important to be left alone and too complicated to be widely understood.

Government is supposed to be bound by the same principles which govern the good man. When social need carries the government into new fields of activity, a theoretical justification is not always ready at hand. Thus, in a situation where social need dictated spending, a rational theoretical justification was necessary. J. M. Keynes provided one answer for academic critics. He offered a bone of contention to the intellectual. The homely rustic symbol of "priming the pump" gave the public a picture to consider while the destitute were cared for. All governmental action must have a philosophical justification. This must also be simplified into an acceptable symbol; a rationale is necessary before action.

Though they become involved in verbal contradictions, public men must say the socially desired thing if they wish to remain in public life. The ideology through which we view public questions tends to make men's words more important than their deeds. They are judged largely by their loyalty to community ideals and ritual. Statesmen occupy positions of symbolic significance. They are expected to stand for the highest principles and aspirations of the community. They are judged by their fidelity to professed social ideals. Conflicts, confusion, and recriminations arise when the voters demand that their high elective officials not only stand for principle but also do something. Such action involves the give-and-take, the dodge-and-push, that is taken for granted in business. It is here that the statesman, in order to accomplish something, becomes a politician.

The increased penetration by government into fields of management means that officials come trailing clouds of symbols that have little to do with their concrete responsibility. Confusion lies in failing to distinguish between problems and our attitude toward these problems. At the present time the obstacle in the way of a balanced budget is as much the attitude toward government as more substantive considerations.

The facts concerning the effect of a particular tax or the economic value of a certain expenditure are exceedingly complex. Nevertheless, since the welfare of individuals or groups may be vitally affected, great effort must be made to rally a mass of supporters. Here accepted symbols or attractive slogans are more useful than facts. The area is too broad, too confused, too technical to be grasped. Politicians are called upon to supply simplifications. Urgent need for generalizations in the field of fiscal policy tends to remove us far from concrete realities. Something called a "balanced budget" is set up as the end that must be achieved. This is attended by various bookkeeping conventions and forms. A balanced budget comes to be treated as an end in itself. This concept of a balanced budget is accepted in principle, and then under a dual bookkeeping arrangement the ordinary budget is balanced and an extraordinary emergency budget unbalanced. Politicians promise to balance the budget—but later— thus kowtowing to the principle and avoiding the fact.

Our ideological confusions about fiscal policy arise perhaps from a basic political conflict between those who favor socialization of wealth for the underprivileged and those who want stimulation or at least stabilization for encouragement of private enterprise. These two forces are in political conflict, and basically contradictory public policies result. Yet this conflict takes place within a political order under which economic interests are expected peacefully to compete through governmental channels. The prevalent ideology casts a mist of unreality over this struggle. Government is the storehouse of social aspirations. Public servants are held to higher standards than those applying to ordinary workers and doers. Yet the individuals and institutions surrounded with such high professions of principle are restricted and even suspected when the time comes for action.

Various writers doubt whether we can properly develop and realize an adequate fiscal policy under our present governmental structure.

"When the President, with heavy majorities in both houses of the Congress, has been unable to secure adherence in such instances to his expenditure recommendations, there is, indeed, ground for apprehension lest the experiment of deficit financing be wrecked by lack of proper timing and control of expenditures [Professor Haig states].[12] Perhaps the pressure groups of special beneficiaries of government spending will decide the issue. Perhaps, before deficit financing can be made safe for democracy, democracy will have to improve its mechanism so that action will be less influenced by the shortsighted and immediate special interests."

If the government is to undertake functions where careful timing is of essential importance, it seems sensible to provide some form of organization that can take this into account. Nevertheless, the calendar and not political expediency or economic conditions determines the timing of election campaigns. Thus, business cycle theory might dictate the reduction of government spending just as a campaign for re-election fell due! It is hardly necessary to elaborate upon the fact that our government is not well designed for the direction of deficit financing.

One or more of our social or institutional factors may, of course, be changed, but this seems unlikely and remains unpredictable. For the present and possibly for a long time to come these conditions constitute the walls within which the politician must work. Some writers take the view that this handicaps the functioning of a "proper" budget system. My point is rather that they merely give the setting to the problem that we are called upon to face. To insist that these conditions must be changed if we desire an improved scheme of financial control seems to me prescribing an anatomical alteration in the patient so that his new suit of clothes will fit.

As R. G. Hawtrey has well stated: "The reason why financial policy is so baffling is that expenditure is not an organic unity, but a mere arithmetic aggregate. Each separate item in the aggregate has been included on account of its merits, and if it is to be suppressed or reduced it must be shown to be less desirable than its rivals." [13]

How can this be demonstrated? Through the persuasive force of superior reasoning? By an authoritative declaration? By skilled political leadership? The totalitarian concept of the state provides one approach: discipline and power are emphasized. Here is government by symbols different from those used under democracy. Our present institutions are surrounded by such symbols as those justifying checks and balances, separation of powers, popular responsibility, states' rights. These phrases do not support the organizational changes needed, for example, in a pump priming program.

Working within the framework of democratic concepts, various scholars have pointed to the advantages of the parliamentary system for the better control of fiscal policy. Here is a system sustained by the symbols and myths of democracy, yet sufficiently well integrated within itself to make the executive effective. At any rate, this seems to be the case in Great Britain. To urge the transference to the United States of such institutions is to assume that our society and economy are sufficiently similar to guarantee the same results. A parliamentary system with real cabinet responsibility depends on a strong party system and a well-organized bureaucracy. These in turn rest upon factors such as the homogeneity of the population, the nature of the national economy, social traditions, and the structure of classes.

Institutional factors are, of course, man-created and susceptible to revision. At the same time this does not mean that they are artificial establishments; they are now deeply rooted and intertwined. Tearing up any one would have such unpredictable consequences that we may well hesitate about altering drastically the system of government. Our government works as it does, not entirely because the machinery is cumbersome, but rather because the propelling power is sporadic and the load is heavy. For example, the difficulties ascribed to federalism would not all disappear if we eradicated state lines. Sectional interests would remain; economic development, cultural characteristics, and even climatic and other geographical conditions would attend to that. The rivalries of sections are at least isolated to some extent within the boundaries of our states. Local leaders are forced to compose the major part of their own quarrels. Our federal system means that the ultimate responsibility for all decision making is not focused in one place. Although the dispersion of responsibility causes some delay and does not appeal to men of strictly logical mind, it at least tempers the intensities of feeling that arise when the onus of decision making is centered upon one governing agency, or even one individual.

To the extent that the executive is able to exercise control, he gathers unto himself the onus of deciding between conflicting interests. Under a system that gives the president a fixed term, focusing responsibility upon him may create antagonisms that cannot be resolved, since the president cannot be expected to resign when he loses the support of Congress.

Our present system has the great virtue of keeping decentralized many of the conflicts within the community. There is no one point where the whole government could be endangered, and hence there is less need for the concentration of governmental force. Such a system, of course, makes for confusion and is not highly suited to straightforward, businesslike management of finance—but government has matters other than finance to manage. Our present form of government is not to be judged simply in terms of its ineptness for fiscal control. Hence, the question is not merely how efficiently fiscal agencies function, but how they do their jobs within the confines of our institutional framework and in view of all the other purposes that the government is supposed to realize.

Our institutional forms prevent the underlying social differences of interest from reaching as sharp a divergence as they would under a system of government that concentrated responsibility more clearly. Today no one view of sound fiscal policy can be pushed through. Men of reason are forced to compromise with men of emotion. No single political group can control the whole machinery of government. This is not the best way to realize a logically consistent policy, but it may be a fortunate thing in a country as diversified as is the United States. Changes in the institutional structure which are desirable from one point of view may be questionable from another.

What are we seeking? Our goal presumably is to develop and apply a rational fiscal policy acceptable to most of the community. But suppose popular government leads to increasing deficits and ultimate inflation? "The acceptance of the view that unbalanced budgets are dangerous, even if at times unreasonable, serves as a check against legislative excesses." According to this view, if legislators only believed that keeping out of debt was more important than representing their constituents, all would be well. "Our fear of unbalanced budgets," we are told, is "a sound conclusion based upon past events. . . . If we lose that fear and in its place accept a belief in the desirability or even in the safety of deficits, we are probably headed toward a ruinous lesson." [14] Is this inference correct?

This exhortation would have us believe that government spending is a bad thing, presumably because this leads to a change in the nature of property relations. But whether such a change is in itself undesirable does not necessarily follow. We can predict a change but we cannot foretell what the nature of this change will be. *Disaster for whom?* Must economic analysis take its stand upon the desirability of preserving the status quo? In facing a long policy of increasing expenditures can we assume a static condition? Disaster is predicated upon the assumption that the present economic system will remain static until its "debt limits" are reached—whereupon it will pop! This must mean either that there is a rigid limit to taxation, or that governmental expenditures will be poured into channels of an unproductive sort that will not make the country better able to carry the increased burden of taxes entailed. We can discover no absolute criterion of what should be—all we can hope to do is to provide a mechanism for channelizing pressures and providing facilities for the formulation and execution of policy that will keep our institutions responsive to our social needs.

Judgment is passed upon the activities of the government in the general field of fiscal relationships largely in terms of the "budget." This administrative machinery of budgetary control we established to increase efficiency of operation. Fiscal policy clearly transcends questions of management. Yet the budget stands as the only summary statement of all federal fiscal policy. No mechanism can automatically settle questions of distributive justice. No objective standards are applicable. Such standards can be developed for management, perhaps, but not for policy.

Viewed as a political problem, budgeting means interest balancing. Thus, no clear economic criterion can be applied in deciding whether millions should be spent on a battleship or on a national park and bird sanctuary. If any scientific adjustment of interests is impossible, we can at least strive for a clear view of the alternatives before us. Officials can be made to offer a program. Means can be provided for weighing the merits of different demands, and shortsighted forces can be urged to seek a longer view. What administrative devices or institutional changes will encourage this approach?

In so far as the purely political problem is concerned, all governments have the basic problem of deciding "who gets what, when, and how." They go about it differently and institutionalize different stages of the process. The outcome in terms of governmental structure shows striking contrasts. An agency that may be provided for by the constitution in one country may be left to private arrangement in another. Thus, persuasion and open bargaining characterize the formulation of fiscal policy in this country. There is a diffusion of responsibility. Differences of opinion and conflicts of interest that would be smothered in party conclave under a dictatorship or privately adjusted between officials and interested groups in Great Britain are bandied about in public debate in the United States.

While we may not hope for an over-all control of fiscal affairs that will lead us to the promised land where milk and honey supplant slumps and depressions, a partial solution may lie in a more realistic attitude toward fiscal policy through clarifying some concepts and discarding others. Other aspects of fiscal policy depend upon the adjustment of group interests. Finally, appropriate institutional changes may lead to the readier compromise of differing habits of thought and conflicting group interests.

While it is arguable that for certain reasons, such as providing a broad basis of responsibility and maintaining a federal structure, bicameralism is desirable, the conclusion does not follow that for other purposes, such as fiscal control, the two chambers should not be brought closer together. Thus, little is gained in thinking of the separation of powers or separation of functions as a *principle* of government. It is nothing more than a form of organization suitable for some functions and unsuitable for others.

To recognize bicameralism, the separation of powers, or the duality between central and state governments as having a political justification is further to recognize chasms that must be bridged rather than eradicated. Yet rivalries between Congress and administrative agencies are not easily set aside.

If our analysis of the politics of fiscal policy is correct, no comprehensive or sweeping reforms are likely to succeed. Congress cannot be expected readily to increase the president's authority at its own expense. Hence, even so defensible a reform as the item veto has received little support in Congress. Various presidents from the time of Hayes have toyed with the idea. The item veto, however, would enable the president to strike at specific appropriations and thus reach back into congressional districts. This might eliminate pork-barrel legislation, but it would also give the chief executive one means of weakening congressmen on their home grounds. Local support means the political life or death of congressmen. They will hardly welcome a whip that may be applied to their own backs.

Under our system of government it is doubtful whether fiscal policy can be successfully approached through the exercise of broad over-all planning and clear responsible authority. To achieve this would necessitate not only a change in the form of government but, what is more difficult, a change in our attitude toward government. Neither our institutions nor our ideology seem suited to meeting in straightforward and foresighted fashion present questions of fiscal policy. This does not mean that careful economic analysis is futile or that all planning efforts should be abandoned. It does mean that the fruits of such forethought are not suited for submission to Congress as a statement of what should be. This can only be finally determined as the result of careful compromise. The legislature may well become impatient with carefully drawn logical blueprints while struggling to find the actual conditions under which men will agree to work together. Because of the very nature of his task the politician cannot follow *a priori* schemes no matter how logically conceived and technically defensible.

Nor are the political difficulties in adjusting differences due solely to the stupidity or the selfishness or the irrational nature of men. Obstacles perhaps more severe arise from the technician's blindness to the limits of his special competence, from the moralist's unmindfulness of the manifold interpretations of justice or social welfare, from the man of reason's disdain for the power of emotional considerations. It is just as important for the expert to see his limitations as it is for the layman to see his. The latter is reminded of his ignorance by the mysteries of technical terms and involved theory; the former has no clear boundary stones to show when he leaves his technical skill to follow his private hunch.

As the value of compromise as a basic political method is realized, the task of carefully adjusting divergent group interests in concrete cases can be tackled. Exhortation will then become less persuasive. Energy can be turned from the defense of abstract principles to the invention of organizations appropriate to doing a job. Here is a task worthy of the expert.

Political issues are not disputes between reasonable men but conflicts of interests between human beings. Fiscal policy must reckon with conflicts and irrational beliefs. The general public can hardly be expected to take a long-term view of fiscal policy; nor is it likely that selfish interests will become unselfish if enough publicists appeal to them through the light of reason to mend their ways. Their ways are well insulated from outside logistic attack by reams of theory concocted by their own apologists. There are victories in the battles between ideals, but the Goddess of Reason has proved herself an undiscriminating camp follower.

The clash of ideologies arises largely from undue emphasis upon principles rather than attention to methods. The thoughtful man should consider particular taxes rather than taxation in general. He has no business believing or disbelieving in sweeping concepts such as "deficit finance" or a "balanced budget." These abstract phrases are more useful for exhortation than for analysis.

In other words, emphasis should be shifted from the vindication of abstractions to the study of concrete data and to the discovery of administrative devices that will get the job done. Is our ideology still fluid and evolving new concepts to meet new needs? Are our institutions sufficiently flexible?

When we note how far England and the Scandinavian countries have moved and how far this country has moved since the turn of the century we need not despair of our capacity to adjust our institutions to changing needs. How have the British been able to go so far toward socialization without affecting business confidence? J. H. Williams calls attention to the lesson to be drawn on this point from English experience or that of the Scandinavian countries:

"In those countries also there has been a large and a growing participation by government in the economic life of the community and in the organization and direction of saving and investment, but, as Colin Clark's figures would seem to prove, such intervention has been effected in ways which have not impaired private initiative and the processes of private capital replacement and improvement to which he mainly ascribes England's post-war economic progress. In England, also, there is a heavy tax burden, probably exceeding ours, but with the important difference that it has accumulated more slowly, so that the process of adjustment has been more deliberate." [15]

Thus the economic question is reduced to skill in adjustment.

This is not altogether a matter of superior foresight and timing by statesmen. As always, we must go back to the social context within which the process takes place. In both Great Britain and the Scandinavian countries there is a long bureaucratic tradition. Skill in the administration of change has reduced friction. Public confidence in the bureaucracy has in turn made their task smooth. Moreover the closer connection and frequent identification between the elite of industry and the ruling class have made it possible for the government to intervene more fully in industry with less disruption to business confidence than otherwise could have been expected.

Where the relationship between the elites of government and of business is direct, no undercover means of persuasion are necessary. With an interlocking membership between the House of Commons and leading corporations, the need for lobbyists is greatly diminished. Wealth and industry can speak directly. For example, in the House of Commons in 1938, 806 directorships, including 181 chairmanships, were held by 198 members of Parliament. R. C. Hall writes: "Every industry in the Empire is represented. Almost every one of the 200 giant corporations in Britain is represented by at least one director, and in many instances that Member of Parliament may be the Chairman of the Board or a managing director of the business." [16]

Attention to such factors is essential to an understanding of the forces which hold the British system together. It is these relations which mark a closely integrated political order. Patronage with its crudity and pettiness has no place. Moreover, so long as the social order rests on a broad acceptance the British probably do not feel that they are paying a high price for continued stability. Every culture has its scale of rewards and its hierarchy that gives strength and permanence. On the other hand the elements in the community who do not share this view seek their own means of expression. The business members of Parliament are counterbalanced by the Labour members drawn from trade union positions.

The legislation that emerges from such a representative assembly authorizing economic shifts has already been broken upon the back of the interests most directly affected. The cushioning of the impact of government intervention is further secured by the British practice of calling in industries and groups which will be affected by proposed regulatory measures, and consulting with them. The drafting of regulatory statutes and their subsequent administrative application can thus be accomplished in the light of information secured from such groups about the probable effects of alternative lines of action. It is easier to understand how the British have been able to intervene so extensively in the industrial life of the nation without creating maladjustments greater than those they sought to remedy. Since they are more intimately acquainted with the interests of both capital and labor, members of Parliament may be able to avoid much of the misunderstanding that makes for friction in our efforts to regulate the economic life of a huge continent.

Brooks Adams, in his analysis of social revolutions, reached the conclusion that the greatest danger to our industrial society arises first from the overspecialization of function which comes as a result of technological advance, and second from the inability of the capitalist mentality to administer the vast centralization of resultant authority and activity.

"I take it to be an axiom," he states, "that perfection in administration must be commensurate to the bulk and momentum of the mass to be administered, otherwise the centrifugal will overcome the centripetal force, and the mass will disintegrate. In other words, civilization will dissolve." [17]

How is this administrative ability to be found in a society dominated by business leaders who have developed "under the stress of an environment which demanded excessive specialization in the direction of a genius adapted to money-making under highly complex industrial conditions"? Adams insists that we have need of the "generalizing mind." [18]

Administration he defines as "the capacity of coordinating many, and often conflicting, social energies in a single organism, so adroitly that they shall operate as a unity. This presupposes the power of recognizing a series of relations between numerous special interests, with all of which no single man can be intimately acquainted." [19]

The dilemma that Adams pictures is acute if we accept his assumptions concerning the narrowness of the capitalist's outlook and his dominant role in government. In fact Adams has created a bogy. He has endowed all businessmen with his abstract characterization of capitalist mentality. The British have proved that a capitalist society can at the same time develop an able administrative class. As already noted, business leaders occupy an important place in Parliament and must consider broad aspects of public policy in both the representative and administrative branches of government. Through force of circumstances, if for no other reason, the capitalist today finds himself considering his relationship to the rest of society.

Claude Robinson, President of the Opinion Research Corporation, writes:

"Heretofore business leaders have been largely occupied with such problems as raw material prices, labor costs, inventories, depreciation, machine obsolescence and so on. Their aim has been to earn a dollar by producing and distributing goods more cheaply. They thought that as long as they were successful in this, they could get along with their several publics. But the social ferment of the past few years has changed this. Nowadays business men not only produce goods and services of better quality at cheaper prices, but they must also justify themselves to the general public on social grounds. If they sell groceries at cheaper prices by quantity methods of purchase and distribution, they must convince the general public that they are not monopolistic, that they pay their labor fairly, and that they contribute something to the community as well as take something out of it. If business makes much profit, it must not only account to the tax collector but also explain to the public why it should appropriate that part of the social surplus. In a hundred and one different ways, the business man is faced with social pressures which before now never entered his consciousness." [20]

Adams, in considering the businessman and the influence of wealth, took a view that has proved too static. He stated that "money is the weapon of the capitalist as the sword was the weapon of the mediaeval soldier; only, as the capitalist is more highly specialized than the soldier ever was, he is more helpless when his single weapon fails him." [21]

This statement overlooks the manifold uses to which money may be put. On the other hand, taxation, monetary and credit controls, spending and relief appropriations are devices for adjustment which may profoundly alter the relations of the capitalist to the society in which he lives. We need suffer no fatal rigidities because the businessman is chiefly concerned with profits. Managerial ability that will direct economic relationships toward broader social objectives can be recruited from many walks of life.

Money is a two-edged sword, and it may be used as a defensive or offensive weapon by numerous groups. But with Adams's main thesis we agree. "There can be no doubt," he writes, "that the modern environment is changing faster than any environment ever previously changed; therefore, the social centre of gravity constantly tends to shift more rapidly; and therefore, modern civilization has unprecedented need of the administrative or generalizing mind." [22] This need is clear, but at the same time if such attitudes of mind are to be protected from the consequences of their own genius their vision must be constantly tested in the daily living of less lofty-minded men. Democracy provides the institutions which make this possible.

☆ *30* ☆

The Animating Spirit of
American Progress

"Experimentation and opportunism rather
than preconceived theories have been the animating spirit of American progress."

ARTHUR SCHLESINGER,
*New Viewpoints in
American History*

IN any concluding evaluation of our political system the word
of the historian must carry great weight. Not in entire forget-
fulness nor yet in utter nakedness do we come to face the future.
Our habits of thought will affect the way in which we meet fresh
problems, however unique these may be. Even though the need
be clear for agreement on long-range objectives and for acceptance
of theories as guides for a consistent progress, past experience
holds little warrant for the assumption that our political behavior can be ordered in such a logical fashion. We have proceeded from one concrete objective to another, but we have seldom followed a plotted course. Short cuts to Utopia have been
eagerly seized upon from time to time, but support has dwindled
when hardheaded men have pointed to impracticalities of application. Hence it seems clear that our course of public policy
will continue to be controlled by the political methods with which
we are familiar. As Carl Becker has written of the political future:

"Whatever it turns out to be, it will have been created by the
traditional American procedure—by fighting for good bargains by
means of ballots and economic pressure, by unlimited indulgence in

the blare and blarney and pandemonium of free propaganda all compact of truth and falsehood, by imputing bad faith to opponent and invoking the American way of life on behalf of every special interest, and by frantically proclaiming that freedom of the press is in danger whenever anyone employs that freedom to promote ideals of which we disapprove. This is the normal American way of life, and whatever comes of it, supposing it to be something less than disaster, we will still call it democracy." [1]

We cannot hope to change profoundly the nature of our politics so long as the democratic order continues; we are wedded for better or for worse. Whether a divorce from this system offers a preferable alternative must remain a subjective decision. With patience and skill we should be able to achieve the kind of life we desire.

For most questions of current policy ways [2] and means of fulfillment can be found under our Constitution. But in the basic law itself is the recognition that no social system or political settlement is to be regarded as final. Through the amending power sweeping changes in our economic structure may be authorized. How drastic change might be without incurring violent resistance we cannot know in advance, but in the extraordinary majorities required for amendments to the Constitution we have a real safeguard. Here is a substantial recognition that as a nation we must be in very general agreement before essential changes can succeed. That a 51 per cent majority is inadequate in such situations is not only based on legal fiat but more importantly on hard social fact.

Adjustment remains the essence of the politics of democracy. Our parties hold political power contingent on popular support and thus provide for a free situation within which intelligence may function. The contribution that parties make to policy is inconsequential so long as they maintain conditions for adjustment. Under the present party system we have political machinery which is able to keep power responsive to change. No one ideology is linked up with any single class-conscious group capable of monopolizing control. Government under the idea of the general interest discourages such an identification.

Democracy provides us with an ideal under which experimentation with institutions and negotiation among interests is tolerated and justified. We are not forced to believe in unity; we may glory in diversity. It is enough if we achieve a working union of interests, ideas, institutions, and individuals. If we would formulate and execute constructive national long-range policies under our democratic ideology, we must face a period of change, of experimentation and of danger. Yet face it we must. Our institutions and current clichés must be altered for these new tasks. Voter, expert, and politician must advance together. The question is how, and how fast. My answer is to keep government close to the individual and move no faster than a strong majority wills.

The function of our party system must be to keep the majority and minority viewpoints from widening to the point where they can no longer be reconciled under our constitutional procedure. In such a time of flux our national party organizations more than ever before must find a common ground for agreement so that the process of policy formulation and execution may proceed under common loyalty to the rule of law. The New Deal demonstrated that rapidity of action was possible within the limits of our present institutions. It also demonstrated consolidation to be as important as change. Programs are nothing more than aspirations except as they are effectively administered.

Our parties may help recruit leaders. Our parties may try to educate their members. Our parties may strive for as broad a following as possible. Yet the politics of democracy cannot stop with the electoral and representative process. Nor can the task be surrendered to neutral administrators however expert. Administration must carry on the representative and unifying process where the parties stop.

The politics of democracy offers a process of adjustment. The United States provides the milieu suitable to its operation. I seek not to urge any substantive goals but rather to stress the profound conviction that our political system provides the means for satisfying our communal needs if we but realize its potentialities. Many writers pose a sharp issue between elements of the community. Theorists forecast an impending struggle sharply drawn between the haves and the have-nots. Such pictures possess a dramatic simplicity. Yet persuasion has proved workable in this country during the past few crucial years. We have all gone along together. We have advanced a long way in a short time.

Many are impatient; others fear the speed of the change. Such differences are inevitable. The important thing is that the country as a whole is united as to its general direction. Social security, the right of labor to organize, the use of the government for positive social ends—these goals are widely accepted.

Our system will work so long as men with widely differing views can content themselves with a middle ground for action. Our two parties must face change together, though one may use caution and the other zest. It is not my object to argue that compromise is a good in itself or that it is necessary to seek compromise in all things. My aim is to explain rather than to advocate. My point is that, no matter what men's visions may be, where their goals differ and where a peaceful adjustment is sought, compromise is the product. In a world already bitterly divided in many areas and easily capable of further cleavages, a system that gives us half a loaf is a system to be cherished. While munching this crust, we can then take thought concerning the next move.

John Morley pointed out long ago:

"Success in politics, as in every other art, obviously before all else implies both knowledge of the material with which we have to deal, and also such concession as is necessary to the qualities of the material. Above all, in politics we have an art in which development depends upon modification. That is the true side of the conservative theory. To hurry on after logical perfection is to show one's self ignorant of the material of that social structure with which the politician has to deal. To disdain anything short of an organic change in thought or institution is infatuation. To be willing to make such changes too frequently, even when they are possible, is fool-hardiness. That fatal French saying about small reforms being the worst enemies of great reforms, is, in the sense in which it is commonly used, a formula of social ruin." [3]

If this be conservatism, let us make the most of it. Conservatism as well as liberalism has a positive contribution to make.

"On the other hand," as Morley cautions, "let us not forget here is a sense, in which this very saying is profoundly true. A small and temporary improvement may really be the worst enemy of a great and permanent improvement, unless the first is made on the lines and in the direction of the second." I argue that our major lines of direction are fairly well determined. Responsiveness to social needs is the inevitable direction of democracy. The problem of politics is how fast we shall go. The great questions relate to tempo and to method. Some argue that it is later than you think. Others say we are going faster than opinion and administrative skill warrant.

Our present party system provides the opportunity for both points of view to compete. Adjustment and compromise are the primary product if not the primary objective of our party system. This displeases both the idealist seeking a much better world and standpatters resisting all change.

A common point of disagreement concerning the nature of our party system arises over different assumptions as to the nature of democracy. One side sees it as a process based on a balance and consolidation of interests; another side sees it as a majority rule with relatively less regard to minority protests.

Our task is to keep politics both representative and integrated: a realization of this dual need is basic to the preservation of democracy. A poison fatal to government in terms of the values we cherish is the belief in an inevitable conflict within our society. A line of policy based on such assumptions leads to intransigence and ultimate breakdown. Such a bifurcation of interests, if it could be institutionalized in parties, would promote stalemate. Whether at a given time and in a given field of policy emphasis should be placed upon renovation or consolidation, depends upon the attitudes and relations among the group interests involved. The basic question is how both the continuity and the adjustment that are essential to the existence of a community can be maintained.

Progressives cannot always be right. Sometimes they are blazing the trail far ahead for the rest of mankind to follow; sometimes they are off on a false lead that could not be taken by all without disaster. Similarly, conservatism within a democratic society may mean stability at one time but rigidity at another. The theories of the left may contribute as much to inflexibility as the dogma of the right. Both sides know the doctrinaire mind.

To believers in democracy there are positive values in compromise and tolerance. Many present-day liberals express great impatience with a system that is not primarily suited to achieving their policies. Democracy may be as much endangered from the left as from the right, however. The conflict between the North and the South points to one way of settling a dispute. But no one could argue that a party of the North and a party of the South could have alternately governed the whole nation from Washington. Party government can function only when both parties seek to represent the whole nation and all classes.

Our task today and for the future is not to set up a system based alone on unskilled labor, or sharecroppers, or small businessmen, any more than it is to take as a basis the welfare of the bondholder or the great wheatgrower. Nor does the consumer alone represent the public interest. Men demand scope as managers, speculators, manipulators, entrepreneurs. These functions sometimes contribute greatly to the community and to the human personality. There can be no employee interest except as against that of the employer. Eliminate the employer and the wage-earner interest breaks up into many divergent parts.

We are witnessing today a fundamental change in the composition of politically effective forces. New groups are finding political and administrative representation in government. They are being sought by both parties. This is the politics of democracy and the path toward union.

How can we get democracy to work in terms of a balance of interests and still evolve public policy? Government, whether by party, president, or bureaucracy, must have a basis in some combination of group interests. These interests can be rationalized in various ideologies. I would defend the myth of the public interest because by its very vagueness it permits the freest interplay of group interests. The dominant combination at any one time can claim that its program expresses the public interest. Yet such a power combination is always contingent. Our loose party system offers an institutional framework suitable to this interplay of forces.

Can government meet the economic needs of the mass if it stops to win consent and compromise? It is argued that the mass is wedded to symbols obstructing action; that unless we cut away abruptly and act, the economic difficulties will ruin the political system of compromise; that national problems demand national thinking; that the weaknesses of federalism and a separation of powers are only too apparent.

In fact we are adapting our system to new needs. More and more we are shifting to a national point of view from sheer force of circumstance. We are facing a transition from a horizontal to a vertical basis of political power. Today political power is partly sectional, partly occupational. Economic organization brings in its train a different political configuration of forces. States' rights are discussed less, and class rights more. Our form of government based on a geographical mold is being readjusted to new conditions.

Our system admirably provides a flexible evolving basis for political power. Checks and balances in their true and original meaning were really a scheme for preventing dominance by any one economic or social class. The Founding Fathers feared factional and group interests—federalism, bicameralism, and our federal system were intended as partial safeguards.

It is well to remember that our scheme of government is an invention of the eighteenth century and that it reflects the values held uppermost by the political thinkers of that time. The members of the ruling group in this country and abroad then knew what they wanted to do—improve economic conditions, keep discontented elements as quiet as possible, and play off interests and appetites one against another. Crane Brinton very aptly suggests that "we cannot . . . in the fourth decade of the twentieth century afford to be too scornful of safety, stability, moderation, harmony, realism, conformity, even conventional good manners and other unromantic ways of adapting ourselves to one another's habits and limitations." He points out how we have aroused the expectation of the mass man. "We shall, indeed, be very lucky if we can get back to the world of values of the early eighteenth century, when the moon was not worth crying for." [4]

Man will not only cry for the moon but also reach for the stars, however, as the late eighteenth century discovered. No ruling clique, however sophisticated and moderate, can deny the will of others to rule in their turn. Aristocrats may cherish stability, but aristocratic government may become static rather than stable. This occurs when class institutions cut off the path of advancement to talent from below. Although the Founding Fathers feared rule by the masses, the Constitution has proved sufficiently flexible to move with the times.

Jeffersonian democracy was succeeded not only by Jacksonian democracy, asserting the right of all citizens to participate in the councils and administration of government, but also by the doctrine of laissez faire. Thus economic theory served to counteract the full effects of equalitarianism in government. Extreme democracy might assert that all men were equally privileged to hold office, but the doctrine of "every man a king" meant little so long as such kingship was in practice a do-nothing monarchy. Thus the effects of popular sovereignty were offset by the acceptance of laissez faire.

The validity of democratic assumptions was seldom questioned while we were attempting to develop this wide continent. The management of human affairs fell largely to those concerned with economic activities. Our elite exercised effective control in the management of industry. The dictates of liberalism were useful in enabling this elite to escape legal disabilities and to challenge those enjoying traditional privileges.

Before the Civil War slaveowners were the dominant interest in the federal government, just as afterwards industry asserted its authority. According to Edward S. Corwin, "the two minority interests which have left the deepest imprint on our constitutional law so far as national power is concerned are slavery and that fairly coherent group of interests which are commonly lumped together as 'Big Business.' " [5]

In addition to the industrialists, there was a clique of professional politicians. Sometimes they worked for industry and sometimes not. Other groups were able to pursue their interest without much direct reference to public policy. The politicos had a greater area of irresponsibility.

As we place greater burdens on the state, do we not necessitate the creation of something very like the corporative state? In the United States the answer, if we are to seek it in democratic terms, will come through preserving in our system all that makes for a continuing adjustment. Democratic government has no final institutional forms; no set of slogans embraces its values; no one combination of interests is determinant. Through its denial of authoritarianism, however, democratic control provides an ideology most conducive to human expression and development.

Totalitarian states preach the myth of self-identification of the individual with one organic whole. If democracy means anything, it means the denial of this creed and the assertion of a faith in the individual and his capacity to adapt the environment to his needs and aspirations. This too is a myth and even an idle dream unless ways and means can be found for its realization. We are discovering that in the face of unemployment and hunger men lose faith in institutions that tolerate such suffering. Suffering, however, need not lead merely to disillusionment; it may also lead to inventiveness and readjustment. Invention cannot be confined to new formulae and slogans but must extend to ways and means of achieving concrete satisfactions.

What philosophic view of the state is most compatible with the politics of democracy? The answer to this must be sought in the main currents of American political thought. While this broad river cannot be explored here, we may note the few assumptions most germane to our argument, namely, the supreme worth of the individual, a government of limited powers, and the experimental attitude. The precise application of these values in concrete instances may lead to debate, but their influence as rationales of behavior is clearly observable. They are basic factors in what Gaetano Mosca would call the "level of civilization" in this country.

Thomas Jefferson, Ralph Waldo Emerson, Henry David Thoreau, William Ellery Channing, Walt Whitman, William James, Charles Beard, Justice Louis D. Brandeis, and Justice Oliver Wendell Holmes have reflected in their different ways these values of American life. They suggest the ideological stuff with which we can work, since their philosophies reflect the attitudes deep-grained in American culture. Our heritage of "experimentation and opportunism" as "the animating spirit of American progress" is joined with a tradition of individual self-reliance and distaste for rulers. It leads to a view of the state admirably summarized by Professor Alpheus Mason as follows:

"There are limits to what government in a democracy can undertake. If men are to be free and democracy to prevail, the functions of government must be shared by many political divisions and functionaries, as well as by non-governmental bodies such as trade unions and co-operative associations. . . . For these are the crucibles whence public opinion emerges, these are the dynamos whence flows the voltage to inspire and control the democratic state. All such bodies provide great forums of discussion and debate, as in ancient Greece and modern Switzerland. To join these voluntary bodies, to participate in their life, to come out into the open and support their chosen purposes, is the effective means whereby the individual grows and fits himself for citizenship." [6]

This creed may not prove workable, but we cannot hope for a new one overnight. We have seen the weaknesses of this view of the state; we have savored also its potentialities. Other political views of statehood more militant and positive we know in this country largely as theories. The results of concentrated authority we can witness abroad and ponder in history.

Mosca has stressed the fact that a conflict of interests seems essential to the preservation of conditions appropriate to political liberty:

"So far in history, freedom to think, to observe, to judge men and things serenely and dispassionately, has been possible—always be it understood, for a few individuals—only in those societies in which numbers of different religious and political currents have been struggling for dominion. . . . In fact, in societies where choice among a number of religious and political currents has ceased to be possible because one such current has succeeded in gaining exclusive control, the isolated and original thinker has to be silent, and moral and intellectual monopoly is infallibly associated with political monopoly, to the advantage of a caste or of a very few social forces." [7]

The liberal can never know the comfort that comes to the true believer who bases his faith on an identification of the public interest with particular classes or institutions and then projects this picture into the future. This is the easy road, but it leads to dogmatism and ends in that bitterest conflict—the battle between true believers.

After long travail men separated church and state. Now, with the economic and political realms becoming merged, another war of isms is threatening. The symbols and the traditions of liberalism offer a means for avoiding internecine struggle. Practical-minded men are not easily led to adopt new beliefs. Deep suffering and heroic intelligence combined with extraordinarily favorable economic conditions brought men finally to accept and later to take for granted the tolerance of difference preached by liberalism and practiced under the politics of democracy. It is a legacy not to be lightly dismissed.

The price of political continuity and peaceful adjustment is the readaptation of institutions and ideals to new needs. The assumption throughout this analysis has been that we are ready to pay this price. It is conceivable that a brave new world might be had if we could manage a clean break with the past and all its clinging tendrils of emotional loyalties, fixed habits, and illogicalities. Yet peaceful change means piecemeal changes—with no surety whatsoever that reform can outdistance disaster. Meanwhile, democracy imposes the ironic insistence that the men who hear time's winged chariot drawing near co-operate with the descendants of those men who at the time of the world's creation looked backward and cried, "Let us preserve chaos." Democracy has been possible in the face of such differences of opinion because the great mass of men have been content to cultivate their gardens. All that such men asked of government was to be let alone. When denied this and confronted by such tragic upheaval as befell the tenant farmers in the Dust Bowl, they question rather than repudiate:

> "We wonder if the liberty is done:
> The dreaming is finished
> We can't say
> We aren't sure . . .
> Or if there's something different men can dream . . .
> Or if there's something different men can mean by Liberty.
> We wonder
> We don't know
> We're asking. . . ." [8]

They cannot long endure without an answer. The suspended judgment of the poor in a land of plenty will be precipitated, and the pattern it takes will be fateful. Democratic government gives us all a share in its crystallization. The real task today is to keep our ideals and institutions meaningful for the diverse interests of society. The grapes of wrath are sown where such meaning is lost. The need cannot be met by saying that the present structure must be scrapped or that it must be kept intact. The doctrinaire approach is useless: patience, subtlety, and imagination are required. Inventiveness is limited by the bounds of political practicality; nevertheless we know that institutions and ideals can be altered and different configurations of interest evolved.

Despite the many petty irrationalities in human behavior and the reluctance to change habitual modes of conduct, men require an environment that has meaning. Peter Drucker goes so far as to argue that where they cannot find meaning in their society through rational concepts, they are forced to accept irrational explanations in order to find some "reasons" for the conditions about them:

> "The individual does not care whether the forces which govern society have become irrational or whether it is the breakdown of his own rational concept of society which deprives them of their rational

function. The fact that the world has no order and follows no laws is all that is important to him." [9]

Drucker argues that "the despair of the masses is the key to the understanding of fascism," not the "revolt of the mob" nor the "triumph of unscrupulous propaganda, but stark despair caused by the breakdown of the old order, and the absence of a new one." [10] It is worth noting that renewed interest in occupational representation and the corporative state arises where the existing system of representation is distrusted and parties are thought slow in responding to social needs. Functional representation came to the fore under the Weimar Constitution; a neocorporativism arose in France during the critical time after 1934; and the push for an economic council was strongest in the United States just before the coming of the New Deal. When men lose faith in existing institutions, they seek substitutes.

The politics of democracy does not flourish on plebiscites, mandates, and disciplined parties bent upon the realization of an announced program. Its strength lies in the multiplicity of avenues of communication between the citizen and the state. The principle of minority protection is as essential for the maintenance of fundamental liberties as is the doctrine of majority rule. The two values may at times compete. The politics of democracy can prevent an impasse by keeping open and extending all channels that promote the continuous permeation of consent and the circulation of social impulses between ruler and ruled. It is unwise to dam up these currents in the hope of using their force for drastic change. Purgings and bloodlettings are bad therapy.

That men both agree and disagree over questions of government gives rise to the struggles we call political. Where they can agree to disagree we have the politics of democracy. Our present party system is based on this mutual toleration of dissent. Here prophets may forecast disaster, scientists may experiment, partisans may squabble, and reformers may offer solutions and panaceas without fear of the chopping block. The verdict is left to time. Meanwhile, some tell us that the public interest demands the general acceptance of some one political doctrine such as socialism or constitutionalism, or some institutional structure such as parliamentarianism or the separation of powers. Others insist that public policy must be based on a recognition of the paramount interests of the consumer, or of business, or of labor, or of agriculture, or of various combinations thereof.

This tendency to identify one's own values and interests with the common welfare is as old as government. Men have defended to the death the doctrine of the divine right of the king or the supremacy of the papacy. They have fought and died over the institutions of democratic Athens, republican Rome, and feudal Europe. As Spartacus, Wat Tyler, and Karl Marx dreamed of political authority based on the interests of the underdog, middle-class and aristocratic and military statesmen have been equally confident that their "power-base" of interests could be identified with the ultimate welfare of their respective societies.

Does the politics of democracy differ in this respect from the politics of monarchy or of communism or of fascism? All of these doctrines in their own ways assert that their ultimate goal is the security and stability of their society. The creed of democracy, however, does not demand, as an act of faith, belief in any one pattern of interests or institutions. Writers and leaders are free to offer their plans for action or their competing theories. Officially there is no one positive way of life—though law sets formal restrictions to misbehavior and custom or economic necessity binds us still more closely. Within these limitations our current ideology of democracy leaves us free to face the fundamental questions of justice and the good life raised by Plato. His dogmatic solution has proved as ineffective as the dreams of many other philosophers; but men continue to insist that each in his generation has the answer. Lo! this is the road to salvation—or there lies the New Jerusalem! Today we are still in an era wherein for a few decades man has been free to take an agnostic view toward the purpose of the state. At the same time as Jacques Barzun remarks: "The man who has at last got hold of THE truth can live among the infidels if his intelligence is as strong as his faith." [11]

The faith of democracy, for all its shibboleths and hypocrisies, is still based on the fundamental tenet that society can continue peacefully even though men agree to disagree. Out of this one attitude we may be able to make the continuing adjustments to each other and to our environment that are inevitable in any social process but which have seldom been accomplished in the past through methods short of violence.

To the extent that the individual has found an opportunity to realize his potentialities, our civilization has advanced. Through this process our culture has slowly reached the point where individual differences of opinion are tolerated even in politics. This has been a long and painful journey, and our present vantage point is not to be lightly relinquished. This heritage is not only denied in totalitarian countries: it is also treated with impatience in democratic countries by men who are eager to realize their view of the good life. They would have their followers close ranks in militant formation against the "economic oligarchs," "incipient fascists," or "subversive elements" who disagree with them. Yet for all its alleged clumsiness and ineptitude, the democratic process is the only path at present discernible for those who value peaceful change and cultural continuity.

The concept which seems most suited to a society of conflicting aims is tolerance. All political struggle is based on a clash of interests or ideals. This conflict is intensified when men insist that their view alone should prevail. Accordingly, men holding to various views of the good life must be willing to compromise on occasion so as to maintain the privilege of advancing their views in competition with other rival views. We, of course, have no guarantee that men will continue to acknowledge this higher loyalty, but through an understanding of its meaning it may possibly be preserved. Adjustment cannot arouse our enthusiasm as an end in itself; but the conditions that it makes possible are worthy of our strongest loyalties. Tolerance of belief or disbelief is basic not only to science but also to the full use of intelligence in the direction of human affairs. Any political or economic purpose which sacrifices this ideal to more immediate ends threatens violent consequences that men have habitually insisted are bad.

This is not to deny that men are easily aroused to resistance when their desires are balked. The liberal democratic tradition persuades its adherents of the validity of a certain procedure for the reconciling of differences. It promises that loyalty to this procedure means the satisfaction of one's more pressing needs at least, through reasonable compromise with the needs of others. In this way social continuity can be preserved. The whole process is a gamble, since we can tell only through trial and error whether we are maintaining the balance of forces necessary for its preservation. Only by experimentation can we know whether the institutional framework is adequate. Only by faith can we feel confident that democracy is any better than other conceptual schemes in the long train of human ideals.

Today our system is endangered by attacks from both the right and the left. This book, by showing how the politics of democracy operates, may serve in some measure to stimulate a new appreciation of its meaning. Some readers may find too much agnosticism in the analysis offered here. Yet what is appropriate to diagnosis may be very inappropriate to a call for action. If we hope to avoid the suffering of violent disruption, we must ever seek a closer relationship between our pressing social needs and our picture world of aspirations, and we must ever scrutinize the adequacy of existing institutions to this end.

The democratic way lies not in the preservation of any fixed set of institutions nor in rule by any one set of interests, but in the constant readaptation of ideals and organizations to answer emerging social demands. No majority is final; the possibility of remaking the pattern of controlling interests must always remain open. The adaptation of man to his environment and the alteration of his surroundings to his desires is the dual struggle of mankind. Democracy as a creed does not deny this inescapable necessity. Although it is capable of much flexibility, men persistently try to identify it with certain interests, institutions, or subjective values of their own.

Democracy provides an ideology conducive to criticism, experimentation, and change. Our parties are perhaps to be judged finally in terms of their contribution to this flexibility. Herein lies their value rather than in the realization of one view as to what society should be. Our present two-party system, with all its flaws, remains a useful implement for democracy.

The practical problem is to discover such a pace of alteration as will enable men to change together through the common sense of conviction resulting from discussion and consent. This is not to preach complacency. Never were the dangers greater, the speed of transition higher, or the demands on forethought and tolerance heavier. The realistic democratic statesman, however, cannot follow Emerson's injunction, "Hitch your wagon to a star." More appropriate for political leadership is the example of the poet who hitched his wagon to a horse: he kept perforce to the middle of the road and his speed was set by the endurance of vital flesh and blood. Tempted to linger in the twilight, he bestirred himself:

> "For I have promises to keep
> And miles to go before I sleep."

Footnotes

CHAPTER I

FOOTNOTE

1 Henry Adams, *The Education of Henry Adams*, New York, The Book League of America, 1928, p. 33.

2 *Ibid.*

3 William James, *Memories and Studies*, New York, Longmans, Green & Co., 1911, p. 316.

4 Maury Maverick, *Blood and Ink*, New York, Modern Age Books, Inc., 1939.

5 Frederic C. Howe, *The Confessions of a Reformer*, New York, Charles Scribner's Sons, 1925, p. 59.

6 *Time*, July 22, 1935, p. 39.

7 See the interesting lectures by Robert Moses in which he discusses the gap between the theoretical and the practical aspects of politics. *Theory and Practice in Politics*, Cambridge, Harvard University Press, 1939.

8 See Max Ascoli, "On Political Parties," *Social Research*, I, 2, p. 203.

9 William B. Munro, "Physics and Politics," *The American Political Science Review*, XXII, 1, 1928, p. 7.

10 *Ibid.*, pp. 4–5.

11 Lincoln Steffens, *Autobiography*, New York, Harcourt, Brace & Co., 1931, p. 618.

CHAPTER II

1 See Crane Brinton, *The Lives of Talleyrand*, New York, W. W. Norton & Co., Inc., 1936. Especially chapters 1, 7, and 8.

2 Charles E. Merriam, *The Role of Politics in Social Change*, New York, New York University Press, 1936, p. 26.

437

FOOTNOTE

3 K. Smellie, *The American Federal System*, London, Williams & Norgate, Ltd., 1928, p. 3.

4 R. S. and Helen Lynd, *Middletown in Transition*, New York, Harcourt, Brace & Co., 1937. See chapter IX, "The Machinery of Government," and chapter XII, "The Middletown Spirit."

5 See Charles E. Merriam, "Government and Society," in *Recent Social Trends*, New York, Whittlesey House, 1933, p. 1511.

6 Arthur N. Holcombe, *The New Party Politics*, New York, W. W. Norton & Co., Inc., 1933, p. 128.

7 Loan Association *v.* Topeka, 20 Wallace, p. 655.

CHAPTER III

1 See Alfred M. Bingham, *Insurgent America*, New York, W. W. Norton & Co., Inc., 1938, and Arthur N. Holcombe, *op. cit.*

2 André Siegfried, *France, A Study of Nationality*, New Haven, Yale University Press, 1930, p. 93.

3 J. A. Spender, *The Public Life*, London, Cassell, 1925, II, p. 33.

4 Walter R. Sharp, "Public Personnel Management in France," in *Civil Service Abroad*, a publication of the Commission of Inquiry on Public Service Personnel, New York, McGraw-Hill Book Co., Inc., 1935, p. 83.

5 *Ibid.*, p. 84.

6 W. L. Middleton, *The French Political System*, New York, E. P. Dutton & Co., 1933, p. 63.

7 William Edward Hartpole Lecky, *Democracy and Liberty*, New York, Longmans, Green & Co., 1903, I, p. xiii.

8 *Ibid.*, p. 235.

9 Arthur N. Holcombe, *op. cit.*, pp. 115–117.

10 Harold J. Laski, *Parliamentary Government in England*, New York, The Viking Press, 1938, p. 165.

11 *The Wisdom of Confucius*, New York, The Modern Library, 1938 (Everyman's edition), p. 200.

12 Max Ascoli and Arthur Feiler, *Fascism For Whom?*, New York, W. W. Norton & Co., Inc., 1938, p. 14.

13 Peter F. Drucker, *The End of Economic Man, A Study of the New Totalitarianism*, New York, The John Day Co., 1939, p. 120.

14 *Ibid.*, p. 124.
See also Albert C. Grzesinski, *Inside Germany*, New York, E. P. Dutton & Co., 1939. "German democracy, as it emerged in 1918, was only an empty shell," he says. "The changes that had taken place and that seemed so far-reaching, were merely outward changes. They failed to turn the German into a true democratic and liberty-loving citizen."

15 E. B. Ashton, *The Fascist—His State and Mind*, New York, William Morrow & Co., 1937, pp. 82–83.

FOOTNOTE

16   *Ibid.*, pp. 61–62.

17   *Ibid.*, p. 64.

18   See the following on the concept of the "gentleman" in public service:
John Gaus, *Great Britain: A Study of Civic Loyalty*, Chicago, University
of Chicago Press, 1929.
Wilhelm Dibelius, *England*, New York, Harper & Bros., 1930, pp. 164 *ff*.
Anthony Trollope, *An Autobiography*, London, Shakespeare Head Press,
1929, p. 29. Also H. J. Laski, *The Danger of Being a Gentleman*, 1940.

19   Peter F. Drucker, *op. cit.*, p. 145.

20   *Ibid.*, p. 118.

21   Carlton J. H. Hayes, *Essays on Nationalism*, New York, The Macmillan
Co., 1928, p. 51.

CHAPTER IV

1   James Truslow Adams, *The Adams Family*, Boston, Little, Brown & Co.,
1930, pp. 94–95.

2   See also the conditions that a real democratic statesman must fulfill in the
opinion of Eduard Beneš, *Democracy Today and Tomorrow*, New York,
The Macmillan Co., 1939.

3   See Henry Jones Ford, *The Rise and Growth of American Politics*, New
York, The Macmillan Co., 1914, p. 11.

4   *Messages and Papers of the Presidents*, 1789–1817, Washington, Government Printing Office, 1896, I, p. 215.

5   *Ibid.*, p. 219.

6   *Ibid.*, p. 218.

7   James Madison, *The Federalist*, New York, E. P. Dutton & Co., 1911
(Everyman's edition), No. X, p. 41.

8   *Ibid.*, p. 47.

9   *Messages and Papers of the Presidents* (see note 4, above), p. 322.

10   Edgar E. Robinson, *The Evolution of American Political Parties*, New
York, Harcourt, Brace & Co., 1924, p. 80.

CHAPTER V

1   B. F. Wright, "Traditionalism in American Political Thought," *International Journal of Ethics*, October, 1937, p. 88.

2   H. A. Washington (ed.), *The Writings of Thomas Jefferson*, Washington,
Taylor & Maury, 1854, IV, p. 246 and p. 562 for Adams Letter.

3   *Ibid.*, VII, p. 376.

4   Henry Jones Ford, *op. cit.*, p. 131.

5   Frank R. Kent, *The Democratic Party*, New York, D. Appleton-Century
Co., Inc., 1928, p. 83.

FOOTNOTE

6   Jesse Macy, *Political Parties in the United States, 1846–1861*, New York, The Macmillan Co., 1900, pp. 32–33.

7   Herbert Agar, *Pursuit of Happiness*, Cambridge, Houghton Mifflin Co., The Riverside Press, 1938, p. 67.

8   James Parton, *The Life of Andrew Jackson*, New York, Mason Bros., 1860, II, pp. 360–361.

9   *Ibid.*, p. 362.

10   *Messages and Papers of the Presidents*, 1789–1897, Washington, Government Printing Office, 1896, II, p. 294. Inaugural Address of John Quincy Adams, March 4, 1825.

11   Claude G. Bowers, *Party Battles of the Jackson Period*, Boston, Houghton Mifflin Co., 1922, pp. 64–65.

12   James Bryce, *The American Commonwealth*, New York, The Commonwealth Publishing Co., 1908, I, p. 92.

13   Lord Charnwood, *Abraham Lincoln*, London, Constable & Co., Ltd., 1917, p. 167.

14   *Ibid.*, p. 168.

15   Richard K. Cralle (ed.), *The Works of John C. Calhoun*, New York, D. Appleton & Co., 1853, I, p. 306.

CHAPTER VI

1   George Boas, "A Defense of Democracy," *Harper's Magazine*, September, 1934, p. 421.

2   Walter Lippmann, *A Preface to Politics*, New York, The Macmillan Co., 1933 edition, pp. 282–283.

3   Quoted by Irving Babbitt, *Democracy and Leadership*, Cambridge, Houghton Mifflin Co., The Riverside Press, 1929, p. 112.

4   James Madison, *op. cit.*, pp. 43–44.

5   *Ibid.*, pp. 45–46.

6   Herbert Agar, *op. cit.*, p. 200.

7   *Ibid.*, p. 199.

8   *Ibid.*, p. 197.

9   Max Lerner, *It Is Later Than You Think*, New York, The Viking Press, 1938, p. 238.

10   Francis Delaisi, *Political Myths and Economic Realities*, New York, The Viking Press, 1927, p. 53.

11   *Ibid.*, p. 68.

12   C. J. Friedrich, "One Majority Against Another: Populus Sempervirens," *The Southern Review*, Summer, 1939, p. 51.

CHAPTER VII

FOOTNOTE

1 Henry Jones Ford, *op. cit.*, pp. 128–129.

2 Graham Wallas, *Human Nature in Politics*, New York, F. S. Crofts & Co., 1921, pp. 103–104.

3 Walter Edward Weyl, *The New Democracy*, New York, The Macmillan Co., 1912, pp. 60–61.

4 Walter Lippmann, "Birds of a Feather," *Harper's Magazine*, March, 1925, p. 411.

5 Frank J. Goodnow, *Politics and Administration*, New York, The Macmillan Co., 1900, pp. 197–198.

6 W. Ivor Jennings, *Cabinet Government*, London, Macmillan & Co., Ltd., 1936, pp. 389–390.

7 Cecil S. Emden, *The People and the Constitution*, London, Oxford University Press, 1933, p. 295.

CHAPTER VIII

1 David Cushman Coyle, "The American Way," *Harper's Magazine*, February, 1938, pp. 232–233.

2 Arthur N. Holcombe, *The Political Parties of Today*, New York, Harper & Bros., 1925 (second edition), chapter II.

3 Andrew C. McLaughlin, *A Constitutional History of the United States*, New York, D. Appleton-Century Co., Inc., 1935 (Student's edition), pp. 403, 402.

4 Arthur Twining Hadley, *Freedom and Responsibility*, New York, Charles Scribner's Sons, 1903, pp. 19–20.

5 John Dickinson, "Democratic Realities and Democratic Dogma," *The American Political Science Review*, May, 1930, p. 298.

6 John Dewey, *The Public and Its Problems*, New York, Henry Holt & Co., 1927, p. 120.

7 Walter Edward Weyl, *op. cit.*, p. 56.

8 Allen Johnson, "The Nationalizing Influence of Party," *The Yale Review*, November, 1906, p. 287.

9 For an excellent discussion of such books see Donald Wallace, "Industrial Markets and Public Policy" in *Public Policy*, Cambridge, Harvard University Press, 1940.

10 See Charles Beard, *Economic Interpretation of the Constitution*, New York, The Macmillan Co., 1929.

11 William Allen White, *Masks in a Pageant*, New York, The Macmillan Co., 1928, pp. 292–293.

FOOTNOTE

12 Charles and Mary Beard, *The Rise of American Civilization*, New York, The Macmillan Co., 1930, II, p. 302.

13 *Ibid.*, p. 295.

14 See Peter H. Odegard and E. Allen Helms, *American Politics, A Study in Political Dynamics* (New York, Harper & Bros., 1938), for an interesting discussion of The Politics of Business, chapter IX.

CHAPTER IX

1 William Ernest Hocking, *Man and the State*, New Haven, Yale University Press, 1926, p. 13.

2 T. V. Smith, *The Promise of American Politics*, Chicago, University of Chicago Press, 1936, p. 248.

3 See the admirable essay by J. T. Salter, "The Politician and the Voter," in *The American Political Scene*, Edward B. Logan (ed.), New York, Harper & Bros., 1938 (revised edition).

4 See John Bright, *Hizzoner Big Bill Thompson*, New York, Jonathan Cape & Harrison Smith, 1930.

5 For extraordinarily interesting accounts of Chicago politics see Charles E. Merriam, *Chicago*, New York, The Macmillan Co., 1929; Harold F. Gosnell, *Machine Politics: Chicago Model*, Chicago, University of Chicago Press, 1937; and Harold F. Gosnell, *Negro Politicians: The Rise of Negro Politics in Chicago*, Chicago, University of Chicago Press, 1935.

6 Alva Johnston, "The Scandals of New York," *Harper's Magazine*, March, 1931, p. 411.

7 *Ibid.*

8 James A. Hagerty, New York *Times*, May 28, 1939, p. 6 E.

9 Harold F. Gosnell, *Machine Politics: Chicago Model*, p. 185.

CHAPTER X

1 "The Kelly-Nash Political Machine," *Fortune*, August, 1936, p. 126.

2 *Ibid.*, p. 130.

3 Brand Whitlock, *Forty Years of It*, New York, D. Appleton & Co., 1925, pp. 217–218.

4 Max Ascoli, *Intelligence in Politics*, New York, W. W. Norton & Co., Inc., 1936, p. 111.

5 E. Simon, *A City Council from Within*, New York, Longmans, Green & Co., 1926, pp. 162–163.

6 William L. Riordon, *Plunkitt of Tammany Hall*, New York, McClure, Phillips & Co., 1905, p. 4.

7 Harold Zink, *City Bosses in the United States*, Durham, Duke University Press, 1930, pp. 37–38.

FOOTNOTE

8   William Anderson, *American City Government*, New York, Henry Holt
    & Co., 1925, p. 646.

9   F. S. Oliver, *The Endless Adventure*, Boston, Houghton Mifflin Co., 1931,
    p. 110.

CHAPTER XI

1   *An Economic Program for American Democracy by Seven Harvard and
    Tufts Economists:* Gilbert, *et al.*, New York, The Vanguard Press, 1938,
    pp. 32–33.

2   See Alvin H. Hansen, *Full Recovery or Stagnation?*, New York, W. W.
    Norton & Co., Inc., 1938, and "Economic Progress and Declining Popula-
    tion Growth," *The American Economic Review*, March, 1939.

3   Wesley Clair Mitchell, "Intelligence and the Guidance of Economic Evo-
    lution," in *Authority and the Individual*, Cambridge, Harvard Tercente-
    nary Publications, Harvard University Press, 1937, p. 26.

4   See Morgan's creed in Frederick Lewis Allen's *Lords of Creation*, New
    York, Harper & Bros., 1935.

5   Alvin H. Hansen, "Economic Progress and Declining Population Growth,"
    p. 13.

6   Douglas Berry Copeland, "The State and the Entrepreneur," in *Authority
    and the Individual*, Cambridge, Harvard Tercentenary Publications, Har-
    vard University Press, 1937, p. 50.

7   Charles A. Beard, "Roosevelt's Place in History," *Events*, February, 1938,
    p. 84.

CHAPTER XII

1   Philip Taft, "Labor's Changing Political Line," *The Journal of Political
    Economy*, October, 1937.

2   From a pamphlet, "Wanted: A New Alignment in American Politics," is-
    sued by the League of Independent Political Action, New York.

3   A. L. Rowse, *Politics and the Younger Generation*, London, Faber & Faber,
    Ltd., 1931, p. 76.

CHAPTER XIII

1   Sidney and Beatrice Webb, *The History of Trade Unionism*, New York,
    Longmans, Green & Co., 1926 (revised edition, extended to 1920), p. 632.

2   Frederick E. Haynes, *Third Party Movements*, Iowa City, State Historical
    Society of Iowa, 1916, p. 2.

3   *Ibid.*, p. 3.

4   Kirk H. Porter, *National Party Platforms*, New York, The Macmillan
    Co., 1924, p. 179.

5   John D. Hicks, "The Third Party Tradition in American Politics," *Mis-
    sissippi Valley Historical Review*, June, 1933, pp. 27–28.

FOOTNOTE

6   *American Messiahs*, by the Unofficial Observer, New York, Simon & Schuster, 1935, p. 156.

7   See John D. Hicks, *The Populist Revolt*, Minneapolis, University of Minnesota Press, 1931, p. 239.

8   George W. Bergquist, "The Dilemma of the Farmer-Labor Party," *Public Opinion Quarterly*, July, 1939, p. 480.

9   See *The Townsend Crusade*, New York, The Committee on Old Age Security of the Twentieth Century Fund, Inc., 1936.

10   Walter Lippmann, *A Preface to Politics*, pp. 258–259.

11   Henry Steele Commager, New York *Times Magazine*, September 4, 1938, p. 15.

CHAPTER XIV

1   Heywood Broun, in his column during June, 1938.

2   Denis Brogan, *Government of the People*, New York, Harper & Bros., 1933, p. 384.

3   Arthur Vandenberg, New York *Herald Tribune*, December 30, 1934.

4   Gallup Poll, October 19, 1938, release.

5   G. W. Hartman, "Party Names and Public Response," *Journal of Social Psychology*, May, 1936, p. 352.

6   Remarks of the Hon. Robert G. Allen in House of Representatives, Monday, August 16, 1937, on Industrial Expansion Act.

7   Wilhelm Dibelius, *op. cit.*, p. 195.

8   Gardner Murphy and Rensis Likert, *Public Opinion and the Individual*, New York, Harper & Bros., 1938, p. 111.

CHAPTER XV

1   New York *Times*, fall of 1936.

2   See *Fortune*, August, 1936, for an excellent discussion. See also James A. Farley, *Behind the Ballots*, New York, Harcourt, Brace & Co., 1938, chapter II.

3   Arthur N. Holcombe, *The Political Parties of Today*, 1924 edition, p. 115.

4   James K. Pollock, "British Party Organizations," *Political Science Quarterly*, June, 1930, p. 163.

5   Herman Finer, *The Theory and Practice of Modern Government*, New York, Dial Press, 1932, p. 421.

6   James K. Pollock, *op. cit.*, pp. 161–181. See also Pollock's "The British Party Conference," *The American Political Science Review*, June, 1938, p. 525, and Joseph R. Starr's articles on British parties in *The American Political Science Review*, October, 1936, and August, 1937.

7   James K. Pollock, "British Party Organizations," p. 167.

8   *Ibid.*, pp. 171–172.

9 *Ibid.*, pp. 169–170.

10 *Ibid.*, p. 180.

11 Marquis James, *Andrew Jackson, Portrait of a President*, New York, Bobbs-Merrill Co., 1937, pp. 26–27.

12 From *Barnes* v. *Roosevelt*, case on appeal, appellate division, 4th Department (New York Supreme Court), p. 1316. Quoted in Harold F. Gosnell, *Boss Platt and His New York Machine*, Chicago, University of Chicago Press, 1924, p. 343.

13 New York *Times*, August 15, 1918, p. 10.

14 Joseph P. Tumulty, *Woodrow Wilson as I Know Him*, New York, Doubleday, Doran & Co., Inc., 1925, p. 330.

15 William E. Dodd, *Woodrow Wilson and His Work*, New York, Doubleday, Page & Co., 1920, chapters 12–13.

16 Henry N. Dorris, New York *Times*, July 30, 1939, p. 7 E.

17 *Ibid.*

CHAPTER XVI

1 Herbert Agar, *op. cit.*, p. 132.

2 M. Ostrogorski, *Democracy and the Organization of Political Parties*, New York, The Macmillan Co., 1902, II, p. 279.

3 James A. Farley, "Selling Roosevelt to the Party," *The American Magazine*, August, 1938, p. 107; see also James A. Farley, *Behind the Ballots*. See also Simeon Strunsky, *The Living Heritage, Change and America* (New York, Doubleday, Doran & Co., 1939), chapter XIX, for an interesting interpretation of party conventions.

4 James Bryce, *op. cit.*, II, pp. 235–237.

5 James A. Farley, "Selling Roosevelt to the Party," p. 98; see also James A. Farley, *Behind the Ballots*.

6 Official Proceedings of the Democratic National Convention, Chicago, 1932, p. 326.

7 See Thomas C. Donnelly and Roy V. Peel, *The 1928 Campaign*, New York, Richard R. Smith, Inc., 1931, p. 27.

8 Harold R. Bruce, *American Parties and Politics*, New York, Henry Holt & Co., 1936 (third edition), p. 357, in New York *Times* of June 28, 1924.

9 Edward M. Sait, "New Parties for Old," *The Forum*, November, 1931, p. 316.

10 Walter Lippmann, *A Preface to Politics*, p. 290.

11 Harry Barnard, *Eagle Forgotten*, the life of John Peter Altgeld, New York, Bobbs-Merrill Co., 1938, pp. 359–360.

12 André Siegfried, *America Comes of Age*, New York, Harcourt, Brace & Co., 1927, p. 247.

13 Robert Luce, *Legislative Procedure*, Boston, Houghton Mifflin Co., 1922, p. 504.

FOOTNOTE

14 John W. Davis, *Party Government in the United States*, Princeton, Princeton University Press, pp. 43–44.

15 James A. Farley, *Behind the Ballots*, p. 128.

16 See Phillips Bradley, "Our Bankrupt Conventions," *The American Review*, III, pp. 153–162; Charles E. Merriam and Louise Overacker, *Primary Elections*, Chicago, University of Chicago Press, 1928; and Ralph Boots, *National Municipal Review*, X, 1921, p. 23, and VIII, 1919, p. 472.

CHAPTER XVII

1 Walter Lippmann, *A Preface to Politics*, p. 259.

2 See Charles E. Merriam and Harold F. Gosnell, *The American Party System*, New York, The Macmillan Co., 1929 (revised edition), p. 301.

3 See Herman Finer, *op. cit.*, pp. 484 and 486.

4 C. A. H. Thomson, "Research and the Republican Party," *The Public Opinion Quarterly*, April, 1939, p. 306.

5 Arthur N. Holcombe, "Present Day Characteristics of American Political Parties," in *The American Political Scene*, New York, Harper & Bros., 1936, p. 2.

6 Edgar E. Robinson, *The Presidential Vote, 1896–1932*, California, Stanford University Press, 1934, pp. 33–34.

7 Jonathan Swift, *Gulliver's Travels*, New York, The Modern Library, 1931, p. 216.

CHAPTER XVIII

1 Herbert Hoover, "Undermining Representative Government." An address delivered to Joint Republican Organizations, Hartford, Connecticut, October 17, 1938.

2 James Truslow Adams, "Our Whispering Campaigns," in *Harper's Magazine*, September, 1932, pp. 447–448.

3 Francis P. Garvan, *Fair Play for Him that Overcometh*, p. 9 (pamphlet).

4 See Frank R. Kent, *Political Behavior*, New York, William Morrow & Co., 1928, p. 151.

5 Peter Odegard, *The American Public Mind*, New York, Columbia University Press, 1930, pp. 160–161.

6 Thurman W. Arnold, *The Symbols of Government*, New Haven, Yale University Press, 1935, pp. 27–28.

7 Drew Pearson and Robert S. Allen, "Political Techniques," from the *Redbook*, in *Review of Reviews*, September, 1926, p. 72.

8 James A. Farley, *Behind the Ballots*, pp. 192–193.

9 *Ibid.*, pp. 319–320.

10 *Review of Reviews*, October, 1928, p. 341.

FOOTNOTE

11 Edward L. Bernays, *Propaganda*, New York, Liveright Pub. Corp., 1928, p. 105.

12 *Ibid.*, p. 102.

13 Francis G. Wilson, *The Elements of Modern Politics*, New York, McGraw-Hill Book Co., Inc., 1936, p. 287.

CHAPTER XIX

1 Edward L. Bernays, *op. cit.*, p. 104.

2 Frederick E. Lumley, *The Propaganda Menace*, New York, The Century Co., 1933; see chapter XV.

3 Leonard W. Doob, *Propaganda*, New York, Henry Holt & Co., 1935, p. 406.

4 "Democratic Strategy Is Told by Michelson," New York *Times*, November 15, 1936, p. 10 E.

5 "The Democratic Party," *Fortune*, April, 1935, p. 136.

6 Ralph D. Casey, "Republican Propaganda in the 1936 Campaign," *Public Opinion Quarterly*, April, 1937, p. 42.

7 *Ibid.*, p. 32.

8 "Democratic Strategy Is Told by Michelson" (see note 4, above).

9 George Gallup, *Public Opinion in a Democracy*, published under the University Extension Fund, Herbert L. Baker Foundation, Princeton University, 1939, p. 14.

10 See *The Fine Art of Propaganda*, edited by Alfred McClung Lee and Elizabeth Briant Lee, New York, Harcourt, Brace & Co., 1939, p. 5.

11 See, for example, New York *Times Magazine Section*, November 26, 1939, p. 1, article by R. E. Turpin, "Democracy Is at Work," and November 5, 1939, p. 5, article by L. H. Robbins, "I Should Like to Ask the Speaker."

12 Jonathan Swift, "A Voyage to Brobdingnag," in *Gulliver's Travels*, New York, The Modern Library, 1931, p. 153.

CHAPTER XX

1 A. L. Lowell, "An Example from the Evidence of History," in *Factors Determining Human Behavior*, Cambridge, Harvard University Press, 1937, pp. 129–130.

2 Karl Mannheim, *Ideology and Utopia*, New York, Harcourt, Brace & Co., 1936, pp. xxiii–xxiv.

3 L. J. Henderson, Lecture III, Introductory Lectures (not yet published), p. 46. See also George C. Homans and Charles P. Curtis, Jr., *An Introduction to Pareto*, New York, Alfred A. Knopf, 1934, p. 34.

4 Wassily Leontief, "The Economics Department Replies," *The Harvard Progressive*, March, 1939, p. 15.

FOOTNOTE

5 Erasmus, *In Praise of Folly*, London, Reeves and Turner, 1876, p. 41.

6 Karl Mannheim, *op. cit.*, p. 36. See also the review by A. L. Rowse, *The Political Quarterly*, October–December, 1937, p. 612.

7 Walter Millis, *The Martial Spirit*, New York, Houghton Mifflin Co., 1931, pp. 58–59.

8 *Ibid.*, pp. 62–63.

9 Wayne C. Williams, *William Jennings Bryan*, New York, G. P. Putnam's Sons, 1936, pp. 211–212.

10 Henry F. Pringle, *Theodore Roosevelt*, New York, Harcourt, Brace & Co., 1931, pp. 350–351.

11 Gerald W. Johnson, "Bryan, Thou Shouldst Be Living," *Harper's Magazine*, September, 1931, p. 389.

12 Alva Johnston, "Political Showmen," *The Forum*, July, 1932, p. 21.

13 Hermann B. Deutsch, "Hattie and Huey," *Saturday Evening Post*, October 15, 1932, p. 90.

14 *New Republic*, August 26, 1936, p. 74.

CHAPTER XXI

1 Matthew Josephson, *The Politicos, 1865–1895*, New York, Harcourt, Brace & Co., 1938.

2 James A. Farley, *Behind the Ballots*, p. 162.

3 Clark Tibbitts, "Majority Votes and the Business Cycle," *The American Journal of Sociology*, January, 1931, p. 605.

4 Paul H. Buck, *The Road to Reunion*, Boston, Little, Brown & Co., 1937, p. 66.

5 *Ibid.*, p. 72.

6 Harrison C. Thomas, *The Return of the Democratic Party to Power*, New York, Columbia University Press, 1919, p. 26.

7 Karl Mannheim, *op. cit.*, p. 170.

8 Allan Nevins, *Grover Cleveland*, New York, Dodd, Mead, & Co., 1933, p. 439.

9 *Ibid.*, pp. 414–415.

10 Harry Barnard, *op. cit.*, p. 75.

11 Francis B. Sayre, *The Way Forward:* The American Trade Agreements Program, The Macmillan Co., 1939; John Day Larkin, *Trade Agreements and the Democratic Process*, Carnegie Endowment for International Peace, 1940.

12 Stuart Rice, *Farmers and Workers in American Politics*, New York, Longmans, Green & Co., 1924, p. 217.

13 Edward P. Cheyney, *Modern English Reform*, Philadelphia, University of Pennsylvania Press, 1931, pp. 194–196.

CHAPTER XXII

FOOTNOTE

1   *Report on the British Press*, London, PEP, 1938, p. 264.

2   M. Ostrogorski, *Democracy and the Party System*, New York, The Macmillan Co., 1910, p. 419.

3   Francis G. Wilson, *op. cit.*, p. 257.

4   Walter Lippmann, *The Phantom Public*, New York, The Macmillan Co., 1925, pp. 61–62.

5   Arthur M. Schlesinger, "Tides of American Politics," *The Yale Review*, December, 1939, p. 220.

6   *Ibid.*, pp. 221–222.

7   *Ibid.*, p. 229.

8   Crane Brinton, *The Anatomy of Revolution*, New York, W. W. Norton & Co., Inc., 1938, p. 243.

9   See John Dickinson, *op. cit.*, p. 291.

10 *Ibid.*, p. 293.

CHAPTER XXIII

1   Peter Odegard, *Pressure Politics*, New York, Columbia University Press, 1928, p. 78.

2   Justin Steuart, *Wayne Wheeler Dry Boss*, New York, Fleming H. Revell Co., 1928.

3   *The New England Journal of Medicine*, July 13, 1939, p. 76.

4   C. C. Catt and N. R. Shuler, *Women Suffrage and Politics*, New York, Charles Scribner's Sons, 1926, p. 27.

5   Kirk H. Porter, *op. cit.*, p. 84.

6   *Ibid.*, p. 81.

7   Harold Underwood Faulkner, *The Quest for Social Justice*, New York, The Macmillan Co., 1931, chapter 7.

8   Kirk H. Porter, *op. cit.*, p. 337.

9   *Ibid.*, p. 385.

10 Doris Stevens, *Jailed for Freedom*, New York, Liveright Pub. Corp., 1920, p. 57.

11 Preston W. Slosson, *The Great Crusade and After*, New York, The Macmillan Co., 1931, p. 160.

12 Doris Stevens, *op. cit.*, p. 288.

13 *Ibid.*, p. 329.

14 John Dickinson, *op. cit.*, p. 291.

CHAPTER XXIV

FOOTNOTE

1 A. D. Lindsay, *The Essentials of Democracy*, Philadelphia, University of Pennsylvania Press, 1929, p. 81.

2 Sumner H. Slichter, in "Social Science and the Future of Democracy," Report of a Colloquium Held at the Harvard Club of New York City on March 23, 1939, p. 7.

3 M. L. Wilson, *Democracy Has Roots*, New York, Carrick & Evans, Inc., 1939, pp. 113–114. See also Simeon Strunsky, *op. cit.*, chapter XIX, for a defense of pressure politics.

4 Lindsay Rogers, *Crisis Government*, New York, W. W. Norton & Co., Inc., 1934, p. 114.

5 Walter Lippmann, *The Good Society*, Boston, Little, Brown & Co., 1937, pp. 110–113.

6 W. Y. Elliott, *The Pragmatic Revolt in Politics*, New York, The Macmillan Co., 1928, p. 436.

CHAPTER XXV

1 "The Influence of Money in Political Campaigns," an address delivered over the radio by Senator Gerald P. Nye, January 10, 1931. Reprinted in the *Congressional Record*, January 14, 1931, at the request of Senator Norris, p. 2158.

2 Representative monographs include:
Louise Overacker, *Money in Elections*, New York, The Macmillan Co., 1932; Earl R. Sikes, *State and Federal Corrupt Practices Legislation*, Durham, Duke University Press, 1920; James K. Pollock, *Party Campaign Funds*, New York, Alfred A. Knopf, 1926. See also Miss Overacker's articles on campaign expenditures in *The American Political Science Review*, October, 1933, and June, 1937. The standard texts on political parties also treat this topic: see Merriam and Gosnell, *The American Party System*, New York, The Macmillan Co., 1929, pp. 337–344; E. M. Sait, *American Parties and Elections*, The Century Co., 1927, chapter XX; and P. O. Ray, *An Introduction to Political Parties and Practical Politics*, New York, Charles Scribner's Sons, 1924 (third edition), chapter XI.

3 "The Influence of Money in Political Campaigns" (see note 1, above).

4 Walter Edward Weyl, *op. cit.*, p. 105.

5 "The Influence of Money in Political Campaigns" (see note 1, above).

6 Simeon Strunsky, *The Forum*, May, 1932, p. 264.

7 Paul W. Ward, "Can the Presidency Be Bought?," *The Nation*, September 26, 1936, p. 354.

8 Louise Overacker, *Money in Elections*, p. 85. For the federal picture, reports of expenditures to Congress required by the Corrupt Practices Act are of some value, though Miss Overacker points out certain limitations

FOOTNOTE

of their accuracy and completeness. Two major congressional investigations —those of the Nye Committee (made pursuant to Sen. Res. 215, 71st Cong.) and of the Lonergan Committee (75th Cong., 1st Sess., Sen. Res. 151)—furnish information as to the nature, extent, and propriety of the use of electoral funds. In addition, Hearings before the Senate Committee on Privileges and Elections and the House Committee on Elections and Election of President, Vice-President, and Representatives in Congress contain pertinent material.

9 Ralph Waldo Emerson, *Considerations by the Way*, New York, Tudor Pub. Co., p. 169.

10 See the article by Delbert Clark in the New York *Times*, July 30, 1939.

11 J. A. Spender, *op. cit.*, II, pp. 86, 88, 89, 92.

12 Tom Harrisson, *Savage Civilisation*, New York, Alfred A. Knopf, 1937. See pp. 25 *ff.*

CHAPTER XXVI

1 J. A. Spender, *op. cit.*, p. 85.

2 See the lively discussion by L. D. White and T. V. Smith, *Politics and Public Service*, New York, Harper & Bros., 1939.

3 W. Ivor Jennings, "Corruption and the Public Service," *The Political Quarterly*, January–March, 1938, p. 32.

4 *Ibid.*, p. 33.

5 Harold Brayman, "Roosevelt and the Spoilsmen," *Current History*, October, 1934, pp. 22–23.

6 Texas delegation letter, *Congressional Record*, 74th Cong., 1st Sess., p. 225.

7 "The Democratic Party" (see chapter XIX, note 5, above), p. 135.

8 Herbert Croly, *Marcus Alonzo Hanna*, New York, The Macmillan Co., 1923, pp. 297–298.

9 *Ibid.*, p. 298.

10 C. J. Friedrich, "Responsible Government Service under the American Constitution," in *Problems of the American Public Service*, New York, McGraw-Hill Book Co., 1935, pp. 14–16.

11 M. J. Bonn, "The Making of a National State," *The Political Quarterly*, October–December, 1937, p. 595.

12 Ernest K. Lindley, *Half Way With Roosevelt*, New York, The Viking Press, 1936, p. 281.

13 Matthew Josephson, *op. cit.*, p. 406.

CHAPTER XXVII

1 Leonard D. White, "British Civil Service," in *Civil Service Abroad*, New York, McGraw-Hill Book Co., 1935, p. 53.

2 Harold J. Laski, *op. cit.*, pp. 209, 265, 266.

FOOTNOTE

3 C. J. Friedrich, *op. cit.*, p. 69.

4 Harold J. Laski, *op. cit.*, p. 267.

5 C. J. Friedrich, *op. cit.*, pp. 69–70.

6 Lewis Merriam, *Public Personnel Problems*, Brookings Institution, 1938.

7 Harold J. Laski, *New Republic*, July 12, 1939, p. 269. See also Arthur W. MacMahon and John D. Millett, Columbia University Press, 1939, for interesting biographical data on important administrators.

8 Arnold Brecht, "Bureaucratic Sabotage," *Annals of the American Academy of Political and Social Science*, January, 1937, p. 55.

9 Graham Wallas, *Public Administration*, III, p. 3.

CHAPTER XXVIII

1 For an interesting view on this general subject see James M. Landis, *The Administrative Process*, New Haven, Yale University Press, 1938, chapter II, "The Framing of Policies: The Relationship of the Administrative to the Legislative."

2 Sumner H. Slichter, *Towards Stability*, New York, Henry Holt & Co., 1934, p. 201.

3 Henry A. Wallace, *New Frontiers*, New York, Reynal & Hitchcock, Inc., 1934, p. 67.

4 Lucius Wilmerding, Jr., *Government by Merit*, New York, McGraw-Hill Book Co., Inc., 1935, p. 26.

5 Harold J. Laski, *Parliamentary Government in England*, p. 273.

6 Henry A. Wallace, *op. cit.*, p. 28.

7 Louis L. Jaffe, "Law Making by Private Groups," *Harvard Law Review*, December, 1937, p. 220–221. See also Lane Lancaster, "Private Associations and Public Administration," *Social Forces*, December, 1934, pp. 283–291.

8 Hearings before the Sub-Committee of the House Committee on Appropriations on the Agricultural Department Appropriation Bill, 74th Cong., 2nd Sess. (1936), p. 1336.

9 See the excellent discussion of administrative responsibility by C. J. Friedrich, pp. 4–24, in *Public Policy*, edited by C. J. Friedrich and Edward S. Mason, Cambridge, Harvard University Press, 1940. See also Fritz Marx, "Bureaucracy and Consultation," *Review of Politics*, January, 1939.

CHAPTER XXIX

1 Jacques Barzun, *Of Human Freedom*, Boston, Little, Brown & Co., 1939, p. 29.

2 George Sokolsky, "The Political Burden of Relief," *Atlantic Monthly*, September, 1936, p. 158.

3 *Ibid.*, p. 339.

FOOTNOTE

4   Ogden L. Mills, *Liberalism Fights On*, New York, The Macmillan Co., 1936, p. 147.

5   "The Fortune Survey: XIX," *Fortune*, March, 1939, p. 135.

6   Alvin H. Hansen, *op. cit.*, p. 329.

7   Committee on National Expenditures, British Report, 1931, p. 223.

8   *Ibid.*, p. 16.

9   *Ibid.*, p. 270.

10 Hearings before Senate Committee on Appropriations on Emergency Relief Appropriation, 75th Cong., 1st Sess., 1937, p. 266.

11 Robert M. Haig, "Facing the Deficit," *The Yale Review*, June, 1936, p. 701.

12 *Ibid.*, p. 693.

13 Ralph George Hawtrey, *The Exchequer and the Control of Expenditures*, London, Oxford University Press, 1921, p. 68.

14 Dan Throop Smith, *Deficits and Depressions*, New York, John Wiley & Sons, Inc., 1936, p. 170.

15 John H. Williams, "The Formation and Use of Capital." An address before the Academy of Political Science at its semiannual meeting on "Essentials for Sustained Recovery," March, 1938.

16 Robert C. Hall, "Representation of Big Business in the House of Commons," *Public Opinion Quarterly*, July, 1938, p. 474.

17 Brooks Adams, *The Theory of Social Revolution*, New York, The Macmillan Co., 1913, p. 204.

18 *Ibid.*, p. 208.

19 *Ibid.*, p. 278.

20 Claude Robinson, "The New Science of Public Opinion Measurement and Its Implications for Business," an address delivered before the alumni of the Harvard Graduate School of Business Administration, June 16, 1939. Reprinted from the *Harvard Business School Alumni Bulletin*, July, 1939.

21 Brooks Adams, *op. cit.*, p. 211.

22 *Ibid.*, p. 216.

CHAPTER XXX

1   Carl Becker, "Democratic Virtues," *The Yale Review*, Summer, 1939, p. 655.

2   See Carl Becker, *Our Great Experiment in Democracy*, New York, Harper & Bros., 1920, p. 107, and *passim*.

3   John Morley, *On Compromise*, London, Chapman & Hall, 1877 (second edition), pp. 184–185.

4   Crane Brinton, *The Lives of Talleyrand*, p. 243.

5   Edward Samuel Corwin, "The Constitution as Instrument and as Symbol,"

FOOTNOTE

in *Authority and the Individual*, Harvard Tercentenary Publications, Harvard University Press, p. 203.

6 Alpheus Thomas Mason, *The Brandeis Way*, Princeton, Princeton University Press, 1938, pp. 148–149.

7 Gaetano Mosca, *The Ruling Class*, New York, McGraw-Hill Book Co., Inc., 1939.

8 Archibald MacLeish, *Land of the Free*, New York, Harcourt, Brace & Co., 1938, pp. 84 *ff.*

9 Peter F. Drucker, *op. cit.*, p. 66.

10 *Ibid.*, pp. 22–23.

11 Jacques Barzun, *op. cit.*, pp. 276–277.

The selections by Robert Frost are from the *Collected Poems of Robert Frost* (New York, Henry Holt & Co., Inc., 1939); the selections by Carl Sandburg are from *The People, Yes* (New York, Harcourt, Brace & Co., 1936).

Grateful acknowledgment is made to all the publishers listed in the above footnotes, who have in each instance granted permission for publication of the quotations taken from books bearing their respective imprints.

Index

Adams, Brooks, 416-417

Adams, Henry, 23-24; definition of a statesman, 68

Adams, James Truslow, 80; on early political leaders, 65; on whispering campaigns, 253-254

Adams, John, 69, 73, 84-85; need for national consolidation, 71; reconciling varied interests, 71

Adams, Mrs. John, letter from Jefferson, 75

Adams, John Quincy, 81, 124; and national unity, 80

Adjustment, in politics, 420; skill in, 414

Administration, Brooks Adams on definition of, 416; skills in, 164

Administrative mind, need of the, 417

Administrative service, proper sphere of, 381

Administrator, relations of, to political parties, 379

Advertising, and campaigning, 269

Advisory committee, of Republicans in 1920, 242

Agar, Herbert, 77; majority rule and major interest groups, 92-95; on national conventions, 226

Aiken, George D., 194

Alcoholism, problem of, 318

Alien and Sedition Acts, 78

Allen, Robert, 258

American Birth Control League, 322

American Federation of Labor, 171-172

American Institute of Public Opinion Poll, 194-195

American Legion, convention, 226

American Revolution, 69

American Woman Suffrage Association, 320

Anderson, William, 157-158

Anti-Masonic party, 182

Anti-Masons, 183

Anti-Saloon League, 314-315, 317; and woman suffrage, 321

Appointments, politics in, 357

Arnold, Thurman, 256-257

Arthur, Chester A., 253-254

Ashton, E. B., on the fascist state, 59

Authoritarian state, 368

Bagehot, W., 54

Balance of interests, 30

Balfour, Lord, 54

Bargaining, 233-234

Barnard, Harry, 231; and the labor problem, 297

Barnes, William, on Boss Platt's methods, 215

Barzun, Jacques, 391, 432

Beard, Charles A., 167, 428; politics and business, 126-127

Becker, Carl, on political future, 419-420

Belief, banners of, 87-99

Bennett, James Gordon, and women's rights convention, 319-320

Bernays, Edward L., 259

Bimetalism, and William Jennings Bryan, 282

Bipartisan alignment, in France, 51

Bismarck, 61

Blaine, Mrs., 253

Boas, George, 88

Bonn, M. J., 174 n.; on civil service, 356

Boss, in politics, 122, 150, 215-216, 238; power of the, 29; see also Frank Hague, Charles E. Murphy, Pendergast, Tom Platt, J. Henry Roraback, Tweed

Brain Trust, 218, 385

Brandeis, Louis D., 428

Brecht, Arnold, 376

Brinton, Crane, 425-426; *Anatomy of Revolution*, 312; on accepted ideals, 37-38; on public feeling, 312

British Cabinet, an integrating device, 53

British civil service, 370 ff.

British Committee on Expenditures, 397, 399

British government, 98

British parties, current trends in, 214

British public servants, 370

British system of honors, 346

Brogan, Denis, 192

Brooks, R. R. R., 170 n.

Broun, Heywood, 192

Bruening, Heinrich, regime, 58

Bryan, William Jennings, 89, 130, 188, 282 ff.; and bimetalism, 282; and imperialism, 283; ultimate influence of, 284

"Bryanism," and tariff revision, 282

Bryce, Lord, 81-82, 101, 270; on public opinion, 313; on shortcomings of party conventions, 227-228

Buck, Paul, political parties after Civil War, 291-292; *Road to Reunion*, 291

Budget, balanced, 294, 404

Bull Moose movement, 130, 185

Bureaucracy, 51, 109; and demands of labor, industry, and agriculture, 376; rivalries of, 389

Burke, Edmund, 68, 78, 89; definition of party, 101; ideal of representation, 89-90

Burr, Aaron, 68

Business cycle, and political adjustment, 395; effect on campaign issues, 290

Businessman, and abstract ideals, 146; after Civil War, 127; and abstract thinking, 198; and the politician, 155

Byrd, Harry, 234

Cabinet, the, 29; appointments to, 79

Calhoun, John C., 80-83, 92-93, 94

Campaign contributions, 335 ff.

Campaign methods, 257

Campaigning, 264-265; honest, 258; political, and commercial advertising, 269

Campaigns, whispering, 253-254

Capitalism, and democracy, 163; labor and, 173

Casey, Ralph, 267

Causation, explanation of, 275

Central Office, of parties, 212-213

Cermak, Tony, 136-137

Chairman, the national party, 204 ff.

Chamber of Deputies, 49

Channing, William Ellery, 428

Charnwood, Lord, 82

Cheyney, Edward P., and party in reform in Great Britain, 302

Chicago, racial groups in, 136-137; complexity of official agencies, 140-141; success of Kelly machine, 148-149

Churches, and propaganda, 264; based on faith, 103

Cincinnati, reform movement in, 148

Citizen, as amateur economist or political philosopher, 271; attitude of average, 270; control of the commonwealth by, 308

Citizens, and popular government, 42; a question for, 84

Citizenship, an interpretation of, 33; conceptions of, 34-35

Civil service reform, 365; in Great Britain, progress of, 351

Civil War, 83-84, 94, 125, 130-131, 160; and slaveowners, 426-427; basic political need after, 292; campaign issues important since the, 290-291; effect on party loyalty, 104

Class basis for parties, 191

Class cleavage, 169-178

Clay, Henry, 81-82

Cleveland, Grover, 172, 253, 255; and the tariff, 296; and the tariff in 1888-1892, 296; victory in 1884, 293

College men, in government service, 363; in local politics, 33

College of Cardinals, 225

Columbus, Christopher, 272

Commager, Henry Steele, 190

Committee, national party, 203 ff.

Committee, Republican advisory, in 1920, 242

Communism, 149

Communist party, 195, 286

Compromise, in democracy, 424; political value of, 413

Confucius, on government, 56

Congress, 167, 183-184, 210-211, 217-218, 223-224; and bills, 380; and national policy, 108; and the president, 219; blocs in, 187; tool of interest, 106

Congress of Industrial Organizations (C.I.O.), 138-139, 171-172

Congressional district data record, 266

Connecticut, 150

Consent, roots of, 326-335

Conservatism, Middleton's views on, 52; and innovation, 74-86

Conservative party, 92; in Great Britain, 54

Conservative-liberal alignment, 193

Conservatives, in British politics, 197

Constitution, United States, 120-121, 131, 162, 185; and public opinion, 309-310; a safeguard against factionalism, 70-72

Consumer, 37; interest of the, 87

Consummating reform, 314-325

Continental Congress, First, 68

Convention, American Legion, 226; see Elks

Conventions, national, Herbert Agar on, 226

Coolidge, Calvin, 192, 254, 333

Co-operative associations, and non-governmental bodies, 428

Co-operatives, 37

Copeland, Douglas Berry, 165 n., 166

Corrupt Practices Act, 347

Corruption, 151 ff.

Corwin, Edward S., 426

Coughlin, Father Charles E., 174 n., 188; appeal of, compared to Marxians', 287; supporters of in 1936, 286

Council, party, 241-242

Cox, James M., 192

Coyle, David Cushman, 120

Crawford, 80

Creeds, in a democracy, 36

Croix de Feu, 51

Cromwell, 42

Davis, John W., 192; on party platforms, 233

Debate, limitations of, 288-302

Debs, Eugene V., 185

Decentralization of conflicts, in government organization, 409

Delaisi, Francis, 98

Demagogue, the, and social demands, 281

Democracy, 36; a definition of, 86; and harmony among groups, 132; and majority and minority groups, 93; and process of adjustment, 279; and roots of consent, 326; and rule by public opinion, 313; and social needs, 48; and the majority will, 67; as a political creed, 99; demand of, 35; experimentation in, 420-421; function of parties in a, 248-249; politics of, 30, 95, 124, 135, 389, 429, 431, 434; politics of, adjust-

Democracy (*continued*)
ment in, 420-421; politics of, administrative service of the, 388; politics of, and adjustment of social problems, 335; politics of, and decentralization of policy forming and executing, 390; politics of, and labor, 169; politics of, a process of adjustment, 421-422; politics of, breakdown during Lincoln administration, 83-84; politics of, campaign methods and, 270-271; politics of, changes today, 424; politics of, the strength of, 25, 431; politics of, view of the state in the, 427-428; success of party government under, 55; successful functioning of, 47; the faith of, 23-35; the future of, 23; the ideology of, 434-435

Democratic administration, 385

Democratic bureaucracy, 368-377; relation between officialdom and citizen, 368

Democratic candidates, and the Townsend movement, 187-188

Democratic convention, dispute in 1932, 237

Democratic dogma, 26

Democratic government, continuance of, 279; possible only in a democratic society, 327; problem of, 40

Democratic governments, capacity of, to meet needs of citizens, 166

Democratic national committee, and job seekers, 352

Democratic party, 138, 159, 176; and liberal policy, 160; policy during first F. D. Roosevelt administration, 177; return to power in 1884, 292-293

Democratic process, and government by aristocracy, 269; protection of political parties by, 246-247

Democratic system, Drucker on collapse of the, 58

Democrats, and sectional interests, 130; during the second F. D. Roosevelt administration, 159

Department of Agriculture, and democracy, 330; unclassified personnel, 352

Dewey, John, on bosses, 122

Dibelius, Wilhelm, 197; on significance of "gentleman" ideal in Great Britain, 59-60

Dickinson, John, 122, 313, 325

Dictatorship, of the proletariat, 307

Distribution of wealth, sought by New Deal, 162

Doctrinaires and demagogues, 272-287

Dodd, William E., 221

Dogma, in religion and government, 42

Doob, 264

Dooley, 25

Douglas, 82

Drucker, Peter F., 28, 60-61, 430, 431

Economic depressions, 128

Economic development and politics, 119

Economic inequality, and theory of political equality, 391; impact on politics, 391-418

Economic system, as related to democratic rule, 57

Economists, theories of, 276-277

Economy, expanding, 123

Electorate, allegiances of the, 112

Elks convention, 227

Elliott, W. Y., 334

Emden, C. S., 113

Emerson, Ralph Waldo, 428, 435

Equal rights movement, and prohibition, 321

Equality, economic and political, 391 ff.

Erasmus, *The Praise of Folly*, 278

Ethics, political, 146-158

Experts, and public policy, 277

Factionalism, 219

Farley, James A., 228, 237, 258, 264; and Democratic National Committee, 204; and organization, 205; and patronage, 352-354; control in

Farley, James A. (*continued*)
1931, 208-209; on the choice of issues, 289; spirit of national conventions, 227
Farm Credit Administration, 386
Farmer-Labor party, 182, 186
Farmers, 198; and political leaders, 173
Fascism, 57-59, 131, 149; see Ashton, E. B., and Italy
Faulkner, H. U., 321
Fay, James H., 222
Federal aid to cities, 361
Federal Reserve System, 387
Federal Trade Commission, 157
Federalist Papers, 90
Federalist party, 68, 77, 79; conservatism of, 194
Federalists, the, 72
Finance, process of British party, 345
Financial policy, difficulties of, 407
Finer, Herman, 121, 212
Fiscal policy, and socialization of wealth, 406; formulation of, 400; politics of, 412; result of, 402
Floating vote, 248
Ford, Henry J., 76; on party action, 103; on political ideals, 151
Fortune, 148-149, 204 n., 354; poll on reaction to spending policies, 394
Founding Fathers, fear of factional and group interests, 425; fear of rule by the masses, 426
France, 131; administration in, 50; bipartisan alignment in, 51; middle class in, 47; party system of, 46 ff.; third party in, 183
Frank, Glenn, 199
Free Soil party, 181, 183
Freudian, the, and conduct as an adult, 274
Friant, Julian, 353
Frick, H. C., 284
Friedrich, C. J., and British civil service, 371, 373; on civil service reform and patronage, 355; on Constitutional democracy, 99
Fuehrerprinzip, 26, 6

Gallup, George, 193, 269-270
Gallup Polls, in 1938, 221
General Federation of Women's Clubs, growth of, 322
"Gentleman," ideal in Great Britain, 59
Georgia, purge of primary, 222
Germany, growth of fascism in, 58-59; National Socialism in, 60, 61; postwar, 58; the middle class in, 57; see also Nazis, Nazism
Gladstone, 350-351
Glass, Carter, 234
Good-citizen ideal, 31
Goodnow, Frank J., 109
Gosnell, Harold F., 141; on Boss Platt's power, 214 n.
Government, and organization, 407; basic assumptions of democratic, 25; broad definition of, 44; challenge confronting democratic, 24; definition of good, 26; demands upon, 45; duties of good, 29; faith in, 42; function of, 40-41; good, 25; meaning of good, 27; policing of, 29; policy of good, 30; popular participation in, 33-34; present system of, and decentralization of conflicts, 409; the relationships of, 26; William Bennett Munro on, 34
Government lawyer, duties of, 381
Governmental activity, extension of, 46
Graft in politics, 140, 157
Granger party, 181, 183
Grangers, 130
Grant, Ulysses S., 253
Greenback party, 181, 182, 183
Greenbackers, 130
Great Britain, 131; alternate political parties in, 78; and changes brought by industrialism, 95-96; civil service reform in, 351; Conservative party in, 54, 197; "gentleman" idea, 59; Labour party in, 54, 179-180; Liberals in, 197; middle class in, 47; party organization in, 52-53; respect for the ruling class in, 376;

Great Britain (*continued*)
third party in, 183; trade union movement in, 179

Greeley, Horace, 259

Group interests, 163, 172, 396; and general welfare, 327; see also Interest groups

Groups, in the control of government, 55

Gulliver, in Brobdingnag, 271; in Laputa, 249-250

Hadley, A. T., purpose of parties, 121

Hagerty, James A., 139

Hague, Frank, 138-139

Hall, R. C., 415

Hallam, on balance in politics, 53

Hamilton, Alexander, 68, 84, 85, 255, 333

Hamilton, John D. M., task before him in 1936, 207

Hamlin, Hannibal, 253

Hand, Judge Learned, on common will, 313

Hanna, Mark, 354-355; and "full dinner pail," 283; and presidential election of 1896, 343

Hansen, Alvin H., 161-162, 164; on capitalism and public investment, 396

Harding, Warren G., 192, 253

Harrison, Benjamin, as a leader, 68

Hartman, G. W., 196

Hatch Act, 223-224

Havemeyer, Henry O., 126

Hawtrey, R. G., on financial policy, 407

Hayes, Carlton J. H., French Revolution and nationalism, 60 n.; on the Industrial Revolution, 61

Haynes, Frederick E., 180-181

Heflin, Tom, 285

Hegelianism, 40

Henderson, L. J., and causation, 275

Hicks, John D., 182-183

Hitler, A., 313; and public opinion, 305

Hobbes, Thomas, 92, 96

Hocking, William Ernest, definition of the politician, 134-135

Holcombe, A. N., 209-210, 247

Holmes, Oliver Wendell, 428

Hoover, Herbert, 208, 236; effectiveness of his campaign speeches, 251-252; election of 1928, 207

House of Commons, 210; connection with commerce, 415

Howe, Bill, 228

Howe, Fred, 28

Huddleston, Representative, of Alabama, 219

Hughes, Charles Evans, hailed as a liberal, 192

Human nature, in politics, 256

Hurja, Emil, 265; and patronage, 352-353

Imperialism, in campaign of 1900, 283

Income Tax Law, 140

Independent party, 182

Individualism, 23

Industrial Expansion Bill, 196

Industrial organizations, 43

Industrial Revolution, 61

Industrial Unions, 37

Innovation and conservatism, 74-86

Institutions, governmental, 45-46

Interest, of the citizen, 34

Interest groups, 32, 109, 176-177; and individuals, 310-311; in a fascist state, 60; political bargaining with, 187; rearrangement of, 308

Interests, and issues, relations of, 300

Interests, sectional diversity of, 119-120

Irrational elements, in campaigns, 255-256

Issues, in parties, 240; and interests, relations of, 300; political, as conflicts of interests, 413

Italian fascists, their justification for totalitarian rule, 57-58

Italy, growth of fascism, 58-59

Item veto, 412

Jackson, Andrew, 79, 80, 81, 84; the party of, 68

Jackson, Robert H., 354

Jackson Day, 193

Jacksonian democracy, leaders before the advent of, 68

Jaffee, Louis L., 386

James, Marquis, 214

James, William, 428; on democracy, 25

Jefferson, Thomas, 72, 74-75, 77-78, 84, 85-86, 253, 333, 428; the party of, 68

Jennings, Ivor, 112-113, 350

Johnson, Allen, 125

Johnson, Gerald, 284-285

Johnston, Alva, 285

Josephson, Matthew, 366; *Politicos, 1865–1896*, 288

Kansas City, Missouri, 28, 139

Kansas-Nebraska Act, 69

Kent, Frank R., and "the plea for sympathy," 255; on the floating vote, 248

Keynes, J. M., 405

Know Nothing party, 182

Labor, American Federation of, 171-172

Labor movement in the United States, 169

Labor party, annual conference of, 212

Labor unions, 43; and propaganda, 264

Labor's Non-Partisan League, 169

Labor's relation to the industrialist, 297

Labour party, in Great Britain, 54, 179-180

La Follette, Robert, 89, 130; in 1924, 185

La Follette Commission, 157

La Follette family, in the Wisconsin Movement, 186

La Guardia, Fiorello, 139

Laissez faire, 163

Laissez-faire doctrines, in the United States, 40

Landon, Alfred, 192, 236, 253, 267; in election of 1936, 170

Laski, H. J., 382; and men in government service, 373-374; on the British civil servant, 371; on political parties, 54

Law and social forces, 45

Lawyer, the government, 381

Leader, the true democratic, 65-66; in New York City, 143

Leaders, a question for, 84; effectiveness of, 64; farsighted, and popular government, 293; labor, status of, 173; labor, work of the, 169 ff.; of democratic politics, 64; on majority will or balance, 67; party, 166 ff.; political, and popular will, 309

Leadership, expression of underlying interests, 67; responsibilities of, 66; task of, in democratic politics, 64; under party government, 64-73

League of Independent Political Action, 176, 177

Lecky, William Edward Hartpole, on parties in Great Britain, 52

Lee, Henry, letter from Jefferson, 75-76

Left, tendency toward the, 48-49

Legislative issues, and Congress, 294

Lemke, William, 188

Lenroot, Irvin, 219

Lerner, Max, view of government, 94-95

Lewis, John L., 175

Liberal, and true believer, 429

Liberal, in Great Britain, compared with Tory, 179

Liberal party, 192

Liberalism, Middleton's views on, 52

Liberals, in British politics, 197

Likert, Rensis, 198

Limitations of debate, 288-302

Lincoln, A., 81, 83, 193; choosing of, 82

Lindley, Ernest K., and the merit system, 356

Lindsay, A. D., 329-330

Lippmann, Walter, 189, 240; and democratic collectivism, 333-334; on group interests, 88-89; on public opinion, 310; on the party system, 106

Lloyd-George, David, 89

Localism, in Congress, 218-219

Locofocos, 183

Lodge, H. C., 300

Lomasney, Martin, 34-35

Lonergan, Senator, 222

Long, Huey, 188, 216, 285-286

Louisiana purchase, 76

Lowell, A. Lawrence, 101, 272

Loyalty, necessity to parties, 111

Luce, Robert, 231-232

Lumley, Frederick E., 262

Lund, Robert S., consequence of progress, 41

Machine, in Chicago, 149; control, explanations of, 153 ff.; survival of the political, 149-150

Madison, James, 69, 70-71, 84, 85; and majority will, 90; on the danger of factionalism, 70

Maine, Sir Henry, 280

Majoritarianism, 85

Majority rule, 95; doctrine of, 92, 431

Majority will, 84; in democracy, 67

Man, description of the political, 31

Mandate, doctrine of the, 113; theory of government, 112-113

Mann Act, 322

Mannheim, Karl, 272-273, 278, 294-295

Marx, Karl, 38, 432

Marxians, appeal of, and Father Coughlin, 287

Marxists, and behavior of industrialists, 274-275

Maryland primary, purge of, 222

Mason, Alpheus, 428

Massachusetts, the Democratic party of, 138

Maverick, Maury, 222; meaning of democracy, 26

McAdoo, William G., in 1932 convention, 229

McAllister, Mrs., 244

McKinley, William, 283, 354; campaign funds of, 343

McLaughlin, A. C., 120-121

Merit system, and political parties, 356

Merriam, Charles E., 241-242; on nineteenth century thinkers, 38

Michelson, Charles, 208, 209, 244, 264, 268-269

Middle class, 47-48; in the United States, 47

Middleton, W. L., 51-52; on French party system, 51 n.

Millis, Walter, 282-283

Mills, Ogden, 255, 393

Milwaukee, reform movement in, 148

Minority protection, principle of, 431

Minority rights, doctrine of, 92

Minority rule, 95

Mitchell, Wesley Clair, 162-163

Monarchy, in Great Britain, 53

Money, in a political system, 151; as political currency, 336-348

Monroe, James, 79

Morley, John, on success in politics, 422

Mosca, Gaetano, 428

Moses, Robert, 29

Mother of Parliaments, 40, 101

Multi-party system, in France, 50

Munro, William Bennett, 34

Murphy, Charles F., and Tammany, 137

Murphy, Gardner, 198

Murray, Alfalfa Bill, 234, 285

Mussolini, Benito, 57, 313

Napoleonic system, 40

Nation, Carrie, 318

National Congress for Uniform Divorce Laws, 322

National Emergency Council, as the administration's propaganda ministry, 244

National Federation of Federal Employees, 364

Nationalism, a force for integration, 57; and popular sovereignty, 61-62

National Labor Relations Board, 37; and employer-employee relations, 298

National League of Women Voters, 355; and government personnel, 362-363

National Liberal Federation, 212

National party committees, 210

National party conventions, and Hatch Act, 224; and consideration of policy, 241; usefulness of, 225-239

National Socialism, 60-61

National Union for Social Justice, 188; 1936 convention, 286-287

National Union of Conservative and Unionist Associations, 212

National Woman Suffrage Association, 323

National Women's Trade Union League, 322

Nazis, 36-37, 158, 237; their justification for totalitarian rule, 57-58

Nazism, 131; and the German nation, 360

Nevins, Allan, 295

New Deal, 113, 130, 159, 161, 162, 166, 175, 176, 177, 197, 267; and patronage, 352; and rapidity of action, 421; and third parties, 187; attempted adjustments, 69; distribution of wealth sought by, 162; in 1938, 222; legislation of, 185; new federal agencies, 141; policies, 132; policies, defended by National Emergency Council, 244; quality of young men in the, 374

New England Journal of Medicine, problem of alcoholism, 318

New York City, Democratic leader in, 143

New York Evening Post, 221

New York Herald, 319

New York Times, 139, 175, 219-220, 222, 263

Nineteenth century doctrines, 38

Nominating machinery, improvements in our, 238

Non-Partisan League, 188

Nye, G. P., 337, 338; on money in campaigns, 336

Odegard, Peter, on prohibition laws, 315

Officials, can they be neutral, 378-387

Old Hickory, 124

Older, Fremont, reform in San Francisco, 150

Oliver, F. S., 158

O'Mahoney, Joseph C., 355

One-party government, necessary function of, 59

One-party systems, in Germany and Italy, 58

Opinion Research Corporation, 417

Organization, in government, 407

Osborne judgment, 180

Ostrogorski, M., on national conventions, 226-227; on improvement of political life, 307-308

Parliament, 50, 210; and the king, 220-221

Parliamentary government, and conflict of parties in Great Britain, 54

Parliaments, Mother of, 40, 101

Participation, by the citizen in government, 34

Parties, based on principle or class, 191; highest function of, 191; in Great Britain, 53; inclusiveness of, 248; major, and public interest, 329; major, criticism of, 175-176; purpose of, 121; take their stand, 119-133; two distinctive, 113-114

Partisan jobbery, 360

Party, an acceptable theory of, 114; A. C. McLaughlin on, 121; irrational loyalty to, 102; judging the, 115; local politics, 33; viewed as an association, 111

Party action, 103

Party allegiance, irrational nature of, 111-112

Party harmony, 229

Party leaders, and a definite program, 106; recruited by parties, 421

Party loyalties, sentimentality of, 133

Party loyalty, 132, 169-179, 382; and voters, 102; expressed in voting, 104

Party organization, 123; after the Civil War, 127; and economic depressions, 128-129

Party organizations, 122; control of, 245

Party platform, 230; terms of beliefs and principles, 249

Party realignment, 176-177

Party system, adjustment and compromise, 423; alignment in the, 55; and governmental machinery, 246-247; British, contrasted to French system, 51; explanation of our, 133; French, 48-50, 51 n.; function of, 421; justification of our, 48; of the present, 131; structure of our, 203-224

Patronage, 215, 361; and a local party machine, 359; and leadership, 352; as reward, 360; C. J. Friedrich on, 355; evils of, compared with money in politics, 349-350; J. C. O'Mahoney on, 355; use of, by politicians, 357

Paul, Alice, 323, 324

Pearson, Drew, 258

Pendergast, Boss, 139-140; formula for ruling Kansas City, Missouri, 28

People's party, 182

Personnel, quality of, in government service, 362

Peter the Hermit, 99

Platform, Democratic, of 1896, 231; Democratic, of 1932, 234-235; Republican, of 1932, 236

Plato, 85, 278

Platt, Tom, 214-215

Plunkitt, George Washington, 157

Policies, the formulating of, 382

Political analysis, 36

Political careers, dependent on home support, 358

Political continuity, price of, 429

Political issues, as symptoms of maladjustments, 300-301

Political parties, and the merit system, 356; as an integrating device, 55; defects in, 301; definition of, 100-101; for organization, 103, 104; function of, in the United States, 289-290; in France, 48; in seventies and eighties of nineteenth century, 109-110; machine, local, and patronage, 359; political battles with, 177-178; protection of democratic processes by, 247; threefold character of, 248-249

Political party activity, 109

Political philosophy, 36-37

Political system, characteristics of our, 107

Politician, adjustment between central and local governmental units, 141; and basis of power, 335; and human relations, 135-136; and patronage, 358-359; and propaganda, 259-260; and the floating vote, 248; as a mediator or adjuster, 129-130; as an intermediary, 146; importance of the, 158; primary task of, 143 ff.; responsibility of the, 154-155; the traditional, 134-145

Politicians, 128; a question for, 84; activities of, 131-132; and art of government, 213; and career men, 364; and simplifications to involved problems, 406; and the long view, 166; and their support, 366-367; new problems of today, 137-138; of today, 29

Politics, and voters, 289; in the nineteenth century, 38; money in, 336-348; propaganda in, 261-271; representative and integrated, 423; search for ideals, 37; sectionalism of, 124; statement of K. Smellie, 39; the struggle of, 46; Thoreau on, 251; see also Democracy

Politics of plenty, in the United States, 131

Pollock, James K., 211-212, 213

Pope, the, and politics, 57

Popular government, requisite for survival of, 55-56

Popular rule, conditions favorable to, 47-63

Popular sovereignty, 61-62

Popular will, concept of, 32

Populist party, 181, 183, 184

Populists, 130

Power, distribution of, 46

Power-units, 43-44; definition of, 43; the state as a, 45

President, the, 29; and Congress, 219

Presidential patronage, 359

Press, 24

Pressure groups, 107; in Washington, 380; see also Interest groups

Pressure politics, 326-327; and state intervention, 334; danger of, 329

Principles, 38

Pringle, Henry F., on Roosevelt's campaign of 1904, 284

Professional associations, 43; and propaganda, 264

Professional politicians, strength of, 215

Progress, the animating spirit of American, 419-435

Progressive party, 181, 182; convention in 1912, 189

Progressives, 423-424

Prohibition, and equal rights movement, 321; national, 314

Prohibition party, 182; and woman suffrage, 320-321

Propaganda, and change, 325; in a fascist state, 60; in politics, 261-271; in totalitarian governments, 56; organizations, 314; strength of, 263-264

Propagandist, 260 ff.; appeal of the, 263; social scientists as, 277

Proportional representation, 49-50

Public administrator, and public policy, 382; and the general welfare, 383; as a student of society, 383

Public expenditures, 403

Public interest, the myth of the, 424-425

Public opinion, 32-33; and general will, 309; a social myth, 307; as a symbol, 305; as attitudes, 310-311; concept of, 306; why believe in, 305-313

Public policy, 378; and economic differences, 301; and public administrators, 382; basis for, 27; concept of, 30-31; prophecy and gamble, 288; working out of, 110-111

Public relations men, 261-262

Public relations problems, 143

Public service, responsibilities of, 369-370

Publicity directors, and rule-of-thumb approach, 268

Racial groups, 136

Raskob, John J., 207, 208, 209

Rational discussion, problem of politics and, 279

Reform, civil service, 365; in San Francisco, 150; progress in Great Britain, 351; consummating, 314-325

Reform movements, see Cincinnati, Milwaukee

Reformer, 135, 147; the successful, 148

Relief, and stamp plan, 344

Relief measures, farm, 188

Religion, faith in, 42; in campaigns, 253

Republican candidates, and the Townsend movement, 187-188

Republican party, 77, 176; after Civil War, 127, 160; during administration of Lincoln, 83; in 1912, 130; program committee of, 243

Republican presidential campaign, of 1936, 267-268

Republican propaganda, 268

Republican Reporter, 243

Republicans, after the Civil War, 125-126; and Congressional district data, 266; breaking of sectional alignment in 1932, 130; failure to

Republicans (*continued*)
build up candidate, 268; in 1938, 199; Old Guard, 176; Radical, in post Civil War years, 176
Research, as a party function, 242-243
Rice, Stuart, 299-300
Ritchie, Albert, 234
"Robber barons," 342
Robinson, Claude, 417
Robinson, E. E., 72-73, 247
Rogers, Lindsay, 160 n., 332; on statesmanship, 66 n.
Roman Catholic Church, 98, 225
Roosevelt, Franklin D., 132, 167, 188, 192, 193, 209, 218, 221-222, 223; election of 1936, 170; physical capacity of, 254; rumor of insanity, 253; second administration of, 159
Roosevelt, Theodore, 89, 188-189, 215, 253, 254, 269-270, 282; 1904 campaign, 284; woman suffrage, 322
Roots of consent, 326-335
Roraback, J. Henry, 150
Rowse, A. L., 177
Ruling class, in Great Britain, 376

Sait, Edward M., 231
San Francisco, reform in, 150
Sanger, Margaret, 322
Scandinavian countries, and changes brought by industrialism, 95-96
Schlesinger, Arthur M., 311
Schools, public, 24
Schurz, Carl, 151
Sectarianism, 151
Sectional interests, 108, 172
Sectionalism, 125
Self-government, 110
Service, administrative, 381
Seward, 82
Share-the-wealth movement, 188
Shouse, Jouett, 208
Siegfried, André, on democracy, 48
Simon, Sir John, experience as Lord Mayor of Manchester, 156
Slavery, as a political issue, 68-69
Slayden, Representative, of Texas, 219

Slichter, Sumner H., 330, 379
Slogans, 37
Slosson, Preston B., 324
Smellie, K., politics and industry, 39
Smith, Alfred E., 138, 234, 236, 253, 255; election of 1928, 207; in 1931, 209
Smith, T. V., on politicians, 135
Social controls, growth of, 44
Social Democratic party, in Germany, 57
Social Labor platform, for 1892, 181
Social responsibility, 167
Social sciences, and social ends, 277
Social scientists, and guides to policy, 276
Social service activities, 141
Socialist party, 184-185; membership in 1936, 286
Socialists, appeal of, and Townsend, 287
Sokolsky, George, 392
Spanish-American War, and national politics, 282
Spartacus, 432
Special-aim organizations, 105; and woman suffrage, 324
Special interests, and governmental politics, 328
Spender, J. A., 346, 350; on British party funds, 345
Spoils, the struggle with, 349-367
Stamp system, and distribution of surplus commodities, 344
Standards, community, 146-158
State, the authoritarian, 369; spiritual and state temporal, 36-46; the service, 134-145
State bosses, 238; see also Boss, in politics
Statesman, responsibility of a, 66; Henry Adams' definition of a, 68
Steffens, Lincoln, 35
Stevens, Doris, 324
Strunsky, Simeon, 339
Suffrage, 24; see also Woman suffrage
Sullivan, Mark, on Democratic platform of 1932, 234-235

Supreme Court, 127, 196; and suffrage for women, 321; theory of our government, 46

Symbols, and liberalism, 429; and the masses, 425; and reality, 41; in the economic sphere, 39; in government management, 405; invocation of, 37; need of, 37

Taff Vale decision, 180

Taft, Philip, description of Labor's Non-Partisan League, 169

Taft, William Howard, 253; and woman suffrage, 322

Tammany, 28, 29; defeat of, 139-140; manipulation of racial groups by, 137; Plunkitt of, 157; work of district leaders of, 142

Tariff, and politicians, 295; as a political issue, 298-299; Cleveland's attitude toward, 296; of interest to many groups, 299

Tariff reform, 295-296

Tariff revision, and Bryanism, 282

Taylor, John, letter from Jefferson, 75

Tennessee Valley Authority (TVA), 142; administration of, 378

Third party, in France, 183; in Great Britain, 183

Third party activities, 179-190

Thomas, Harrison, and return of Democratic party to power, 292-293

Thomas, Norman, 185

Thompson, Big Bill, 136, 149, 285

Thoreau, Henry David, 251, 428

Toledo, Ohio, 150-151

Tolerance, 433

Tories, 73

Tory, in Great Britain, compared with Liberal, 179

Totalitarian countries, 433

Totalitarian government, 56; as an integrating device, 55

Totalitarian state, basis of appeal, 57-58; identification of the individual with the state, 427; life in the, 313

Totalitarianism, 23, 26; function of, 59

Town Hall of the Air, popularity of, 270

Townsend, 174 n.; appeal of, compared to socialists, 287

Townsend movement, 97

Townsend plan, 187-188

Trade union movement, in Great Britain, 179

Trade unionism, 180

Trade unions, and nongovernmental bodies, 428

Traditional institutions, inadequacy of, 107

Twain, Mark, 305

Tweed, Boss, 139

Tyler, Wat, 432

Unemployed, the, 26, 97

Union, in American politics, 131; search for, 131-132

Unions, industrial, 37; see also Labor unions

United States Bank, 78

Urban areas, per cent living in, 45

Urban society, demands of, 45

Vandenberg, Arthur, 193

Vardaman, Senator, of Mississippi, 219

Veto, item, 412

Walker, James J., 285

Wall Street, 42

Wallace, Henry A., 384, 400-401; on pressure groups, 380

Wallas, Graham, 376; on political parties, 103-104

Ward, Paul, 340

Washington, George, 69, 73, 84-85; Farewell Address of, 69-70; on dangers of party, 70; sees need for national consolidation, 71

Webb, Sidney and Beatrice, 180

Webster, Daniel, 81-82

Wehrwirtschaft, 60

Weyl, Walter E., 123, 338; on party loyalty, 104

Wheeler, Wayne B., 316, 318; and prohibition, 315

Whig party, 68, 72-73

White, Leonard D., 370

White, William Allen, 126, 235 n.

Whitlock, Brand, difficulties in Toledo, 150

Whitman, Walt, 428

Williams, 283

Williams, J. H., 414

Wilson, Francis G., and propaganda, 260; theory of opinion, 308-309

Wilson, M. L., *Democracy Has Roots*, 330

Wilson, Woodrow, 101, 188-189, 220-221, 333; and Congress in 1918, 219; and party council, 241; and woman suffrage, 322-324; hailed as a liberal, 192

Woman suffrage, growth of, 322-324

Woman suffrage movement, 318-319

Women's rights convention, 1853, 319-320

Workers' Alliance, 138

Works Project Administration (WPA), 139, 197

Wright, B. F., 74

Yankees, 138

Zink, Harold, on honesty in business and politics, 157